The Cambridge Companion to Debussy

Often considered the father of twentieth-century music, Debussy was a visionary whose influence is still felt. This book offers a wide-ranging series of essays on Debussy the man, the musician and composer. It contains new insights into his character, his relationship to his Parisian environment and his musical works across all genres, with challenging views on the roles of nature and eroticism in his life and music. His music is considered through the characteristic themes of expression, sonority, rhythm, tonality and form, with closing chapters considering the performance of his music and our view of Debussy today as a major force in Western culture. This wide-ranging view of Debussy is written by a team of specialists for students and informed music lovers.

Simon Trezise is a Lecturer in Music at Trinity College, Dublin. He is the author of *Debussy: La mer* in the series Cambridge Music Handbooks and has written on French music and on Schoenberg.

Cambridge Companions to Music

Composers

The Cambridge Companion to Bach
Edited by John Butt

The Cambridge Companion to Bartók
Edited by Amanda Bayley

The Cambridge Companion to Beethoven
Edited by Glenn Stanley

The Cambridge Companion to Benjamin Britten
Edited by Mervyn Cooke

The Cambridge Companion to Berg
Edited by Anthony Pople

The Cambridge Companion to Berlioz
Edited by Peter Bloom

The Cambridge Companion to Brahms
Edited by Michael Musgrave

The Cambridge Companion to John Cage
Edited by David Nicholls

The Cambridge Companion to Chopin
Edited by Jim Samson

The Cambridge Companion to Debussy
Edited by Simon Trezise

The Cambridge Companion to Handel
Edited by Donald Burrows

The Cambridge Companion to Ravel
Edited by Deborah Mawer

The Cambridge Companion to Schubert
Edited by Christopher Gibbs

The Cambridge Companion to Stravinsky
Edited by Jonathan Cross

Instruments

The Cambridge Companion to Brass Instruments
Edited by Trevor Herbert and John Wallace

The Cambridge Companion to the Cello
Edited by Robin Stowell

The Cambridge Companion to the Clarinet
Edited by Colin Lawson

The Cambridge Companion to the Guitar
Edited by Victor Coelho

The Cambridge Companion to the Organ
Edited by Nicholas Thistlethwaite and Geoffrey Webber

The Cambridge Companion to the Piano
Edited by David Rowland

The Cambridge Companion to the Recorder
Edited by John Mansfield Thomson

Cambridge Companion to the Saxophone
Edited by Richard Ingham

The Cambridge Companion to Singing
Edited by John Potter

The Cambridge Companion to the Violin
Edited by Robin Stowell

Topics

The Cambridge Companion to Blues and Gospel Music
Edited by Allan Moore

The Cambridge Companion to Jazz
Edited by Mervyn Cooke and David Horn

The Cambridge Companion to the Musical
Edited by William Everett and Paul Laird

The Cambridge Companion to the Orcheatra
Edited by Colin Lawson

The Cambridge Companion to Pop and Rock
Edited by Simon Frith, Will Straw and John Street

The Cambridge Companion to

DEBUSSY

....

EDITED BY
Simon Trezise

CAMBRIDGE
UNIVERSITY PRESS

CAMBRIDGE UNIVERSITY PRESS
Cambridge, New York, Melbourne, Madrid, Cape Town, Singapore, São Paulo

Cambridge University Press
The Edinburgh Building, Cambridge CB2 2RU, UK

Published in the United States of America by Cambridge University Press, New York

www.cambridge.org
Information on this title: www.cambridge.org/9780521652438

© Cambridge University Press 2003

First published 2003

A catalogue record for this publication is available from the British Library

Library of Congress Cataloguing in Publication data
The Cambridge companion to Debussy / edited by Simon Trezise.
    p.   cm. – (Cambridge companions to music)
Includes bibliographical references and index.
ISBN 0 521 65243 X (hardback) – ISBN 0 521 65478 5 (paperback)
1. Debussy, Claude, 1862–1918. – Criticism and interpretation.   I. Trezise, Simon.   II. Series.
ML410.D28 C26   2002
780´.92 – dc21   2001043703

ISBN-13 978-0-521-65243-8 hardback
ISBN-10 0-521-65243-X hardback

ISBN-13 978-0-521-65478-4 paperback
ISBN-10 0-521-65478-5 paperback

Transferred to digital printing 2007

In memoriam François Lesure, 1923–2001

Contents

Contributors

Mark DeVoto, composer and writer, has been Professor of Music at Tufts University, Medford, Massachusetts since 1981. He edited the fourth and fifth editions of Walter Piston's *Harmony*; edited *Altenberg Lieder*, Op. 4 for the Alban Berg *Sämtliche Werke*; he recently completed *Debussy and the Veil of Tonality: Essays on His Music.*

Déirdre Donnellon graduated in music from the University of Manchester in 1993 and completed her M.Phil. at the University of Liverpool in 1996. She recently completed a Ph.D., 'Debussy, Satie and the Parisian Critical Press', at the University of Liverpool.

David Grayson is Professor of Music at the University of Minnesota. He wrote *The Genesis of Debussy's* Pelléas et Mélisande, and contributed to the Cambridge Opera Handbook on *Pelléas, Debussy Studies* and *Debussy and His World.* He is editing *Pelléas* for the *Œuvres complètes de Claude Debussy* and is on the editorial board of *Cahiers Debussy.* He has also written a Cambridge Music Handbook on two Mozart piano concertos.

Barbara L. Kelly is Lecturer in Music at Keele University. She is author of the Ravel article for *New Grove* 2 and of a forthcoming book on Darius Milhaud. Her research is focused on late nineteenth- and early twentieth-century French music, and on issues of French national identity from 1870 to 1939.

Julie McQuinn is a Ph.D. candidate and part-time lecturer at Northwestern University. In her dissertation she examines the forces behind perceptions of gender and sexuality in Parisian society at the turn of the twentieth century and their connection to the creation and reception of a handful of highly individual operas performed at the Opéra-Comique.

Roger Nichols read music at the University of Oxford and subsequently lectured at various universities before becoming a freelance writer and broadcaster in 1981. He has published widely on French music of the last 200 years, including *Ravel* (Dent, 1977), *Ravel Remembered* (Faber, 1987), *Debussy Remembered* and *A Life of Debussy.*

Robert Orledge is Professor of Music at the University of Liverpool. His research field is French music between 1850 and 1939 and his main publications are *Gabriel Fauré* (Eulenburg, 1983), *Debussy and the Theatre, Charles Koechlin: His Life and Works* (Harwood, 1995), *Satie the Composer* (Cambridge University Press, 1992) and *Satie Remembered* (Faber, 1995).

Richard S. Parks is Professor of Music Theory at the University of Western Ontario in Canada. He has been exploring theoretical-analytical issues in Debussy's music for thirty years and has published articles on the subject in *The Journal of Music Theory, Music and Letters* and *Music Theory Spectrum,* and a chapter in *Debussy* *in Performance*. His *The Music of Claude Debussy* appears in the Yale University Press series Composers of the Twentieth Century.

Boyd Pomeroy is Assistant Professor of Music Theory at Georgia State University in Atlanta. A former professional double-bass player, he holds degrees from Edinburgh University, Guildhall School of Music and Drama and Cornell University, where his doctoral dissertation dealt with issues of tonality and form in Debussy's orchestral triptychs. Aside from the music of Debussy he specialises in Schenkerian theory and analytical approaches to form in the Classical period.

Caroline Potter is a Senior Lecturer in Music at Kingston University. A graduate in both French and music, she is the author of *Henri Dutilleux* (Ashgate, 1997). Current projects include a volume on French music since Berlioz, jointly edited with Richard Langham Smith, and a book on Nadia and Lili Boulanger.

Nigel Simeone is Senior Lecturer in Music at the University of Wales, Bangor, and has written widely on twentieth-century French music. His publications include *Olivier Messiaen: A Bibliographical Catalogue* (Schneider, 1998); *Paris: A Musical Gazetteer* (Yale University Press, 2000); and articles on Ravel, Poulenc, Messiaen and the *Concerts de la Pléiade*. Current projects include a documentary biography of Messiaen (with Peter Hill) and a study of music in Paris under the German Occupation.

Charles Timbrell is Professor of Music and Coordinator of Keyboard Studies at Howard University, Washington, DC. He has given concerts extensively in the United States and Europe and performed all-Debussy recitals. He is the author of *French Pianism* (2nd edn, Amadeus Press, 1999) and numerous articles in *Cahiers Debussy*, *Music and Letters* and *New Grove* 2.

Simon Trezise is Lecturer in Music at Trinity College, Dublin (also known as the University of Dublin). His research areas include various approaches to music analysis, performance-practice analysis, history of recording, Debussy and Wagner. He has written on Schoenberg and is author of the Cambridge Handbook *Debussy: La mer*. He is currently working on the impact of recording upon the performance and reception of classical music.

Arnold Whittall is Professor Emeritus of Music Theory and Analysis at King's College London. He has written extensively on the technical and historical nature of music since Wagner. His large-scale *Musical Composition in the Twentieth Century* was published in 1999, and he has recently been working on a series of substantial articles on twentieth-century composers from Debussy to Birtwistle and beyond.

Acknowledgements

The work of Edward Lockspeiser and François Lesure continues to set the tone and standards for Debussy scholarship. The Debussyan world is growing at a fast and furious rate, greatly aided, and not a little excited, by the continuing production of the *Œuvres complètes de Claude Debussy*, now under the fastidious editorship of Denis Herlin. Working on Debussy remains a pleasure, not just because the music is intoxicating, but because Debussy scholars are so supportive of each other. Now that I have had the enjoyable experience of meeting young, up-and-coming scholars recruited for the companion, things seem unlikely to change. Thanks are due to all the contributors for their good will and input.

Thanks are also due to Jonathan Dunsby, David Grayson, Roy Howat, Richard Langham Smith and Robert Orledge for advice on contributors and subject areas, and to John Flood-Paddock and Tamsin Simmill for their advice on translations (most translations in this volume not accredited to English-language sources are the work of contributors). Penny Souster at Cambridge University Press has been patient and immensely supportive of the whole project. Top Type Music Bureau (Dublin) did a marvellous job on the production of many of the music examples, as did Richard S. Parks on the music examples in chapter 11. I should also like to acknowledge financial and other support I have received from Trinity College, Dublin, including the Taylor Bequest.

Chronology of Debussy's life and works

Various excellent chronologies are available. I have drawn on several here, including Briscoe, *Claude Debussy: a Guide to Research* (my main source); Goubault, *Claude Debussy*; Lesure and Nichols, *Debussy Letters*; Gerald Abraham, *100 Years of Music* (London: Duckworth, 4/1974). Below completed and premiered works by Debussy in the third column I have added a handful of important contemporary works in the years of their first performance. Debussy's works are given by their completion dates unless indicated otherwise by (P), which indicates that the year given is of the first performance; for some of the most important works I have given both dates (works in collections such as the orchestral *Images* were composed over often quite extended periods, but only the date of the collection's completion is given). The best introduction to Debussy's life is Nichols, *The Life of Debussy*, which includes critical discussion of much of his music. An attractive critical apparatus for Debussy's life and works (in French), albeit slightly out of date now, is Goubault, *Claude Debussy*, which includes short analyses of all his main works, a detailed chronology, and a dictionary of terms (including a list of incomplete and abandoned works and other useful information).

Year	Life	Works
1862	Born at Saint-Germain-en-Laye near Paris, 22 August.	Berlioz, *Béatrice et Bénédict*
1867	Family settles in Paris.	Gounod, *Roméo et Juliette*
1872	Enters Paris Conservatoire.	
1875	Receives first certificate of merit in piano at Conservatoire.	Bizet, *Carmen*
1877	Enters harmony class of Emile Durand.	
1878	No prizes.	
1879	First known and dated compositions.	*Ballade à la lune*; *Madrid, princesse des Espagnes*
1880	Becomes pianist in Mme von Meck's entourage (she was Tchaikovsky's patron). Meets Mme Vasnier with whom he has an affair (the Vasniers became the chief benefactors of Debussy's youth).	Piano Trio in G
1881	In Russia with von Meck. Composes several songs for Mme Vasnier.	Symphony in B minor

Year	Life	Works
1882	Attends premiere of Lalo's *Namouna* and is ejected for his excessive enthusiasm. Meets Gounod. First public appearance as composer accompanying his song *Les roses*. First published work (*Nuits d'étoiles*).	*Mandoline* Wagner, *Parsifal*
1883	Comes second in Prix de Rome.	*Le gladiateur*
1884	Wins Prix de Rome on 28 June.	*L'en fant prodigue*
1885	Leaves for Villa Medici in Rome. Hears Liszt play. Hears Palestrina and Lassus at church of Santa Maria dell'Anima.	Brahms, Fourth Symphony; Franck, *Variations symphoniques*
1886	Takes leave from Rome to be in Paris.	*Diane au bois* (fragments only) Saint-Saëns, 'Organ' Symphony (No. 3)
1887	Returns to Paris for good. At premiere *Printemps* is accused of 'vague Impressionism'.	*Printemps* (for chorus and orchestra) Verdi, *Otello*
1888	First Bayreuth visit (*Meistersinger* and *Parsifal*). Publishes songs.	*La damoiselle élue*
1889	Second Bayreuth visit (*Tristan*). Famous conversations with Guiraud. Universal Exhibition in Paris at which Debussy hears Javanese gamelan music and Musorgsky.	*Petite suite* for piano duet Franck, Symphony Strauss, *Don Juan*
1890	Publishes *Cinq poèmes de Baudelaire*. Starts opera *Rodrigue et Chimène*. Breaks with Académie.	*Fantaisie* for piano and orchestra; *Suite bergamasque* (early version); Mazurka
1891	Asks Maeterlinck for permission to set *Princesse Maleine* to music (is refused).	*Trois melodies de Paul Verlaine*; *Fêtes galantes*, series 1
1892	Meets Gabrielle (Gaby) Dupont with whom he lives until 1899. Works on *Trois scènes au crépuscule*.	Nocturne for piano
1893	Abandons *Rodrigue* and starts work on *Pelléas et Mélisande*. Hears *Die Walküre* and plays in four-handed *Rheingold* and *Walküre* excerpts.	String Quartet; *La damoiselle élue* (P)
1894	Gets engaged to singer Thérèse Roger, but returns to Gaby. First	*Prélude à l'après-midi d'un faune*

Year	Life	Works
	performance of *Prélude à l'après-midi d'un faune*. Plays Act I of *Parsifal* at private gathering. First all-Debussy concert (Brussels).	
1895	Completes first version of *Pelléas*.	
1896	Works on abortive theatrical projects.	
1897	Gaby attempts suicide.	
1898	Ravel's 'Habanera' makes great impression on him. Meets Rosalie (Lilly) Texier. In debt.	*Chansons de Bilitis*
1899	Marries Lilly.	*Nocturnes*
1900	Debussy named the 'Verlaine of music' by *L'écho de Paris*.	'Nuages' and 'Fêtes' (P) Puccini, *Tosca*
1901	Monsieur Croche (Debussy's critical alter ego) begins his brief existence.	*Pour le piano*; *Nocturnes* complete (P)
1902	Falls out with Maeterlinck over casting of Mélisande. Premiere of *Pelléas*. Debussy first visits London. Begins work on Poe operatic projects.	*Pelléas et Mélisande* (P)
1903	Writes music criticism for *Gil blas* and *Mercure de France*. Reviews *Ring* in London. Meets Emma Bardac. Begins *La mer*. Receives Légion d'Honneur.	*Estampes*
1904	Leaves Lilly for Emma. Makes his only gramophone recordings.	*Fêtes galantes*, series 2; *Deux danses*; *L'isle joyeuse* Ravel, String Quartet
1905	Emma and Debussy both get divorced. Daughter 'Chouchou' (Claude-Emma) born. Signs exclusive contract with publisher Durand. Finally moves to 80 Avenue du Bois de Bologne (where he remains).	Piano *Images*, series 1; *La mer* Strauss, *Salome*
1906	Critic Pierre Lalo writes that 'The religion of Debussyism has replaced the religion of Wagnerism.'	
1907	Emma is disinherited in her uncle's will. Debussy worries about his	Piano *Images*, series 2

Year	Life	Works
	flagging inspiration. Meets André Caplet.	
1908	Marries Emma. First biography of Debussy, by Louise Liebich. Contract with Metropolitan opera for Poe operas *La chute de la maison Usher* and *Le diable dans le beffroi.*	*Children's corner*; *Rapsodie* for saxophone; *Trois chansons de Charles Orléans*
1909	Still working on Poe operas and other theatrical projects. Louis Laloy's biography of Debussy published.	*Hommage à Haydn*
1910	Meets Mahler but leaves during performance of Second Symphony. Hears Stravinsky's *Firebird*.	*Préludes*, book 1; *La plus que lent*; *Première rapsodie*; *Trois ballades de François Villon*
1911	Again in debt and suicidal. Conducts in Turin with assistance of Vittorio Gui.	
1912	Around this time makes piano rolls. Reads through *Le sacre du printemps* at piano with Stravinsky. Nijinsky's choreography of *Prélude* provokes a scandal.	*Khamma* (orchestrated by Koechlin); *Images* (orchestra) Schoenberg, *Pierrot lunaire*
1913	Attends premiere of *Le sacre du printemps* Conducts in Russia. René Lenormand publishes his *Etude sur l'harmonie moderne*.	*Trois poèmes de Stéphane Mallarmé*; *Printemps*, orchestrated Busser (P); *Images* for orchestra (P); *Jeux*; *Préludes*, book 2
1914	Conducts in Rome, The Hague and Amsterdam.	*Six épigraphes antiques* Vaughan Williams, *London Symphony*
1915	Last bout of creative energy in summer. Edits Chopin for Durand. Rectal cancer diagnosed. Undergoes surgery in December.	*Etudes*; Cello Sonata; Sonata for flute, viola and harp; *En blanc et noir* Ravel, Piano Trio Sibelius, Fifth Symphony
1916	Completes final revision of libretto for *La chute de la maison Usher*.	
1917	Last public appearance as a performer, in Violin Sonata. Hears premiere of Satie's *Parade* ballet. Edits solo violin sonatas of Bach for Durand.	Violin Sonata

Year	Life	Works
1918	Dies on 25 March in Paris to the sound of Germany's bombardment of Paris. 'It's unbelievable. I don't know how I stay alive, and I can't believe the awful truth.' (Chouchou's letter to her brother Raoul Bardac on her father's death, 8 April 1918, *Debussy Letters*, 336).	Holst, *The Planets*
1919	Chouchou dies on 16 July.	
1934	Emma dies.	

Note on the text

References to the most common Debussy texts are given in short-title form in the endnotes with the full reference in the Select Bibliography. In most instances these refer to the most recent edition of the publication. Full publication details are provided for more occasionally referenced sources on their first citation in each chapter. Mindful of the needs of readers of this volume, I have added a few volumes to the Select Bibliography that, for any number of reasons, receive little or no attention in the chapters but are, in my opinion, important for the study of Debussy.

References to musical texts vary according to author. Preference is generally given to the most commonly available source, so Dover scores of the orchestral works are often used (they are based on the original Durand editions). In order to make references as straightforward as possible, rehearsal figures and bar numbers are sometimes given together when available. Definitive texts for some of Debussy's works are available in the *Œuvres complètes de Debussy* under the general editorship of Denis Herlin (the edition is a long way from completion). It is assumed that readers will have access to scores when reading chapters that deal in detail with the music.

Introduction

SIMON TREZISE

Debussy occupies a place apart from his contemporaries in the history of music. He is a composer who has, though the sheer quality and originality of his work, plus a character far removed from the average, 'run-of-the-mill' composer of the period, placed himself in a hallowed position in the richly coloured years around the end of the nineteenth century. I say this not because I find his music highly attractive – I do, of course – but because intellectual circumstances have conspired in Debussy's favour in a quite unusual way.

Before the Second World War, and even for a few years after it, one could legitimately find fault with Debussy. As far back as 1924, Cecil Gray, a cantankerous, erratic but often illuminating writer, acknowledged that Debussy was a Symbolist not an Impressionist, for Debussy's purpose was 'not to evoke a definite picture, but to suggest the mood or emotion which the particular image in question aroused in the artist's mind'.[1] All of which bodes well, but on the music itself he is less likeable: 'in his harmony, Debussy is as curiously limited, monotonous and restricted as in his melody. His rhythms too are singularly lifeless and torpid.'[2] Gerald Abraham fell into a trap Debussy set for musicologists when he wrote that 'Debussy's work was still for the most part far too closely linked with literature and painting and nature impressions to be absolute music. [It was] a half-way house between romanticism and a new classicism.'[3]

A few residual grudges against him might have trickled out in the years following Europe's orgy of destruction. I recall a distinguished and well-respected music analyst and musicologist in the late 1970s evincing some disdain for the solo-violin passages in 'Ibéria', which struck him at the time as trite – another example of the 'too pictorial' vein of criticism (he wasn't overly impressed by Debussy's orchestration either). But nowadays much has changed: no composer fits the modern psyche better than Debussy. Triteness is now just one facet of Debussy's independent brand of modernism, which we can accept because there are no rules in Debussy and no etched-in-stone critical yardsticks. If this sounds far-fetched, just think of current critical encounters with Richard Strauss, who is let away with far less and is regarded with greater suspicion than Debussy.

Late twentieth-century reductionism faced its most uphill struggle in Debussy. Boulez assured us of his paramount importance in the history of music and the profound effect he had had on the avant garde, but how was so much intellectual integrity going to 'explain' a composer who was openly contemptuous ('We must not turn it [music] into a closed and academic art' he declared[4]) of the intellectual rationalisation of music? It was also a contempt that was effectively composed into the music. Indeed, just as perplexing for the musicologist were the many contradictions in his character, which ranged from rebellious and anti-establishment to snooty, racist and exclusive, reaching the most ethereal realms of absolute quality in his 'fineness', as Roy Howat so eloquently puts it. For Debussy pleasure and associated instinct were the law: he wrote parallel dominant-ninth chords because they pleased him. However, the nature of that 'pleasing' was not random: Debussy wrote slowly and meticulously. If pleasure was the law, it was a very learned genus of pleasure. Nevertheless, compared with Strauss and Schoenberg, who gave ample evidence of intellect in their musical structures (not in the sense that they showed off, but simply that they used procedures that are easily understood as being manifestations of musical ingenuity, such as counterpoint, complex motivic development and so on), which we can disentangle rather more easily (or so we may often think), the intellectual properties of Debussy's music are located on a different plane to these contemporaries of his, and it is a plane we are still prone to tackle with less confidence, if we are even able to tackle it at all. It is a satisfying mystery. Debussy would have been pleased with himself and probably euphoric that strict Schenkerians found his music unanalysable.

All this makes Debussy a unique composer in the great canon of Western music. He occupies a position that seems to become more unassailable at every stride taken in theory and musicology. He must suit many post-modernists, post-structuralists and new musicologists to a tee. New approaches to analysis have been formulated in recognition of the failure of the old. New systems of thinking, not of course peculiar to Debussy, but better suited to his music than his contemporaries, are providing us with sophisticated, exciting areas for the mind to explore in the labyrinth of Debussy's 'rhythmicised time', his 'vegetative circulation of form'. But it is also a paradox that a man who pleased himself, who eschewed an intellectual style of composition in favour of instinct and pleasure, should have necessitated such a feast of intellectual activity. He places a mirror before us that can well prove disconcerting, for we may not always like what we see reflected back at us. As we 'perform' Debussy in multifarious attempts to explain the structure of his music through a long-overdue investigation of his association with *fin-de-siècle* eroticism, a re-evaluation of his links with painting and sculpture and so on, perhaps we should ask just how well we are able to know Debussy and how well the early twenty-first-century psyche is adapted to a union with such a mind. Then in the real performative zone

Briscoe's ominous words from his stimulating chapter 'Debussy and orchestral performance' in *Debussy in Performance* come to mind:

> Since 1950 with the exception of Ansermet, Inghelbrecht, and more recently Boulez, conductors' tempi have sagged noticeably. At the same time, the sense of the exquisite moment is too seldom conveyed for the early scores, and nuance becomes note-to-note tedium. Many recordings of the *Faune* are notorious in this regard. The remarkable art of the early conductors lay in balancing the aesthetic tendencies of nuance and of structural linearity in Debussy's music.[5]

The last sentence is especially worrying. If the sound conjured up in Debussy's name by conductors (and with them singers, pianists and other instrumentalists too) is as far removed from the spirit of the letter as Briscoe suggests, many concerns surrounding his reception now have to be confronted: analysis is only part of a broader cultural process of assimilation and understanding.

It is wholly consistent with these views that the contradictions in Debussy's character and music are so refreshingly and diversely traversed by contributors to this Companion. One conclusion that comes round several times is that we have a long way to go before the mysteries of Debussy the man and Debussy the musician are solved. Indeed, we are not given a great deal of encouragement to think that the man who made pleasure a principle – the law in fact – of the greatest art (and yet who became quite a bourgeois snob once ensconced in his fashionable suburb of Paris) will ever be fully explained in a set of essays. If this sounds discouraging we should hastily add that the attempt to explain and understand has been enthralling, and there are many new insights in the pages that follow. We are at an interesting time in Debussy studies, for the musicological bias of so much distinguished work has been redressed by several important analytical works, the number of which is set to increase. Richard Parks has given us a major study of his musical structures which complements the musicological slant of an excellent volume of *Debussy Studies* (ed. Smith). On the biographical side of things we at last have a single-volume biography that can gracefully supersede the long-established volume by Edward Lockspeiser in the Master Musicians series: we are all indebted to Roger Nichols for his *The Life of Debussy*. Two new studies, too late for references to them to be given in the Companion, include Jane F. Fulcher (ed.), *Debussy and His World* (Princeton: Princeton University Press, 2001) and Mark DeVoto, *Debussy and the Veil of Tonality: Essays on His Music* (Hillsdale, NY: Pendragon Press, 2002).

The Companion is divided into four parts, the first of which deals with the man, his cultural environment and his critical writing. Part II looks closely at different aspects of his aesthetic outlook and approach to cultural forces around him. Part III is a theoretical and analytical study of different facets of Debussy's compositional technique. Part IV looks at two aspects of Debussy as he is displayed to us now: in performance and through scholarship – an evaluation of his impact in our own time.[6]

Chapter 1, 'Debussy the man', is a re-evaluation of Debussy's character in the light of the primary sources that became available to scholars during the twentieth century. Although it is an assimilation of printed information that is generally available, through the concentration on certain facets of his life, such as his collecting mania, his relationships with women, and others, a strikingly vivid and unusual portrait of him emerges.

Given the relatively uneventful character of Debussy's life, at least to outward appearances, it is important to understand his fixation on Paris, the city of most of his youth and all his adult life – nowhere else would do. In chapter 2, 'Debussy's Parisian affiliations', Barbara L. Kelly examines some of the intellectual currents that drew Debussy to the city and also his response to these currents, including the considerable influence of Baudelaire and the extent to which this literary figure stimulated Debussy's musical innovations with respect to timbre and form. His relationship with great Parisian institutions such as l'Opéra and the Conservatoire is explored, and a final section assesses his growing nationalism in the war years.

Throughout much of his life Debussy wrote about music, mainly as a reviewer, and he was interviewed on his music. Debussy's approach to the word was as uncompromising and controversial as his music. In chapter 3, 'Debussy as musician and critic', Déirdre Donnellon takes the important step of combining a survey of these writings, adding to the tally of known writings, and assimilating them as a basis for understanding Debussy as a musician – an important departure.

Chapter 4 is one of two exceptions from the overall plan of the companion, which is to eschew a generic treatment of the music in favour of a thematic approach. Debussy's numerous dramatic projects, and proto-dramatic projects in the early years, demanded extensive and separate treatment; and this is what they receive in chapter 4, 'Debussy on stage', which sheds light on Debussy in many ways. While Debussy's choice of, say, song texts was pretty much his own, when it came to theatre music, especially opera, the substantial social pressures that came into play (collaborators, institutions, etc.) caused him grave difficulties. Succumbing to pressures to conform may have helped him win the Prix de Rome, but thereafter he suffered whenever he compromised his principles. The chapter also offers fresh angles on *Zuleima* and *Pelléas*.

The other exception to the thematic approach is chapter 5, 'The prosaic Debussy'. Roger Nichols discusses Debussy's word setting in the light of the brief period in his long-standing devotion to song writing when he chose prose poems. Given that his only completed opera was a setting of a prose libretto, this is a valuable addition to our understanding of Debussy's settings in general and his approach to rhythm in the French language. By extension, as Nichols shows, we can, in the light of these prose-poem settings, re-evaluate his many settings of verse poems.

Debussy used a great many poetic and evocative expression marks in his music that specify the expressive content of his music with a level of precision entirely new in French music. He was surprisingly ambivalent about being labelled an Impressionist composer; he was irritated by the term but proud to be described a disciple of Monet. Chapter 6, 'Debussy and expression', considers Debussy's use of expression markings as a vital component of his mature compositions, and examines the evidence for aesthetic concerns which have parallels in the work of Monet, Cézanne and others.

Chapter 7, 'Exploring the erotic in Debussy's music', ventures into a realm that is not usually believed to have an important place in the study of music. Yet it seems undeniable that elements of eroticism have always swirled around Debussy and his music, serving as tiny threads connecting life and art in a complex, reflexive manner. This chapter includes startling information about Debussy's friends and offers readings in the erotic nature of the music itself.

Few of Debussy's works are entirely independent of nature or other external sources (such as poems, the carnival, etc.), but as Caroline Potter argues in chapter 8, 'Debussy and nature', Debussy's music is not a conventional attempt to represent nature in musical language; neither is nature used as a metaphor for human emotion in the Romantic manner. We discover here a quite different relationship between composer and nature, which is pursued in discussion of passages from a number of works in which nature is evoked.

In chapter 9, 'Debussy's tonality: a formal perspective', application of certain traditional concepts of formal syntax to a composer usually thought resistant to them results in a reappraisal of what are now received views on Debussy, not least his status as a proto-avant-gardist.

Chapter 10, 'The Debussy sound: colour, texture, gesture', offers the only survey in this companion of Debussy's music from some of his earliest to the last works. Understanding the colour of the music is of great importance; indeed, for many years writers would argue that this was the main subject of the music. For all that our current theoretical understanding of Debussy may have proved them misguided, the sonority of Debussy's music is unique and quite evidently a primary structural element in his compositional process.

Much analytical-theoretical literature devoted to Debussy has focused in some fashion upon pitch, rhythmic materials, and forms despite lip service to the notion that chief among his innovations was his attention to the structural properties of sound divorced from these three elements. Chapter 11, 'Music's inner dance: form, pacing and complexity in Debussy's music', examines the motive aspect of musical form. Easily understood and applied techniques for plotting tendencies in various domains are presented first in theoretical form and then in a series of practical analyses of three works (with reference to many others).

As an alternative to pitch-centred analyses of Debussy's music, chapter 12, 'Debussy's "rhythmicised time"', enters the maze-like domain of the temporal in music. Little attempt is made to construct a theory for the endeavour, though some theoretical precepts are reviewed; the chapter draws on various sources to underpin studies of several works. A clearer picture of how Debussy 'rhythmicised time' emerges, as does the fair prospect for future work in this rewarding field.

Chapter 13, 'Debussy in performance', is an overview of a large and sometimes elusive topic that provides some parameters for modern performers by reference to recordings and other documents by Debussy and those in his immediate circle, including the piano rolls and gramophone recordings made by the composer himself.

Finally, chapter 14, 'Debussy now', considers changing attitudes to Debussy, not least in theory and analysis, where major developments have taken place over the last decade or so. Arnold Whittall conveys the excitements of new discoveries as well as suggesting that there is still much to come. In particular he examines how Debussy successfully encapsulates a form of classicism and a form of modernism – a paradox that was not lost on his contemporaries.

PART ONE

Man, musician and culture

1 Debussy the man

ROBERT ORLEDGE

Creating a balanced picture of such a deliberately enigmatic character as Claude Debussy is no easy task. But so great is the fascination that his life and music have exerted that 'performers, writers and analysts have been peeling away the layers of the onion that is Debussy'[1] ever since Louise Liebich first approached the chopping board way back in 1907. And as Roger Nichols aptly continues: 'I think it is some measure of his greatness that the more we peel, the more we find.' Coincidentally, both Liebich and Nichols ninety years on begin by quoting Debussy's veiled warning to future biographers that 'Another man's soul is a thick forest in which one must walk with circumspection',[2] and I make no excuse for reusing this ideal quotation here, or for assuming that readers will refer to the accompanying chronology on pp. xiv–xviii above for the well-known landmarks in Debussy's career.

Debussy very rarely bared his own secretive soul, and if he was hardly a model of circumspection himself, he disliked its absence in others. The thick forest in which his shadowy operatic masterpiece *Pelléas et Mélisande* begins can be seen to have parallels with his own life, for it surrounded a dream-world controlled by destiny in which happiness was rare, and from which there was no escape except in death. If Maeterlinck's Symbolist play provided Debussy with a musical way forward in 1893 and eventually brought him the fame he had dreamed of when it was staged in 1902, it nevertheless did not satisfy the cravings of the 'happiness addict'[3] who, for a variety of reasons, became increasingly reclusive and miserable during his final years.

The frustrated desire to be a man of action provides an important key to Debussy's elusive inner world. As the first of the following, strikingly similar, revelations predates *Pelléas*, it can be seen that his focal opera solved none of his underlying psychological problems. As he told the banker and writer Prince André Poniatowski in September 1892,

> alongside the man who spends his days at the work-table, whose only delight is catching butterflies at the bottom of an inkwell, there is another Debussy who is receptive to adventures and mixing a bit of action with his dreams. As long as he can return to them afterwards and not have to watch them being mown down, as they so often are, by worthless reality.[4]

On 8 July 1910 we again find Debussy lamenting his fate to his chief *confidant* of the post-*Pelléas* years, his publisher Jacques Durand, as follows:

Those around me simply don't understand that I've never been able to live in a world of real things and real people. That's why I have this insurmountable need to escape from myself in adventures which seem inexplicable because they reveal a man that no one knows; and perhaps he represents the best side of me! Besides, an artist is by definition a man accustomed to dreams and living among apparitions . . . In short, I live in a world of memory and regret . . . They are two gloomy companions! But at least they are faithful ones, more so than pleasure and happiness![5]

Outwardly, Debussy was now an acclaimed composer, whose transformation from the poor left-wing Bohemian of the 1890s to the apparently wealthy bourgeois in his well-appointed and luxuriously furnished house on the Avenue du Bois de Boulogne was now complete. But very few people knew that he was continually in debt and that his second marriage to the possessive and capricious Emma Bardac was already floundering. From these letters it is also clear that Debussy saw himself as set apart from ordinary mortals by his talents as a composer, although the only artistic escapism he now felt able to indulge in lay in his operas based on stories by Edgar Allan Poe. And if Debussy's only real 'adventures' that we know of before 1900 were amorous ones which merely produced short-lived periods of happiness, then we need to look farther back into his psychological make-up to find the root causes of his prevailing melancholy.

One such cause lay in his difficult relationship with his parents before the success of *Pelléas*. If he kept it secret during his lifetime, he felt deeply ashamed that his father was imprisoned for revolutionary activities after the defeat of the Commune in December 1871, and that prior to this he had had difficulties holding down even menial jobs. Debussy's unsettled working-class background made him selfish, stand-offish and insecure. His lack of any regular education contributed to this (though it made him into a voracious reader of everything from Mallarmé to adventure stories), and his mother's strictness helped make him an 'affection addict'[6] too, who desperately needed friends throughout his career. Moreover, his father wanted his eldest son to rescue the family fortunes by becoming a virtuoso pianist, but even if he was snobbishly billed as 'Achille De Bussy' and hailed as 'this little Mosart [sic]' at his first public concert at the age of thirteen,[7] he secured only a single Second Prize in piano during his unhappy years at the Paris Conservatoire, gaining greater success in *solfège* and as a sensitive (though not entirely reliable) accompanist. His switch to studying composition with Ernest Guiraud in 1880, of course, led to his winning the Prix de Rome with his cantata *L'enfant prodigue* in 1884. Here he played the official game with skill, but was horrified when he discovered he had won and would have to leave Paris and his mistress, Marie-Blanche Vasnier, for several years. We still find him trying to please his father by setting Catulle Mendès's uncongenial libretto for *Rodrigue et Chimène* in 1890–2, and it was only after he was made a Chevalier de la Légion d'Honneur in 1903 that the sincere affection he showed his parents in their declining years seems to have developed.

The second cause of Debussy's unhappiness was also linked to his parents, whose precarious financial situation was carried to the verges of bankruptcy by their irresponsible son. Doubtless because they were always having to move house, Manuel and Victorine never acquired many luxury items, and Debussy developed a passion for these from an early age. If anything, collecting oriental artefacts was his true passion throughout his life, whether he could afford them or not, and his first known letter of 1884 was to borrow 500 francs from Count Primoli, ostensibly to buy flowers for Mme Vasnier before leaving for Rome.[8] Earlier that year, Paul Vidal (who had won the Prix de Rome in 1883) told Henriette Fuchs that

> He's incapable of any sacrifice. Nothing has any hold over him. His parents aren't rich, but instead of using the money from his teaching to support them, he buys new books for himself, knick-knacks, etchings, etc. His mother has shown me drawers full of them.[9]

Debussy's first wife, Lilly, frequently despaired when he selfishly spent the money from piano lessons in an antique dealer's shop on the avenue Victor Hugo while she 'was anxiously awaiting his return to be able to go out and buy the dinner',[10] and Raoul Bardac recalled that, after marrying his mother in 1908, 'he never went out anywhere if he could possibly avoid it, except to the bookseller's or to shops that sold Chinese *objets d'art* and engravings'.[11]

Debussy was nevertheless well aware of the pitfalls inherent in the 'Cult of Desire' as he followed the dictates of his *plaisir* in his life as well as his music. As he told André Poniatowski in February 1893,

> You have this crazy but inescapable longing, a need almost, for some work of art . . . and the moment of actual possession is one of joy, of love really. A week later, nothing. The object is there and you spend five or six days without looking at it. The only time the passion returns is when you've been away for several months . . . You could write down a formula for desire: 'everything comes from it and returns to it'. By a rather elegant piece of trickery, the desire to be happy works pretty much on the same lines. One is never happy except by comparison or by giving oneself a certain limit to aim at . . . to provide some relaxation from the onward drive to glory.[12]

This artistic quest, of course, he pursued with utter dedication. In the periods when he escaped from the 'usines de Néant' and his compositions flowed freely, as in his final productive summer at Pourville in 1915, he came as close as he ever did to achieving true inner happiness. But if his oriental collection, in the end, only inspired a single piano piece, 'Poissons d'or', it was nonetheless vital in creating the refined, luxurious surroundings Debussy needed to be able to compose. Like Le Cousin Pons in Balzac's novel, he was smitten by the collecting bug, and the quest for the exquisite also provided an essential antidote to the mediocrity and shabbiness of the world about him, of which he frequently complained.

Another fundamental need was a circle of close friends, preferably ones he did not need to explain things to. His moral irresponsibility and pursuit of pleasure rather than passion with women caused many of his male friends to desert him (chiefly after Lilly's attempted suicide in 1904). Only three remained faithful despite everything: Paul Dukas, Robert Godet and Erik Satie – though even Satie broke off relations for a while in 1917 when Debussy kept on making fun of his ballet *Parade*. As Louis Laloy later observed, their friendship was 'tempestuous . . . each constantly on his guard against the other, without being able to stop loving him tenderly. A musical brotherhood, yet a rivalry of musicians.'[13] Debussy got on best with Satie before he achieved fame on his own account in 1911. While Debussy loved playing games like cards and backgammon with Satie and others, he was, from all reports, a bad and rather childish loser who was not averse to cheating.

By and large, Debussy required his friends to come to him (especially after 1905) and regarded each friendship as exclusive, with a set weekly visiting time. As he was often depressed and there was invariably someone ill in the Avenue du Bois de Boulogne in later years, it is small wonder that his circle remained small. Visitors were more likely to be performers (who were invariably in awe of him), younger composers (whom he encouraged) and journalists. But if he welcomed diversions from the difficulties of composition, it was not from his musical colleagues, for he always preferred discussing the other arts. He could be charming (especially when cultivating wealthy potential patrons), but in the main he was shy and reclusive, not a fluent conversationalist, and often appeared grumpy and opinionated.

Moreover, it cannot have escaped other than the least perceptive that Debussy was two-faced, especially about performers and conductors (except for a very few, like Mary Garden, André Caplet and Walter Rummell, whom he admired unreservedly). In short, he had a public and a private persona. Thus, however much he may have praised Maggie Teyte to her face, he complained to Durand on 8 June 1908 that she 'continues to show about as much emotion as a prison door' and was 'a more-than-distant Princess'.[14] But this must have been after a particularly unsatisfying performance of *Pelléas*, for he added that 'Périer [in the title-role] mimes admirably to my music' and 'Dufranne [as Golaud] thunders away'. In reality, these barbs rather show how concerned he was about the future of his creations, which he saw as his children, who grew ever more difficult to control after they had left the nest. The way that he blurted out his immediate reactions is confirmed by his vacillating opinions of Rose Féart, who did not always match up to the ideal Mélisande he had originally found in Mary Garden (despite or even because of her Scottish accent). On 6 December 1908 he wrote that 'her voice and musicality please me enormously', whereas on 18 May 1909 he found Féart's London performance 'indescribably ugly and lacking in poetry', though five days later she was miraculously 'transformed and almost pretty!'[15]

It is doubtful if Debussy's views were any more sexist or racist than the rest of his politically incorrect generation. Both aspects reached their nadir in his strained relations with the exotic dancer Maud Allan, who had commissioned the ballet *Khamma* in 1910 and persisted with her ir-rational demands for Debussy to make the score he had sent her both twice as long and scored for half as many players.[16] Apart from wanting to give 'la "Girl" *anglaise*. . . a good spanking', he complained to Durand that she had supplied him with 'a scenario so boring that a Negro could have done better'.[17] And when he had not heard from her for a while in 1913, he imagined that 'the undulating Miss Allan was dancing for some Negro race in darkest West Africa'![18] As always, Debussy's letters to his long-suffering publisher contain his frankest and most personal admissions, many of which (as above) Durand wisely chose to suppress when he published them in 1927.

Amongst Debussy's more endearing traits were his love of children and animals, and the chief joy of his later life was his daughter Chouchou. But if this sounds like a standard apology for a thoroughly unpleasant character, it is far from the truth, for there are numerous tributes to Debussy's essen-tial kindness and perceptive encouragement towards artists he considered worthwhile. The violinist Arthur Hartmann was one such recipient who received a signed photograph of the composer after his first visit, and even managed to get the reticent Debussy to accompany him in public in 1914 (in a concert which included his specially made arrangement of 'Minstrels'). Hartmann also gives some good examples of Debussy's delightful sense of humour. As he recalled:

> One morning I found him in his garden with his little girl, and a trowel in his hands. Suddenly the gate bell rang and ere I was aware of what was happening, he had seized me by the neck and dragged me with himself behind a bush. Peering forth to see who it was, while we heard the servant calmly saying, 'Monsieur is not at home', he winked at me and we emerged.[19]

Then, when Hartmann remarked that 'Vincent d'Indy's religious fanaticism coupled with medieval learning made of him quite a figure of, let us say, the fourteenth century', Debussy immediately brought him down to earth with the brief retort: 'Oui, en bois!'[20] No composer was exempt from his ready wit, especially Wagner, and his French love of puns and fantastical imagination can be seen in the following recollection by René Peter:

> He wrote to me, speaking about Siegmund and Sieglinde: 'They love each other ... very *wälse!*' (Wälse being, as you know, the name of their father) 'and he issues her with an invitation to the *wälse* ... upon which she invites him to lunch; pale ale and *wälse* rarebit!'[21]

Although he was an Anglophile, it is unlikely that Debussy would ever have chosen this sort of fare in a restaurant (even in its French form of Croque Monsieur). All accounts testify that he was a gourmet of refined tastes rather than a gourmand and, as early as the 1870s, Gabriel Pierné remembered

> the way he used to savour the cup of chocolate which my mother would buy him at Prévost's, when he came out of the Conservatoire; or the way at Borbonneux's, where there was a window reserved for de luxe items, he would choose a tiny sandwich or a little dish of macaroni, instead of gorging himself on more substantial cakes, like his colleagues. Poor as he was, and from the humblest of origins, he had aristocratic tastes in everything.[22]

Similarly, around 1912, Alfredo Casella frequently came across Debussy scrutinising the food displays 'in the avenue Victor Hugo, accompanied by his favourite dogs and much engaged in selecting some choice fruit and superfine cheese to take home for luncheon'.[23] And it was Debussy's 'delightful lunches' on Fridays that Satie recalled in 1921 as the high spot of his visits to the rue Cardinet in the later 1890s:

> Eggs and lamb cutlets were the centre of these friendly occasions. But what eggs and what cutlets! I'm still licking my cheeks – on the inside, as you can guess. Debussy – who prepared these eggs and cutlets himself – had the secret (*the innermost secret*) of these preparations. It was all washed down with a delicious white Bordeaux whose effects were touching, and put us in just the right mood for enjoying the pleasures of friendship and of living far from 'Mutton Heads', Mummified Relics' and other 'Old Chaps' – those scourges of Humanity and the *poor in pocket.*[24]

Lunches and dinners *chez* Debussy were always intimate affairs, never exceeding a total of eight.[25] In congenial company the dinners could last until the early hours of the morning, and the pianist Ricardo Viñes found him

> neither pompous nor austere. At times he could enjoy himself in quite childish ways. I remember on one occasion, after dinner, we spent the

whole evening, with two other guests, drawing pigs with our eyes closed, and being allowed to take the pencil off the paper only once, to make dots for the eyes![26]

This comes as a stark contrast to the 'official' lunch arranged by his publisher in 1906 when Richard Strauss reduced Debussy to 'obstinate silence' with his lengthy account of the workings of the German copyright society he had founded.[27] But if Debussy really preferred playing party games, he was nonetheless prepared to expound on the 'damage done by the mediocrities' at the Schola Cantorum with Louis Laloy and Viñes the following year, and his discussion of 'the Chinese and their revolution' with the latter in 1912 shows that he did at least read the papers and keep abreast of major political events.[28]

Debussy's anglophilia led him to attach great importance both to afternoon tea and to the regular consumption of Scotch whisky. 'A simple tea at Debussy's was as lavish as most dinners', Hartmann recalled,[29] while Mme Gérard de Romilly says that 'At tea, he had the habit of absent-mindedly tracing imaginary patterns on the table with his knife while he was talking'; he was well aware of the anguish it was causing to the owner of the tablecloth.[30] 'He was fond of his whisky', Raoul Bardac remembers, 'which he used to drink every evening around ten o'clock, served in *his* special graduated decanter, and of *his* tea, which he drank only out of *his* teacup.'[31]

This fastidious and quasi-superstitious ritual was even more evident in the studio in the Avenue du Bois de Boulogne where Debussy composed. Numerous accounts attest to its almost obsessive neatness, and most agree that there was never a music manuscript in sight, either on his piano or work desk (or an ink stain on his blotter). 'The objects of his work-table were arranged in an order which never changed', Dolly Bardac recalls. 'He was never parted from a big wooden toad, a Chinese ornament, called "Arkel"... he even took it travelling with him'[32] when he went on the lucrative conducting trips he hated so much, 'claiming he could not work unless it was in sight'.[33] In fact, his expansive desk was cluttered with these essential familiar objects, most of them oriental, which were complemented by the Japanese prints on the walls – including Hokusai's 'Hollow of the Deep-sea Wave off Kanagawa', part of which he used as the cover of the first edition of *La mer*. Nothing, of course, could ever be out of place, and Maggie Teyte was involved in two (apparently) separate occasions when rehearsals were delayed by a stray pin and a piece of thread on the carpet.[34] Meticulous carpet care was equally in evidence in the 1890s at 58 rue Cardinet, according to René Peter. Discovery of additional impressions to the four he allowed his chair to make led to the following, almost incredible demonstration of how Debussy reached his composing position without shifting the chair from its habitual place:

It was a simple piece of acrobatics. It consisted of carefully tipping up the back so that the front legs were clear of the floor, thereby creating a little space between it and the desk. Into this space Claude gradually inserted himself, facing the desk, until he judged that he had moved far enough to be able to sit in the middle of the chair. At that point he lowered (1) the chair, (2) himself into it. After which:

'Well then, what do you think?'

'Magnificent', I replied admiringly. 'You're the composer of *Pelléas*, all right!'[35]

The same meticulous attention to detail that characterises his music and manuscripts also applied to Debussy's garden, when he eventually acquired one in the Avenue du Bois de Boulogne. Again, Raoul Bardac gives the best account of the way it provided him with both inspiration and some much-needed exercise:

He loved his garden, laid out to his own plans, which contained flowers and shrubs chosen by him, and which he looked after himself. He would walk round it slowly for a long time, in silence, then, suddenly, he would turn back towards the house where he would ask the upright Bechstein or the Blüthner [grand] . . . to repeat for him the musical idea he had just had. At other times he would rapidly and clearly jot this idea down (always in ink) in a bound notebook, or perhaps he would just come back to the house to arm himself with garden implements, with which he would perform a painstakingly delicate operation on some undesirable growth or some withered twig.[36]

As always, everything had to be exactly in place, and in this at least he was at one with Ravel and his self-designed, though more Japanese-inspired, garden at Montfort l'Amaury. Both composers chain-smoked too, even when engaged in their horticultural diversions, though Debussy meticulously rolled his own.

For all his reticence (and at times disdain), Debussy made a memorable impression on those he met. At the age of sixteen, Paul Vidal was 'immediately struck by his singular appearance, his burning eyes and the fierce concentrated expression on his face'.[37] Nine years later, Raymond Bonheur was impressed by his

powerful forehead with the strange faun-like cast, which he thrust ahead of him like the prow of a ship . . . With his dark hair, sensual nose and pale face surrounded by a light fringe of beard, Debussy in those days made you think of one of those noble portraits painted by Titian.[38]

Artistic comparisons, which no doubt pleased Debussy, frequently emerge: for the poet Léon-Paul Fargue in 1895 'he resembled a faun-like version of Jean Richepin, or better still Solario's "Head of St. John" in the Louvre',[39] whereas for Jacques-Emile Blanche in 1900 his 'sculptured face looked . . . like a fourteenth-century mask'.[40] Georges Jean-Aubry also commented on his physical resemblance to Dante Gabriel Rossetti in 1908.[41] The protruding forehead, which Debussy hated to be photographed at close quarters,[42] contributed to an exotic impression that was variously described as Moorish, Asiatic, or 'like an Assyrian prince'.[43] Apart from his exceptionally large ears and thick black, curly hair (which he never lost), his other most striking feature was his dark, penetrating eyes. 'From the shadows of his forehead, two immense, catlike eyes kept watch, casting ironic and ambiguous looks', Ricardo Viñes recalled,[44] and another pianist, George Copeland, spoke of them as 'like two pieces of shiny black jet'.[45] He invariably wore a smart, dark, three-piece suit and a bow tie (even on the beach) and, like Satie in later life, appeared in public as a typical French professional member of the bourgeoisie. But whereas Satie retained his left-wing views to the end, he observed after his friend's death that

> Debussy was far more inconsistent in his political and social tastes than he was musically. This artistic revolutionary was extremely bourgeois in his daily life. He disliked the 'eight-hour day' and other social customs . . . Raising salaries – other than his own, of course – was disagreeable to him. He had his own fixed 'opinions'. A strange anomaly.[46]

For someone as widely read and cultured as Debussy, who wrote some of the most perceptive letters that ever came from a composer, this indeed seems strange until we remember that Debussy's only real interest lay in artistic matters and that the mundanity of everyday life was not there to be argued about, especially in ever-diminishing social circles. He simply did not have the time or the energy for this, and it seems unlikely that he entered into detailed discussions (of which Satie had a similar horror) even with the most intelligent of his friends. Thus René Peter, to whom he gave lessons in writing for the theatre around the turn of the century, also found that Debussy

> held more or less categorical opinions about everything in life, principles from which he would not depart lightly: for instance, that superficial kindness is often no more than laziness; that obliging a borrower in whom you have no personal interest is in most cases the result either of the embarrassment you feel about getting rid of him, or else of your fear of appearing attached to money . . . that if a man holds to one idea in the face of everyone, he is necessarily in the right, given the fallibility which is the defining element of the human spirit – from which it follows that the more people agree about something, the more chance it has of being wrong.[47]

In fact, one of the best descriptions of Debussy's character came from a perceptive acquaintance rather than a close friend. His fellow composer Alfredo Casella remembered him as being extraordinarily nervous, impulsive and impressionable, and he was easily irritated. The oddity of his appearance, his unprepossessing voice, a strong dose of *gaucherie*, and finally an almost incredible shyness which he disguised under a show of paradox and often sarcastic and unkind irony, all made for a certain awkwardness in one's first relations with him. But then he was capable of deep and loyal friendship, and his affection for a few persons was boundless. He was generous, and he delighted to aid the needy – not seldom anonymously and with exquisite delicacy.[48]

On the other hand, as Paul Dukas observed, some found him 'heartless, an egoist, a trifler with the feelings of others', but 'you had to have known him in his adolescence really to understand him and, indeed, really to love him'.[49]

In general, Debussy's slowness of movement and uninterested manner often suggested laziness, an aspect that was reinforced by the numerous theatrical projects he embarked upon in bursts of enthusiasm but never completed. It might well be said that we owe much of his later piano music to the need to pay off at least part of his enormous financial debt to his publisher Durand, though he never relaxed his high standards in the process. In reality it was Debussy's perfectionism, his hours spent in spacing a single chord and making each work new and utterly distinctive, which led to what might be regarded as a relatively slender output. What Roy Howat has aptly described as the 'fineness', and Nichols as the 'transience' of his work was, in fact, laboriously achieved, for Debussy found composition far more difficult than Satie and Koechlin, and probably even more so than the equally secretive Ravel and Dukas. Indeed, as Debussy left few sketches, it is only recently that musicologists have even begun to understand his complex creative processes and his musical 'onion' still has many layers to be peeled away.

Debussy's reputation for immorality, as 'a trifler with the feelings of others', is less easily dismissed. We have already seen him as a man in quest of pleasure rather than passion, and one has only to read his letters to Lilly Texier to see such passion as existed evaporating after his marriage to her. Even so, his reputation as a roving Don Juan, especially in the 1890s, has been much exaggerated, for he had fewer affairs (or 'adventures') than most of his contemporaries. Pierre Louÿs told his brother Georges in 1915:

I don't know a man who was less of a rake than Debussy. In 1896, aged thirty-five, he was a handsome man, very masculine and extremely ardent; but in fifteen or twenty years of love-life he only knew five women, one of whom (Mme Hochon) ravished him. Therefore, five was the total. No prostitutes whatsoever. He used to say: 'It was purely by chance, but all five of them were blonde. I don't know what a brunette is like.'[50]

Several of Debussy's conquests were, however, married women. The first was Marie-Blanche Vasnier, whose civil servant husband, Henri, was eleven years older. When Debussy first met her in 1880 (as accompanist for the singing classes of Mme Moreau-Sainti) he was eighteen to Marie-Blanche's thirty-two. If there seems to be an element of artistic toy boy meets bored housewife here, the truth is that Mme Vasnier, with her agile coloratura soprano voice and professional standards, turned Debussy into a serious songwriter, inspiring twenty-three songs (with devoted dedications) over the next four years. 'Everything he writes is for her and owes its existence to her', Paul Vidal observed,[51] and if she actually had reddish hair, she had the green eyes that were to attract Debussy to Gaby Dupont in the 1890s. Enforced absence in Rome, of course, gradually cooled Debussy's ardour, though while he was there his long, friendly letters to Henri Vasnier suggest that he was either a willing accomplice in the affair or was ignorant of its existence (which seems unlikely). As his daughter Marguerite recalled, 'when he [Debussy] came back for good [in 1887], the intimacy was no longer there. He had changed, as we had.'[52]

Whilst in Rome, however, Debussy's existence was not as dreary and unfulfilling as his letters make out. As the diaries of Gabrielle Hébert (the wife of the director of the Villa Medici) show, Debussy led an active social life with society figures, like Count Primoli and the Princess Scilla, after Hébert took over in June 1885, and the arrival of the Hochons in January 1886 livened things up still further. Louise Hochon – known to her intimate friends as Loulou – developed a crush on Debussy, and on 9 February Gabrielle Hébert recorded in her diary that Count Primoli 'tells me that they have seen Loulou and Debussy kissing in the Villa'.[53] As Lesure suggests, the contemporary setting of Verlaine's 'Green' (published in the 1888 *Ariettes*), with its restrained ecstasy, may well have been inspired by the brief Loulou affair rather than 'the lady far away in Paris'.[54]

Between 1890 and 1898, Debussy pursued a much longer relationship with the alluring Gaby Dupont, finally leaving his parents to set up house with her at 42 rue de Londres in March 1892. To all outward appearances, these were Debussy's happiest and most carefree years, though we have to remember that they were years of artistic struggle (with the uncongenial *Rodrigue et Chimène*, the operatic revolution of *Pelléas*, and the problematic *Nocturnes*). They also saw Debussy's two rather unconvincing attempts at a respectable marriage, which (coupled with his financial irresponsibility) caused havoc in his domestic life.

First came the soprano, Thérèse Roger, whom he accompanied in the last two of his *Proses lyriques* at a Société Nationale concert on 17 February 1894, but who was no second Marie-Blanche in the looks department. Within days Debussy had proposed to her, to the amazement of his friends and, it would seem, principally to impress his benefactor Chausson, who disapproved of his living in sin with Gaby. What was worse was that Debussy lied both to Chausson and to Thérèse's mother about their engagement, which was equally quickly broken off. But if he lost Chausson as a friend, he gained another in Pierre Louÿs (who stood by him until he deserted Lilly in an equally hypocritical way in 1904).

Debussy's second proposal to Catherine Stevens shows him in a rather better light. The family of the painter Arthur Stevens had run into severe financial difficulties in early 1896 and, according to Lesure, Debussy proposed to his daughter to alleviate her distress, promising her that *Pelléas* would secure their future financially. 'She refused prettily, telling him they would speak of the matter again once *Pelléas* had been performed.'[55]

Then, in a letter to Louÿs of February 1897 (which brings his feminine total up to eight, counting Lilly and Emma), Debussy confessed that

> Gaby of the piercing eye found a letter in my pocket which left no doubt as to the advanced state of a love affair, and containing enough romantic material to move even the hardest heart. Whereupon . . . scenes . . . tears . . . a real revolver and *Le petit journal* there to record the lot . . . It's all so uncivilised and pointless, and it changes absolutely nothing: you can't wipe out a mouth's kisses or a body's caresses by passing an india-rubber over them. But all the same, it would be a handy invention, a rubber for expunging adultery.[56]

Gaby's attempted suicide was also exacerbated by the death of her father on 7 February, and if things were never the same again in the rue Cardinet, Gaby soon recovered and, rather unexpectedly, became a close friend of Debussy's next affair, the beautiful mannequin Lilly Texier, whom he met in the spring of 1899. As well she might, Gaby warned her of Debussy's roving eye. But to no avail, for he married Lilly on 19 October (with Satie as a witness), paying for the wedding breakfast from the proceeds of a piano lesson that morning!

Although Lilly remained devoted to Debussy, jealously guarding his privacy and remaining content to live in poverty in his shadow, he soon found her unstimulating and overly possessive. It is tempting to see a glimpse into their domestic life in his contemporary play *Les 'Frères en art'* for, according to its co-author René Peter, Marie represents Lilly, and the main character, Maltravers, has views which strongly resemble those of Debussy at the time (in terms of intellectual anarchy, elitism and pantheism). Debussy's revised version probably dates from 1903 because of its references to telephones and cinematographic techniques, and here he adds the remark that Maltravers and Marie 'are as silent as little goldfish', implying that they have little to say to each other and live an enclosed, goldfish-bowl existence. Marie is 'a delightful woman, nothing more', with an ideal of cosy domesticity that threatens to stifle her creative partner. At the only moment when the couple embrace, Debussy adds the cool stage direction 'nothing more, nothing less', and the demise of his relationship with Lilly was surely hastened by her inability to bear children.[57]

On 1 October 1903 he met yet another soprano, Emma Bardac, who was no stranger to extra-marital affairs herself. Indeed, her liaison with Gabriel Fauré had inspired his song-cycle *La bonne chanson* in the early 1890s. Emma was intellectually far more of a match for Debussy, and their friendship developed rapidly during the early months of 1904. By June at least they were lovers. On 15 July, Debussy packed Lilly off by train to her parents in Bichain, referring ominously to the 'new path' he had found which 'he dare not abandon' in an ostensibly caring letter to her the following day.[58] Late in July he and Emma eloped to Jersey (the 'Isle joyeuse' of his most extrovert piano piece) and Dieppe for the summer, and in October they set up house together in the fashionable sixteenth district of Paris. But their idyll was short-lived for, just before what would have been her fifth wedding anniversary, Lilly shot herself in the breast. Although she survived, the bullet remained with her until she died in 1932. Thanks to his growing international fame, Debussy's personal life now received extensive press coverage, and his treatment of Lilly before and during their protracted divorce settlement does him little credit. He kept her entirely in the dark about Emma, for instance, until 13 September 1904, and had pretended he was going to London with the painter Jacques-Emile Blanche a month earlier.[59] In February 1908 the whole Lilly scandal even reached the stage in a thinly disguised melodrama by Henry Bataille called *La femme nue*, just over a month after his eventual marriage to Emma. Equally seriously, Emma's uncle, the financier Osiris, had disinherited her in his will a year earlier, even though they now had a fifteen-month-old daughter to support. So Debussy had good reason to be pessimistic about his future prospects.

In fact, married life with Emma was anything but idyllic. She was frequently ill, constantly possessive and extravagant, and far less easy to pacify than the naively devoted Lilly had been. Debussy frequently retreated to the sanctuary of his study and wrote notes to Emma in preference to the fraught confrontations he so loathed.[60] Financial pressures forced him to undertake conducting trips abroad between 1908 and 1914, but Emma sometimes insisted on coming too, and equally insistently stopped him going to the States in 1912 to hear Caplet's superb Boston production of *Pelléas*. Family holidays proved a particular trial, and although Debussy loved the sea and playing games with his young daughter, we find him telling Durand from Houlgate in 1911 that 'the truth is that at the end of this holiday we have to admit we don't know why we came. Is it really that we've lost the ability to enjoy things together?'[61] The fault was by no means all Emma's. It was she, not Debussy, who wrote to her lawyer to enquire about a trial separation during a matrimonial crisis in 1910, and as Mary Garden concluded in her autobiography: 'I honestly don't know if Debussy ever loved anybody really. He loved his music – and perhaps himself. I think he was wrapped up in his genius.'[62] The external signs of devotion remained to the end: the touching letters from abroad, the affectionate dedications 'A La Petite Mienne', and so on. But as early as March 1905 we find the dedication of *La mer* to Emma, 'whose eyes sparkle in the dawn',[63] withdrawn in favour of his publisher Durand, and even during their 'honeymoon summer' in 1904 we find the composer nostalgic for 'the Claude Debussy who worked so enthusiastically on *Pelléas*'.[64]

The truth is that Debussy brought many of his problems on himself. However often he maintained that he was 'as simple as a blade of grass',[65] for him that grass was always greener somewhere else, and Emma must have come to despise his inaction, moral cowardice, self-pity and much-vaunted hypersensitivity. As he admitted to Durand after another, particularly bad crisis in July 1913,

> Struggling on one's own is nothing! But struggling 'en famille' becomes odious! . . . In my case I only struggle to uphold a point of honour . . . Perhaps I'm to blame, because my only energy is intellectual; in everyday life I stumble over the smallest pebble, which another man would send flying with a light-hearted kick![66]

One might well wonder why Debussy got married once, let alone twice, for he seems to have been well aware of the pitfalls. He tried, for instance, to placate Lilly in 1904 with the observation that 'an artist is, in short, a wretched indoors man and perhaps also a wretched husband. Besides, the reverse, a perfect husband, often produces a contemptible artist . . . It's a vicious circle.'[67] Perhaps his chief reasons for marriage lay in his selfish desire for outward respectability, and in Emma's case there was also the need to make Chouchou legitimate. But within his own circles no one achieved lasting happiness through his action (or inaction), least of all himself.

The war years only brought more misery as the patriotic Debussy lamented his inability to be of practical use to his beloved France and found his inspiration drying up. Only in the summer of 1915 did he experience a return of his former creative powers, but that winter his rectal cancer became serious and, apart from the Violin Sonata and a draft setting of Louis Laloy's *Ode à la France*, his composing career was over and his existence was only made bearable through morphine.

As for his philosophy of life, this is more difficult to determine. He once told Pierre Louÿs that 'Life is a compromise between instinct and civilisation. The nobility of the human condition consists in aspiring to the freedom which nature has given us.'[68] Certainly, he was artistically at his happiest in nature, as he delightedly told Caplet in 1910, noting 'how naturally the transition works between "Parfums de la nuit" and "Le matin d'un jour de fête". *It sounds as though it's improvised.*'[69] But if he composed some of the most evocative and spontaneous nature music ever written, he could still say just after he had finished his orchestral *Images*: 'Only souls without imagination go to the country for inspiration . . . I can look into my garden and find there everything that I want.'[70] Similarly, he admitted in an interview in 1914 that

> the sea fascinates me to the point of paralysing my creative faculties. Moreover, I've never been able to write a page of music under the direct, immediate impression of this great, blue sphinx, and my 'symphonic triptych' *La mer* was entirely composed in Paris.[71]

So it would seem that the ideal surroundings he found in the Avenue du Bois de Boulogne, after a lifetime of changing addresses, more than compensated for the trauma of his second marriage; for which posterity must be grateful.

All of this reinforces just how interiorised Debussy was both as a man and as a composer. As Roger Nichols says: 'This reluctance to engage with what the material world calls "realities" was something that all the women in Debussy's life had to try to accept, with greater or lesser success.'[72] As increasing age and the fame thrust upon him after *Pelléas* made him ever more reclusive, it would seem that Emma suffered the most. For in the 1890s Debussy was perfectly gregarious, enjoying the daily round of cabarets, cafés, bars, salons and bookshops. If his musical motive was 'toujours plus haut', then the same cannot be said about his personal life, where his immorality and deviousness caused innumerable problems. He wanted his life to be straightforward, but his desires made it complicated. If his desires led to the experiences he craved, then few remained unaffected in the process: friends were compartmentalised or lost. He could take Gaby to bars and cabarets, but not to bourgeois salons or public concerts, which is one reason why he had to marry Lilly. Then, when her child-like devotion palled, his initial desire for Emma led him to feel trapped in a world of domestic upheaval, in which what are frequently described as his own childish attitudes only exacerbated matters. From this imprisonment there was now no escape except into the inner world of creativity, though deep down this may have been what Debussy really wanted in the end. When even this creativity deserted Debussy it is easy to see why he considered suicide on more than one occasion, especially in 1916–17.

None of this, of course, detracts from the greatness of his music, but it surely accounts for some of the sinister undercurrents that lurk beneath its attractive surface, and which contribute so much to its mystery and profundity. As Debussy told another interviewer, in 1910:

There will always be an enormous breach between the soul of a man as he is and the soul he puts into his work. A man portrays himself in his work, it is true, but only part of himself. In real life, I cannot live up to the ideas I have in music. I feel the difference there is in me between Debussy the composer and Debussy the man.[73]

Yet if many people during his life wanted Debussy the man to be different, there are few who would now seek any changes in Debussy the composer.

2 Debussy's Parisian affiliations

BARBARA L. KELLY

Paris: the importance of geography

In 1928 a handful of Debussy supporters formed a committee to raise money to erect a monument to Debussy. Initially the location for the monument was to be in his birthplace, Saint-Germain-en-Laye, but it was soon felt that Debussy's significance and profile were too great and that two statues should be erected, with the main one in Paris in the Bois de Boulogne. The conductor Gabriel Astruc gave a speech entitled 'Le Monument de "Claude de France"' at an official concert on 17 June 1932 to celebrate the unveiling of the monument; he revealed that the aim was 'to honour ... the memory of Debussy, who so many times had led the great battle of music'.[1] This shift in the monument's location from the periphery to the centre was symbolic of Debussy's own artistic relocation from the margins of Parisian musical life to the centre as the symbol of French musical identity.

By the time of Debussy's birth in Saint-Germain-en-Laye, Paris was consolidating its position as a hub in all aspects of social, political and cultural life. When he came to Paris to enter the Conservatoire in 1872, he experienced a city recently invaded and defeated by the Prussians, and reduced to turmoil by the Commune. Given his father's imprisonment on account of his involvement in the Commune, his memory of these events was painful and personal. In a letter to Jacques Durand at the beginning of the 1914 war he admitted the lasting impact of this time: 'the memories of 1870 ... prevent me from yielding to enthusiasm'.[2] While Haussmann had already put his mark on Paris, the city was constantly in the process of reconstruction. In his youth Debussy must have seen the expansion of the railways under Charles de Saulces de Freycinet's direction.[3] On his return from Rome in 1887 Debussy would have witnessed the construction of the Eiffel Tower, which was completed for the 1889 Exhibition and soon came to symbolise Paris's patriarchal might and innovation. Henri Rivière's engravings entitled *Trente-six vues de la Tour Eiffel* (1888–1902) demonstrate the dominance of this new image on the Parisian landscape through his purposefully distorting and exaggerating eye. His engravings also emphasise the vital role of the workers in modernising the city.[4] In addition, Debussy would have witnessed the building of the Paris metro, which was planned in 1871, but only begun in 1898. Line 1 was opened on 19 July 1900 in time for the

1900 Exhibition.[5] Finally, on Debussy's deathbed in March 1918, Paris was being invaded once more and German guns were changing the landscape of the city.

François Lesure has emphasised the accidental nature of Debussy's place of birth in his opening line of his book *Claude Debussy avant Pelléas*: 'It is rather by chance that Achille-Claude Debussy was born in Saint-Germain-en-Laye.'[6] In 1882 Mme von Meck observed in a letter to Tchaikovsky that Debussy 'is a Parisian to his fingertips, a real *gamin de Paris*'.[7] Once in Paris Debussy was very reluctant to leave it, as his two unhappy years in Rome testify. Yet separation was fruitful in consolidating his artistic ideas. This chapter examines the nature of Debussy's attachment to place – Paris – in terms of his intellectual and musical development. It considers this alongside the composer's real openness to other musics; just as the Paris Exhibition was the controlling space wherein the Parisian public (including Debussy) could sample foreign wares – in Debussy's case, the Javanese gamelan and Musorgsky – so Paris remained the site where Debussy could assimilate and naturalise a range of foreign musical influences.[8]

Debussy evoked Paris in only a few works. Villon's ballad 'Ballade des femmes de Paris' from *Trois ballades de Villon* (1910) says nothing about the city or the character of Parisian women; it merely boasts that they can gossip better than women from elsewhere. We have to take Villon's word for it, however, for we do not hear them chattering. Debussy's letters reveal that he was attracted to the ballad's historical remoteness; and the antique character of his musical setting confirms this.[9] Debussy also evoked Paris in the orchestral *Nocturnes* of 1897–9. In 'Nuages' we hear a rare instance of Parisian sounds in the hooting of barges. Nichols has observed that his allusion to the *Garde republicaine* in 'Fêtes' was the nearest Debussy ever got to the everyday world of Charpentier's *Louise*, but he argues that even this procession 'is poeticised through its stereo treatment'.[10] By way of contrast, Debussy much more readily located many of his Spanish works, for example, the early song *Madrid*; 'La Soirée dans Grenade', *Estampes*; and 'La puerta del vino', *Préludes*, book 2. These titles represented exotic places in his musical imagination. His relationship with Paris went far beyond the need to evoke its physical presence or the sounds associated with it. As Debussy's early letters reveal, he was involved in redefining the nature of French music, and in this process Paris was the source of his intellectual and artistic stimulus.

Debussy's attachment to the capital was essential for making an impact on France as a whole, because Paris was the space where Frenchness was defined. Theodore Zeldin emphasises the role of Paris for constructing notions of nationhood:

> To be a Frenchman, in the fullest sense, meant to be civilised, which
> required that one accept the models of thought, behaviour and expression
> held in esteem in Paris. At one level, to accept civilisation meant to accept
> cultural uniformity and centralisation.[11]

As a result, intellectuals and artists were drawn to Paris from the provinces in
search of intellectual sustenance and a successful career. Composers whose
interests were predominantly regional tended to be marginalised: Déodat de
Séverac, for instance. Vincent d'Indy, who was committed to regionalism,
as evinced by his educational programmes throughout France in connection with the Schola Cantorum, still made his reputation in the capital.
A minority of intellectuals felt they could keep abreast of Parisian intellectual developments by reading books and reviews.[12] Debussy's discomfort in
being forced to do this in Rome confirmed his need to be physically present
in the city. According to Zeldin, Paris was particularly anxious to claim and
retain the arts:

> Paris got its population from the provinces but gave it back its worst
> features – like its fashions – and kept for itself everything worth keeping,
> like painting and music.[13]

Thus, although the idea of France as a unified nation is open to scrutiny,
the power of the centre in fashioning a national artistic identity should
not be underestimated. If Debussy could conquer Paris with his musical
innovations, then he had taken hold of France.[14]

Debussy and the Conservatoire: conformity and innovation

Debussy's uneasy relationship with authority manifested itself clearly during his years at the Paris Conservatoire. There was considerable tension
between Debussy's wilful and experimental nature and his ability to play
the game by winning the necessary prizes and achieving status and recognition. Debussy's attitude to his harmony teacher Emile Durand was telling:
he declared that the only rules were 'mon plaisir'. He alluded on several
occasions to the restrictive teaching of his teacher in his writings in the
press.

   Maurice Emmanuel, a few years Debussy's junior, recalled how Debussy
had shocked a class of students by experimenting with daring harmonies
at the piano while his teacher, Léo Delibes, was absent. This gave Debussy
a following, but they were disappointed when they realised that Debussy
had conformed in his winning Prix de Rome cantata; they had anticipated
a public outcry:

> Nearly all of us had managed to get into the sanctuary. When
> Claude-Achille's turn came, and the air was filled with the opening chords
> of *L'enfant prodigue*, we exchanged delighted glances. But these soon faded.
> Instead of the scandal we were counting on, and despite occasional signs of
> agitation on the part of one or two elderly conductors who looked
> surprised and inclined to protest, compared with the outrageous
> harmonies which Debussy had served up to us previously, Claude-Achille's
> cantata struck us as debonair! It triumphed, in spite of some opposition.
> And while we did not grudge its success, we felt seriously let down that the
> expected brouhaha had not materialized.[15]

Debussy admitted in an interview for *The New York Times* (1910) that he realised he must conform if he hoped to win. During his student years Debussy
was already setting contemporary literature by Paul Verlaine, Paul Bourget,
Stéphane Mallarmé and Théodore de Banville. His setting of Banville, *Diane
au bois*, dates from this period (1883), but the young composer heeded his
teacher, Ernest Guiraud, when the older man remarked: 'This is all very
interesting, but you must put it away for later or you will never have the Prix
de Rome.'[16]

It is worth comparing Debussy with Ravel, who also struggled with
Conservatoire authority, but who entered for the Prix de Rome five times,
and on the final occasion did not get beyond the first round because his fugue
contained parallel fifths and ended on a chord containing a major seventh.
Ravel was less skilled in keeping up a pretence and admitted in 1926 to feeling
an impostor.[17] Satie, who was uncompromisingly anti-establishment, left
the Conservatoire without any qualifications, though he received a certificate
in counterpoint from the more authoritarian Schola Cantorum at the age of
thirty-nine. However, Debussy's success was at some personal cost; in 1903
he recalled his reaction to the news of his achievement:

> Suddenly, someone tapped me on the shoulder and said in a breathless
> voice: 'You have won the prize . . . !' Believe it or not, I can assure you that
> my heart sank! I had a sudden vision of boredom, and of all the worries
> that inevitably go together with any form of official recognition. I felt I was
> no longer free.[18]

Roman exile: imagined communities

Debussy regarded his two-year stay at the Villa Medici as an enforced exile
from the familiar setting of Paris. His letters are full of references to his lonely,
miserable state. In a letter to Antoine Marmontel he opined that Parisians
were 'disoriented and crushed by Rome'.[19] He also spoke of feeling artistically
impotent in Rome, and certainly his letters reveal that he struggled with his

composition. However, absence from his cultural home gave Debussy the opportunity to reflect on and test his ideas. It could be argued that it was during this period that he experimented with the musical ideas that were to make him distinctive and original. In the process of this discovery Debussy revealed his active engagement with the vibrancy of French intellectual life.

Once in Rome Debussy no longer felt able to please the authorities and struggled to produce his yearly composition as required by the Institut. However, despite his sense of musical impotence through lack of stimulus in Rome, he was by no means idle: he strove to articulate – in letters mainly to Henri Vasnier – his notion of the ideal composition, which involved a new approach to form and colour. In a letter to Vasnier of 4 June 1885 he expresses his disatisfaction with *Zuleima* (his first *envoi*), stating that 'I don't think I will ever be able to cast my music in too rigid a mould.'[20] In this instance his difficulty relates to the task of combining text with music. His recent experiences of setting 'ces grands imbéciles de vers' for the Prix de Rome competitions were clearly fresh on his mind, and his determination to opt for wordless chorus in *Diane au bois* and *Printemps* resolved this dilemma as well as allowing him to experiment with the voice as musical colour.[21]

Debussy had a strong sense that his ideal was beyond his abilities.[22] Writing again to Vasnier he explains his difficulty in trying to achieve something new: 'perhaps I have undertaken a task that is beyond me; there being no precedent to go on, I find myself obliged to invent new forms'.[23] He acknowledges but dismisses as ridiculous one possible model, Wagner, though this was certainly the phase when he experienced Wagner's positive influence most keenly. It is significant that he felt that there were few musical models at his disposal. It suggests that the main source of his ideas was coming from outside music, as Dukas was to remark during the 1890s.[24] While he felt the need to resist Wagner's musical influence, he responded to literary Wagnerism as defined and discussed by Baudelaire and the Symbolists.

Debussy's letters during this period reveal the impact of Baudelaire's ideas on the young composer. Lesure and Jarocinski have identified an instance where Debussy rephrases Baudelaire in a letter to Vasnier. Writing about his difficulty in achieving his musical ideal in *Zuleima*, he declares: 'I want music that is supple and concentrated enough to adapt itself to the lyrical movements of the soul and the whims of reverie.'[25] This is remarkably close to Baudelaire's comment in the dedication letter to Arsène Houssaye, director of *La presse*: 'Who among us has not . . . dreamt the miracle of poetic prose without rhyme and rhythm, which is supple and striking enough to adapt itself to the lyrical movement of the soul and to the undulations of reverie?'[26] It is significant that Debussy saw a parallel between his musical aims and the literary struggle against the traditional strictures of verse and rhyme. Jarocinski regards Debussy's assimilation of Baudelaire in this letter as a measure of the 'lasting impression of Baudelaire's ideas in the memory of Claude Debussy' and as an indication that Debussy 'was very much *au courant* with the artistic life of Paris'.[27] Debussy's assimilation of Baudelaire goes far beyond this one paraphrase.

Debussy mirrored Baudelaire's tendency to draw connections between the arts in his own quest for an ideal musical form and expression. Writing about *Printemps* to Emile Baron, he insisted that the work was to be 'without a programme, as I have a profound dislike for music that follows one of those leaflets which they are so careful to give you when you enter the concert hall'. Music could only evoke the other arts in a general way. He continued: 'You should understand the extent to which music must have evocative power.'[28] This emphasis on the evocative power of music can be compared to Baudelaire's comments about Wagner's *Tannhäuser* in which he addresses the issue of 'translating' or describing music in terms of the other arts: 'It translates in its own fashion and in its own appropriate way. In music, as in painting and even in the written word . . . there is always a gap which is completed by the imagination of the author.'[29] Musical, literary and artistic expression were not interchangeable; all required the imprecise but vital role of the listener's imagination.[30]

Debussy also followed Baudelaire in writing about music in terms of the visual arts. In the same letter to Baron he describes *Printemps* as 'a work with a special colour, recreating as many sensations as possible'.[31] One of the ways in which he wanted to achieve this was by using the choir for its orchestral/timbral qualities: 'it is the ensemble – the blending of colours – which is tricky to achieve'.[32] In his pamphlet on Wagner, Baudelaire made a similar connection between music and colour. He writes of his experience of listening to *Tannhäuser* as 'an immense horizon and a large, diffuse light. I experienced the sensation of a luminosity that was more alive, with increasing intensity of light and with such speed.'[33] Whereas Baudelaire was compelled to make these connections because of his technical inability to write about music in musical terms, for Debussy establishing these connections with art provided a useful way of thinking about musical timbre. Baudelaire's idea of correspondences between the arts may well have emerged from his art criticism; in *Le salon de 1846* Baudelaire not only immersed himself in an art different from his own, he explored connections between the visual and musical arts:

> Harmony is at the root of the theory of colour. Melody is the unity in colour, or colour in general. Melody wants closure; it is an ensemble where all the effects converge into a general effect.[34]

In the same essay Baudelaire expounds his notion of the colour spectrum with its musical equivalents, which he finds in the gradation of colour from shade to light in nature.[35] Similarly, Debussy in the letter to Baron describes the gradual process of rebirth in nature, which he wants to capture musically in *Printemps*: 'I would like to express the slow and laborious genesis of beings and things in nature, then the gradual blossoming, culminating in a burst of joy at being reborn into a new life.'[36]

Debussy's aim was to depict not simply nature but rather 'le côté humain'.[37] Baudelaire also linked nature to human concerns and passions in his letter to Wagner of 17 February 1860, in which he detected in Wagner 'great aspects of nature, and the solemnity of great human passions'.[38] Furthermore, in expressing his impressions of *Tannhäuser* he describes the gradual emergence of red, which represents passion, from 'the transition of red and pink to the incandescence of the blazing fire'.[39] This notion of the scale and range of artistic and human emotions was an important idea for literary Wagnerians and for the Symbolists. Paul Claudel, who had also come under the Wagnerian spell in the 1890s, was similarly preoccupied with the range of musical and dramatic expression, which, by his own admission, had its roots in Wagner. Furthermore, both Poe and Wilde were interested in the interchangeability of nature, human life and art.[40]

It appears that Debussy's life-long fascination with the intricacies of musical colour was stimulated by Baudelaire's ideas on the correspondences between the arts. Indeed, Debussy's and Ravel's approaches to colour are often compared. Ravel admitted that while orchestration for him was a technical exercise after composition, Debussy's treatment of timbre is integral to the composition process.[41] Debussy certainly conceived *Jeux* instrumentally, and his comment in a letter to André Caplet that 'I'm thinking of that orchestral colour which seems to be lit up from behind' indicates that Baudelaire's ideas had not been forgotten.[42] Indeed, despite Marie Rolf's manuscript studies which suggest that Debussy often conceived his works in piano arrangement before orchestrating,[43] Debussy tended to allow timbres to transform slowly over time and to appear to dictate structure, as in 'Feuilles mortes' and 'Ondine', *Préludes*, book 2.[44] Baudelaire's observations from nature that harmony is created in the subtle blend of gradations of colour and shadow, and that form and colour are one, constitute important aspects of Debussy's originality. Debussy expressed the inseparability of form, rhythm and colour in a letter to Durand in 1907: 'Generally speaking, I feel more and more that music, by its very essence, is not something that can flow inside a rigorous, traditional form. It consists of colours and of rhythmicised time . . .'[45]

Debussy's *Cinq poèmes de Baudelaire* are probably the most Wagnerian works he ever wrote. In part they could be regarded as a homage to the poet, whose impact had been so important during these formative years.

Nichols and Holloway argue that the works do not fit comfortably with the rest of Debussy's oeuvre in that Wagner's influence is unchecked.[46] By 1889 Debussy had made two pilgrimages to Bayreuth where he heard *Parsifal, Die Meistersinger* and *Tristan*.[47] This also represents the beginning of Debussy's disillusionment with Wagner, though not the end of his absorption in his music (however much he revolted against his influence). While working on *Printemps* in 1887, he admitted to Ernest Hébert that the first act of *Tristan* 'is definitely the most beautiful thing I know in terms of emotional depth'.[48] His principled rejection of Wagner was on musical and cultural grounds: Wagner was unsuitable as a model for French composers because he was inimitable and not French. It was a rejection his literary Symbolist friends found hard to understand.

Baudelaire was one of several influences that connected Debussy to Parisian intellectual life in Rome. Friends, such as the poet Paul Bourget and Emile Baron, the Paris bookseller, supplied him with the most recent French literature. By this route he read Jean Moréas, Huysmans and Dumas *fils*.[49] Debussy also showed his determination to keep abreast of contemporary debates and read a number of new periodicals, including *La revue indépendante, La vogue, La revue contemporaine* and *La revue wagnérienne*.[50] While the contents of *La revue wagnérienne* are well known, the other periodicals have not received much scrutiny and reveal his Parisian intellectual diet. Already familiar and recurring names occur in these reviews, including articles in *La revue contemporaine* on Baudelaire, Poe, Wagner, Rimbaud and Huysmans, and literary contributions by Bourget, Moréas, Barrès, Villiers de l'Isle-Adam, Dujardin and Verlaine. In its first year of publication, 1885, two authors stand out for special mention: Théodore de Banville and Dante Gabriel Rossetti. The former's publication of *Nocturne* is significant in that 1885 was the year in which Debussy was struggling with Banville's setting of *Diane au bois*.[51] More significant is the publication of Rossetti's poem *La damoiselle élue* translated by Gabriel Sarrazin.[52] Debussy embarked on his own setting in 1887 and it is likely that he first read it in this review. Richard Langham Smith identifies the impact of Pre-Raphaelite tendencies generally in 1887, exhibited in Debussy's desire for 'une belle froideur' (a beautiful coldness) in *Diane au bois*.[53] The Parisians' interest in English literature is evident from the frequent presence in the review of translations and commentaries – often by Sarrazin – of Walter Pater's *The Renaissance* (1877), *Marius the Epicurean* (1885) and Shelley's *Cantilènes*. Rossetti's and Pater's work would certainly have appealed to the artistic sensibilities of this emerging group.

Many similar names appear in *La vogue*, which in the eight months of its existence (1886) reveals its proximity to Symbolist ideals. In the October issue Paul Adam reproduces Moréas's manifesto, which first appeared in the supplement of *Le figaro*, 18 September 1886. Moréas's advocacy of 'a new vocabulary where harmonies combine with colours and lines' highlights the interchangeability of musical, literary and artistic vocabularies.[54] *La vogue*'s director, Gustave Kahn, defended this exposé of the group's ideals in *L'événement*, 28 September, which Adam reproduces, thus confirming the orientation of the review. He draws comparisons with Wagner and Impressionism, reflects on the interchangeability of dream and reality, and, in his discussion of the representation of the Idea in the material world, he suggests but does not assert Schopenhauer's influence. Finally, his celebration of the rhythmic flexibility of prose poems, which follow 'the allures, the oscillations, the twists and the naiveties of the Idea', not only recalls the Baudelaire passage Debussy half quoted in his letter to Vasnier, but suggests the stimulus for another of Debussy's preoccupations and innovations, his rhythmically flexible vocal writing.[55]

As an avid reader of *La vogue* Debussy is also likely to have come across Theodor de Wyzewa's article on Mallarmé's *L'après-midi d'un faune*, entitled 'M. Mallarmé: Notes' (5–12 July and 12–19 July 1886). Discussing the musicality of Mallarmé's writing in *L'après-midi d'un faune*, he opines: 'I believe that . . . the poetic work of M. Mallarmé remains today the best model that exists of the music of words.'[56]

Artistic formations and patterns of allusion

Once back in Paris Debussy realised his ambition to integrate himself into Parisian intellectual life. Most influential were the unofficial networks – the artistic formations. These gatherings took place in Bailly's bookshop and in cafés and bistros, such as the Brasserie Pousset in Montmartre, Café Vachette, which was frequented by Jean Moréas, and the Café Voltaire at l'Odéon, the haunt of Charles Morice. Debussy also mixed with intellectuals in the homes of the Chaussons, Henri Mercier and Pierre Louÿs. Debussy began to frequent the most prestigious group – Mallarmé's Tuesday evenings from c. 1892 – where he met many of the writers he had read in the reviews, including Verlaine, Villiers de l'Isle Adam, Huysmans, Dujardin and Wyzewa.[57] There has been some uncertainty about exactly when the young composer first came to the poet's attention. It now seems that they met in autumn 1890 as a result of hearing the *Cinq poèmes de Baudelaire*.[58] In Lesure's view 'The *Cinq poèmes* did more for his growing reputation than *La damoiselle élue* and the Quartet' because it drew him to the attention of prominent figures such as Mallarmé, Catulle Mendès and the critic Willy.[59] Debussy and Mallarmé planned a collaboration on *Prélude à l'après-midi d'un faune* for a projected performance with Paul Fort at the Théâtre d'art. In fact a performance was announced for 27 February 1891: '*L'Après-midi d'un faune*, 1 tableau en vers de Stéphane Mallarmé, partie musicale de Mr. de Bussy'.[60] For unknown reasons Mallarmé delayed the performance and the project never materialised.

It was, perhaps, more appropriate that their works remained distinct, and that Debussy was able to take the idea of 'evocation' a stage further in his *Prélude* than he had managed in setting Baudelaire's poems; it also enabled him to realise his aim in *Diane au bois* to 'sacrifice dramatic action to an expression of the long exploration of inner feeling'.[61] Just as Mallarmé was seeking to capture the qualities of music through poetry, which may explain his desire to withdraw from the collaboration, Debussy was seeking his own distinctively musical ends, with ideas clearly derived from Baudelaire and the Symbolists. Mallarmé wanted to take from music its ability to suggest rather than to describe.[62] He declared that 'Henceforth literature will seek to express only the mood or attitude of the poet in the presence of Nature, the atmosphere of the wood rather than the exact form of the trees.'[63] Debussy was drawn to Mallarmé's subject in which music, love, the natural and the dream world interact. For Mallarmé as for Schopenhauer, whose impact on the Symbolists was considerable, music provides momentary release from the cycle of desire and fulfilment. In addition, the world of dreams and sleep provides a similar release:

> Passive,
> The whole scene burns in this fierce hour without a sign
> Of what craft whisked away the wished-for nuptial
> As I tune up my A; so that I wake again
> To warmth, just as before, erect, alone,
> Under a long familiar wave of light, O lilies![64]

Like Baudelaire, Mallarmé linked music to the visual image of light and shade in nature; in Mallarmé's poem nature, light and shadow provide the backdrop to the faun's reverie and music making. Music is close to nature in borrowing such effects, but also more obscure and mysterious than nature or poetry in its imprecision and detachment from the phenomenal world.[65] This view led Mallarmé to consider poetry superior in terms of clarity and meaning, but also to envy music's mystery.[66]

The form of Debussy's *Prélude* arises out of the poem: the line 'A single line of sound, aloof, disinterested' inspires the flute theme, which generates the piece. In his invitation to Mallarmé of 20 December 1894, Debussy acknowledged the importance of the flute:

> I need not say how happy I should be if you were kind enough to honour
> with your presence the arabesque which, by an excess of pride perhaps,
> I believe to have been dictated by the flute of your faun.'[67]

Here he uses 'arabesque' to describe the foregrounded flute and, by extension, the whole work.[68] This term was popular with the Symbolists, particularly with Mallarmé, who, according to Jean-Jaques Eigeldinger, used the word regularly between 1893 and 1895.[69] Debussy found in the Symbolist idea of arabesque a means of inventing 'new forms'.[70] Jarocinski concurs when he writes that 'the notion of the "arabesque", which recurs so often in his writings, is in itself proof that the composer was thinking along new lines'.[71] The arabesque, as he understood it, is an undulating melodic line, independent of any notion of the development of themes or 'motifs'. Indeed, the flute melody functions as the melodic, tonal and structural foundation of the work. The ornamented flute line is subject to varied repetition; just like the ever-changing orchestral background on which it is imposed, the melody only appears in the same shape in its first two statements; it is always recognisable but never fixed. Its recurrence at the pitch C♯, on all but two occasions (bars 79 and 86), and on the flute, except in one instance (bar 86, oboe) reinforces the extent to which pitch (although not necessarily tonal centre) and sonority are embedded in the structure of the work. Here the arabesque is the melodic kernel, tonal pivot (C♯) and structural device.[72]

Lockspeiser has identified parallels between Debussy's desire in *Diane au bois* to record fleeting moments – 'les mille sensations d'un personnage'[73] – and Mallarmé's similar aim while he was working on an early version of the faun poem, which he outlined in a letter to Henri Cazalis in March 1865. He writes:

> I have found an intimate and peculiar manner of depicting and setting down very fugitive impressions. What is frightening is that all these impressions are required to be woven together as in a symphony, and that I often spend whole days wondering whether one idea can be associated with another, what the relationship between them may be and what effect they will create.[74]

The poem contains many references to both static and active transient images; references to sleep and dreams are juxtaposed with images of breezes, flight, flowing and running. The momentary nature of the faun's desire is captured in the line: 'Ah well, too bad! Toward happiness there will be others to draw me.'[75] In evoking Mallarmé's subject, Debussy achieved moments of stasis and structural coherence through the recurring flute melody and ostinato elements. His predilection for short phrases, flexible rhythmic patterns, and an ever-changing sonorous and harmonic background indicate his continuing desire to record fleeting moments. Using Mallarmé's poem and ideas as a source of inspiration for the realisation of his musical ideals, Debussy moved beyond homage to Mallarmé in the *Prélude*; in so doing he revealed crucial aspects of his originality.

Debussy's receptivity to foreign musical sources, in particular Russian music and the gamelan, during this formative period has been well documented.[76] Lockspeiser has detected Tchaikovsky's specific influence on the *Prélude à l'après-midi d'un faune*.[77] However, there are some striking similarities between Rimsky-Korsakov's *Antar* and Debussy's work. The symphony was first published in 1880 in St Petersburg, but was distributed in France through Leduc.[78] Immediately striking is Rimsky-Korsakov's use of a repeated flute line from bar 42 of the first movement, which is subject to varied repetition and is accompanied by horns, harp and violins. The theme is heard eight times, five times starting on the pitch A. This theme returns in the fourth movement, thus providing some structural coherence. Parallels can also be drawn between the third movement and the relatively static middle section of the *Prélude* (from bar 55). The comparable section of *Antar* is in common time with regular phrasing, and moves quickly from A major to the same key of Db. It is dominated by a theme – first heard in the violins and cellos and then the oboes and violins – which has a similar downward thrust and is accompanied by syncopated strings.[79] Debussy's apparent knowledge of this work reveals his receptivity to a range of sources, both musical and literary, which provided him with the inspiration he needed to realise his own ideas.

Lockspeiser and Boulez, among others, have identified an important departure in this work. In Boulez's view the *Prélude à l'après-midi d'un faune* signalled the beginning of modern music:

> What was overthrown was not so much the art of development as the very concept of form itself. Here freed from the impersonal constraints of the schema, giving wings to a supple, mobile expressiveness, demanding a technique of perfect instantaneous adequacy. Its use of timbres seemed essentially new, of exceptional delicacy and assurance in touch . . .[80]

For Boulez the work's modernity lies in its treatment of form and timbre, the two elements Debussy had sought to refashion in Rome. Lockspeiser goes further when he claims that these innovations were specifically French:

> A new spirit, a new world was magically conceived. Yet its novelty consisted, then, as still today, in revivifying the age-long French traditions. It was a world that was inevitably to be born to prove the continuity of these traditions, whose sweet and powerful renascence was now evident to give the lie to Déroulède's pessimistic vision of his country in decline.[81]

This chapter examines the process by which these purely musical innovations, inspired by a variety of sources, came to be recognised as identifiably French, and, given the cultural dominance of the centre in France, as Parisian.

Official institutions

Debussy continued to have an ambivalent relationship with the musical establishment. On the one hand he showed a willingness to establish himself in the musical scene, declaring in a letter to Chausson in 1889 that he wanted to keep in with the Société Nationale.[82] He maintained this commitment; even after his supporters established the Société Musicale Indépendante in 1910, Debussy remained a member of the Société Nationale and kept his distance from the new organisation, which was set up partly to champion him. In 1909 he was elected to the Superior Council of the Conservatoire under Fauré's reforming leadership. Unlike Ravel, he accepted the order of Chevalier de la Légion d'Honneur in 1903. However, in some respects Debussy found it difficult to gain a foothold in the establishment. Prix de Rome winners returning from Italy were required to write an orchestral overture for an annual public concert. Debussy refused and wrote to the Institut that he had to 'decline this honour because I am not in a position to accomplish any work worthy of the Institut'.[83] He did, however, work on his fourth *envoi* – *Fantaisie* for piano and orchestra – in 1889, but he never sent it to the Institut. As Lesure comments, 'The Institut was definitely not the direction in which Achille directed his hopes for becoming known.'[84] Instead, it was programmed for a Société Nationale concert for 21 April 1890 to be conducted by d'Indy. However, he withdrew the parts from the music stands, having learned that only the first movement was to be performed. His letter to d'Indy of 20 April indicates that rather than intending to slight the older composer or annoy the Société Nationale, he felt that a partial hearing would distort the whole.[85]

Debussy anticipated some of these tensions with the establishment in a letter to Hébert shortly after leaving Rome:

> When I reached Paris, I felt like a little boy tentatively trying to make his way in the world . . . I have spent these months in a dream world, absorbed in my work, all my efforts directed towards a lofty artistic ideal, without bothering in the slightest as to what anyone else might think of it . . . Now I'm wondering how, in my exaggeratedly uncultivated state, I shall find my way as I struggle in the midst of this 'success market', and I foresee innumerable anxieties and conflicts . . .[86]

Debussy's difficulty in finding a stage for *Pelléas* reflects the unease with which his musical innovations were regarded at this stage by the establishment. His article on the Opéra of 1901 reveals his bitterness towards the institution and its repertoire, and hints at his own frustrating struggle for recognition:

> Of all these there is not a thing that is really new. Nothing but the churning of a factory, the same old things over and over again. You'd think that

music had to put on an obligatory uniform as it entered the opera house, as if it were a convict. It assumes all the false grandeur of the place, competing with the celebrated Grand Staircase that an error in perspective and too many details made . . . well . . . not so grand.[87]

Perhaps it was appropriate that the more modest Opéra-Comique provided the location for *Pelléas*, which, after its scandalous premiere, became the focus of debates concerning Debussy's originality and Frenchness. Young enthusiasts, such as Ravel and his fellow Apaches, celebrated its experimental treatment of Symbolist drama, operatic structure, colouristic harmonic language and instrumentation, and a text setting that was responsive to Dargomizhsky and Musorgsky's innovations, but applied to a French context.[88] Enthusiastic critics, such as Vuillermoz (an Apache) and Jean Marnold, were active in promoting the work they had for so long anticipated. Jann Pasler observes that

> Debussy kept many Symbolist writers on board because he frequented those circles and had already built substantial support and interest . . . by frequently playing excerpts of it in various salons and literary circles – especially those of Pierre Louÿs, Mme de Saint-Marceaux, and the *Revue blanche* . . .[89]

– Debussy's literary connections had paid off. For the opera's supporters, the issue of originality was one of the most important and yet one of the most divisive. While Gaston Carraud could celebrate an orchestra 'd'une variété, d'une finesse et d'une nouveauté de coloris extraordinaires', and Jean Marnold could herald it as the new 'music of the future', others perceived its danger.[90] Conservative music critics and Monarchist publications were critical of the harmonic language, detecting decadence and moral decay in the opera and the composer. Henri de Curzon, writing in the *Gazette de France* (3 May), dismissed the work as 'morbid'; he opined:

> We now have music lacking in form, method or harmonic design, and without motives. Of course, one can discuss and condemn the brutal realism of a Charpentier, but this is, without doubt, robust and healthy music. M. Debussy's is deceptive, sickly and almost lifeless.[91]

His objections were on musical, aesthetic and moral grounds.

Perhaps more surprisingly, d'Indy reviewed the work favourably in the June issue of *L'occident*. While criticising the harmonic experimentation, he linked Debussy's treatment of text to earlier Italian operatic practices. Both left and right approved of Debussy's declamation, with more conservative writers tracing Debussy's treatment of language back to France's ancient and pre-Revolutionary past, drawing parallels with plainchant and the importance attached to language by Lully and Rameau.[92] Similarly, Debussy's sensitivity to dramatic expression could be perceived either as a return to earlier French opera or as a response to Wagner's ideals (or both). For Wagner supporters and detractors, the opera could be construed as a French response to Wagner; it was similar in its adherence to important Wagnerian ideas such as leitmotif, response to text and the drama, but different in its realisation, especially in not allowing the orchestra to commandeer the drama.[93] The fact that *Pelléas* was unlike French opera to date and could not be neatly categorised contributed both to its notoriety and to its success.

The issue of what constituted Frenchness in music had not been resolved beyond such elusive qualities as *clarté* and concision. It was therefore possible for aesthetically and politically opposed groups to interpret Debussy's innovations as French. It is surely no coincidence that Debussy was offered the Légion d'Honneur in 1903, a year after *Pelléas*. From that moment Debussy's musical achievements were linked to national and political aspirations. Astruc, in his speech on the unveiling of the Debussy monument, spoke of 'the great battle of *Pelléas*', and André Suarès, in the commemorative issue of *La revue musicale* (1920) devoted to Debussy, singled out *Pelléas* for having 'liberated both music and harmony'.[94]

Paris and the construction of national traditions

Debussy became increasingly explicit about what constituted Frenchness in music in his public pronouncements. In his contribution to Landormy's survey of the state of French music in 1904 he revealed his preoccupation with the French musical past, linking French qualities to his musical heritage:

> French music . . . is clarity, elegance, and simple and natural declamation; above all, French music wants to please – Couperin and Rameau are the ones who are truly French![95]

In 1903 Debussy praised the Schola Cantorum's performance of Rameau's *Castor et Pollux*. It was the first time his views on Rameau, and his importance for French music, had appeared in print, but it was a topic to which he was to return many times:

> Rameau, whether one likes it or not, is one of the surest musical foundations and one can follow in the beautiful route he has traced without fear, despite the barbarous trampling down, the errors in which he is mired.[96]

In his view, the foreign influences of Gluck, Wagner and Franck had diverted French music from its true direction. This statement was followed by his 'Hommage à Rameau', *Images*, series 1 (1905), which does not allude stylistically to Rameau in the way one might expect; in some ways the homophonic textures are actually closer to Musorgsky. This is an important instance of Debussy paying tribute to French tradition while, whether consciously or not, revealing the mixed progeny of his own. The music of 'Hommage à Rameau' has an expansive, monumental quality; the work can be read as a claim for equal status: the tribute of one French master to another.

Debussy engaged more closely with Rameau's style when he edited *Les fêtes de Polymnie* for the complete Rameau edition in 1908 (*Œuvres complètes*, vol. XIII). Scott Messing has argued that the works in which this close study of Rameau's style manifests itself most are the late sonatas.[97] Debussy was certainly portraying himself as an inheritor of French Baroque traditions by conceiving them as a set of six sonatas and by describing himself as 'Claude Debussy, musicien français'.[98] Messing notes rhythmic and some melodic similarities between Rameau's *Les fêtes de Polymnie* and two of the late sonatas. There are also further similarities between the descending motive heard in the violins and flute from Rameau's overture and the flute and viola theme in the Interlude from Debussy's Sonata for flute, viola and harp. Although these and other similarities are likely to be accidental, they reveal Debussy's engagement with Baroque gestures, such as dotted figures, syncopation, pedals, contrapuntal textures, Baroque bowing techniques and uncharacteristically expansive melodies.

Even so, these sonatas rarely achieve a Baroque sound. Debussy's choice of instrumentation in the Sonata for flute, viola and harp evokes familiar *fin de siècle* sonorities, albeit within a stricter formal context. The Violin and Cello Sonatas do, however, reveal a new austerity and anticipate the war-time and post-war aesthetic of *dépouillement*, where musical elements are reduced to their minimum. Indeed, Ravel claimed that post-war austerity could be traced to Debussy.[99] Once again Debussy was continuing to innovate while looking back. His sonatas are not a homage in the manner of Ravel's *Le tombeau de Couperin*, in which (despite his disclaimers), Ravel found a specific model in Couperin's 'Forlane'. Neither are Debussy's sonatas nostalgic: he was using the past to justify innovation.

En blanc et noir (1915), written in the same year as the Sonata for flute, viola and harp and the Cello Sonata, gives further insight into Debussy's preoccupations. The work alludes explicitly to war, quoting from 'Ein' feste Burg' and embedding a portion of *La Marseillaise*, which is marked *de très loin*. This and his tendency to sign himself 'musicien français' and 'Claude de France' are evidence of an increasing chauvinism, which was heightened by the war. His writings from this period are preoccupied with notions of French musical purity. Most striking is his article, also from 1915, which appeared on the front page of *L'intransigeant*, in which his call for a pure French music lay alongside descriptions of military atrocities. He equated military victory with musical liberation and viewed war as the catalyst for returning French music to its true path, as outlined by Rameau.[100] This demonstrates Debussy's involvement in the war propaganda machine.

Unlike Ravel and Satie, who were more directly involved in defending their country, Debussy became involved with war on the musical front. Owing to his own failing health it was the only area in which he could be combative. His letter to his former pupil Nicolas Coronio, proclaiming that 'French art needs to take revenge quite as seriously as the French army does!', confirms his musical war-time aims.[101] His personal identification with the war effort is revealed in a letter to Durand of 1914 in which he indicated his willingness to die for the cause, stating that if there was need for one more life to assure victory, he would give his willingly.[102] Perhaps this is how he viewed his own struggle against cancer, a struggle he lost in March 1918 as Paris was being bombarded by Big Berthe. His death was seen by many as a national sacrifice.

Debussy's reputation took some time to consolidate in Paris. The articles of 1918 reflecting on his death and achievement were mixed. For instance, Alfred Mortier's obituary in *Le courrier musical* (1 April 1918) emphasises Debussy's fascination with danger, describing the author of *Pelléas* as 'an isolated artist, who is prestigious, seductive and, in short, as unforgettable as a rare flower whose troubling perfume one happens to smell one day'. Describing the 'pseudo Debussysme' as one of the musical maladies of our time, he concludes: 'Debussy is more of an isolated figure than a pillar of musical evolution.'[103] This assessment was contested by the establishment figure, Julien Tiersot, in the following issue of *Le courrier musical* (15 April 1918). In his view Debussy's harmonic and melodic innovations make him a master, but he hesitates to judge whether or not he is a great master on account of his disrespectful attitude towards 'heroes of art' such as Gluck, Wagner and Beethoven. It is Debussy's championing of the French musical past that convinces Tiersot that he is a master of the new art he has inaugurated. His role as cultural ambassador is significant in contributing 'to the wide dissemination of the spirit of French art'.[104] For Camille Bellaigue, writing in the *Revue des deux mondes*, Debussy deserves to be recognised as 'Claude Debussy the musician of French race' on account of his return to a French interest in language, which links him to Rameau, and also because he delivered French music from Wagner. This endorsement is significant, because Bellaigue had spoken out against *Pelléas* in 1902; it demonstrates that Debussy's activities as upholder of French traditions had worked.[105]

The verdict on Debussy was only finally consolidated after the victory; Debussy was increasingly seen as heroic alongside Magnard.[106] The Debussyste Vuillermoz was important in pushing for Debussy's status as a national hero, as his articles in *Le ménéstrel* (11 and 18 June 1920) reveal, despite claiming otherwise. In emotive language he argues that

> Debussy was not one of the glorified candidates in whose honour one offered banquets, bronze statues or honorary presidencies ... It was not his calling to preach ... He was neither a great citizen, nor an apostle, nor a saint; he was only a musician ... Debussy was never presented to us as a prophet or Messiah.[107]

Despite these protestations, Vuillermoz's role in presenting Debussy as a Messiah figure was considerable; it was motivated by the loss of his musical figurehead and by Vuillermoz's inability to adapt to the changed post-war musical context. In his article of 18 June 1920 he portrays Debussy as the saviour who has given the younger generation their freedom and in so doing alludes to the language of war. Indeed, in the early 1920s disrespect for Debussy was interpreted by critics as both blasphemous and a threat to 'national security' in the realm of music.[108] Debussy had come to symbolise Frenchness in music at a time of national political upheaval. He had also realised his personal aim to capture Paris musically.

3 Debussy as musician and critic

DÉIRDRE DONNELLON

Beethoven's *Pastoral* Symphony was mocked for conjuring up a 'wooden nightingale' and a 'Swiss cuckoo', Richard Strauss's *Till Eulenspiegel* resembled 'an hour of new music written for lunatics'; Wagner's Wotan was 'majestic, empty and insipid'; Gluck's music was 'almost uniformly pompous'; and modern composers, in catering to the tastes of their public, were reduced to 'something midway between the monkey and the servant'.[1] Debussy was certainly not afraid to speak his mind and his published articles will always make entertaining reading. In contrast to the musical reviews of his peers his comments were hard-hitting, uncompromising and, on occasion, deliberately inflammatory. What prompted him to publish such savage remarks and what he hoped to achieve by them are no less fascinating; an examination of the issues concerned provides insight into the concerns of Debussy the musician.

When Debussy's first articles appeared in *La revue blanche* between April and December 1901, they met with a mixed response that ranged from laughing indulgence to downright hostility. That any young composer, as yet relatively unknown, should have the presumption to challenge the supremacy of composers like Beethoven and the current idol, Wagner, was beyond the comprehension of most. However, it was not unexpected by those who had been unpleasantly surprised at the recent premiere of the first two *Nocturnes* at the Concerts Lamoureux on 9 December 1900. Debussy's music was also a marked departure from what one was accustomed to hearing, and the scorn for the musical past and criticism of the musical establishment in his articles was just what one would expect from such an 'original' composer, a term that quickly acquired negative as well as positive connotations in relation to Debussy's music.

On the other hand, Debussy's supporters welcomed the audacity of his words as much as they did his musical innovations. For both supporters and detractors Debussy's articles were seen as a confirmation of the qualities found in his music. As the critic Henry Gauthier-Villars (Willy) slyly remarked: 'all the paradoxes do not just appear in *La revue blanche*, but are entered on paper ruled in five lines of five lines'.[2] In more recent times Debussy's articles, which were collectively published in the posthumous *Monsieur Croche antidilettante* (1921), have been criticised for their apparent inconsistencies, subjectivity and, at times, carelessness. However, it is precisely these qualities that make them so interesting. While Debussy's occasionally brutal honesty presents a clear picture of his likes and dislikes, the apparent contradictions that appear from time to time are often a reflection of his own artistic development.

It is worth considering how Debussy's critical writings compare with those of his peers. During the course of his career the profession underwent rapid change: there were far fewer critics and they were far better qualified than their predecessors. At the turn of the century, however, drama and literary critics frequently doubled as music critics when called upon to do so by their editors, and what frequently passed for music criticism was often little better than the subjective views of those who had little or no understanding of music. Debussy himself suffered at the hands of fellow critics, and this is touchingly revealed in his reviews of the works of young composers. Generally, critics felt no need to spare the feelings of young composers. If anything, as Gustave Doret remarked,

> you know with what severity, with what injustice even, the attempts of young artists are met. It seems as if beginners are the enemy, and so it is generally their flaws rather than their, at times hidden, qualities that [critics] are hell-bent on finding.[3]

By comparison Debussy was a fair and sympathetic critic. In particular, negative remarks about the music of young composers were tempered with gentle encouragement. Typical of this was his review of Gustave Samazeuilh's Piano Suite, which he felt was 'un peu verte' but nonetheless boded well for the future.[4] When he felt unable to say anything complimentary (as he frequently did) Debussy (like Fauré) skilfully dodged the issue by discussing a more general aspect of music.

On the other hand, Debussy's harsh treatment of some composers was both shocking and unusual to readers used to gentler comments from the press. In particular, his lament on the decline in quality of Saint-Saëns's musical output since the *Danse macabre*, and his uncompromising attitude toward the 'elder statesman' of French music, were a far cry from the platitudes uttered by the majority of critics. The blandness of most music criticism made Debussy's forthright comments appear all the more colourful. In particular, readers were taken aback by the outspoken Monsieur Croche, who first made his appearance in *La revue blanche* on 1 July 1901. A reflection of the literary circles Debussy was frequenting, these articles are among his most self-conscious literary efforts. But it was their content that drew the attention of fellow critics, and the use of Monsieur Croche for the introduction of contentious issues quickly brought fame to Debussy's crotchety old alter ego. However, Monsieur Croche was not the sole mouthpiece for Debussy's more controversial ideas, and he did not shy away from broaching more contentious issues in his own name, for example in his damning indictment of modern symphonic music in *La revue blanche* of 1 April 1901. In later articles, moreover, Monsieur Croche did not feature very much. Debussy himself may have been aware of the rather contrived nature of Monsieur Croche's appearances and, despite further articles penned by Monsieur Croche being solicited by Louis Laloy for the *Mercure musical* in 1905, these were not forthcoming. In all, Debussy's alter ego featured in just six of his articles, and many of these were no more than fleeting references.[5] Viewed in this light the importance of Monsieur Croche has certainly been exaggerated, though to a certain extent this may be attributed to the posthumous publication of Debussy's collected articles under the umbrella title of *Monsieur Croche antidilettante.*

Debussy himself repeatedly claimed that his articles were nothing more than his 'impressions' recorded in writing.[6] Yet they provide a useful insight into the concerns of the composer. Purely musical issues aside, Debussy used his articles as a platform from which to launch attacks on what he viewed as the *malaise* pervading modern French music. In various hard-hitting articles, he repeatedly attacked the inertia of the French musical world (particularly institutions such as the Opéra and the Conservatoire) and expressed his disillusionment with modern concert audiences (whom he chastised for their lack of discrimination). In particular, the conservative Société des Concerts du Conservatoire was condemned by Debussy as nothing more than a 'music hall for weak minds'.[7] In making such attacks Debussy had the support of many of his fellow critics and composers. His tirades against the poor quality of productions, the uninspired programming and the inferior qualities of many of the Opéra's troupe were issues lamented by the musical press as a whole.[8] Similarly, his attacks on the teaching at the Conservatoire (although mostly restricted to bitter remarks about the Prix de Rome) coincided with a wider debate that culminated in the sweeping changes implemented by Gabriel Fauré once he became its director in 1905.

From a musical viewpoint, Debussy's 'impressions' of composers both past and present are particularly revealing. Debussy refused to unquestioningly accept established opinion regarding both past-and-present 'masters'. As he made clear in an interview in 1911, 'I admire Beethoven and Wagner, but I refuse to admire them without exception just because I was told they are masters. That, never!'[9] Instead, Debussy subjected the works of past masters to the same critical scrutiny as those of lesser known composers. Despite the popularity of both composers he proffered the view that Beethoven's piano sonatas were 'very badly written for the piano', while Wagner's orchestral music was unflatteringly likened to a 'piece of multi-coloured putty'.[10] Neither did he spare the feelings of his contemporaries. While Ernest Reyer's music was only admired by 'people who listen to music with cotton-wool in their ears', Camille Saint-Saëns wrote operas with the 'soul of an unrepentant old symphonist'.[11]

Wagnérisme

In these outspoken attacks Debussy showed himself a fearless and provocative music critic. However, among contemporaries, his incendiary opinions further served to enhance his reputation as a young radical intent on revolutionising French music. This was held to be particularly true of Debussy's complicated attitude towards Wagner. Although French *Wagnérisme* had reached its peak during the 1880s, the composers of Debussy's generation grew up in its shadow and, throughout Debussy's own career, Wagner's music continued to be beloved of Parisian concert goers. However, in contrast to the infatuation of many of his peers, Debussy saw no future in the continued application of the Wagnerian style. As he explained in an article published in *Le mercure de France* in January 1903,

> Wagner, if I may be permitted to express myself with the pomposity befitting him, was a beautiful sunset that was mistaken for a dawn.[12]

Despite this and other more blatantly hostile comments about Wagner, Debussy made the pilgrimage to Bayreuth in 1888 and 1889 and later also attended productions of both *Lohengrin* and *Die Walküre* at the Paris Opéra, which establishment he also chided for failing to perform *Der Ring* in its entirety.[13] This ambivalence toward Wagner finds a mirror in Debussy's own compositional efforts: his attitude toward the German giant was far from straightforward. On a purely musical level Debussy faced an on-going struggle with the legacy of Wagner, for he was attempting to forge an independent path for himself. Notwithstanding the composer's dislike of celebrity, this private struggle came under public scrutiny with the premiere of *Pelléas et Mélisande* in 1902. Moreover, this was still at a time when, as the editor and critic Paul Flat remarked, 'one must always come back to it [*Wagnérisme*] when one speaks of music today'.[14] In their reviews of the opera both supporters and detractors resorted to comparison with Wagner, but even among supporters there was confusion as to the degree of Wagner's influence. Alfred Bruneau welcomed *Pelléas* because 'it pushes Richard Wagner's patented imitators and their bastard productions into the grave'. On the other hand, Pierre Lalo, critic for *Le temps* and the opera's most powerful advocate, less convincingly argued that 'there is nothing, or almost nothing, of Wagner in *Pelléas et Mélisande*'.[15] These frequent references to Wagner by the first critics of *Pelléas* explain the defensive tone of Debussy's vehement refutation of Wagnerian influence on his opera in an interview with the critic Louis Schneider in April 1902.[16] Debussy's struggle to devise an operatic form that was true to Maeterlinck's drama but which avoided the crassness of the leitmotif, or 'visiting card technique', of Wagnerian drama was ultimately successful. In place of the heroic leitmotifs characteristic of Wagner's scores Debussy created brief, subtle motifs that implied rather than signalled both the main characters of the opera and certain recurrent symbols, such as the fountain, the forest and the sea. These leitmotifs are often little more than brief rhythmic cells or oscillating intervals that hint at, rather than declare, the emotions and events depicted on stage. They are certainly a far cry from the Wagnerian leitmotif, which Debussy irreverently dismissed as a helpful device designed to accommodate 'those who are unable to follow a score'.[17]

In fact Debussy's abhorrence of the Wagnerian leitmotif also coloured his judgements of other composers. It formed a key criticism of Alfred Bruneau's *L'ouragan*: although he applauded the remarkable harmonic inventiveness of the score, he felt it was tainted by its use of Wagnerian leitmotifs.[18] Wagner's influence on Massenet's *Grisélidis* was also deplored and Massenet was counselled to abandon his experiments in that direction.[19] Similarly, although he acknowledged the musicality of Albert Savard's overture *Le roi Lear*, which was premiered at the Concerts Colonne on 17 March 1901, he felt it had 'a little too much of the Wagnerian accent for my taste'.[20] However, in this instance it was Savard's Wagnerian orchestration that met with Debussy's displeasure. Here too was an aspect of Wagnerian art to which Debussy sought an alternative in his own opera. Again, his instinct did not fail him. The introduction of unusual sonorities, the variety of textures and the restrained, chamber-like quality of the orchestra in *Pelléas* form a notable contrast to the rich Wagnerian style.

In later articles Debussy's views on Wagner's music were more forgiving. Although aesthetically he was as far removed from Wagner as ever, he was prepared to offer more neutral statements. Despite mischievously referring to the *Ring* cycle as the 'telephone directory of the Gods', in 1913 he conceded that 'for a long time to come it will still be necessary to consult this admirable repertoire'.[21] Similarly, in private correspondence with the conductor André Caplet at the time he was composing *Jeux*, Debussy admitted his admiration for the orchestral effects in *Parsifal*.[22] This more conciliatory tone may have been a sign of Debussy's successful efforts to develop a personal musical language; in later years he was certainly less defensive about Wagner's influence on his music. More generally, any fears Debussy may have had concerning Wagner's influence on French musicians were fading. As early as 1908 the critic Gaston Carraud had confidently declared: 'Among new generations of composers, the disappearance of the Wagnerian influence appears to be complete';[23] and although Debussy may have felt Carraud was somewhat premature in his assessment, it is true that by the second decade of the twentieth century Wagner's influence on French music was waning.

Symphonic music: tradition versus innovation

Debussy's ambivalent attitude towards Wagner mirrored his desire to develop an individual musical style. This bid for artistic freedom was central to Debussy's aims and, musically, it manifested itself in his reluctance to limit himself to composing within canonical forms. With *Pelléas* he had cast aside the traditional operatic formulae of aria, recitative and ensemble, because, as an interviewer paraphrased,

> when a person has something natural to say, the musical phrase is natural;
> it becomes lyrical only when necessary. M. Debussy repudiates lyricism in
> a continuous stream, because one is not lyric in life, one becomes lyric
> only at certain decisive moments.[24]

Thus in *Pelléas* we find vocal writing that follows the natural inflections of the language, avoids large intervals (except at moments of heightened emotion) and is rhythmically very free. In his instrumental music Debussy also turned his back on canonical forms, gradually moving away from traditional symphonic structures and rejecting what he saw as the inadequacy of purely programmatic content. His views on programme music are best exemplified by an unfavourable review of Beethoven's *Pastoral* Symphony in which he exclaimed:

> how much more certain [other] pages of the old master profoundly
> express the beauty of the countryside, simply because they are not a direct
> imitation but a sentimental depiction of that which is 'invisible' in
> nature.[25]

This belief in the need to progress beyond traditional symphonic writing informed his reviews of composers past and present, including the symphonic music of Schubert, Schumann and Mendelssohn, and contemporaries such as Joseph-Guy Ropartz, André Gedalge and Théodore Dubois, which were indirect propaganda for Debussy's own experiments in orchestral composition. He repeatedly took advantage of the opportunity to trumpet his opposition to the use of formal sonata structure and, in particular, the use of large-scale motivic development. In this regard his review of the premiere of Georges Witkowski's First Symphony, Op. 14 served as a launch-pad for an *exposé* of the modern symphony. His declarations that 'since Beethoven the proof of the uselessness of the symphony has been shown' and that, since then, the symphonic efforts of Schumann and Mendelssohn, for example, had been nothing more than a 'respectful repetition of the same forms but already with less conviction',[26] reflect Debussy's attempts to create a style of instrumental writing uninhibited by formal convention.

Given that Witkowski was a pupil of Vincent d'Indy, it may also be regarded as an indirect challenge to d'Indy, the Schola Cantorum, and all those who had lambasted the lack of structure in Debussy's own music. The use of the cyclic form associated with César Franck was a favourite structural device of Debussy's contemporaries, including many of his fellow members of the Société Nationale, and the acolytes of the Schola Cantorum. D'Indy, one of Franck's many pupils, was one of its staunchest advocates. As director of the recently founded Schola Cantorum and a member of the committee of the Société Nationale, he was an influential figure in French musical life. Contemporary music critics made much of the supposed dichotomy between the musical paths of the revolutionary Debussy and the traditional d'Indy, and there were many heated exchanges between Debussystes and d'Indystes. In this highly charged atmosphere, Debussy's rather unflattering opinion that Witkowski's willingness to submit to the voices of authority was 'preventing him from hearing a more personal voice' in his music was interpreted by critics as a direct rebuttal of the supremacy of the Franckian model as promoted by d'Indy.[27]

As ever with Debussy it was not as straightforward as that. Debussy had attended Franck's organ class at the Paris Conservatoire and his own compositions, particularly the early *Fantaisie* (1890) and the String Quartet (1893), show Franck's influence. Yet Debussy's dislike of lengthy developments, and his aversion to traditional forms, drove him to develop the cyclic technique beyond accepted convention. This led him in the *Nocturnes* to explore a less obvious cyclic form, free of the traditional conflict and resolution of primary themes; it made use of elaborate thematic transformations that were not in the traditional mould. This formal ambiguity was a device that came into its own in mature works such as *La mer* and 'Ibéria', which confounded contemporary critics and confirmed Debussy's reputation as an advanced composer. However, as can be heard in both these works, Debussy never fully renounced Franck's influence, and in his articles and interviews this ambivalent attitude towards the Belgian composer is evident. Despite being called upon to review numerous concerts featuring Franck's music, Debussy rarely discussed it except in passing, and on the one occasion that he discussed Franck's music at length he gave a rather unflattering assessment of the *Les Béatitudes*.[28]

Debussysme

Debussy's dislike of formal constraint in music also found expression in his admiration for Musorgsky's *The Nursery*. The song cycle was praised because there is 'no question of any such thing as "form", or, at least, the form is so complicated that it is impossible to relate to the accepted forms – those one might term the "official" ones'.[29] Similarly, Paul Dukas's Piano Sonata was applauded for its freedom from 'parasitic developments', in direct contrast to the majority of reviewers who chided Dukas for the sonata's unwieldy length and structural weaknesses.[30] However, Debussy's desire for 'freedom in music' was not a renunciation of form. He admired Bach because, despite the 'strict discipline' which he imposed on music, he also imbued it with a 'free imagination'.[31] Freedom in music was a recurrent theme in Debussy's articles and, in his quest for it, his admiration extended beyond Western music. On more than one occasion he expressed his admiration for cultures whose music was independent of 'arbitrary treatises'.[32] His admiration for folk music went hand in hand with a Utopian vision of music and nature as one, removed from the 'little idiosyncrasies of form and of arbitrarily decided keys that so clumsily congest music'.[33] Freedom in music also extended to harmonic innovations, though Debussy argued that he was not revolutionising but developing Western harmony. The influence of the exotic sounds of the Far East, his recreation of the sounds of the Javanese gamelan and adoption of modal, pentatonic, octatonic and whole-tone chords enriched Debussy's harmonic language. His contemporaries were, unsurprisingly, dazzled by his audacious innovations. When René Lénormand published a study in modern harmony in 1913, he confidently heralded Debussy, 'by virtue of the audacity of his harmonies, their charm and their musicality', as the head of 'la [nouvelle] école'.[34]

Indeed, following the *succès de scandale* of *Pelléas*, Debussy was hailed as the leader of a new school of music, *Debussysme*; yet when called upon to define the music of *Debussysme* most critics were hard pushed to do so and for the vast majority Debussy's music proved difficult to analyse. Even the learned d'Indy had trouble analysing Debussy's *Nocturnes*, as is evident from a letter he wrote to Auguste Sérieyx, in which he exclaimed that there was

> no literary programme, no explanation of a dramatic nature [that] gives a reasonable explanation for the range of keys and the agreeable, but uncoordinated, themes in these three pieces.[35]

The increasing incomprehension of critics brought hostility, as exemplified by Pierre Lalo's proclamation that 'ordinary musicians, in imitating him, are on the road to ruin. May they beware of the prince of darkness, of his pomps and of his works'.[36] Despite this dire warning from one of the most powerful critics of the day, young students of the Paris Conservatoire, under the more liberal reign of Gabriel Fauré, did experiment with Debussy's innovations. However, as a composer, Debussy was determined not to repeat himself and, while other composers clung to the novelties unveiled in *Pelléas*, Debussy himself quickly progressed beyond the musical efforts of the Debussystes. As a result, he repeatedly issued denials in his articles regarding the formation of a school of *Debussysme*. In fact, he was deeply unhappy with the idea – the impetus for *Debussysme* certainly did not come from him. As he stated in an interview in 1910, 'There is no school of Debussy. I do not have disciples.'[37] The following year he reiterated this claim, saying that 'I have neither theory nor methods . . . I do not at all claim that it [my music] should be imitated, or that it should exercise any form of influence on anybody.'[38]

Debussy the reluctant interviewee

This and other occasional interviews were only reluctantly granted, for as Debussy increasingly came to realise, few of those who interviewed him had the musical expertise to report his views accurately. Those who did all too often had their own decided opinions, which coloured the manner in which they quoted the composer. This was something Debussy realised quite early in his career. After commenting on 'L'état actuel de la musique française' to the critic Paul Landormy for *La revue bleue* in 1903, Debussy later remarked to Louis Laloy, 'It's extraordinary how hard of hearing this so-called musician is'.[39] Over the years Debussy's disillusion with (often well-meaning) interviewers deepened, as can be seen from Louis Vuillemin's account of an interview with a taciturn Debussy in 1910.[40] An increasingly cynical Debussy reported himself delighted with the spoof interview given by him to the critic of the 'Scène de la fard' written by his friend, Paul-Jean Toulet, and published in *Les marges* in 1912 in which Debussy's monosyllabic responses are transformed beyond recognition by an imaginative journalist desperate for good copy.[41]

Given his scant regard for the ability of contemporary critics to accurately record his views, Debussy only very reluctantly submitted to being interviewed in his later career. Similarly, the frequency with which his articles were misquoted was certainly a contributing factor to the dearth of articles published by him in the immediate wake of those he contributed to *Gil blas* in 1903. No doubt this unwillingness to commit himself to paper was partly due to the fact that his words had frequently been quoted out of context, or been so inaccurately paraphrased as to distort their original meaning beyond all recognition. Although he had only himself to blame for the undeniably provocative nature of some of his earlier statements,

Debussy's views, particularly regarding past masters, were certainly exaggerated by a press keen to provoke debate. As he angrily announced to the interviewer Georges Delaquys, in 1911,

> I was accredited with I don't know what sort of attitude which I never actually had with regard to the masters, and I was reported as having said things that I had actually never said about Wagner and Beethoven.[42]

An end to this lull in his written output came with his agreeing to review the Concerts Colonne for *La revue musicale S.I.M.* in late 1912. As he explained in a letter to Robert Godet, in these later articles he was hoping to

> put things back in their place, [by] trying to rediscover the values that arbitrary judgements and capricious interpretations have warped to the point of no longer being able to distinguish between a Bach fugue and *La marche lorraine*.[43]

His stated purpose in his later articles, therefore, was to educate the misguided majority about the need to recapture the qualities of clarity and simplicity that he felt formed the very essence of French music both past and present. Debussy's articles also came to play an increasingly important role in ensuring that both his music and his musical preferences were properly portrayed in the partisan and acrimonious musical world of early twentieth-century Paris.

Renewal through simplicity: Debussy and d'Indy

This partisanship particularly applied to the debate over the merits of both the so-called Debussyste and d'Indyste creeds, which was partly due to the revolutionary light in which Debussy was regarded by contemporary critics; his lively attacks on established masters, both past and present, did little to counter this image. As a revolutionary Debussy was frequently posited by the critics as the alternative to the teachings of the more conservative d'Indy. While Debussy came to be seen as the revolutionary head of the unhealthy school of *Debussysme*, d'Indy was the pioneering figure behind the traditional Schola Cantorum.[44] The emotional basis of Debussy's Symbolist music was contrasted with the intellectual basis of d'Indy's art.

However, aside from the contentious issue of Wagner,[45] Debussy and d'Indy shared more common ground than the contemporary press (and some modern scholars) would have us believe. Although Debussy's espousal of a free, pantheistic art was at odds with d'Indy's rather more structured and dogmatic concept, it is certain that the quasi-religious devotion to music inherent in the Schola's teaching appealed to the errant Conservatoire pupil. As he commented approvingly,

> for some years, this school [Schola], using only its students plus a few rare artists, has rediscovered for us the beauty of ancient music, not to mention what it has made known of the works of young, hitherto unknown composers.[46]

More particularly, the two composers found common cause in their championing of the music of Rameau. In articles which appeared in *Gil blas* as early as 1903, Debussy applauded d'Indy for staging the first two acts of Rameau's *Castor et Pollux* and shortly afterwards attacked what he felt was the detrimental influence of Gluck on the clarity that he identified as a key component of French music.[47] Debussy's advocacy of Rameau was a symptom of his search for what he felt to be a distinctive French musical voice, which was needed to replace the *néant* or nothingness left in the wake of Wagner's detrimental and over-long reign. In Debussy's music this preference for clarity and lightness was always present, but in the midst of the polemics surrounding the more 'revolutionary' aspects of his music it was initially overlooked. Ironically, one of the few reviewers who identified the clarity of Debussy's text setting in his formative years was d'Indy himself, who proved a far more perceptive critic of Debussy's music than many of the younger man's avowed supporters. In his supportive review of the premiere of *Pelléas*, he remarked that

> there is, indeed, probably without the composer having thought about it, a close connection between his [Debussy's] method of noting the words of the text and the 'stile rappresentativo' of Caccini, of Gagliano [and] of Monteverdi.[48]

Despite d'Indy's perceptive identification of this key element of Debussy's musical style, it was not until the appearance in 1908 of the *Trois chansons de Charles d'Orléans*, settings of sixteenth-century French verse, that more of his contemporaries were prepared to acknowledge the link to musical tradition in Debussy's music. That Debussy was aware of the irony of his image as a revolutionary and his advocacy of the lessons of the past is clear from his remark that 'it is strange how dreams of Progress lead one to become conservative'.[49]

Conservative and revolutionary: *musicien français*

For all the 'conservative' advocacy of tradition in his later articles, Debussy retained many of those ideals that had originally led others to class him as a revolutionary. He managed to combine the two in such a way that the freedom in music he had preached in his earliest articles, and his pantheistic vision of the fusion of music and nature, were not brought into conflict with his interest in the music of the past. While acknowledging that the aims and lifestyles of Renaissance composers were probably 'no longer compatible with our times', he declared his admiration for the freedom with which they were allowed to learn their craft; he coupled this with previously voiced beliefs regarding the special relationship between music and nature, the idea that 'music is precisely the art that is closest to nature; that which offers it the most subtle trap'.[50] However, compared to the vaguer musings on these and other subjects in his earlier articles, Debussy now had a far more definite agenda. He reconfirmed his rejection of the perceived benefits of Wagner's influence on French musicians, remonstrated with French musicians for their comparative neglect of the music of Rameau and Couperin, and declared their need to rediscover the simple virtue of 'taste', which he felt had been sadly lacking in French music of recent times. This deplorable demise in 'taste' had been brought about by Debussy's old *bête noire*, the 'administration of the arts'.[51] He also railed at what he felt was the continued dull acceptance of musical formulae, which indicated a worrying 'laxness, and almost discourteous indifference towards art' among his peers.[52] Debussy asserted that a true artist was one who recognised that 'art is a sacrifice' and who acted accordingly, in stark contrast to the attitudes of young composers.[53] For him, the common link with the past was the humble nature of past composers who showed 'no desire for quick glory'.[54] This attack on the *arrivisme* of young composers, which, incidentally, was also a war cry of d'Indy during these years, was a symptom of Debussy's growing alarm at the emergence of what he felt were short-lived artistic 'fashions' (he went so far as to describe Futurism as such) with little or no substance.[55]

This is not to say that Debussy wished to halt the progress of music; neither did he wish to confine new music to the lessons of the past. In his own music he continued his harmonic and structural innovations (the colourful and exuberant orchestral *Images* being a good case in point) while marrying them with a greater clarity and sparsity of means. Debussy certainly did not have regression in mind: he firmly maintained that 'the age of the aeroplane has a right to its own music'.[56]

The war years: French and 'Boche' music

Notwithstanding his preaching of the need to revitalise French music, Debussy's ideal music was not nationally exclusive and he was quite prepared to admit the lessons of other nations. Mozart's music was frequently cited as a salutary lesson in the application of taste and clarity to composition. Similarly, while Debussy continued to praise the music of Palestrina, Bach was repeatedly lauded for his rich imagination and inventiveness. This continued generosity towards foreign composers in Debussy's later articles is of particular importance in the light of the cultural climate leading up to the First World War. In the immediate pre-war years the seeming inevitability of war fostered a climate of cultural isolationism that increasingly found expression in open hostility to the 'Boche' music of contemporary German composers such as Strauss and Reger.[57] Debussy had long since made plain his dislike for the music of Strauss and did not revise his opinions with time, but he did not adopt the chauvinist tone adopted by so many of his contemporaries. His pleas for the renewal of French music became more focused, but not to the exclusion of the beneficial lessons of foreign composers. With the outbreak of war Debussy did briefly succumb to the epidemic of war fever. His single article of 1915, which appeared in *L'intransigeant*, repeated his previous exhortations to French musicians to revitalise their national music, but these were now couched in such terms as must have pleased the nationalist and conservative readers of the newspaper. Victory in war was to give French artists a sense of the purity and nobility of French blood, an idea that was a recurrent theme in the French cultural press as a whole at this time.[58] This initial burst of wartime patriotism is also echoed in Debussy's correspondence from the time, but was to be short-lived.

Debussy's rallying calls to French musicians were not intensified by the reality of war, although it is certain that they met with a more receptive audience than previously. As he made clear in a letter to Georges Jean-Aubry, he did, at least initially, see in the war

> an opportunity to return, not to a narrow and contemporary French tradition, but to the true one; one which can be placed after Rameau, at which point it began to lose its way![59]

However, this statement was relatively benign in the context of the vitriolic climate pervading French musical circles during the war. With many of the younger generation in the trenches, an older generation of composers and critics held sway.[60] The calls made for both the exclusion of German music from Parisian concert halls and the banning of the music of all Austro-German composers whose works were not yet in the public domain were symptomatic of the prevailing cultural isolationism. This contrasts with Debussy's modest but long-standing plea to rid French music of the nefarious influence of Wagner. His distance from the former point of view is clear from the brief preface he wrote for Paul Huvelin's 1916 publication, *Pour la musique française,* in which he remarked of this vilification of all German composers that

> one hears in certain circles strange comments about Beethoven, who – Flemish or German – is a great musician, and Wagner, more great artist than musician. That has been understood for many years.[61]

Neither was Debussy prepared to produce overtly patriotic war music because, as he made clear in a letter to Jacques Durand on 9 October 1914,

> if I dared and, above all, if I did not fear the particular 'pomposity' which is associated with this kind of composition, I would happily write a Heroic March . . . But, as I have said, to play the hero peacefully, safe from the bullets, seems ridiculous to me.[62]

Debussy's more obviously war-inspired pieces were true to this. The *Berceuse héroïque,* which Debussy composed at the request of the *Daily Telegraph* as a contribution to *King Albert's Book* (a publication intended as a tribute to occupied Belgium and the part Belgians were playing in the war), was dark, sombre and introspective and contains far more of the berceuse than the heroic. Similarly, his *Noël des enfants qui n'ont plus de maisons,* far from exhorting Frenchmen to battle, laments the effect of war on the civilian population, as does the *Ode à la France,* which he started to compose to words by Louis Laloy in 1917 but never completed. All these pieces deal with the harsh reality of war and there were certainly no attempts by Debussy to glorify war.

Last works and last words

Alongside these, Debussy's other wartime compositions, coming as they did at the end of his career, form a mature body of work in which his efforts to unite inspiration with clarity of expression and simplicity of line are fully realised. The two books of *Etudes,* the *Epigraphes antiques* and the caprices for two pianos, *En blanc et noir,* are all evidence of a new stage in Debussy's career as a composer. In particular, the group of six instrumental sonatas, only three of which he managed to complete before his death in March 1918, reveal a clarity and often joyous expansiveness that belie his terminal illness and their wartime creation, particularly as we know from correspondence that Debussy found composition very hard during the war years. This was partly due to the increasingly debilitating nature of his illness, and also to the depression wrought upon him by war. As he wrote of the previous two months in a letter to Durand dated 21 September 1914, 'I have not written a note, or touched a piano: it is unimportant when put into the context of events.'[63] This sober attitude was remote from the more patriotic outbursts of other prominent French musicians. The war inspired a flood of patriotic music, including the rather sentimentally titled *Prière du petit garçon fusillé* by Gabriel Grovlez and, among more established composers, one could cite the several 'couplets patriotiques' and marches written by Saint-Saëns.[64] A more restrained Debussy refused to fall victim to this fashion for patriotic marches, for, as he laconically remarked in a letter to Nicolas Coronio in September 1914, 'After all, who would dream of buying music? One is far more concerned with the potato crop!'[65]

This was a stance he also maintained when asked, during a survey of the great intellectual figures of contemporary France published in *Le figaro* in 1916, whether the war had affected his creative abilities. Debussy's response was true to the sober comments made in private correspondence. While offering his illness as a partial reason for having composed so little, he also declared that

> It seems to me that nobody has been able to work, or at least not with the necessary freedom of spirit. And yet, those who, like myself, have been unable to serve [in the military], have a duty to prepare for after the war to the best of their abilities.[66]

This was in marked contrast to the buoyant responses of others questioned. In particular, both Saint-Saëns and d'Indy gave cheerful accounts of their industriousness during the previous two years. It was left to Debussy's music to speak for him at this point. The progression of his illness and his efforts to complete his sonatas meant that these were his last known words submitted for publication. In the meantime he had consented to Louis Laloy's suggestion that his previous articles be prepared for collective publication. Debussy did play a role in the proof-reading of the articles and suggested some minor cuts, but a combination of his illness and the war meant that this project was not realised until after his death – *Monsieur Croche antidilettante* did not appear in print until 1921.

Debussy's articles are an accurate account of his uncompromising musical beliefs and tastes. Compared to fellow composer-critics such as Charles Koechlin and Paul Dukas, he was controversial, unquestionably biased and frequently dismissive of the efforts of others. Debussy had decided views on contemporary musical concerns and, while he was certainly responsive to outside influences, he clearly knew his own mind. The issues he addressed are especially revealing when examined in the context of contemporary musical life and Debussy's own role in French music. Some common threads emerge: concern about the extent of Wagner's influence on contemporary French music, a semi-mystical belief in the freedom of music and its oneness with nature, a belief in the overwhelming need to de-institutionalise music and free it from artificially imposed restrictions, and a conviction that this could best be achieved by incorporating the clarity and simplicity found in the music of Rameau and Mozart. An understanding of these beliefs is all the more important when one examines their impact on Debussy's music. His musical struggles to resist Wagner's influence, his innovations in timbre, harmony and musical structure, and the gradual evolution of his own distinctive musical style all show the extent to which he applied his beliefs to his music. It is precisely this use of his articles as propaganda for his own musical aesthetic that gives them their true value.

PART TWO

Musical explorations

4 Debussy on stage

DAVID GRAYSON

[T]he atmosphere of a theatre is made up of contradictions and of unforeseen influences. And one does not submit easily to advice given through incomprehension. DEBUSSY, MAY 1902[1]

For the aspiring young French composer of the nineteenth century, the Prix de Rome represented the capstone of musical study, and winning it signalled the start of a promising career. Claude Debussy, winner of the 1884 competition, later remarked on this popular perception: '[A]mong certain people the Prix de Rome has become something of a superstition: to have won it, or not to have won it, answers the question of whether one has any talent or not. Even if it is not infallible, at least it is a useful standard by which the general public can easily judge.'[2] Characteristically, Debussy was ambivalent about the honour, proud to be among its recipients but sceptical of the competence of state-sponsored institutions to recognise, assess or inspire great art. He later recalled the moment he learned that he had won the prize: '[M]y heart sank! I had a sudden vision of boredom, and of all the worries that inevitably go together with any form of official recognition. I felt I was no longer free.'[3]

First awarded in 1803, the Prix de Rome in musical composition was administered initially by the Institut de France and later by the Académie des Beaux-Arts, a division of the Institut.[4] Although details of the award varied over time, the winner of the Prix received a stipend to subsidise two years of residence at the Villa Medici in Rome, a third year of travel, preferably to Germany or Austria, and a fourth year spent either back in Rome or in France. Each year the laureates were required to submit musical compositions, called *envois*, as evidence of their progress. The competition itself was conducted annually in two rounds. For the preliminary round (*concours d'essai*), scheduled in early May, competitors had six full days to write both a fugue on a given subject and a work for chorus and orchestra on a specified text. The final round (*concours définitif*) required a lyric scene for three different voice types and orchestra, which competitors had twenty-five (later thirty) days to complete.[5] The text, selected through competition, provided an aria or extended solo for each of the three characters, plus a duo and trio. Recitatives were to connect the vocal numbers and the scene was to open with an orchestral introduction. Debussy later disparaged this so-called cantata as 'an awkward hybrid form that unfortunately shows up all the worst faults of operatic writing. Or else it is a "symphony with singers", a really institutional form; I wouldn't advise anyone to admit that he has composed one of these.'[6]

These obligatory genres, however artificial, were not arbitrary: the *fugue d'école* represented the highest level of scholastic discipline, formal rigour and technical (contrapuntal) skill, while the chorus and cantata were academic exercises preparatory to writing opera, which was implicitly being promoted as the appropriate career ambition. Indeed, Debussy considered the Prix de Rome and the values it fostered partly responsible for the relative paucity of French symphonies and chamber music in that they encouraged

> young musicians to neglect pure music; this wretched 'cantata' whets their appetite for the theatre rather too early. (And in many cases their later theatrical pieces are no more than frantic reworkings of their early cantatas.) Hardly are they back from Rome than they are already in search of a libretto, overtaken with a feverish desire to follow in the footsteps of their forebears. Renan said somewhere (unless it was M. Barrès) that it is merely pretentious and quite disastrous to write before one is forty. This could also be said of dramatic music, which, unless one is an exceptional genius, is really of any value only when one is approaching middle age.[7]

There is a pronounced autobiographical resonance to these remarks, which date from 1903. Although Debussy undoubtedly considered himself to be 'an exceptional genius', he was also forty years old at the time. Only a year had passed since the premiere of his sole completed opera, *Pelléas et Mélisande*, and he may have been recalling, with a mixture of embarrassment and remorse, his own early 'cantatas' and a series of aborted operatic ventures.

Debussy cynically described the path to the Prix de Rome: 'Someone looks up the winning formula in all the previous prize-winning cantatas, and that's all there is to it.'[8] His own manner of preparing was rather more ethical. In the early months of 1882, as practice for his first run at the Prix de Rome, he worked on a setting of *Daniel*, the lyric scene by Emile Cicile that had served as the required poem for the 1868 competition.[9] An extended, though incomplete, short-score draft of this Biblical scene survives, but the exercise was wasted as Debussy failed to pass the first round and was therefore denied the opportunity to apply his acquired experience to Edouard Guinand's *Edith*, the cantata text for the 1882 competition. When Debussy competed again the following year he succeeded in advancing to the final round. As a result, between 19 May and 13 June 1883 he and the four other competitors – Paul Vidal, Charles René (Bibard), Xavier Leroux and Edmond Missa – set Emile Moreau's *Le gladiateur*, and their cantatas were performed with piano accompaniment on both 22 and 23 June: the first reading was for the music section of the Académie des Beaux-Arts, and the second a public performance for the entire Académie.[10] Debussy was fortunate to have had excellent singers: baritone Emile-Alexandre Taskin, who had sung at the Opéra-Comique since 1879; tenor Antoine Muratet, a student at the Conservatoire who was to make his debut at the Opéra-Comique the following year and at the Opéra in 1886; and the celebrated Viennese soprano Gabrielle Krauss, who had sung at, among other places, the Vienna Opera and in Paris at the Théâtre-Italien and the Opéra. The first grand prize went to Paul Vidal, and the second to Debussy, who received the verdict: 'A generous musical nature but ardent sometimes to the point of excess; some convincing dramatic accents.'[11] The consensus of the newspaper critiques was that Vidal's cantata, which was published in 1883, was technically more expert, but that Debussy's, which remained unpublished, was the more imaginative.

Le gladiateur is set in a prison cell beneath a gladiatorial arena, and its action unfolds in three short scenes for one, two and three characters respectively. Narbal (tenor), the title character and son of the Numidian king, has been captured by the Roman consul, Métellus (baritone), and is about to be escorted into the arena. Enchained, he invokes the god Baal to avenge his countrymen and destroy their foes. Fulvie (soprano), Métellus's daughter, is in love with Narbal and urges him to escape with her, but he refuses lest he be branded a coward. An angry Métellus interrupts their embrace, but rather than submit to his will they consume poison. Narbal thus evades a dishonourable death in the arena before his jeering enemy, and the lovers experience joy as they die in one another's arms. Métellus's consequent agony is Narbal's revenge.

The jury's terse assessment of Debussy's cantata, quoted above, was not unjust. The final trio drew particular praise from the press, though one critic properly faulted an excessive reliance on vocal unison. Léon Vallas was right, however, to single out the central portion of Fulvie's aria in the second scene, where she imagines a blissful exile with Narbal 'in the land of palms'. Here Debussy's personal stamp is most clearly in evidence, and the cantata most nearly approaches the level of his *chansons de jeunesse*. Elsewhere the music is marked by stock clichés, with dramatic tension achieved through tremolos, ostinatos and diminished-seventh chords.

In 1884, in his third attempt at the Prix de Rome, Debussy finally triumphed, defeating some familiar competition – Leroux, René, Missa, and a newcomer, Henri-Charles Kaiser – with his setting of Edouard Guinand's lyric scene *L'enfant prodigue*.[12] Composed from 24 May to 18 June and performed on 27 and 28 June, Debussy's cantata was sung by soprano Rose Caron, who had just made her debut at the Théâtre de la Monnaie in Brussels and was to appear the following year at the Paris Opéra; the

Belgian tenor Ernest Van Dyck, who made his stage debut the same year in Antwerp and later achieved fame as a Wagnerian tenor; and baritone Emile-Alexandre Taskin, who had sung the previous year in Debussy's *Le gladiateur*. The composer provided the piano accompaniment, assisted in the four-hand sections by his friend René Chansarel. The musicians on the jury did not support him, but thanks to the painters and pressure from Charles Gounod, Debussy received twenty-two of twenty-eight votes. A similar reaction awaited him upon his arrival at the Villa Medici when he played the cantata for his fellow laureates: he found that some liked it, but not the musicians.[13] On the advice of his teacher, Ernest Guiraud, Debussy had deliberately curbed his progressive impulses, persuaded that a more conservative style would appeal to the jury.[14] The strategy worked, although Conservatoire students, like Maurice Emmanuel, who were familiar with Debussy's bold harmonic experiments, registered surprise and even disappointment that the cantata was so 'debonair'.[15] The Académie found it to possess a '[v]ery marked poetic sense, brilliant warm colours, the music has life and drama'.[16] Perhaps Debussy was belatedly repaying the work's evident debt to Massenet when he later wrote of that composer: 'His influence on contemporary music is clear enough, although it is not acknowledged by some who owe him a great deal – ungrateful hypocrites!'[17]

As the title indicates, the plot of *L'enfant prodigue* is related to the Biblical parable of the prodigal son. The action begins at sunrise in a village near the Lake of Gennesaret (Sea of Galilee) as joyous songs are heard in the distance. Lia (soprano) laments the long absence of her son, Azaël (tenor). Her husband, Siméon (baritone), impatient with her incessant weeping, directs her attention to the approaching procession of merrymakers ('Cortège et air de danse'). As they all depart, Azaël, the prodigal son, arrives. He expresses remorse for the pain he has caused his mother and, weakened from hunger and injury, loses consciousness within sight of his home. Lia's voice revives him and they enjoy a joyous reunion. When Siméon enters, Lia urges him to forgive their son, who is prostrate before him. Siméon confesses the grief he has long concealed and orders a celebratory feast. The reunited family sings in praise of God.

The Middle Eastern setting (and the success the previous year of Léo Delibes's *Lakmé*) inspired a host of exotic touches in the music, including incomplete and static harmonies, drone fifths, modal melodies, a pronounced pentatonicism in the 'air de danse', grace notes, and the use of tambourine (*tambour de Basque*) and cymbals.[18] The opening prelude introduces two main motives: a Phrygian arabesque, which represents distant songs and serves as the scene's unifying motive, and a lyrical horn melody that seems to symbolise the bond between mother and son; it reappears several times, to moving effect, but disappears around the middle of the scene. In purest

Wagnerian fashion a leitmotif associated with Azaël is introduced as the figure to which Lia sings his name; it recurs tellingly thereafter.

The cantata was reprised at the Institut de France on 18 October 1884 (with Mme Boidin-Puisais replacing Rose Caron, who was unavailable), and that same month Durand–Schoenewerk & Cie published the vocal score. The score currently available, which was published in 1908, differs considerably from the version that won the Prix de Rome, not only in its orchestration, which was substantially redone, but also, in places, in the substance of the accompaniment. Debussy might have preferred that the cantata be forgotten, but he succumbed to pressure from his publisher, always eager for new works but content to fill lapses in productivity by issuing (or reissuing) 'old' compositions. In fact, Debussy had a sentimental fondness for the cantata because it was apparently one of the few works of his that his father admired.[19] In 1906 Durand published, in full score, Debussy's revisions of two cantata excerpts: 'Récit et air de Lia', which justifiably became (and has remained) the cantata's most popular portion, and 'Cortège et air de danse'. The composer was nevertheless unwilling to let the conductor Edouard Colonne include the latter excerpt in a projected chronologically arranged all-Debussy programme. As Debussy explained in a letter to Jacques Durand, he considered the selection 'too slim, both in interest and in duration', and feared he would be 'accused of rummaging around in [his] bottom drawer just to keep [his] name on the posters'.[20] A performance of this orchestral excerpt nevertheless took place in Paris the following year, on 12 December 1907 at Salle Gaveau by the Concerts Séchiari.[21] In mid-July 1907, after the English conductor Henry Wood had expressed a desire to perform the entire cantata, Debussy felt compelled to redo its orchestration, which he feared 'smells of "exams", "the conservatoire" and tedium'.[22] He began the revision, but a month later found that the task was greater and more time-consuming than he had anticipated.[23] In June 1908, eager to bring the assignment to a rapid conclusion, he enlisted the aid of André Caplet. The engraver's copy (*Stichvorlage*) of the revised score is thus a compilation that surrounds the three revised excerpts already published – 'Récit et air de Lia' (with further autograph corrections) and 'Cortège et air de danse', both from 1906, plus 'Récit et air d'Azaël' from 1908 – with manuscript pages: these are initially autograph, but the concluding pages are apparently by Caplet, though surely prepared in consultation with the composer.[24] The first performance of the revised cantata was led by Henry Wood at the Sheffield Musical Festival in October 1908.[25] Although conceived for the concert hall, *L'enfant prodigue* received theatrical treatment during Debussy's lifetime.[26]

When Debussy later commented of Prix de Rome winners that writing the 'wretched' cantatas 'whets their appetite for the theatre rather too early', he was speaking from experience. For his first *envoi* from Rome he considered several dramatic and para-dramatic projects, and ultimately decided to submit the first part of a projected three-part 'symphonic ode' entitled *Zuleima*, a setting of a poem by Georges Boyer, based on Heinrich Heine's *Almansor*.[27] Heine's tragedy is set in the vicinity of Granada around 1500, after the Moors were expelled from Spain. Almansor, a Moor, returns to his homeland and visits his late father's castle. He is urged to lead an insurrection, but his true aspiration is to elope with his beloved Zuleima, now a Christian convert. Their religious differences, parental enmity and her betrothal to a Spaniard present obstacles, so he abducts her. Atop a cliff in an imaginary heaven they declare their mutual love, but to escape the Spanish knights who pursue them they leap to their deaths. Life separated them, but in death they are united.

Since Debussy's score is lost, our knowledge of *Zuleima* is based primarily on references to it in his correspondence and the official report of the Académie des Beaux-Arts, published following the work's December 1886 performance.[28] It is in this report that *Zuleima* is described as an 'ode symphonique', suggesting a connection to the 'ode-symphonie', a multi-part work for voices, chorus and orchestra, of which Félicien David's *Le désert* (1844) was the prototype. This oratorio-like symphonic genre enjoyed a fleeting popularity in mid-century France. David's *Christophe Colombe* (1847) is another example, and Georges Bizet cultivated the genre during his own residence at the Villa Medici: he began but discarded *Ulysse et Circé* (1859) before submitting *Vasco de Gama* (1859–60) as his second *envoi*.

Debussy's work on *Zuleima* was plagued by doubt. On 4 June 1885 he resolved not to make it his first *envoi*: '*Zuleima* is decidedly not for me. It's too old and fusty. The long stupid lines – great only in length – bore me and my music would be stifled by them.'[29] By the end of the month he was recommitted to the project, but content with only the first part, which he feared was too short for an *envoi*. The second part no longer pleased him, the third was 'too stupid', and he preferred to work on something else rather than return to them.[30] On 19 October he again declared the project 'dead', explaining that it was not the kind of music he wanted to write – 'too much like Verdi and Meyerbeer'.[31] More than a year passed between this self-assessment and his submission of the score, so the music was presumably revised. Nevertheless, Debussy's correspondence suggests that, even though his artistic ambitions lay elsewhere, he truly wanted to please the Académie. If so, he misjudged badly. The official report expressed great disappointment, apparently detecting little that resembled either Verdi or Meyerbeer. Debussy, they found, was intent on writing music that was 'strange, bizarre, incomprehensible, and unperformable. Despite a few passages that display a certain individuality, the vocal part of the work is uninteresting, with respect to both its melody and declamation.'[32]

While forging ahead with the uncongenial *Zuleima*, Debussy also laboured on two other projects, presumably operas. He worked briefly on *Salammbô*, based on Flaubert's novel, a historical romance set in Carthage during the third century BC. The novel combines elements of the exotic, the epic and the decadent, and its poetic style shows Parnassian affinities.[33] In the novel barbarian mercenaries, owed wages for service to the Carthaginians, plot to conquer the city and manage to steal the sacred veil of the moon-goddess. Salammbô, daughter of Carthage's leader and priestess of the moon-goddess, performs a ritual dance with a sacred python, then sets off to recover the veil, though she loses her virginity in the process. When a Numidian mercenary helps to slaughter the barbarians, he is rewarded with Salammbô's hand in marriage, but she dies during the ceremony while toasting the Carthaginian victory. Debussy claimed in October 1885 to have produced 'one or two sketches which could be worked up' when he returned to Paris, but no trace of them has been found.[34] Of course, rather than an opera, Debussy's *Salammbô* could have been conceived as a purely orchestral work or even as a cantata or lyric scene, all of which were options for *envois*. It is not known what poem or libretto he might have used for a vocal setting, but as an opera *Salammbô* had no possible future since the composer Ernest Reyer already had exclusive rights to the subject.[35] Indeed, Debussy's discovery of that fact might account for his sudden abandonment of the project.

In contrast, he was long preoccupied with a setting of Théodore de Banville's two-act *comédie héroïque, Diane au bois*.[36] His interest in the play extended back at least to 27 November 1881, which date is inscribed at the end of the manuscript of his four-hand *Diane* overture. Between 1880 and 1882 he set thirteen Banville poems, and the earliest of these songs, *Nuits d'étoiles*, was his first published work. In 1882 he set portions of Banville's *Hymnis*, a *comédie lyrique* in seven scenes,[37] and composed at least three movements of a four-movement suite for orchestra, *Triomphe de Bacchus*, inspired by a Banville poem; the first, second and fourth movements survive in a four-hand piano version. Another operatic 'trial' from the period, also set in the world of classic myth, is a fragment of *Hélène*, Leconte de Lisle's *poème antique*, which dates from the first half of 1881. According to Raymond Bonheur, a classmate at the Conservatoire, Debussy also considered setting Banville's four-act *comédie, Florise*.[38]

Mallarmé described Banville as 'the very voice of the lyre', and Baudelaire said of him: 'Like the art of antiquity, he expresses only what is beautiful, joyous, noble, great, rhythmic.'[39] Banville's *Diane au bois* was published in 1864 and drew its subject from Ovid: Diane, the virgin goddess of the hunt, has had Eros, the god of love, banished from Olympus, and the latter takes vengeance by seducing her, disguised as the shepherd Endymion. Her 'weakness' exposed, Diane rescinds Eros's banishment and, with some reluctance, terminates their relationship: 'To love! to live! O my heart, that was the dream. Farewell!' The extant portion of Debussy's score comprises the seduction of Diane (soprano) by Eros (tenor), corresponding to portions of scenes 3–4 of act II. Detailed stage directions in the manuscript suggest that a theatrical performance was ultimately envisioned, although admittedly similar instructions are found in the cantata *L'enfant prodigue*. The title page is generically ambiguous, describing the selection as 'Fragments lyriques. / 1$^{\underline{\text{e}}}$ Duo. = Eros et Diane', though this designation may merely characterise the work's current material state rather than his ultimate ambition for it.[40] The generic classification of many of Debussy's early works for voices and orchestra is oftentimes speculative and precarious, but in a letter of 4 June 1885 the composer lauded *Diane* as 'nothing at all like the usual poems set for "envois," which are basically no more than glorified cantatas. Heaven knows, one was enough!'[41] Transcending the category of 'glorified cantata' does not necessarily make for an opera, but that seems to be Debussy's implication. Handwriting analysis indicates that the extant duo was composed during the first half of 1883, just prior to the composer's second failed attempt at the Prix de Rome. It therefore predates his extensive work on the opera in Rome and may represent the very portion that he presented, 'not without pride', in Guiraud's composition class, eliciting the advice that he 'save it for later' if he wished to win the Prix de Rome.[42] If this duet was indeed a 'trial' to test his affinity for the work, it is interesting that he chose scenes from the play's ending, rather than its beginning. (His setting of *Pelléas*, more than a decade later, was similarly to begin with the love duet scene.)

Debussy evidently took Guiraud's advice and resumed work on *Diane* at the Villa Medici. In it he found the antidote to all that displeased him in *Zuleima*, and he seriously considered making it his first *envoi*. At issue were not only its generic superiority and the quality of its poetry, but above all its depiction of human emotions. In the same letter quoted above, he contrasted it with *Zuleima*, explaining: 'I would always rather deal with something where the passage of events is to some extent subordinated to a thorough and extended portrayal of human feelings. That way, I think, music can become more personal, more true to life; you can explore and refine your means of expression.' Banville's text, he felt, would allow him to write his own 'sort of music'. So committed was he to the project that later in the month he announced his intention to contact the poet through his stepson, the painter Georges Rochegrosse, presumably to secure authorisation to proceed with the setting, but also to request the addition of 'some choruses'.[43] Although

Diane was clearly congenial, it was not without its own challenges. After four months of work Debussy announced the completion of one scene, but he was still far from satisfied with it. He worried that he had 'taken on something too ambitious', elaborating:

> There's no precedent to go on and I find myself compelled to invent new forms. I could always turn to Wagner, but I don't need to tell you how ridiculous it would be even to try. The only thing of his I would want to copy is the running of one scene into another. Also I want to keep the tone lyrical without it being absorbed by the orchestra.

In contrast to what he had composed for *Zuleima*, he aspired to write music 'that is supple and concentrated enough to adapt itself to the lyrical movements of the soul and the whims of reverie'.[44] Clearly, he was intent on breaking away from received operatic conventions. As he put it a year later in another context, 'I think [the public has] had enough of cavatinas and all that rubbish, showing off the singers' technique and the heroes' pectoral muscles.'[45] In late November 1885 *Diane* was still giving him trouble, but now the difficulty was one of musical characterisation: 'I can't manage to find a musical idea that gives me the look of her [Diane], as I imagine it. In fact it's quite difficult, because the idea must be beautiful but cold – it mustn't give any hint of passion. Love comes to Diane only much later and then it's only really by accident; I'll have to get it across through the transformation of this idea, step by step as Diane loses her resistance to love, but the idea must keep the same contour throughout.'[46] These comments not only illuminate Debussy's developing concept of the leitmotif, but imply that he was working on the beginning of what he planned would be a substantial dramatic work. In late January 1886, he continued to experience misgivings:

> It's so difficult to portray the countless emotions a character undergoes and still keep the form as simple as possible; and in *Diane* the scenes were constructed with no thought of their being set to music, so they could seem too long and it's the very devil to keep up the interest and ward off yawns of boredom. But there's no point complaining about the text; I chose it, and I must take responsibility for the decision.[47]

One obvious solution would have been simply to cut and rearrange the text, precisely as he had done three years earlier in setting the act II duo. There he transferred some of Eros's lines from the middle to the end of the scene and set them as a duet, producing a more conventionally arranged libretto and in the process betraying the mentality of a Prix de Rome competitor. By 1886 he seems to have become more deferential towards the text, more disposed to write an 'opera as sung play' (to adopt the formulation used by Joseph Kerman to describe *Pelléas*). He anticipated completing *Diane* later that year, but, unable to do so, reverted to *Zuleima* as his first *envoi*. Although his comments about *Diane* reveal directions in his musical and dramaturgical thinking, he seems not have found satisfactory solutions to the formidable challenges he undertook. Lacking the 1885–6 drafts, we cannot judge for ourselves. Alas, nothing of *Diane* survives other than the overture of 1881 and the duo of 1883. Both deserve occasional hearings. The overture juxtaposes two 'hunt' themes: a whole-tone horncall that outlines an augmented triad and seems to represent Diane the huntress, and a more lyrical theme that recurs in the duo, accompanying Eros's impassioned vow to pursue her.

For his second and third *envois*, Debussy retreated from opera and produced *Printemps* (completed 23 February 1887), a two-movement symphonic suite for orchestra, piano, and wordless chorus, and *La damoiselle élue* (1887–8), *poème lyrique d'après D.-G. Rossetti* for women's voices (solos and chorus) and orchestra, which Debussy himself described as a 'little oratorio in a mystic, slightly pagan vein'.[48]

Still, he aspired to write opera and, as was the case with *Diane*, looked to progressive drama for his text. According to Vallas he set one scene of the dramatic prose poem *Axël* by Philippe Auguste Villiers de l'Isle-Adam, but Debussy's manuscript has vanished and its contents have never been described.[49] The first part of Villiers's *Axël* appeared in *La renaissance littéraire et artistique* in 1872, but the four-part symbolist play was not published in its entirety until its serialisation in *La jeune France* between November 1885 and June 1886. The first edition, which incorporated the author's revisions, was issued posthumously in January 1890, and this publication may well have been the stimulus for Debussy's interest. More an armchair drama than a stage play, *Axël* follows the mystic initiation of a couple willing to renounce everything worldly, and ultimately, life itself. Its first performance, in 1894, with incidental music by Alexandre Georges, lasted five hours. Obviously, considerable cuts would have been required to convert it into a viable libretto, and Debussy apparently decided not to proceed beyond the single 'trial' scene.

By April 1890 he had already begun a new opera, *Rodrigue et Chimène*, based on the legendary eleventh-century Spanish hero El Cid.[50] There were already more than two dozen operas (mostly Italian and German) on this popular subject, and in 1878, when Catulle Mendès wrote the libretto, it was but one of six 'competing' versions discussed in the musical press. Two of these were already out of the running: Aimé (Louis) Maillart was reported to have been composing *Le Cid Campéador* to a text by Auguste Maquet at the time of his death (1871), and in 1873 Georges Bizet had drafted but left unfinished *Don Rodrigue*, to a text by Louis Gallet and Edouard Blau. The three 'active' projects, in addition to Mendès's, were a libretto by Emile de la

Rue, another by Jules Barbier for composer Victor (Félix-Marie) Massé, and most importantly, because it was the only one to reach the stage, Massenet's *Le Cid*, based on a reworking by Gallet and Blau of their libretto for Bizet, with further contributions by Adolphe d'Ennery. Although Massenet's opera was not completed until 1885 (and staged that same year at the Opéra), the collaboration was announced as early as 1878. By June 1879, Mendès's libretto seemed to have found its composer, François-Auguste Gevaert, who prior to 1870 had accepted but abandoned yet another libretto for *Le Cid* – by Victorien Sardou. Perhaps Gevaert had some sketches he thought he could put to use, but in the end he did no better by Mendès, who had to wait until 1890 (by which time Massenet's *Cid* had received over eighty performances) to snare another composer – Claude Debussy.

Debussy's agreement to undertake *Rodrigue et Chimène* (as Mendès's *Le Cid* was renamed to distinguish it from Massenet's opera) is surprising in the light of his literary sympathies, which had already shifted from the Parnassians to the Symbolists. Apparently pragmatic interests outweighed aesthetic considerations. First of all, Mendès offered to underwrite the publication of Debussy's recently completed *Fantaisie* for piano and orchestra. Secondly, quite apart from his own ambition, Debussy was feeling parental pressure to achieve the kind of fame that brought financial rewards, and he must genuinely have felt that *Rodrigue* held that potential. This did not prevent him from expressing grave misgivings, as he did on 30 January 1892 when he announced to his friend Robert Godet that he had completed two acts of the opera: 'My life is hardship and misery thanks to this opera. Everything about it is wrong for me. . . . I'm afraid I may have won victories over my true self.'[51] He complained similarly to Gustave Charpentier, 'It is the exact opposite of everything I should like to express', and in particular, 'The traditional nature of the subject demands a type of music that I can no longer write.'[52] In 1892 he drafted the third act, and as late as the summer of 1893 still treated the opera as a work in progress destined for performance. On 10 August he played it for Paul Dukas, who had the impression that *Rodrigue* was nearly complete, although no trace of its concluding fourth act has survived, if indeed it was ever written. A few weeks later Dukas wrote to Vincent d'Indy that 'the dramatic breadth of certain scenes' was something he had not expected: 'It is moreover perfectly *natural*. In addition, all of the episodes are exquisite and in their harmonic finesse recall his earliest songs. . . . The text, however, is completely uninteresting: a mélange of Parnassian bric-a-brac and Spanish barbarism.'[53] For his part, Mendès was especially proud of the Spanish flavouring. In a press release published on 21 December 1878, Mendès even stressed that he had 'gone back to the original legends' precisely in order to 'add the strange and powerful local colour and all the unique atmosphere of Castilian and Moorish customs'.[54]

Our knowledge of *Rodrigue* is considerably hampered by the condition of the sources. The libretto survives only in Debussy's score, which contains gaps in the first three acts and is lacking the fourth act altogether. Mendès drew from Corneille's *Le Cid*, Guilem de Castro's *Las Mocedades del Cid*, and earlier, anonymous *Romanceros*.[55] Act I begins before daybreak. Rodrigue (El Cid), the son of the elderly Don Diègue de Bivar, visits his fiancée, Chimène, at the castle of her father, the brash Don Gomez de Gormaz. They sing a love duet, then part when Gomez's lusty soldiers enter singing a drinking song. Diègue prevents them from harassing a group of frolicsome girls from Bivar but is in turn humiliated by Gomez for reprimanding the men. Gomez accuses Diègue of lying about his military record, but the latter is too feeble to defend his honour. At the start of act II Rodrigue pines for Chimène while his two younger brothers, Hernan and Bermudo, play chess. Their father enters, so broken that they initially mistake him for a beggar. He asks them to defend his honour by killing Gomez. Rodrigue is torn between his sense of duty and his love for Chimène, but decides that duty takes precedence. Gomez taunts Rodrigue, who then kills him in a duel. With his dying breath Gomez asks Chimène to avenge his death. Act III opens with a drinking chorus, after which the soldiers are joined by groups of esquires, mountaineers and monks, among others, in support of King Ferdinand's battle against the Moors. Despite Diègue's attempts to justify Rodrigue's action, the King agrees with Chimène that her father's murderer should be punished. Now it is Chimène's turn to choose between love and duty. She cannot hate her lover but must avenge her father. Rodrigue requests death by her hand, but she cannot do it, and besides, he is needed on the battlefield. He hopes to lead the soldiers to victory but die in combat in order to satisfy Chimène's need for vengeance. In the missing act IV Rodrigue presumably returns triumphant and is reconciled with Chimène so they can marry.

The three extant acts of Debussy's setting are incomplete in various ways, a situation which created considerable challenges to the team that produced the truncated three-act performing version of the opera, first performed in 1993 and subsequently recorded.[56] The manuscripts of acts I and III survive only in short score. Since these were working drafts intended solely for the composer's personal use, the notation is often sketchy, sometimes with layers of hasty revision and lacking accidentals, clefs, words and even lines of text. Sometimes the vocal parts themselves are missing, as in part of the choral confrontation between the men of Gormaz and the girls of Bivar in act I. Moreover, a page from act III is missing, as is the very end of act I. (Would this have been the act end where, according to Raymond Bonheur, 'one already felt the rough expression [*rude accent*] of Golaud'?[57]) Act II, in contrast, represents the next compositional stage: it is a piano-vocal reduction, created both for rehearsal purposes and for publication.

Its very existence demonstrates the extent of Debussy's commitment to the opera and inspires the hope that additional manuscript material may yet come to light, including the missing act IV. Unfortunately, two portions of the act II vocal score are missing: a speech delivered by Hernan during the chess game and, more crucially, the duel between Rodrigue and Don Gomez plus its immediate aftermath. The absence of these pages from the vocal score suggests that, subsequent to its preparation, these passages were so extensively revised (in the missing short score) that Debussy could not merely retouch the vocal score, as he did elsewhere in the act, but needed actually to replace the pages. Apparently he never got around to doing it. Hernan's missing speech may be the material roughly sketched (without text) at the end of the act I short score (fols. 53–4), but the duel is nowhere to be found. Debussy's emendations present other problems as well. At points throughout the opera the often hastily scrawled revisions offer a choice between the relatively clearly notated original version that Debussy rejected and a revision that is to varying degrees incomplete and ambiguous.

Commentators have identified a number of non-French musical influences in *Rodrigue*: exoticism in the evocative melody based on a non-traditional scale, which complements the picturesque scene on the banks of the Duero River at the start of the second tableau (scene 5) of act II; sixteenth-century polyphonists, whose music Debussy had heard in Rome, in the marvellous seven-part sacred chorus at the end of act II; Borodin, whose music he had encountered in the early 1880s while working for Mme von Meck, in the Hernan–Bermudo act II duet in which they offer hospitality to the beggar; and Wagner, not only for echoes of *Tristan* and *Parsifal*, operas Debussy had heard during visits to Bayreuth in 1888 and 1889, but also for the general abandonment of self-contained set pieces in favour of a more through-composed drama, sustained by a symphonically developed accompaniment dependent on a system of leitmotifs. All of the principal characters have leitmotifs which follow them throughout the opera. To give some examples: the prelude to act I introduces three main leitmotifs, representing Chimène, Rodrigue and their love for one another. This last is 'defined' in the act I love duet and returns in act III, scene 3, as Chimène realises that her heart cannot accommodate hate since it is filled with love for Rodrigue. In act II, scene 3, as Rodrigue agonises over having to choose between love and duty, the two sentiments are musically represented by the themes of Chimène and Don Diègue respectively, which alternate synchronously with his vacillations.

Until he discovered *Pelléas* Debussy was perpetually torn between operatic projects that truly appealed to him and those he felt obliged to undertake. Thus, even while forging ahead with *Rodrigue* he actively sought a more congenial alternative. In 1891 he requested but was refused authorisation to set

Maurice Maeterlinck's recent Symbolist play *La princesse Maleine*. As the playwright explained in a letter of 23 June 1891 to the intermediary, Jules Huret, even though the play hardly lent itself to musical treatment, others had approached him with the same request, and he had refused them all because Vincent d'Indy had expressed a vague intention to set it some day.[58] In 1892 Debussy and Gabriel Mourey planned a lyric drama 'on the theme of *Being*', whose 'first tableau opened with the mad dancing of monks and rustics in the cloister', but nothing came of it.[59] Then in 1893 Debussy found the operatic project that finally enabled him to abandon *Rodrigue*: another Symbolist play by Maeterlinck, *Pelléas et Mélisande*.[60]

Maeterlinck's *Pelléas* was published in May 1892, but Debussy did not read it until 1893, probably before attending its first performance by Lugné-Poe's Théâtre de l'Œuvre, on 17 May 1893. Although immediately convinced of the play's operatic potential, he waited more than two months to seek authorisation from Maeterlinck, whom he approached through the symbolist poet Henri de Régnier. The playwright granted the rights in a letter of 8 August, and just two days later Debussy sought Dukas's opinion of *Rodrigue*, perhaps secretly hoping for confirmation of his own misgivings. Notwithstanding Dukas's enthusiasm, Debussy seems at this juncture to have definitively abandoned *Rodrigue* in favour of *Pelléas*. Armed with the playwright's authorisation he set to work, and by early September completed a draft of the love scene at the opera's climax (act IV, scene 4). This strategy of starting with the climactic love duet to test both the play's operatic potential and his affinity for it is one we have already witnessed in the composition of *Diane au bois*. (In *Rodrigue* the love duet comes near the start of act I.) The *Pelléas* love scene may have been the first composed, but it was also the one most frequently revised, and the first revision came hard on the heels of its initial completion. On 2 October he wrote to Ernest Chausson that he tore up the first version because of its conventionality, 'and worst of all the ghost of old Klingsor, alias R. Wagner, kept appearing'. In seeking something more personal he discovered a way of using 'silence' as 'a means of expression'.[61] Debussy was particularly sensitive to traces of Wagnerian influence as he had announced the previous month a forthcoming article – never published and probably never written – 'On the Uselessness of Wagnerism'.[62]

By mid-October he completed the new version of act IV, scene 4 and played it for his friends. In early November in the company of Pierre Louÿs he visited Maeterlinck in Ghent both to play the scene for him and, more importantly, to discuss the adaptation of the play as a libretto.[63] Although Debussy's earliest extant complete draft of the love scene set the play virtually verbatim, he was probably anticipating the need to make cuts elsewhere in the drama and for that needed the playwright's approval. Maeterlinck not only granted him permission to make whatever cuts he liked, but even suggested 'some important ones – *extremely useful ones even!* '[64] In addition to numerous cuts throughout the drama, Debussy eliminated four entire scenes, two of which involved the servants rather than the principals.[65]

Francisque Sarcey's plot summary, in an unfavourable review of the play's premiere ('It is the incestuous love of a married woman for her brother-in-law; the outraged husband surprises the guilty ones, kills the one and wounds the other, who dies afterwards.'), stresses the naturalistic level on which the symbolist play also operates, its representation of the tragic collision of natural and social laws.[66] But in keeping with the Symbolist aesthetic, there is an overriding atmosphere of mysterious vagueness. To begin with, the setting is indefinite in both time and place. Maeterlinck's attempt to bring precision by describing its era as the eleventh, twelfth or possibly the fifteenth century only muddled matters further.[67] The name of the imaginary kingdom, Allemonde, combines the Greek word *allos*, meaning 'other', with the French word *monde*, meaning 'world', to suggest an 'other-world' that is both self-contained and separate from the 'real' one. The action is largely confined to the castle and its grounds, and the main characters avoid contact with the outside world. Pelléas and Mélisande recoil from the silent beggars they encounter in the grotto, the servants never speak (in the opera), and the sailors' and shepherd's voices are only heard from a distance. There is even a certain vagueness about the relationships among the principal characters, who belong to four generations. Geneviève, the mother of the half-brothers Golaud and Pelléas, is generally taken to be the daughter of King Arkel but must be his daughter-in-law: she speaks of having lived in the castle nearly forty years, which, given the age of her elder son, means that she was not born there but, like Mélisande, arrived as a bride. Her second husband, Pelléas's unnamed father, never appears; her first, Golaud's father, is never mentioned and is presumably dead. Is it possible that this generation too was marked by fratricide – that the two sons of Arkel quarrelled over Geneviève, that Pelléas's father killed Golaud's and then married his wife? One is probably not supposed to speculate about such things, but doing so leads to a crucial point. This is a family shaped by a powerful destiny – the force of fate is constantly felt and discussed – and patterns of behaviour repeat generation after generation, often with tragic consequences. As Arkel says of Mélisande's daughter in the opera's closing lines (shortly after Mélisande dies): 'She must now live in her [mother's] place. It is the poor little girl's turn now.' If Geneviève was a past Mélisande grown old, the little girl is the infant Mélisande for the future.[68]

Instead of a continuously developing narrative, the opera's action unfolds in a series of vignettes connected by orchestral interludes: fifteen short scenes organised into five acts.[69] One entire scene (act IV, scene 3) is purely symbolic (and therefore sometimes omitted in performance):[70] Yniold,

Golaud's son, cannot extricate his golden ball, wedged between a rock and a heavy stone.[71] (Human will is powerless in the pursuit of perfection, hence Pelléas and Mélisande are unable to 'seize' love and are 'trapped' in their pursuit of it.) The sun vanishes. (King Arkel fails to provide guidance.) The invisible shepherd keeps the crying sheep on the path. (Our lives are controlled by fate.) The sheep stop bleating as they realise that they are no longer on the path to the shed. (The innocent lambs are being led into the unknown – presumably to be slaughtered – and they accept their fate; Pelléas and Mélisande are also innocents submissive to destiny and destined for death.) Yniold complains that it is too dark. (He fails to comprehend; hope is lost.) As René Terrasson has observed, Yniold's final remark, that he will tell something to somebody, reconnects this symbolic scene to the plot. Yniold needs to share his experience with the person to whom he feels closest, his stepmother. (In the final scene of act III Golaud observed that he is always with her.) When Yniold discovers that Mélisande is not in her room he perhaps unwittingly discloses her absence to his father, who then goes looking for her, sword in hand.[72]

The libretto abounds in symbols and recurring images. Mélisande's long hair, an attribute of femininity and, because it emanates from her head, of her spiritual force, is one such recurrent symbol. She allows it to plunge into Blindman's Well in act II, but the well, which in normal circumstances cures and purifies, has lost its power. In act III Pelléas caresses her unbound hair and entangles it in the willow branches to prevent her from leaving him. In act IV Golaud brutally reinterprets this gesture: he yanks her hair, blasphemously drags her by it in the shape of the cross, and invokes the name of Absalom, the traitorous son of King David, who was killed when his hair became entangled in tree branches. Hands and touching also play a critical role, and water images (the spring, the well, the sea, even a drink of water) abound. In act I Mélisande has dropped her crown (the symbol of her past, her title, and her previous marriage) into the shallow spring and does not want Golaud to retrieve it. Then in act II she jeopardises her marriage to Golaud by tossing her wedding ring into the air, and when it falls into Blindman's Well she discourages Pelléas from recovering it. (He suggests they might find another ring – by marrying one another? – but she rejects that too.) Since the well where they meet is deeper than the spring where she met Golaud, are we to conclude that her love for Pelléas is deeper than her love for Golaud? Does the name of the well connote that Pelléas and Mélisande are as yet 'blind' to their mutual love? She loses her ring precisely at noon, when the sun is at its height, symbolising a moment of revelation. Then in act III her song from the tower reveals that she was born at noon. Is this an allusion to her metaphorical birth in the previous act, a rebirth through love made possible by her symbolic renunciation of her marriage to Golaud?

Mélisande is the mysterious outsider in this drama. Golaud wants to know where she comes from, but she will not say. From one point of view, her undisclosed background facilitates perceiving her less as a person than as a symbol – a symbol of love, which briefly brightens a desolate world but 'brings in its train misery and horror, jealousy, murder, and intolerable suffering'.[73] On the other hand, from a later Maeterlinck play, *Ariane et Barbe-bleue* (set as an opera by Paul Dukas), we learn that she was one of Bluebeard's imprisoned and terrorised wives. This explains why she recoils from Golaud's touch in the opening scene. Like the wounded boar that Golaud is pursuing, she too is an injured, hunted creature. As a battered woman she is obviously a victim, but as the 'provocation' to fratricide she also becomes an agent of fate. Her kinship with Mélusine, the archetypal siren of French mythology, is suggested by the similarity of their names, and like the sirens of Greek mythology, she seduces with her voice. Her song from the tower in act III lures Pelléas, and in the act IV love scene he rhapsodises over the beauty of her voice, unintentionally invoking the sirens that enticed sailors to their deaths: 'Your voice seems to have wafted across the sea in spring!' When Mélisande tells Pelléas that she loves him is she telling the truth, or as seductress and/or battered woman (take your pick), is she only saying what she thinks he wants to hear? Pelléas questions her veracity; Golaud is sure she is a liar (we catch her in the act and she readily admits to it); the blind Arkel 'sees' nothing but innocence. She enables all males, from the child Yniold to the old Arkel, to project their fantasies onto her. This is at once the source of her power and ultimately the cause of her ruin, when the fantasies of Pelléas and Golaud come into conflict.

In December 1893, temporarily satisfied with his setting of the love scene and authorised by the playwright to make cuts, Debussy turned to the beginning of the play. He eliminated the first scene and set the remaining three of act I, composing them roughly at the rate of a scene per month. While the balance of his compositional schedule cannot be determined with absolute certainty, he seems next to have turned to act III and between May and August 1894 completed its first three scenes (scenes 2–4 in Maeterlinck's play). During August he also worked on the final scene of act III, but only after completing act IV, scene 3, the other scene involving Yniold. The balance of the year was devoted to other compositions: *Nocturnes* for violin and orchestra, of which no trace survives; the orchestration of *Prélude à l'après-midi d'un faune*; and three *Images* for piano, which were published in 1977 as *Images (oubliées)*. He resumed *Pelléas* in January 1895 (act IV, scenes 1–2?), and between April and June completed act V, although work on this act was interrupted by yet another revision of act IV, scene 4 (in May) and by his collaboration with Pierre Louÿs on a scenario for *Cendrelune*, an unrealised *conte lyrique* in two acts and three tableaux, commissioned by the Opéra-Comique for Christmas 1895. In June he undertook act II, the last remaining act, and completed the opera (in short score) on 17 August. Debussy's comments about his scenes in progress, voiced in letters to friends, reveal the intensity of his involvement with the opera and offer insights into his aspirations. Of act I, scene 1: 'I've spent days trying to capture that "nothing" that Mélisande is made of'. Of act I, scene 2: 'At the moment it's Arkel who's tormenting me. He comes from beyond the grave and has that objective, prophetic gentleness of those who are soon to die'. Of act II, scene 2: 'That's the point where things begin to move towards the catastrophe, and where Mélisande begins to tell Golaud lies and to realise her own motives.' Of act II, scene 3: 'I tried to capture all the mystery of the night and the silence in which a blade of grass roused from its slumber makes an alarming noise. And then there's the sea nearby, telling its sorrows to the moon and Pelléas and Mélisande a little scared of talking, surrounded by so much mystery.' Of act III, scene 2: 'It's full of impalpable terror and mysterious enough to make the most well-balanced listener giddy.' Of act III, scene 3: 'full of sunshine but a sunshine reflecting our mother the sea'. Of act III, scene 4: 'It's terrifying, the music's got to be profound and absolutely accurate! There's a "petit père" that gives me nightmares.' Of act IV, scene 3: 'Here I've tried to get across something at least of the compassion of a child who sees a sheep mainly as a sort of toy he can't touch and also as the object of a pity no longer felt by those who are only anxious for a comfortable life.'[74]

As a prose play, *Pelléas* presented special challenges. As Debussy commented while composing act II: 'Anything resembling conversation doesn't really work in music and the man who discovers the secret of the "musical interview" ought to be generously rewarded.'[75] Nonetheless, the absence of verse inviting treatment as self-contained arias or ensembles, which might have thwarted other composers, was an attraction for Debussy, given the direction of his operatic goals. The only verse in the libretto is the mock folk song that Mélisande sings from the tower, and it is essentially unaccompanied. Otherwise, Debussy created his own musical 'language': a highly expressive recitational 'chanting' over an orchestral background. On one level the vocal style aims to convey the pacing and inflection of stylised, theatrical speech (perhaps influenced by the actors' 'psalmodising' in the original production of the play), though at moments of emotional climax it soars into pure melody, producing 'arias' of extraordinary beauty but lasting only seconds. In both tangible and subliminal ways the orchestra not only supports the characters' words and actions, but reflects their thoughts and feelings. At times it even contributes 'stage' sounds, ranging from Golaud's coughs and Mélisande's sobs to the noisy bolts and chains of the closing castle doors. Ultimately, Maeterlinck's prose style was ideal for Debussy's purposes. While the sparseness of words and frequent silences left 'room' for orchestral expression and 'commentary', the constant repetition of words and phrases served to sustain emotions, allowing time for appropriate musical expression. Furthermore, the recurring poetic images and symbols that fill the text inspired a corresponding system of associated leitmotifs – a kind of musical symbolism – although character leitmotifs predominate, just as in *Rodrigue*. Symbolic meanings are also associated with various rhythmic, harmonic, dynamic, timbral and tonal elements.[76]

In early September 1893, as he was finishing his first draft of a scene from *Pelléas*, Debussy proposed the formation of a Society of Musical Esotericism as an alternative to 'spreading music among the populace'. 'Music really ought to have been a hermetical science', he explained, 'enshrined in texts so hard and laborious to decipher as to discourage the herd of people who treat it as casually as they do a handkerchief!'[77] This Society may have been no more than a passing fancy, but in 1895 Debussy's initial prospects for performances of *Pelléas* came not from opera companies but from the avant-garde theatre. To protect Lugné-Poe's proprietary interest in the play, Maeterlinck intervened to dissuade Debussy from pursuing a proposal from Paul Larochelle's Théâtre Libre, but then an alternative offer from Lugné-Poe's Théâtre de l'Œuvre failed to materialise.[78] Debussy contemplated a private performance at the home of Count Robert de Montesquiou, in his 'Pavillon des Muses', but he rejected suggestions that he arrange portions of the opera as incidental music for the play[79] or that he allow excerpts to be performed in concert. Finally, in May 1898 his publisher Georges Hartmann helped him bring the opera to the attention of the new administration of the Opéra-Comique: Albert Carré, its director, and André Messager, its music director and conductor. Carré immediately accepted *Pelléas* 'in principle', but Debussy still had to wait another three years, until 3 May 1901, before he received Carré's written promise to stage *Pelléas* in the coming season.

Since the playwright wanted his mistress Georgette Leblanc to sing the role of Mélisande, casting the relatively unknown soprano Mary Garden caused a permanent rupture in Debussy's relationship with Maeterlinck. After his appeal to the Société des auteurs et compositeurs dramatiques failed,[80] Maeterlinck denounced the production in the press. Difficulties of a different sort resulted from casting a boy, Blondin, as Yniold. Act IV, scene 3 had to be cut and was only reinstated the following season when the part was assigned to a woman. Although Yniold remained a trouser role in subsequent seasons, Debussy never completely abandoned his original wish to have the part sung by a child.[81] For *Pelléas* Debussy wanted a tenor with a youthful quality, but the part went to Jean Périer, a *baryton Martin*[82] who was considered to have the necessary look and acting ability. The role had to be adapted to his range. The rest of the cast included Hector Dufranne as Golaud, Félix Vieuille as Arkel, Jeanne Gerville-Réache as Geneviève and Viguié as the doctor. During rehearsals it became apparent that the equipment and facilities of the Opéra-Comique were inadequate to manage the rapid set changes that Debussy envisioned when he composed the orchestral interludes that connect the scenes. Working under pressure and with some reluctance, Debussy expanded the interludes in time for the premiere, on 30 April 1902, but, since the full score was not published until August 1904, he had – and took – the time to revise these expanded interludes to his satisfaction.[83] Other changes were imposed on the score following the dress rehearsal when Henry Roujon, Director of Fine Arts, who had the authority to censor dramatic works presented in state-supported theatres, called for the excision of act III, scene 4, in which Golaud forces Yniold to spy on the suspected lovers. Debussy agreed instead to change certain expressions and make several cuts, two of which were incorporated into the published full score: a fifteen-bar discussion between Golaud and Yniold over whether or not Pelléas and Mélisande are near the bed and Golaud's exit line, with its implication that he and Yniold will charge into Mélisande's room to see what is going on.[84]

Originally a *succès de scandale*, *Pelléas* rapidly became a *succès d'estime*, consistently attracting contingents of passionate admirers. Until the outbreak of the First World War it was revived at the Opéra-Comique nearly every year, and it was soon introduced in many of the world's operatic capitals, including Brussels and Frankfurt in 1907; New York, Milan, Cologne, Budapest, Prague, Munich, Berlin and Lyons in 1908; Rome, London, Boston and Philadelphia in 1909; Chicago in 1910; Vienna in 1911; Nice, Geneva and Buenos Aires in 1912; Birmingham in 1913; and St Petersburg in 1915. The attendant international publicity entitled Debussy to tell a *New York Times* reporter in June 1910: 'I returned to France [from Rome] and didn't know exactly what to do with myself, until I came across "Pelléas et Mélisande". Since then you know what I have done.'[85]

When he offered this biographical summary, Debussy could not have imagined that *Pelléas* would turn out to be his only completed opera. In April 1895, even before he had finished his initial draft of that opera, he was already planning his next, the collaboration with Pierre Louÿs on *Cendrelune*, mentioned above.[86] This was just one of numerous operatic projects he entertained over the years. In September 1895, a month after completing the *Pelléas* draft, he announced that he was working on a libretto for *La grande bretèche*, after Balzac.[87] This was followed over the years by other theatrical ventures, presumably operas, and pursued to varying degrees: *Les uns et les autres* (Verlaine), *Comme il vous plaira* (Paul-Jean Toulet, after Shakespeare), *Joyzelle* (Maeterlinck), *Don Juan, Roméo et Juliette, L'histoire de Tristan* (Gabriel Mourey), *Siddartha* (Victor Segalen), *Orphée-roi* (Segalen) and *Crimen amoris* (opera-ballet by Charles Morice, after Verlaine).[88] And although nothing came of it, in November 1903 he was receptive to a request from the publisher Enoch that he complete Chabrier's *Briséïs*, an undertaking that would have necessitated renewing contact with Catulle Mendès, one of the opera's librettists and his former collaborator on the long-abandoned *Rodrigue*.[89] (Ironically, only six months earlier Debussy had written disparagingly of posthumous adaptations in a review of a stage version of Berlioz's *La damnation de Faust*: 'to step into a dead man's shoes without any specific invitation seems to me to go beyond that special feeling of respect which we usually reserve for the dead.'[90])

Perusing the list of unrealised operatic projects, one is struck by how frequently – with *Orphée-roi*, *Don Juan*, *Tristan*, *Roméo* – he contemplated 'challenging' staples of the repertoire, much as his *Rodrigue* would inevitably have invited comparison with Massenet's *Le Cid*. It is almost as if, by so doing, he imagined that he might usurp the place of a Gluck, Mozart, Wagner, or Gounod, in the pantheon of opera composers. While the thought may have stimulated his imagination (and his ego), he had the good sense to withdraw from contests he probably could not win, much as the advent of *Le sacre du printemps* in the wake of *Jeux* sent him in a new musical direction, resulting in the late neoclassical instrumental works.

Debussy's major post-*Pelléas* operatic project was the double-bill based on tales by Edgar Allan Poe, which he read in Baudelaire's translations: *Le diable dans le beffroi* ('The Devil in the Belfry') and *La chute de la maison Usher* ('The Fall of the House of Usher').[91] These one-act operas occupied him, off and on, from June 1902, just a few weeks after the premiere of *Pelléas*, until 1917, shortly before his death. In a letter of 9 June 1902 he mentioned that he was working on *Le diable* and on 12 September 1903 announced that the scenario was 'more or less complete'. (The surviving scenario is dated 25 August 1903.[92]) In this same letter, to André Messager, the conductor of the *Pelléas* premiere, he divulged that he viewed the new opera as an opportunity to go 'beyond' *Pelléas*:

> Those who are kind enough to hope that I will never be able to forsake [the style of] *Pelléas* are carefully averting their eyes. They simply don't understand that if that were to happen, I would immediately turn to growing pineapples in my bedroom, believing as I do that repeating oneself is the most tiresome thing. Moreover, these same people will probably find it scandalous to have abandoned Mélisande's shadow for the Devil's ironical pirouette, and yet another pretext for accusing me of bizarrerie.[93]

On 9 July 1906 he disclosed to Jacques Durand his secret invention of 'quite a novel way of writing for voices' which had 'the further merit of being simple'.[94] Unfortunately, the 'secret' was never revealed. Only three pages of untexted musical sketches survive, apparently dating from August 1903, some of which Debussy used to compose the *Morceau de concours*, a short piano piece published in the January 1905 issue of *Musica*.[95] When Henri Busser visited the composer on 31 March 1912, he noted that Debussy had written numerous sketches for *Le diable*: 'He plays some of it for me on the piano, fragments which are very colourful ['pittoresques'], entertaining, with a feeling very different from his usual style.'[96] In February 1910 Debussy gave the following plot synopsis to a Roman interviewer: *Le diable*

> is a fantasy in the manner of [Laurence] Sterne. A waggish devil hides one day inside the belfry of a peaceful little Dutch village, and instead of letting the clock strike noon, he forces it to strike thirteen o'clock. From that ensues a very amusing confusion among these solid Dutch folk.[97]

The second scene takes Poe's final paragraph as a point of departure. Order is eventually restored, but achieved through the prayer of a devoted fiancé whose love had made him immune to the devil's influence.

By mid-June 1908 Debussy was at work on his second Poe opera, *La chute de la maison Usher*,[98] and on 5 July he offered first refusal on the Poe double-bill 'to the Metropolitan Opera and to its affiliated theatres in the United States of America, including the Boston Opera Company'. (The same contract offered the Metropolitan the first option on future operas, 'and in particular on the "Légende de Tristan"'.[99]) During the next nine or so years, Debussy wrote several drafts of the *Usher* libretto and set a substantial portion of it. In addition to various sketches, he produced in 1916–17 a short-score draft that represents the entire first scene but less than one-third of the second (and final) scene. The surviving music for the second scene has numerous gaps, some obviously quite large, but its state raises the hope that 'missing' pages may yet be found. It is unlikely, however, that Debussy completed the opera, even in draft form. Of the various attempts to create a performable score from the surviving materials, the most complete to date is that of Juan Allende-Blin, whose version of the opera was published and staged in 1979 and was later recorded.[100] The following synopsis derives from Debussy's 1910 Roman interview, mentioned above:

> Roderick Usher, fearing that his sister Madeline is not truly dead, as the doctors maintain, places her body in a deep underground vault beneath the house, awaiting the occasion to bury her. On a stormy night, during a tragic vigil where the fury of the elements combines with the anguish of the human beings, the young woman, who is not dead, after a desperate battle to escape from the vault comes to die beside her brother, whose life is also extinguished in this dreadful moment. And the entire house vanishes, collapsing into a tarn whose water lapped against the walls.[101]

This summary fails to indicate the expanded role that Debussy was to give the sinister doctor, but it does bespeak the opera's expressionistic qualities. Like *Le diable*, it represented a conscious departure from the style of *Pelléas*, though obviously in a very different direction.

In June 1908, when he was just starting to work on *Usher*, Debussy described it in therapeutic terms as 'an excellent means of strengthening the nerves against all kinds of terror'.[102] By 1917, with the First World War raging and Debussy himself battling a painful terminal illness, these words would have taken on an altogether more harrowing meaning. One would like to think that it was only the composer's death in 1918 that prevented him from completing at least one of the Poe operas – and producing his second operatic masterpiece.

With good reason we think of Debussy as a one-opera composer – like Beethoven, Bartók, and Messiaen. Yet like the typical French composer of his generation, who coveted the Prix de Rome as the necessary spring-board to launching a successful career in opera, he was occupied with operatic and other theatrical projects throughout his life, not merely the para-dramatic vocal genres mentioned above but ballet and incidental music as well. Certainly he did not pursue these interests singlemindedly at the expense of instrumental music, which was the accusation he made of some of his fellow winners. Still, the theatre was a lifelong fascination. In early childhood he would entertain himself and his sister Adèle for hours by putting on plays in a toy millboard theatre, which was fully equipped with scenery and with built-in 'incidental music' provided by a mechanism beneath the stage. Adèle recalled that when engaged in this activity he cast aside his habitual taciturnity and became talkative, even rambunctious.[103] If his attraction to the stage began at a very early age, its continuation was too often spoiled by the 'contradictions and unforeseen influences' that he believed inevitably clouded 'the atmosphere of the theatre'.[104]

5 The prosaic Debussy

ROGER NICHOLS
for Margaret G. Cobb

As the conventional distinction between recitative and aria weakened in late-nineteenth-century opera under the Wagnerian assault, it was only natural that other ready-made forms should be more closely scrutinised, among them the use of metrical verse and rhyme for musical settings. France proved to be particularly fertile soil for such debate. As Hugh Macdonald has pointed out:

> French poetry had always contained a degree of artificial emphasis that required rules and conventions to hold poetic forms in check. French composers found themselves setting verse which might be stressed in one way according to metrical convention, but differently if read in an ordinary speaking voice. The temptation to abandon verse for prose was thus greater for French composers than elsewhere . . . [1]

Macdonald quotes Gounod's eloquent preface to his unpublished opera *George Dandin* in which the composer claims that 'The infinite variety of stress, in prose, offers the musician quite new horizons which will save him from monotony and uniformity.'[2]

Whether the young Debussy ever read Gounod's words we do not know. What is certain is that among his café acquaintances was the poet and full-time aesthete Catulle Mendès, who had his own solution to the facture of librettos:

> Certainly I'm not hostile to the idea of prose in opera. It may well lead to curious effects. But don't you think that what's wrong with some contemporary operas is the uniformity in the structure of the libretto? Poetry has a considerable number of different rhythms at its disposal. Need I remind you how many there are in Banville? Why, when it comes to opera, should we not use these rhythms to lend the libretto variety, picturesqueness, colour and originality? But more often than not, people use the alexandrine or lines of eight or ten syllables which, in bulk, give the spectator an impression of fatigue and monotony.[3]

Despite the hammering given to Mendès's libretto for Chabrier's *Gwendoline*, he persisted in this approach when writing the one for *Rodrigue et Chimène* on which Debussy laboured between 1890 and 1892. In abandoning this project, the composer laid the blame firmly on the heroic subject matter, tactfully saying nothing about the nature of Mendès's versification (or nothing that has come down to us). But at the least, this libretto must have alerted him to the problems and possibilities inherent in the use of varied metres. From here the setting of prose might have seemed a natural extension, not only for opera but also for *mélodies*.

The great majority of Debussy's ninety-or-so songs are settings of verse. But over a six-year period towards the middle of his career, between 1892 and 1898, he confined his song setting to nine pieces of free verse and prose (hereafter referred to as Group B),[4] in addition to the prose text of Maeterlinck's *Pelléas et Mélisande* and an attempt on *La saulaie*, Pierre Louÿs's free-verse translation of Rossetti's 'Willow-wood'.[5] Why did he temporarily abandon strict verse forms? And why, after the production of *Pelléas* in 1902, and with the single exception of *Noël des enfants qui n'ont plus de maisons*, did he then return to them exclusively for the rest of his life?

It is natural that we should look for an answer in Debussy's own words. No less naturally our eyes light up when we see the title of the questionnaire sent out by one Fernand Divoire for the magazine *Musica*, answers to which, including Debussy's, were printed in its edition of March 1911.[6] As often with Debussy it takes time for him to stoop to the matter in hand, but he does eventually make three points relevant to our inquiry. First, 'real poetry has its own rhythm which is rather awkward for us [composers]'; secondly, despite this 'I've just set three Villon ballades . . . because I'd been wanting to for a long time'; and thirdly, 'with rhythmic prose one is more comfortable, one is more able to turn round in every sense' (avec la prose rythmée, on est plus à son aise, on peut mieux se retourner dans tous les sens).

Readers familiar with Debussy's writings will recognise not only the call for 'freedom' and 'more elbow room', but the ultimate resort to the pleasure principle when the intellectual going gets slightly sticky: why Villon? 'parce que j'en avais envie'. The same readers may intuit that Debussy is not coming quite clean on the subject. In this chapter I shall try to discover what new techniques, if any, Debussy adopted for his 'prose patch' and whether he was able, or chose, to take any of them over into his strict verse settings of 1903–4.

Words and structures

The two basic questions to be answered are: were there things that free verse and prose enabled Debussy to do which he could not do easily or at all with strict verse? and conversely, were there things that strict verse enabled him to do which he could not do easily or at all with free verse and prose? As examples of 'before' I adduce the six Verlaine songs, 'La mer est plus belle', 'Le son du cor s'afflige', 'L'échelonnement des haies' together with the first set of *Fêtes galantes*, series 1, all of which date from 1891 and/or 1892 (Group A); and as examples of 'after', seven songs on poems by different authors, *Dans le jardin* of 1903 (Paul Gravollet) and *Trois chansons de France* (Charles d'Orléans and Tristan Lhermite) and the *Fêtes galantes*, series 2 of 1904 (Group C).

More attention has been paid so far to the form, harmony and piano writing in Debussy's songs than to the details of his word-setting. Of those who have gone below the surface of his prosody, Peter Ruschenberg has perhaps been the most perceptive.[7] But a number of points remain to be made. Anyone who has ever accompanied these songs will know that, by and large, the piano part consists of 'onbeat' phrases filling one or two bars (I trust the epithets 'onbeat' and 'afterbeat' used from here on are self-explanatory). The piano therefore acts as a framework over which is stretched the rhythmically much looser vocal line. Debussy never saw any reason to modify this basic arrangement and it is still plain to see in the *Trois poèmes de Stéphane Mallarmé* of 1913.[8] As far as settings of free verse and prose were concerned, this piano framework was obviously useful in supplying a regularity the texts now lacked and it may have been the proven validity of such a framework that gave Debussy the courage in the first place to set what I shall call 'free texts' incorporating both free verse and prose.

Another feature that any performer soon appreciates is that whereas the piano is typically onbeat, the voice entries are either upbeat or, more usually, afterbeat. The pianist's job is to start the proceedings of each phrase, to set the atmosphere, often with the lion's share of the melodic interest; and a crucial contribution lies in judging the weight and colour of these onbeat entries, which the singer must be felt to respond to and not merely to follow in a mechanical manner. In Groups A and C the proportion of vocal onbeat entries to the whole is relatively constant (24/98 lines = 24 per cent and 21/92 lines = 23 per cent). But in the free text settings of Group B the proportion is significantly lower (14/177 = 8 per cent). This suggests that Debussy was aware of the need in Group B for the piano framework to be heard more clearly, to make good the loss of regularity in the texts.

These statistics also start alarm bells ringing. Was Debussy in 1911 wholeheartedly advocating being 'à son aise' in writing *mélodies*, and was the ability 'mieux se retourner dans tous les sens' an unmitigated blessing? Another set of statistics may be relevant here. In every one of the nine songs of Group B, the piano introduction is rhythmically firm and decisive, the framework

Example 5.1 'Le son du cor' (bars 1–7)

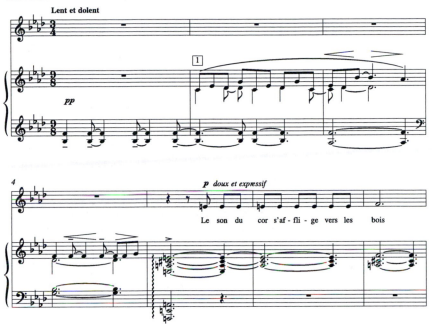

in place from the very start. This may well have stemmed from the need outlined above. But in both Groups A and C there are examples of the piano introduction sowing disorder, which the voice then sets to rights. In 'Le son du cor' any listener without a score will have difficulty identifying the beat until the voice enters, although even then there is a struggle between 9/8 and 6/8 metres (Example 5.1).[9] Here Debussy seems to be turning his habitual piano–voice relationship on its head. He then pursues the logic of the voice's controlling intervention by placing all eight end rhymes of the first two verses, as well as the first two of verse 3, on the first beat of the bar. In French songs of thirty years earlier this was common enough (see, for example, Fauré's Op. 1, No. 1, 'Le papillon et la fleur' of 1861), but for Debussy this rhythmic rhyming is highly unusual: normally he takes great care to 'bury' the rhyming syllables by placing them on different beats. The effect of the reversal here is to paint a picture of a chaotic, dangerous world that one can control by treading carefully, preferably in regular, repeated steps.

Parallel examples can be found in Group C, in *Dans le jardin*, 'Le temps a laissé son manteau' and, most notably, in 'Colloque sentimental'. Here the voice's role is not so much controlling as clarifying. After the vagueness of bars 1–3, bar 4 seems to plead for some light to be shed (Example 5.2).

Example 5.2 'Colloque sentimental' (bars 1–8)

This notion of clarification is indeed the driving force behind the poem, as the first ghost tries desperately but unsuccessfully to wring reassurance and explanation from the second. It also underpins Debussy's flights of harmony. The song ends in A minor, but that key is not heard until the final chord. It is reached only by a B♮ clarification in the penultimate bar of the B♭ with which the song began, so that we almost find ourselves saying, 'Ah! It was the B♭ that was wrong!' But, as I have pointed out, Debussy denied himself this important resource in the songs of Group B.

Perhaps the most obvious problem with the so-called 'freedom' of Group B is that of diminishing returns. The delights of musical deviation, in which Debussy was already well versed by the 1890s, are felt most keenly when there is some clear pattern to deviate from; or to put it another way, nuance makes more impact within a context of regularity. It strikes me (and this is necessarily a personal view) that it is above all in the strict verse settings of Groups A and C that we find the most subtle *frottements* between the regular and the irregular.

Here are three examples. In 'Clair de lune', after a standard, static four-bar piano introduction,[10] the first two of Verlaine's three four-line verses are both set to eight-bar phrases, the bars clearly grouped in pairs. Working against this extreme regularity is the irregular disposition of syllables:

verse 1	6 5 8 2	verse 2	6 7 6 2
	6 4 7 4		9 1 9 2

In verse 1 the accelerations in the middle of lines 2 and 4, producing eight and seven syllables in bars 7 and 11 respectively, are each launched from key words: from 'vont', giving the sense of movement, and from 'tristes', which flies against the hitherto idyllic tone of the first three lines and seems to throw the music into temporary disarray, underpinning the deception of the 'déguisements fantasques'. In verse 2 the final word 'lune' is similarly emphasised in two ways: by a rhythmic rhyme with 'opport*une*' (the first in the song) and, more startlingly, by an absolute rhythmic correspondence between lines 3 and 4 (Example 5.3). The message seems to be that just as their happiness is insubstantial through disbelief, so their singing becomes insubstantial through blending with the moonlight. Such a correspondence is unusual. Insofar as Debussy ever obeys any rules about anything, the rule in his songs is that the vocal rhythm in each bar tends to be unique, as opposed to those in the piano part where the rule is repetition. This is true in verse 1 of 'Clair de lune'. Where Debussy breaks the rule, he usually does so with a purpose: in verse 3 the almost exact similarity in vocal rhythm between bars 27 and 28 over the same D♯ minor chord helps the singer with the marvellously apt yet surprising 'sveltes'.

Example 5.3 'Clair de lune' (bars ##)

Two eight-bar verses in succession are tolerable; three might sound like carelessness. Debussy extends the words of the third verse over ten bars but, to maintain the sense of control, now 'rhymes' the words 'beau' with 'd'eau' on the first beat of the bar and partially rhymes 'arbres' with 'marbres'. In this decorous, ordered world of *fêtes galantes*, small gestures such as the stretching of 'marbres' over three notes have a huge emotional impact – like the opening of a fan just so . . .

My other two examples come from the *Trois chansons de France* (Group C). These were the first songs with piano for which Debussy used pre-nineteenth-century texts (until that time the most historically distant of his poets being Alfred de Musset, born in 1810). Although Debussy had sharp things to say about respect in art, which he felt could never be obligatory,[11] there is something almost respectful about these settings of Charles d'Orléans (1394–1465) and Tristan Lhermite (1601–55).

In 'Le temps a laissié son manteau', Charles d'Orléans built in some asymmetry in the three verses of four, three and five lines respectively.[12] Debussy added slightly to this through the occasional extra bar (e.g. bar 5), but his syllabification is decidedly sober with a narrow range of mostly three to seven syllables per bar and a constant pace of around two bars per line. Within this regular structure the tiny but unexpected syncopation on 'soleil raiant' shines out memorably. The regular pacing also means that on the first line of verse 3, 'Rivière, fontaine et ruisseau', Debussy can indulge his water fixation without histrionics merely through halving the pace of the line, extending two bars to four; and just as we relax into this he strikes us amidships with the first onbeat entry, 'Portent en livrée jolye', a phrase also marked by two successive triplets, the only ones in the song (of which more below).

My third example of the friction between regularity and irregularity comes from Lhermite's 'La grotte'. Here the three verses each contain four octosyllabic lines (if one ignores the mute 'e', which Debussy does not) with an ABBA rhyme scheme. The juxtaposition of the B rhymes (in verse 1 'doux' and 'cailloux') should alert the most sluggish listener to the presence of end rhymes, and the more responsive will be waiting for the appearance, after the regulation seven syllables, of a rhyme for 'sombre' (the answer, 'l'ombre', will come as no surprise to Debussystes). The composer, as usual, has got there well ahead of them. The first two bars of the song are unambiguously in 3/4 metre, but the piano part in bars 3–6, although notated in 3/4, sounds as if in 2/4; and a look at the vocal line will show that this is in agreement. The return to 3/4 finally happens in bar 7 and it is precisely on 'l'ombre' that the opening threeness reasserts itself (Example 5.4).

The final words of the other two verses are similarly privileged. 'Narcisse' marks the point where the harmony returns to its obsessive F♯–G♯ (G♭–A♭) after a three-bar excursion; 'sommeille' rhymes harmonically with 'vermeille' and continues to fight the 3/4 corner ('de*dans* les songes de l'eau qui som*meil*-le') against the piano which has reverted to 2/4 phrasing in bar 18. Who wins? Debussy leaves the question open. But one can imagine that the song might simply start again ('l'eau qui sommeille auprès de cette grotte sombre').

I submit that these *coups de salon*, while maybe not impossible to achieve with free texts, were at least made a great deal easier for Debussy by metrical regularity and even by verbal rhyme. To this extent he was perhaps being disingenuous when he complained that 'les vrais vers ont un rythme qui est plutôt gênant pour nous'. But it would be strange if a composer of Debussy's genius had found nothing new and valid in the employment of free texts.

Example 5.4 'La grotte' (bars 1–8)

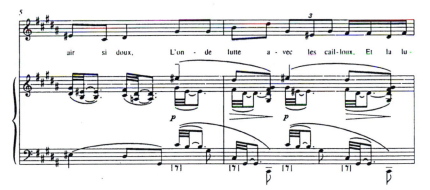

Debussy as poet-composer

In the case of Debussy's own texts for the four *Proses lyriques* and the two
completed *Nuits blanches*, the word 'free' obviously has to be qualified. The
texts of the first two *Proses lyriques* were published in *Entretiens politiques
et littéraires* in December 1892. Since the autograph of the first song is in-
accessible and that of the second is lost, we cannot tell whether he had
already set them to music or was merely considering doing so. Theoret-
ically he could, I suppose, have intended them initially to be just poems
and only at some later stage have had the idea of setting them to music;
but I find this unlikely. In any event, all these six poems sprang from
the same brain that, sooner or later, produced the music for them and
it is surely reasonable to imagine that music and poetry would show common concerns, even if not necessarily common techniques. The titles of the
Proses lyriques – dreams, the sea, flowers, evening – form a kind of aesthetic
Debussy biography and are 'free' in the sense of 'freely chosen'. They deal
with subjects that mattered to him and about which he held his own views,
even if the poetic language owes something to Baudelaire, de Régnier and
Laforgue.

It may, therefore, come as a surprise to find that in 'De rêve', for instance, the poet's dream is not expressed in the piano part through some
vague, amorphous mush, but through two- and four-bar phrases. In the
ninety-nine bars of the song this phraseology is broken only four times: in
bar 5 through repetition of bar 4, in bar 46, in bar 75 through extension
of bar 74, and in bar 94 through extension of bar 93. Of these four exceptions only one (bar 46) has the temerity to introduce material unconnected
with what comes immediately before it. It may be argued that dreams do
proceed largely by extension and varied repetition and that, even if their
premises are sometimes bizarre, they do tend to be driven by some kind of
logic.

As for the floating quality of the dream, Debussy entrusts this to the voice,
aided by plentiful quantities of whole-tone harmony. After the opening five
bars of 12/8, the piano settles into a regular eight-bar phrase for the 3/4
Andantino. Over this the voice sings a five-bar phrase ('A celle qui vient de
passer la tête emperlée'), entering at the end of bar 3. The two end together,
but until then the disjunction between them seems to support the vision
of the She of the poem, processing past, her head crowned with pearls
(Example 5.5).

Debussy engineers a similar disjunction in bars 67–75. First, the lengthening of 'âmes' throws the voice out of kilter with the piano; then, to accommodate 'si frêles', the piano has to insert the extra bar 75, as noted above.
The relationship of these disjunctions with the words 'folles' and 'frêles' is

Example 5.5 'De rêve' (bars 6–13)

clear enough. The final 'dreamy' extension comes in bar 94 where, to accommodate the voice's final six-bar phrase ('Mon âme! c'est du rêve ancien qui t'étreint!'), the piano expands to a seven-bar phrase.

Not everything, though, in the poems is irregular. Debussy follows Mendès's advice in providing a mixture of elements, and it becomes clear that one of the benefits of free texts is that they are also free to incorporate strict ones, whereas the reverse is not true. There is therefore no impediment to free verse including alexandrines, for example.

The alexandrine did not have a uniformly respectful press in the late nineteenth century, even though Baudelaire, Verlaine and Mallarmé all used it (*L'après-midi d'un faune* is written entirely in alexandrines). So did Henri de Régnier, whose alexandrine 'Dieu fluvial riant de l'eau qui le chatouille' would shortly stand at the head of Ravel's *Jeux d'eau*. Debussy stated bluntly in March 1911 that 'Henri de Régnier, who writes long, classical verses, cannot be set to music.' Whether or not this was a hit at Ravel whose not particularly successful setting of de Régnier's octosyllabic *Les grands vents venus d'outre-mer* had been published four years earlier, it would seem to accord with Debussy's general belief that less is more. The facts, though, tell a different story.

Example 5.6 'De rêve' bars (3–4)

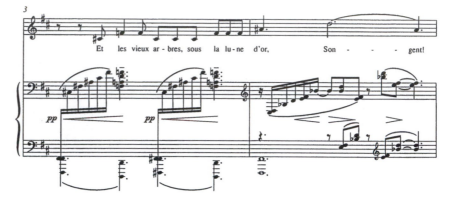

No fewer than fourteen of Debussy's song-texts are written wholly in alexandrines, and four others partially so, accounting in all for nearly a fifth of his output in the genre and stretching over a thirty-year period from 1881 to 1913.[13] There is no real cause for surprise then in finding the occasional alexandrine in Debussy's own free texts, as well as a number of near misses. These are not without interest, especially where an alexandrine seems to be in the offing, only to be headed off at the last moment, as in the second line of 'De rêve', where 'songent' replaces the expected iambus to dreamlike effect (Example 5.6).

There are altogether five strict alexandrines in *Proses lyriques*, although only the three marked * observe the midway caesura both in word and in phrase structure:

'De rêve'
    *Hélas! de tout ceci, plus rien qu'un blanc frisson.
    *Les chevaliers sont morts sur le chemin du Grâal!

'De fleurs'
    Les chères mains si tendrement désenlaceuses?
    *Et les lys, blancs jets d'eau de pistils embaumés,

'De soir'
    Et c'est Dimanche dans les avenues d'étoiles;

The starred example in 'De fleurs' is of no particular significance, but both examples from 'De rêve' are interesting. In the first Debussy points up rhythmically the symmetry between the two halves of the line and this symmetry helps take the ear over the extra bar 46 (or was the extra bar made necessary by the alexandrine?) (Example 5.7). In the second, the baleful,

Example 5.7 'De rêve' (bars 40–7)

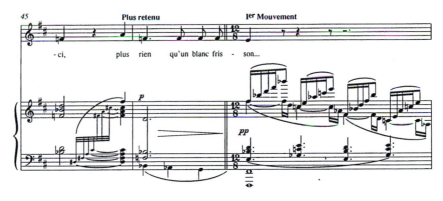

iconic sentiment lies at root of the song; the alexandrine, together with the low tessitura and the pseudo-plainsong outline, lends the line due weight. Clearly, where alexandrines occur either continuously or as part of a regular pattern, this kind of emphasis is harder to achieve.

Another of the main benefits offered by free texts was in the chance to use triplets in the vocal line. The strong piano framework allowed this line to spread freely over its two- and four-bar phrases, giving Debussy more opportunity to turn to the triplet rhythms that occur perhaps most famously in *Pelléas*. He seems to have used these for two reasons: always, to follow the rhythm of the spoken French; and sometimes, to give life to particular phrases.

In 'De soir', for instance, '*pour* quelques jours' sits well in triplets, as does '*ne* veulent plus', but neither phrase can claim to be especially poetic. Elsewhere though, Debussy seems to be aiming at effects of life, energy, lightness, charm and surprise:

> 'De rêve'
>> aux *bri*ses frôleuses
>> ca*re*sses charmeuses

> 'De grève'
>> petites *fil*les sortant
>> par*mi* les frou*frous* de leur robe
>> *lèv*res aimantes

> 'De soir'
>> chan*tant* d'une *voix* informée
>> *feux* d'arti*fi*ces manqués'

In the third verse of 'De soir' Debussy opts for his favourite ploy of mixing triplets with duplets, here to evoke things mechanical: 'des *im*pressions tou*tes* mécaniques'. In 'De fleurs' he develops this to include monotony and gloom –

> 'De fleurs'
>> si dé*so*lement vert
>> é*ter*nellement
>> des *pé*tales noirs
>> tom*bant* goutte à goutte'

– a usage that recurs in the second line of 'Nuit sans fin', the first of the *Nuits blanches*: 'Tristesse *mor*ne des *heu*res où *l'on* attend!'

At this juncture a cynic might complain that Debussy changed certain words in the published 1892 version of the first two *Proses lyriques* for the first edition of the songs in 1895, that he may well have tinkered with the texts of the last two similarly, and that the viability of his free-text approach can only really be judged against words which he was not at liberty to change if ever they turned awkward. At which point we turn to the *Chansons de Bilitis*.

Free morals: free metre?

'They are miracles of "speaking" French in music, and true models of the genre', wrote Romain Rolland to Richard Strauss and, as far as I know, no one has ever disputed this.[14] Of the three songs, the first and last are, as Ruschenberg noted,[15] the closest to *Pelléas* in their style of declamation (all phrases are afterbeat); the central 'La chevelure' rises to more lyrical heights. This investigation of 'the prosaic Debussy' may fittingly conclude with a consideration of the first song, 'La flûte de Pan', where many of the features discussed so far coincide.

The first thing to be said is that the beginning of this piece of 'free' prose is not really free at all:

> Pour le jour des Hyacinthies, il m'a donné
> Une syrinx faite de roseaux bien taillés,
> Unis avec la blanche cire qui est douce
> A mes lèvres comme le miel.

Louÿs here has behaved in precisely the opposite way to those numerous 'poets' of our own time who write prose and then chop it up arbitrarily into lines: his prose can be reset as three more or less respectable alexandrines, crowned by an octosyllabic *envoi*. But Debussy, just as he kept the secret of Louÿs's spoof, did not give the metrical game away either, being guided instead by the author's commas. The text, then, sounds free. But the piano part, for all its triplets and sextuplets, its tied quavers and the oscillating metre, continues its accepted role as a framework. The difference in this first verse is that, instead of two- and four-bar phrases, we find a pair of three-bar phrases, organised in typically Debussyan fashion as ABC–ABD. Arthur Wenk has said of this song that 'the mythological associations of the text preserve the metaphor of the closed circle. Syrinx was a nymph pursued by Pan who, to escape, was changed by Diana into a reed from which Pan made a flute.'[16] Since three is the minimum number that may be used to define a circle, the presence of three-bar phrases, of copious triplets in both voice and piano, and of three songs in the cycle is perhaps not accidental. Louÿs's launching of the poem with three pseudo-alexandrines may not have been accidental either.

No sketches for these songs survive, so we cannot know for certain that Debussy planned the piano framework before tackling the prosody, but it is hard to see that he could have worked in the reverse order. If we assume that the framework came first, then it is reasonable to suppose that the next stage was the apportioning of the clauses within that framework. It is entirely in keeping with Debussy's habits that, whereas the movement of the piano is relatively constant, the sung syllables accelerate through the paragraph (or verse); in general, sometimes they decelerate towards the end, forming a curve of movement, sometimes the acceleration continues to the end, as here with a syllable count 8–8–12–20. In that respect, verse 2 is unusual in beginning with a marked deceleration (12–7–7–10–2). Verse 3 conforms to a third pattern of greater consistency (3–9–8–10–9), reinforced here perhaps by words such as 'près', 'se répondre', 'tour à tour' and 's'unissent';[17] but verse 4 returns to the cumulative pattern of verse 1 (2–1–12–5–7–17–1), with wider variation between the elements, emphasising once again the circular shape of the song.

Rhythmic variation is only one of the many ways in which Debussy accentuates particular words or phrases. It is instructive, for instance, to look at those which join the 3/4 and C sections. With the exception of 'avec', straddling bars 5–6, all are central to the song's message: 'syrinx' (4–5); 'genoux', the first sexual image (7–8); 'nous n'avons rien', establishing the non-happening nature of the song (12–13); 'sur la flûte' (16–17). Then there are the words which are emphasised by the regularity of the piano phrasing. The most obvious of these is, again, 'flûte', which rounds off the two-bar + two-bar phrase of bars 13–16, but parallel to this is 'Hyacinthies', which straddles the two three-bar phrases of bars 1–6. Rather more contentiously there are words underlined by harmonic change, as in the last verse where the words 'tard', 'commence', 'mère', 'croira', 'jamais', 'suis', 'longtemps' and 'perdue' constitute a fairly comprehensible précis of the whole. Finally, no two bars contain the same vocal rhythm. The nearest Debussy comes to this is in bars 13 and 14 – 'tant nous sommes près l'un de l'autre'.

Here perhaps are some of the fruits of the freedom Debussy was looking for, emancipated from that 'rythme propre qui est plutôt gênant pour nous' into which composers might find themselves bound when setting strict verse. Given that through all these concerns in 'La flûte de Pan' Debussy had also to maintain what I might call his 'Arcadian plainsong', we could understand that he might not relish additional constraints of metre and rhyme (to bury it or not to bury it?), and that in any case the song is quite well enough structured without them.

Rappel à l'ordre

After composing the second of the projected five songs of *Nuits blanches*, Debussy abandoned free texts for good (until, as noted above, his own free text for *Noël des enfants* of 1915 which, as one dictated by the 'real', outside world, may be regarded as a special case: perhaps Debussy, having to invent his own text, distrusted his talent as a writer of strict verse). As to what he proceeded to take over from free texts and apply to strict ones, I shall in true Debussyan fashion decline to give anything like a definitive answer. I confine myself to three suggestions. First, although he returned, as noted above, to a greater number of onbeat vocal entries, these now stand

Example 5.8 'Colloque sentimental' (bars 42–8)

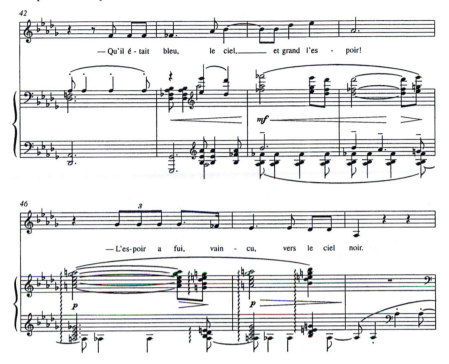

out less obviously because his prosody is more fluid, developed from the unconstrained 'speaking' style of the *Chansons de Bilitis*.

Secondly, because he had been working without rhyme for a decade, he returned to it with a greater appreciation of what it had to offer if used sparingly. The three songs of the second set of *Fêtes galantes* contain eighteen rhyming pairs of lines. Debussy draws attention to these only twice. In 'Le faune', Verlaine continues the rhyme scheme of verse 1 into verse 2, and Debussy chooses to make a rhythmic rhyme *across* the verses (instants sereins/mélancoliques pèlerins), so emphasising the oxymoron. His second rhythmic rhyme is much darker in tone, locking in the final exchange between the two ghosts (Example 5.8). Not only does the final 'noir' rhyme with the first 'espoir' but, as indicated on the above example, the rising Fb–Bb–Eb ('BLEU', 'ciel', 'es(poir)') of the first ghost is negated by the falling Gb–Db–Ab ('espoir', 'ciel', 'NOIR') of the second.

My final suggestion underlines the value of isometric lines within a poem. The narrator's last two lines in 'Colloque sentimental', two of the most heartrending lines in all French poetry, sum up what we have heard. How could Debussy refer back simultaneously both to the narrator's introduction and to the ghost's conversation without overloading the texture

Example 5.9 'Colloque sentimental' (bars 9–11; 53–5)

(never again would his songs approach the density of the *Proses lyriques,* let alone of the *Cinq poèmes de Baudelaire*)? The conversation can be neatly resumed in the nightingale's song, but the *correspondance* with the narrator's introduction is achieved through rhythm, in a way effective only with isometric lines (Example 5.9). Here Debussy applies across a whole song the technique we observed between consecutive lines in 'Clair de lune', which must surely be counted as a gain in subtlety; and in combining a rhythmic technique with a motivic one he is encouraging us to hear rhythm as an equal partner with melody – one of his greatest legacies to the twentieth century and beyond.

It goes without saying that a mere analyst is never going to discover all the struggles Debussy went through in writing his songs. Nevertheless, I hope this article will allow the reader to see another sentence from Debussy's 1911 profession of faith as identifying at least part of the challenge he set himself with his return to strict verse in 1903. Maybe, for once, we should entirely believe him when he writes:

> Well, you know, it's very difficult to follow the rhythms closely, to 'fix' them, and keep your inspiration at the same time. If you cheat and are happy just to juxtapose words and music, obviously that's not difficult, but then it's not worth doing either.[18]

6 Debussy and expression

NIGEL SIMEONE

I feel more and more that music, by its very essence, is not something that can flow inside a rigorous, traditional form. It consists of colours and of rhythmicised time . . . [1]

The works to be discussed in this chapter include three of Debussy's greatest pieces for orchestra, all of them explicitly evocative: the *Nocturnes*, *La mer* and 'Ibéria' from the orchestral *Images*. In addition, the three piano pieces composed at about the same time as *La mer* – *Masques*, *D'un cahier d'esquisses* and *L'isle joyeuse* – will be considered from the point of view of Debussy's expressive intentions. Among his orchestral works, the score of 'Ibéria', in particular, is teeming with expression marks which give important clues to the atmospheric evocation he sought to achieve – an innovative practice at the time and one which has sometimes been misunderstood as the quest for a rather generalised kind of poetic or naturalistic allusiveness in music, or simply a vaguely defined effect. But the very precision of Debussy's performance instructions in this instance suggests an entirely different interpretation: that as he refined his command of music's expressive potential, so his intentions were not only to give indications of tempo, dynamics and articulation, but also to specify the emotional and expressive content of a note, a phrase, a section or even a whole piece. For other works the scores themselves contain many fewer clues, but valuable evidence of Debussy's expressive and musical thought processes can be found in his letters and writings – both rich seams of self-revelation.

'Vague impressionism'?

In a letter written on 9 February 1887 from the Villa Medici in Rome, Debussy described his latest *envoi* for the Académie des Beaux-Arts to his bookseller friend Emile Baron:

> I've decided to write a work of special colour, recreating as many sensations as possible. I'm calling it *Printemps*, not 'spring' from the descriptive point of view but from that of living things. I wanted to express the slow, laborious birth of beings and things in nature, then the mounting florescence and finally a burst of joy at being reborn to a new life, as it were. There's no detailed programme, of course, as I have nothing but

contempt for music organised according to one of those leaflets they're so careful to provide you with as you come into the concert hall. I'm sure you see how powerful and evocative the music needs to be, and I'm not sure I shall be wholly successful in this.[2]

Debussy's preoccupation with the most effective way of depicting nature was shared by the greatest visual artists of the same period. In 1897 Paul Cézanne wrote that 'art is a harmony parallel to nature';[3] and in 1902 he stated that 'the transposition made by the painter, from a perspective of his own, gives a new interest to that part of nature which he has reproduced; he renders as a painter that which has not yet been painted; he makes it into a painting in an absolute sense – that is to say something other than reality. This is no longer straightforward imitation.'[4] Two decades earlier, in 1883, Jules Laforgue described a specifically Impressionist approach to nature: 'Where the academic sees only things set down in regular, separate positions within an armature of purely theoretical lines, the Impressionist sees perspective established by thousands of imperceptible tones and touches, by the variety of atmospheric states, with each plane not immobile but shifting. The Impressionist sees and renders nature as she is.'[5]

The reaction of the Establishment to *Printemps* also suggests strong parallels with conservative responses to the 'new art' a decade earlier.[6] The report by the Secretary to the Académie des Beaux-Arts in 1887 described the works as follows:

> Monsieur Debussy does not lapse into banality, nor is he platitudinous. On the contrary, he has a pronounced tendency – too pronounced – towards an exploration of the strange. One has the feeling of musical colour exaggerated to the point where it causes the composer to forget the importance of precise construction and form. It is to be strongly hoped that he will guard against this vague impressionism, which is one of the most dangerous enemies of truth in works of art.[7]

As Roger Nichols has observed, this was the earliest known use of the term 'Impressionism' in connection with Debussy's music.[8] Debussy's reactions during his career to being dubbed an 'Impressionist' are not as unequivocally hostile as might at first be imagined. In March 1908 he wrote to Jacques Durand (his publisher and – years earlier – his fellow pupil in Guiraud's composition class at the Conservatoire) about the expressive and pictorial nature of the orchestral *Images*: 'I'm trying to write "something else" – *realities*, in a manner of speaking – what imbeciles call "impressionism"', but he goes on to bemoan the use of the term in connection with painting as well as music, describing Impressionism as 'a term employed with the utmost inaccuracy, especially by art critics who use it as a label to stick on Turner, the finest creator of mystery in the whole of art!'[9] And yet on

26 January 1916, at a time when his late style had moved decisively towards an almost neoclassical abstraction, he wrote to Emile Vuillermoz, editor-in-chief of *La revue musicale S.I.M.* (and a critic with a passionate enthusiasm for modern music): 'You do me a great honour by calling me a pupil of Claude Monet.'[10]

Parallels with Monet will be considered in greater detail in the discussion of *La mer* below, but the paradox exemplified in these two quotations is apparent in many of the musical observations to be found in Debussy's letters and writings. The search for a clearly expressed and very particular musical evocation of a seemingly imprecise or intangible poetic or visual image (often from nature), or of a sensory intoxication (such as 'Les parfums de la nuit' in 'Ibéria'), is sometimes described with startling clarity and precision by Debussy. For example, on 26 June 1909 he wrote to Jacques Durand about a particular effect in his operatic setting – soon to be abandoned – of *La chute de la Maison Usher*. We find him glowing with pride at a new discovery – in this case finding a musical equivalent for an aptly Poe-like atmosphere and odour: 'It smells charmingly of mildew, obtained by mixing the sounds of a low oboe with violin harmonics . . . I'm very proud of it, so don't tell anyone.'[11]

Nocturnes

The *Nocturnes* provide a fascinating example of a work where Debussy's writings and correspondence reveal his detailed expressive intentions for a large-scale composition. The genesis of the *Nocturnes* is complex: in a letter to Prince André Poniatowski of 8–9 September 1892 he mentioned 'Three *Scènes au crépuscule* almost finished – that's to say the orchestration is all worked out, it's just a matter of writing it down.'[12] In another letter to Poniatowski from February 1893 he referred to the work again: 'I've revised the *Scènes au crépuscule* quite extensively.'[13] By the following year the title had been modified and so had his conception of the work. To his friend Henri Lerolle he wrote on 28 August 1894 that he had 'started some pieces for violin and orchestra which'll be called *Nocturnes*. I'm going to split up the orchestral groups so as to achieve nuances with the groups by themselves. Composers aren't daring enough.'[14] A few weeks later, on 22 September 1894, he wrote to Eugène Ysaÿe giving the first clues about the expressive content of the pieces: 'In the first one the orchestra is strings only, in the second flutes, four horns, three trumpets and two harps and in the third one both groups come together. It's an experiment, in fact, in finding the different combinations possible inside a single colour, as a painter might make a study in grey, for example.'[15] This plan, like the first, was abandoned,

but not until after 13 October 1896, when Debussy suggested to Ysaÿe that
he could put in a concert '*Trois nocturnes* for violin and orchestra, written
for Eugène Ysaÿe, a man I like and admire. Furthermore these *Nocturnes* can
be played only by him: if Apollo himself were to ask for them I should have
to refuse. What do you say to that?'[16] By the following year, the work is being
discussed in very different terms. Debussy wrote to his publisher Georges
Hartmann (also the eventual dedicatee of the *Nocturnes*) on 31 December
1897, explaining what he hoped to achieve: 'I've tried to give orchestral music
a little life and freedom. Unfortunately I haven't finished them and am rather
discouraged.'[17] He developed this in another letter to Hartmann, written
on 16 September 1898: 'You're going to hear, and own, the *Nocturnes*, which
together have given me more trouble than the five acts of *Pelléas*. I hope
it'll be open-air music that will vibrate in the breeze of Freedom's mighty
wing. (Goodness, what fine writing . . . !)'[18] The firm of Fromont, under
Hartmann's guidance, published the work in February 1900; Hartmann
died two months later on 23 April 1900.

Debussy was unusually revealing about the moods and senses he wanted
to conjure up in the *Nocturnes*. His commentary is a document of the greatest
importance in explaining his intentions:

> The title *Nocturnes* is to be interpreted here in a general and, more
> particularly, in a decorative sense. Therefore it is not meant to designate
> the usual form of the nocturne, but rather all the various impressions and
> the special effects of light that the word suggests. *Nuages* renders the
> immutable aspect of the sky and the slow, solemn motion of the clouds,
> fading away in grey tones lightly tinged with white. *Fêtes* gives us the
> vibrating atmosphere with sudden flashes of light. There is also the
> episode of the procession (a dazzling fantastic vision) which passes
> through the festive scene and becomes merged with it. But the background
> remains persistently the same: the festival, with its blending of music and
> luminous dust, participating in the cosmic rhythm. *Sirènes* depicts the sea
> and its countless rhythms and presently, among the waves silvered by the
> moonlight, is heard the mysterious song of the Sirens as they laugh and
> pass on.[19]

Even more explicit commentaries by Debussy are quoted by Marcel
Dietschy (from the 1932 *Festival Claude Debussy* programme).[20] The subject
of 'Nuages' is described as 'night on the pont de Solférino, very late. A great
stillness. I was leaning on the railing of the bridge. The Seine, without a
ripple, like a tarnished mirror. Some clouds slowly pass through a moonless
sky, a number of clouds, not too heavy, not too light: some clouds, that is all.'
A similarly poetic account is given of 'Fêtes': 'It is the Bois de Boulogne. A
retreat with torches, evening in the woods . . . I have seen from afar, through
the trees, lights approaching, and the crowd running towards the path

where the procession is going to pass. Then ... the horsemen of the Garde
Républicaine, resplendent, their arms and helmets lit by the torches, and
the bugles sounding their fanfare. At last, all that fades and grows distant.'[21]

In his review of the first performance of 'Nuages' and 'Fêtes' in the *Revue
hebdomadaire* (February 1901), Paul Dukas wrote in detail about the expressive essence of the pieces; his comments deserve quoting at some length:

> M. Debussy himself seems to delight in surprising his admirers, of whom
> some are very enthusiastic; none of his works seems to be the expected
> consequence of the previous ones; each of them brings something
> individual which denotes, if not a complete transformation of his manner,
> at least a different and unexpected point of view. These sudden changes of
> horizon are reflected in his works, through uses of different and often
> contrasting colours, and these alternations are troublesome in trying to
> judge his output as a whole. For example, nothing could be less like
> *L'après-midi d'un faune* than the *Nocturnes* from which we were introduced
> to two movements by M. Chevillard. The external procedures scarcely
> differ at all from one composition to the next; the musical language
> remains more or less the same ... But if the tone of the discourse is similar,
> its object is altogether different: that is sufficient to change the perspective
> from which feelings are communicated to us.
>
> So each work by M. Debussy springs a new surprise on us ... In fact, M.
> Debussy is unclassifiable.
>
> The majority of his compositions are symbols of symbols, expressed in a
> language so rich and so persuasive that it attains the eloquence of a new
> word, with its own laws, and often much more intelligible than the
> language of the poems on which it is based. Such is the case, for example,
> with *L'après-midi d'un faune*.
>
> We find all these characteristics again in the *Nocturnes* ... though here
> the personality of M. Debussy is not at the service of poetry, but, as he
> says, to some impressions which are all 'decorative'. In the first of these
> *Nocturnes*, the 'decor' consists of unfurling clouds on an unchanging sky,
> their slow progress achieving "in anguished grey tones lightly tinged with
> white" music which does not set out to be a meteorological representation
> of such a phenomenon, as one might think. It is true that it makes allusion
> to it, through the continual floating of sumptuous chords whose rising and
> falling progressions recall the architecture of the skies. So imitation is
> there, but at a distance. However, the real significance of the piece still
> remains symbolic, and, though different from the composer's previous
> works, it shares a common trait with them: it translates analogy through
> analogy in the medium of music in which all the elements, harmony,
> rhythm and melody, seem in some way to have vanished in the ether of the
> symbol, as if reduced to an imponderable state. As always with M.
> Debussy, it should be added that this music justifies itself through its
> subtlety and through its musicality.

In the second part, *Fêtes*, we encounter a means of transposition which most resembles the play of light through sound . . . I would not be surprised to discover that it was the music which motivated the analogy and marked out the programme: the episode of the 'ghostly procession' which imbues the instrumental development made me think about this. In any case, whether the programme came before the music or not, the piece shows the most marvellous handling of the orchestra. It would be impossible, perhaps, to cite another symphonic episode in which the composer succeeds so well in producing such a vertiginous and scintillating impression, such a hubbub in the crowd, intercut by fanfares, without clashing sonorities, without discordant timbres . . . His music produces a rare impression of a festival seen in a dream, in which its vivid brilliance is skilfully softened and its rhythms mollified by the use of distance in its sonic perspective. However, despite these rare qualities, I still prefer the first of these *Nocturnes*: this perhaps has less to do with the music itself than with the nature of the art which is truly M. Debussy's own, which seems more distinctive [in 'Nuages'].

It's a great pity that we didn't hear the work in its entirety. Because of the need for a female chorus, M. Chevillard cancelled the performance of the finale, entitled *Sirènes*.[22]

Debussy wrote to Dukas on 11 February 1901 a delighted response to this important and sensitive account of his aims as a composer. In this letter he also outlined the origins of 'Fêtes' about which Dukas had speculated: 'In fact the music of "Fêtes" was based, as always, on distant memories of a festival in the Bois de Boulogne; the "ghostly procession" was, on that occasion, made up of cuirassiers!'[23]

Seascapes: metronomes and Monet

L'isle joyeuse was composed in 1903 and revised the following year. As Roy Howat has convincingly argued, it was originally intended as the finale to a set of three pieces, a putative second 'Suite bergamasque' comprising *Masques, D'un cahier d'esquisses* and *L'isle joyeuse*.[24] The result of such a juxtaposition is by far the most symphonically conceived of Debussy's piano works, a three-part cycle (one of which even alludes to 'sketches' in its title) which has clear spiritual, musical[25] and structural connections with *La mer*, the 'Trois esquisses symphoniques' on which he was working at exactly the same time, during his passionate elopement with Emma Bardac. As for the expressive content of *L'isle joyeuse*, Debussy conceived it as an unusually demanding *omnium gatherum* of the instrument's technical and emotional possibilities. In September 1904 he wrote to Jacques Durand from Dieppe: 'My God! it's hard to play . . . This piece seems to me to bring together every different way of striking the piano, since it unites force and grace.'[26] Despite this eminently reasonable claim, the printed text of *L'isle joyeuse* is remarkably free of expression marks, certainly in comparison with slightly later works such as 'Ibéria' or the piano *Préludes*. However, the marking 'Quasi una cadenza' over the first six bars, and the broad chordal theme which first appears at bar 67, marked 'Un peu cédé, Molto rubato' with the further instruction that it is to be played *ondoyant et expressif* all suggest that Debussy intended a flexibility here which is somewhat at odds with the claims of Marguerite Long and others that he preferred strict tempos.[27] Long's insistence on strictness is something of an over-simplification – albeit an understandable and well-intentioned one – and Debussy's wishes could perhaps be expressed more accurately as a scrupulous observation of musical detail, including freedom and suppleness where this is called for. Certainly, the composer himself was very equivocal about the matter of metronome marks. On 12 July 1910, in a letter to Edgard Varèse he reluctantly agreed to add some markings to Varèse's score of *Pelléas et Mélisande*: 'although I have no confidence in metronome markings, I'll do what you ask.'[28] No metronome marks are printed in the *Nocturnes* or in *L'isle joyeuse*, but they do appear in *La mer* and in two of the orchestral *Images*. Debussy returned to the matter of the metronome in a letter to Jacques Durand sent from Pourville on 9 October 1915: 'You know what I think of metronome marks: they're right for a single bar, like "roses, with a morning's life". Only there are "those" who don't hear music and who take these marks as authority to hear it still less!'[29] Marie Rolf quotes a letter written to her in 1974 from Fernand Gillet, oboist at the first performance of *La mer* on 15 October 1905, recording a delightful moment at the rehearsals for the premiere:

> he is reputed to have said to the conductor Chevillard, 'un peu plus vite ici...' So Chevillard said: 'mon cher ami, Yesterday you gave me the tempo we have just played.' Debussy looked at him with intense reflection in his eyes and said: 'but I *don't feel music* the *same way every day*'.[30]

As well as metronome markings, the score of *La mer* also includes a number of carefully placed tempo modifications. In some cases these extend over several bars; for example the instruction *Cédez très légèrement et retrouvez peu à peu le mouvement initial* is applied to an entire sixteen-bar section in 'Dialogue du vent et de la mer' (bars 56–71); and elsewhere in this movement other instances of tempo alteration or modification are described with precision, even if the results are sometimes potentially confusing if treated too literally: thus the interpreter is faced with the dilemma of considering what distinction can (or should) be made between *Retardez un peu pendant ces 4 mesures* (bar 159) and *Cédez pendant ces 4 mesures* (bar 171) in two otherwise musically identical passages.

The sea's central importance to Debussy as the mightiest and most ineluctable of natural phenomena is well documented in his letters and is also readily adduced from an examination of his list of works.[31] On 12 September 1903 he wrote to André Messager from Bichain about his work on *La mer*. This is a fascinating document; it includes two movement titles which were later changed, notes the amusing irony of composing the piece at Bichain (near Villeneuve-la-Guyard) in the resolutely landlocked *département* of the Yonne in north-west Burgundy, and describes his approach to the work with an interesting analogy to landscape painting:

> I'm working on three symphonic sketches entitled: 1. 'mer belle aux îles Sanguinaires'; 2. 'jeu de vagues'; 3. 'le vent fait danser la mer'; the whole to be called *La mer*.
>
> You're unaware, maybe, that I was intended for the noble career of a sailor and have only deviated from that path thanks to the quirks of fate. Even so, I've retained a sincere devotion to the sea.
>
> To which you'll reply that the Atlantic doesn't exactly wash the foothills of Burgundy . . . ! And that the result could be one of those hack landscapes done in the studio! But I have innumerable memories, and those, in my view, are worth more than a reality which, charming as it may be, tends to weigh too heavily on the imagination.[32]

In July 1904 Debussy left Lilly Texier and fled to Jersey with Emma Bardac. In an undated letter from the Grand Hotel in St Helier he wrote to Durand that 'The sea has behaved beautifully towards me and shown me all her guises.'[33] He returned to the subject with Durand a year later while he was staying at the Grand Hotel in Eastbourne, by now correcting the proofs of *La mer*: 'It's a charming, peaceful spot. The sea unfurls itself with an utterly British correctness.'[34] The critical reaction to the first performance of *La mer* included a stinging review by Pierre Lalo in *Le temps* (16 February 1905) which concluded by levelling at Debussy the very charge of studio-bound artificiality which he had so strenuously sought to avoid:

> It seems to me Debussy has willed himself to feel, rather than feeling really deeply and naturally. For the first time, listening to a descriptive work by Debussy, I have the impression of standing, not in front of nature, but in front of a reproduction of nature; a wonderfully refined, ingenious and carefully composed reproduction, but a reproduction none the less . . . I do not hear, I do not see, I do not smell the sea.[35]

To this Debussy responded with wounded vigour:

> You say – keeping your unkindest cut for the last – 'that you do not see or smell the sea throughout these three sketches'! That's a large claim and I don't know who is going to evaluate it for us . . . I love the sea and I've listened to it with the passionate respect it deserves. If I've been inaccurate in taking down what it dictated to me, that is no concern of yours or mine.

You must admit, not all ears hear in the same way. The heart of the matter
is that you love and defend traditions which, for me, no longer exist or, at
least, exist only as representative of an epoch in which they were not all as
fine and valuable as people make out[36]

Louis Laloy, a staunch supporter of Debussy's music, had some interesting reflections on the reasons for the work's comparative failure at its
first performance, also alluding to the work's differences from *Pelléas* (and,
indeed, the *Nocturnes*) and to the disappointment of the opera's devoted
admirers:

They could no longer rediscover him in the clouds or under the branches
of a legendary park, for he had set up his easel on the edge of a sheer cliff
where he sought to paint three parts of a composition laid out like a
classical symphony with large formal schemes and sustained lines, unfussy
and uninhibited – three landscapes evoking the force, the splendour, the
joy, and the fear of the sea. It was treason.[37]

Edward Lockspeiser is unhesitating in describing *La mer* as 'the greatest
example of an orchestral Impressionist work'[38] and it does not seem unduly
far-fetched to see a parallel in Monet's seascapes from the 1880s and 90s
with Laloy's vision of Debussy the composer with his 'easel on the edge of
a sheer cliff'. Guy de Maupassant wrote in 1886 about watching Monet at
work on some seascapes, painted in Etretat the previous year, describing the
artist's method in dramatic terms:

With both hands he took hold of a shower that had fallen on the sea and
flung it down upon the canvas. And it was indeed the rain that he had thus
painted, nothing but rain veiling the waves, the rocks, and the sky, which
were barely visible . . . Last year . . . I often followed Claude Monet in his
quest for impressions . . . the painter stood before the motif, waiting,
examining the sun and the shadows, in a few brushstrokes capturing a ray
of sun or a passing cloud, which, scorning the fake or the conventional, he
rapidly set down on canvas.[39]

Such 'scorn of the fake or the conventional' would certainly find an echo
in Debussy. But more interesting for the purposes of considering shared
artistic attitudes are the relatively little-known 'series' paintings executed by
Monet of seascapes at Pourville and Varengeville (just to the west of Dieppe)
from the mid-1890s, and the remarkable group depicting mornings on the
Seine. As Debussy himself remarked in a letter to his stepson and occasional
pupil Raoul Bardac: 'Collect impressions. Don't be in a hurry to write them
down. Because that's something music can do better than painting: it can
centralise variations of colour and light within a single picture – a truth
generally ignored, obvious as it is.'[40] It is only in 'series' paintings – most

famously those of haystacks and Rouen Cathedral – that Monet was able to attempt visual art which could suggest the passing of time and the consequent changes of mood in a landscape. During his work on the Pourville series, he endured squalid accommodation and dreadful weather, but the slightly later series of 'Mornings on the Seine' was a less arduous and perhaps finer achievement: 'Far smoother than the Rouen [Cathedral] pictures, they chart the gradual growth of light at daybreak on a summer morning with astonishing purity.'[41] Surely the expressive aim here is very similar to Debussy's in the first movement of *La mer* and through use of a series of paintings, time can appear to be momentarily unfrozen as the viewer passes from image to image.[42] It is interesting to note that Monet's working method for these paintings was unusually painstaking: his 'impressions' were the result of many hours' work in his studio. Maurice Guillemot, describing Monet's latest pictures in 1898, declared, in fact, that 'Nature is his studio.'[43] So, whatever the propriety of transferring Impressionism as a term from painting to music might be, Debussy's admiration for Monet may well stem from shared aesthetic concerns – though necessarily not technical ones. A frequently suggested position is that Debussy was closer to Symbolist poets – to Baudelaire and Mallarmé in particular. But it should also be remembered that there is at the very least a common stem from the poets into both painting and music: Baudelaire was a trenchant and brilliant art critic whose writings on Delacroix, Jérôme, Ingres, Millet and Corot often found a receptive response among the young Impressionists (though their enthusiasm presumably did not extend to embracing his loathing of nature); and *Les fleurs du mal* (published in 1857) had a profound impact on younger visual artists as well as on musicians and poets. Baudelaire admired Manet and knew Fantin-Latour and Monet; and in the last, desperate, months of his life (he died in 1867), his greatest solace was reported to be listening to Manet's wife playing Wagner to him on the piano.[44] As for Mallarmé, his death in 1898 was a loss to several friends among the surviving Impressionists. He had been one of Manet's closest friends and wrote to Verlaine in 1885: 'I saw my dear Manet every day for ten years, and I find his absence today totally incredible.' It was at Manet's studio that he met and befriended Monet, Degas, Renoir and Berthe Morisot, for whose daughter Julie he acted as guardian after the artist's death.[45] One of his most interesting articles on painting was originally published in English. 'The Impressionists and Edouard Manet' includes the following analysis of the Impressionist aesthetic:

> The search after truth, peculiar to modern artists, which enables them to
> see nature, and reproduce her, such as she appears to pure and just eyes,
> must lead them to adopt the air almost exclusively as their medium, or at
> all events to work in it freely and without restraint; there should at least be

in the revival of such a medium, if nothing more, an incentive to a new manner of painting. This is the result of our reasoning and the end I wish to establish. As no artist has on his palette a transparent and neutral colour answering to open air, the desired effect can only be obtained by lightness or heaviness of touch, or by the regulation of tone. Now Manet and his school use simple colour, fresh, or lightly laid on, and their results seem to have been attained at the first stroke, so that the ever-present light blends with and vivifies all things. As to the details of the picture, nothing should be absolutely fixed in order that we may feel that the bright gleam which lights the picture, or the diaphanous shadow which veils it are only seen in passing, and just when the spectator beholds the represented subject, which being composed of a harmony of reflected and ever-changing lights, cannot be supposed always to look the same, but palpitates with movement, light, and life.[46]

Stefan Jarocinski has produced some compelling arguments for considering Debussy neither as an Impressionist nor as a Symbolist, but as a figure who held a unique position in the arts at the turn of the century.[47] His ideas are supported by an impressive amount of evidence and his position is often brilliantly argued. However, such is his (understandable) reluctance to allow Debussy to be pigeon-holed as a member of a group or school that he perhaps puts insufficient weight on those aspects of Debussy's work where congruent activity in the other arts has similarities with his music. To be fair, Debussy himself was at pains to stress the uniquely rich expressive possibilities of music over and above all of the other arts. In an article for the *Revue musicale S.I.M.* in November 1913, he set out his views with a rare eloquence and clearsightedness:

Our symphonic painters do not pay nearly enough attention to the beauty of the seasons. Their studies of nature show her dressed in unpleasantly artificial clothes, the rocks made of cardboard and the leaves of painted gauze. Music is the art that is in fact the closest to Nature, although it is also the one that contains the most subtle pitfalls. Despite their claim to be true representationalists, the painters and sculptors can only present us with the beauty of the universe in their own free, somewhat fragmentary interpretation. They can capture only one of its aspects at a time, preserve only one moment. It is the musicians alone who have the privilege of being able to convey all the poetry of night and day, of earth and sky. Only they can recreate Nature's atmosphere and give rhythm to her heaving breast.[48]

On a less exalted note, Debussy was quite capable of poking fun at himself – and some of his greatest music, as can be seen in a letter to Durand, sent from London on 13 May 1909:

My Dear Jacques,

The sea was in D♭, in 6/8 time.

(See *La mer*, esquisses symphoniques, first part, published by Durand et fils.)

So, a pleasant crossing.[49]

'Ibéria' – expressive precision

Among orchestral works, the *Images* include some of Debussy's most explicit expression marks on the scores, especially in 'Ibéria' and 'Rondes de printemps', both of which are equipped with metronome marks (unlike 'Gigues' which has none). The first of the *Images* to be composed was 'Ibéria', which Debussy optimistically reported as being almost finished in a letter to Jacques Durand on 7 July 1906: 'I should have *Ibéria* finished next week and the two other pieces by the end of the month.'[50] In fact the autograph full score of 'Ibéria' is dated Christmas Day 1908 and the 'two other pieces', far from being written by the end of July 1906, as Debussy suggests in his letter, were not completed until 1909 ('Rondes de printemps') and October 1912 ('Gigues'). On 8 August 1906, Debussy was agonising over the end of 'Ibéria', writing to Durand that 'at the moment I have three different ways of finishing *Ibéria*. Should I toss a coin to see which one to use or look for a fourth?'[51] Two years later, on 10 August 1908, he was still five months from completing the work but was clearly absorbed in the task, if somewhat confused by a profusion of ideas and sensations; he wrote to Durand that 'at the moment, I hear the sounds of streets in Catalonia at the same time as the music of the streets in Granada'.[52]

In 'Ibéria', the care with which expressive indications are written in the score is somewhat at odds with the free and extemporised feeling of the work, a characteristic which has been so well described by Pierre Boulez:

> What I find most attractive in this work . . . is the freedom of symphonic invention given to the basic elements selected. I particularly admire 'Les parfums de la nuit', one of Debussy's most inventive pieces, not so much for its thematic content as for the novel way in which he 'creates' the development, and makes the orchestral sound evolve, by the subtlety of the transitional passages. Even when themes reappear, the music never looks back: everything suggests a superior, polished kind of improvisation, so great is Debussy's control of his inventive skill and therefore his ability to do without any immediately recognisable formal framework. This art of transition is particularly noticeable in the passage linking the second and third movements, where 'Les parfums de la nuit' is gradually absorbed as the new elements – particularly the rhythmic elements – of 'Matin d'un jour de fête' become increasingly clearly defined. From Debussy's letters

we know that he himself was particularly pleased with this subtle transition from darkness to light.[53]

The letter to which Boulez refers is presumably the long one to André Caplet, written on 25–6 February 1910, describing the rehearsals of the Colonne Orchestra:

> This morning, rehearsal of *Ibéria* . . . it's going better. The aforementioned young Capellmeister [Gabriel Pierné] and his orchestra have consented to be less earthbound and to take wing somewhat . . . You can't imagine how naturally the transition works between 'Parfums de la nuit' and 'Le matin d'un jour de fête'. *It sounds as though it's improvised* . . . The way it comes to life, with people and things waking up . . . There's a man selling watermelons and urchins whistling, I see them quite clearly . . . Mind you, not everyone finds it all so obvious – some people thought it was a serenade.[54]

In the original French the phrase underlined by Debussy reads '*Ça n'a pas l'air d'être écrit . . .*' which implies an additional allusion to 'écriture', that is to say the craft of composition and of putting musical notation on paper. It is particularly interesting – though perhaps less surprising – that the care with which Debussy notated the transition to which he refers here is even more punctilious than usual, including very careful stage management of the changing perspectives of the images evoked. The marking at the head of the third movement is *Dans un rythme de Marche lointaine, alerte et joyeuse*, interrupted four bars later with *Mouvt. précédent, encore plus lointain* for two bars, then back to the main 'march' tempo, this time with a metronome mark of crotchet = 112. This is followed at fig. 54 by a gradual speeding up (*animez peu à peu*) over the next twenty bars until there is a sudden return (at fig. 56) to the opening tempo of crotchet = 112. Just at the moment when the march might be expected to settle into a steady tread, Debussy destabilises the rhythm again, marking the 'vamp' at fig. 57 *En cédant et plus libre* and the rather wild clarinet melody *gaiement, et très en dehors en exagérant les accents*. The sultrier idea five bars after fig. 58 (flute and bassoon, then solo violins) is marked *Rubato* then *expressif et un peu moqueur*.

These instructions are sometimes very subtly differentiated. The quirky solo violin theme at fig. 61 sees a reappearance of the metronome mark of crotchet = 112 but now the tempo is described as *Modéré (sans lenteur)* and the solo line is marked *libre et fantasque*; in a very slight shift of expressive emphasis, the repetition of the same tune starting in the seventh bar of fig. 61, now on the oboe, then cor anglais, is marked *gai et fantasque*.

This careful description of different nuances is evident from the very start of 'Ibéria'. In 'Par les rues et par les chemins' the first main melodic idea (one bar after fig. 1) is marked *élégant et bien rythmé*, but on its return at fig. 24 the marking is *gaiement en dehors*. Elsewhere in the first movement, Debussy attempts to notate the kind of metrical flexibility he also sought in parts of *La mer*, but the markings remain ambiguous. At fig. 22, *Expressif et souple* is qualified by the metronome marking quaver = 132 *pour commencer*, though apart from the passage at fig. 23 with its pair of four-bar phrases marked *Rubato* for two bars followed by *a Tempo* for two bars, it is not clear what kind of tempo modification Debussy intended after the 'starting' speed of quaver = 132. The opening marking of quaver = 176 is reiterated at fig. 24. The sultry opening of 'Les parfums de la nuit' is marked *Lent et rêveur* with a metronome mark of quaver = 92. But sweetness and warmth of expression are specified with great care throughout the movement. At the start, the oboes are marked *expressif un peu traîné*. The glorious sliding chords in the lower strings (just after fig. 39) are to be played *Sans rigueur, expressif et pénétrant* and the latter adjective is particularly interesting as the music is marked *pp*: it seems that what Debussy wants here is the musical equivalent of a stage whisper – a really projected *pianissimo*. When the idea returns on all the strings (fig. 41) it is still marked *pp* but contains no further performing instructions. At fig. 43 there is great attention to detail and the markings indicate different expressive effects from different instruments. The general marking is *Un peu plus allant*, but the harp is marked *doux et léger*, the celesta *doux et égal* and the first horn *doux et mélancolique*. The same care over minute expressive differentiation is exemplified by a passage of fourteen bars beginning two before fig. 45. Here the first violins are marked *expressif et passionné* with the sustained woodwind lines marked *expressif* and the doubling of these lines in the lower strings completely unmarked. At fig. 45 itself, the flute and clarinet lines are marked *expressif et soutenu*, though the same music in the violas has no marking; and two bars later the rising bassoon motif is marked *doux et soutenu*. The oboe two bars further on is asked to play *doux et pénétrant*, and the supporting clarinets simply *doux*. At fig. 46 the two flutes are marked *expressif, soutenu dans la douceur*, while the cellos underneath have *expressif et doucement soutenu*. In the third bar of fig. 46, the six solo violins are marked *pp doux et pénétrant* and two bars later, with a change of tempo (*En animant peu à peu*), the solo violin and bassoon have *lointain et expressif* while the first clarinet has *très doux*. A few bars on, at fig. 48, the marking on the melody – *doux et soutenu dans l'expression* – is followed by a tempo (rather than expression) marking of *En animant avec une grande intensité dans l'expression*, while the individual oboe and cor anglais lines are pushed to ever greater expressivity: *très appuyé dans l'expression*. It should be apparent from the sheer resourcefulness of Debussy's markings in this movement that he was seeking a hitherto unprecedented precision of expressive effect in order to bring the work's musical ideas vibrantly to life.

'Plein-air' music and the limits of expression

On at least two occasions Debussy wrote about a specific and radical expansion of music's expressive possibilities. 'Open Air Music' was the subject of an article published in *La revue blanche* on 1 June 1901 in which he proposed the composition of music as an act of communion with nature:

> why is the adornment of our squares and boulevards left solely to the military bands? I like to imagine more unusual happenings, ones that would blend more completely with the natural surroundings... For the trees we should have a large orchestra with the support of human voices (No! Not a choral society, thank you!). I envisage the possibility of a music especially written for the open air, flowing in bold, broad lines from both the orchestra and the voices. It would resound through the open spaces and float joyfully over the tops of the trees, and any harmonic progression that sounded stifled within the confines of a concert hall would take on a new significance. Perhaps this is the answer to the question of how to kill off that silly obsession with overprecise 'forms' and 'tonality' which so unfortunately encumber music. She could certainly be regenerated, taking a lesson in freedom from the blossoming of the trees... It would be a mysterious collaboration between the air, the movement of the leaves and the scent of the flowers – all mingled into music. She would be reunited with all these elements in such a natural marriage that she would seem to live in each one of them. Then, at least, we could prove once and for all that music and poetry are the only two arts that live and move in space itself...[55]

A later article, published in *Gil blas* on 19 January 1903, returns to the same subject and indeed includes several passages repeated word for word from the *Revue blanche*, now prefaced by a humorous discussion of the barrel organ and the desirability of making mechanical instruments which would be able to 'play the complete *Ring!*'[56]

Debussy took up the same theme in an interview with Georges Delaquys published in *Excelsior* on 18 January 1911, describing music as 'a free art, a wellspring, an art of the open air, an art comparable to the elements – the wind, the sea, and the sky! It must not be an art that is confined, academic.' He goes on in this interview to offer some interesting ideas about musical notation in relation to expression: 'this *method* of writing [music] would benefit by being simplified, the means of expression being made more direct'.[57] But Debussy was acutely aware of the shortcomings of notation. He wrote to Manuel de Falla on 13 January 1907 about these problems in relation to the score of the *Danses* for harp and orchestra: 'It's not possible to write down the exact form of a rhythm, any more than it is to explain the different effects of a single phrase! The best thing, I think, is to be guided by how you feel . . . The colour of the two dances seems to me to be clearly defined.'[58]

Debussy's quest for an ideal in which music would represent a true expression of nature is readily apparent in a letter to Charles Levadé, written on 4 September 1903: 'To be honest, you learn orchestration far better by listening to the sound of leaves rustling in the wind than by consulting handbooks in which the instruments look like anatomical specimens.'[59] Eight years later, on 18 December 1911, in a magnificent letter to his life-long friend Robert Godet, his thoughts ranged far and wide – to the Salon d'Automne, to Stravinsky, to Poe, to Geneva ('a hive of professors'), to his beloved daughter Chouchou – and, especially, to two abiding musical concerns: the need for simplicity and the absolute truth of nature (the latter with a small dose of self-deprecating humour):

> The longer I go on, the more I detest the sort of intentional disorder whose aim is merely to deceive the ear. The same goes for bizarre, intriguing harmonies which are no more than parlour games . . . How much has first to be discovered, then suppressed, before one can reach the naked flesh of emotion . . . pure instinct ought to warn us, anyway, that textures and colours are no more than illusory disguises!
>
> . . .
>
> No, what I'd much rather do is climb a mountain with you and listen to the wind . . . ! You may be sure it would sing only that music made of all the harmonies it gathers as it passes over the treetops (a sentence all the more beautiful for being utterly meaningless!) . . .[60]

7 Exploring the erotic in Debussy's music

JULIE McQUINN

And when all's said and done, Desire is what counts . . . You could write down a formula for desire: 'everything comes from it and returns to it'. DEBUSSY[1]

The word *erotic* does not rest quietly on the page. It is a word that tempts and eludes us. It hides behind its dictionary definition – 'of, devoted to, or tending to arouse sexual desire' – which cannot begin to touch the numerous spheres that it encompasses. For this term is heavily laden with ideological baggage. It darts through our minds, drawing out questions; we want details. And always there is a tinge of excitement as we tread into a secret, forbidden land. Eroticism mingles with anticipation and imagination; it dangles possibilities before us. The evasive nature of eroticism makes writing about it a challenging task. For the scholar's goal is to attempt to explicate, to reveal, to clarify, and this contradicts eroticism's most basic end, which is 'to take knowledge and render it uncertain, ambiguous'.[2] John L. Connolly, Jr claims, for example, that the paintings of Ingres 'generate erotic power precisely because they elude the imagination's hot embrace'.[3] And eroticism, like beauty, lies in the eye of the beholder. As Robert Stoller concisely states, 'Eroticism is a matter of taste.'[4] So how is it possible to speak objectively about a concept that is so intensely personal? Marcia Allentuck's description of eroticism as 'an area in which the public and private perennially converge, with varying degrees of conflict, diversity, enigma, absurdity and even, occasionally, fulfillment'[5] suggests an exploration of the nature of the erotic as understood within the context of *fin-de-siècle* Paris.

Eroticism's association with sex carries with it Parisian society's ambivalent attitude towards sex at the end of the nineteenth century, an attitude shaped by a tangle of forces. First, there was the ever-present threat of syphilis and the longstanding 'Christian reading of syphilis as the scourge of God directed against the sexually sinful'.[6] Linda and Michael Hutcheon demonstrate how this 'intertwining of syphilis and sexuality'[7] intensified in the nineteenth century, especially in France, where the Christian view 'merged with societal sexual anxieties about the effects of syphilis on the general social fabric and . . . on the family in particular'.[8] This anxiety was the result of a unique set of circumstances, beginning with France's embarrassing loss in the Franco-Prussian War, followed by a decline in the French birth-rate.[9]

The obsessive search for solutions to the depopulation crisis urged an examination of the proper role of women in society and the responsibility of the individual to the nation.[10] This endeavour was complicated by the beginning of a feminist movement in France, the passing of the Naquet Law in 1884 permitting divorce, never possible through mutual consent but only as the result of 'moral delinquencies',[11] and the rapid expansion of prostitution in the second half of the nineteenth century, which increased the threat of syphilis.[12] Crime and decadence were on the rise and society was perceived to be at an all-time moral low. As more and more people patronised commercial entertainments, fears of degeneracy, laziness, immorality and hedonism began to surface, and 'a debate about the enjoyment of life began to simmer'.[13] Many identified the Republic and its advocacy of liberty as the source of the problem: 'To conservative moralists, the Republic was unleashing unprecedented license: divorce, pornography, alcoholism, nudity on stage, egoism, all seen as ever worsening symptoms of sickness and decline.'[14]

Together these elements generated a sense of social disorder and panic. It became clear that the cultivation of the family was the only path towards the survival of the nation. Thus women were expected to be wives, and wives were expected to be domestic angels, sexless and selfless. 'Maternity defined the essence of womanhood'[15] and male sexual fantasies were saved for the brothel. But prostitutes were classic degenerates, even running the risk of becoming lesbians; they therefore represented 'a terrible threat to the sexual order'.[16] Alain Corbin writes of men's irresistible pull toward prostitutes and subsequent remorse, and observes that 'the counterpoint being woven between *fear and male desire* ordered in a broader way many other aspects of the history of sexuality in the second half of the nineteenth century'.[17]

Michel Foucault distinguishes between Eastern and Western views of sexuality and asserts that in the West sex became associated with sickness and danger as a result of the nineteenth century's obsession with scientific classification. With the advent of psychiatry, sex became something to be interpreted and cured, an object of suspicion, 'the point of weakness where evil portents reach through to us', 'the fragment of darkness that we each carry within us', 'a fear that never ends'.[18] In fact 'there was scarcely a malady or physical disturbance to which the nineteenth century did not impute at least some degree of sexual etiology'.[19] For Foucault, true eroticism is a secret knowledge of pleasure that is passed from master to initiate; it is 'an absolute mastery of the body, a singular bliss, obliviousness to time and limits, the elixir of life, the exile of death and its threats'.[20] This form of eroticism was completely annihilated in the West through the practice of confession, where sex became 'a privileged theme'.[21] Sex was still secret knowledge, but a secret to be confessed, a secret to be ashamed of.[22] He writes, 'With these confessed truths, we are a long way from the learned initiations into pleasure, with their technique and their mystery.'[23] But to say that nineteenth-century Paris simply repressed sexuality is to simplify a complex situation. For as both Foucault and Antony Copley observe, the very fact that the subject was discussed in such profusion suggests an obsession. Foucault even asserts that all this discourse was simply a form of erotica.[24] Sexual perversions 'captured the popular imagination',[25] not only in fiction, but also in medical texts.

Vernon Rosario maintains that 'all eroticism in the modern Euro-American context is perverse because of the way sexual behaviour and fantasy were theorised by physicians since the eighteenth century.'[26] Thus the endpoints for numerous continuums encompassing the erotic are established: desire and fear; heavenly, spiritual love and earthly, sexual love; languor and horror; domestic angels and seductive *femmes fatales*; pleasure and death; pleasure and responsibility; the erotic and the perverse; the beautiful and the grotesque; sex and violence; fear and obsession. And the eroticism of Debussy's time and music is rooted in the tension between these endpoints.

The seductive power of Debussy's music

Linda Nochlin argues that all erotic art of the nineteenth century involved images of women and was created only for the enjoyment of men.[27] But the eroticism floating around the works of Debussy seems to resist this assertion. The very notion of erotic music presumes a relationship between a human being and some aspect of that music. In the case of Debussy, every possible relationship seems to have carried with it an erotic tinge, and thus a web of relationships filled with erotic possibilities, all orbiting around a music that defied convention, connected composer, poet, lover, performer and listener with the music and with each other, regardless of their sex. Debussy's music seduced (and repelled) men and women alike.

Women were drawn to a man whom they had never met through experiencing his music, whether performing it or watching and hearing it performed. Alfredo Casella writes, 'Physically Debussy was very unlike the willowy and soulful-looking aesthete fondly imagined by so many of the young women who with all too faulty fingers were wont to essay the first *Arabesque* and the "Jardins sous la pluie".'[28] It seems that his music was also partially responsible for the seduction of both his wives. Mary Garden explains how both she and Lilly Texier were first drawn to Debussy through his song 'C'est l'extase', published in *L'illustration*:

It wasn't until some years later that I discovered that the same song had also brought Debussy and his first wife, Lilly, together. She, too, had seen the song in *L'Illustration* and said to herself, 'I'd like to know the man who wrote this song – I've *got* to know him.' Lilly would say to me, 'Mary, I fell in love with Claude through that song, didn't you?'[29]

And Emma Bardac was singing his songs long before he came to play at her salon. Marcel Dietschy writes:

Unbeknownst to him, Debussy had already charmed her for a year or two before their first meeting by means of his songs, which she sang to the accompaniment of Charles Koechlin, who has described the eager understanding she displayed towards this music and her feverish curiosity when she asked him to tell her about the composer and the man.[30]

Even Debussy himself seemed to acknowledge this seductive power. In 1913, while he was in Moscow, Emma wrote of her jealousy of his music and he replied:

if I go on creating it and loving it it's because this music, which you're so unfair to, was responsible for my meeting you, loving you and so on. The chances are that if I were never to compose again, you would be the one to stop loving me, because I could hardly rely on the somewhat restrained charms of my conversation or on my physical advantages to keep you by me.[31]

Roland Barthes writes of the sensual physicality of music in performance, whether it be the performer's relation to the music and the instrument or the listener's relation to the physicality of the performer within the music, and its utter difference from the passive sort of listening that dominates today. The music one plays is more sensual; it is 'a muscular music in which the part taken by the sense of hearing is one only of ratification, as though the body were hearing – and not "the soul"'.[32] The live performance, especially that of an amateur, evokes 'not satisfaction but desire',[33] the desire to act, to do, and for Barthes desire is highly preferable to satisfaction.

I am determined to listen to my relation with the body of the man or woman singing or playing and that relation is erotic – but in no way 'subjective' (it is not the psychological 'subject' in me who is listening; the climactic pleasure hoped for is not going to reinforce – to express – that subject but, on the contrary, to lose it).[34]

According to George Copeland's recollection of Debussy's words regarding how to play his music, Debussy agreed: 'It is necessary to abandon yourself completely, and let the music do as it will with you.'[35] All people 'come to music to seek oblivion'.[36]

Others too felt the erotic nature of his playing, especially when he was 'caught up in the heat of improvisation'.[37] Karl Lahm writes that 'there was in his gentle playing a narcotic/erotic note, a sweet dreaminess like that of a woman's hand'.[38] And Léon-Paul Fargue attests both to his physical reaction to the music and Debussy's own physical relationship to it:

> Debussy would sit himself down without speaking at the piano of the little study-cum-library and start to improvise. Anyone who knew him can remember what it was like. He would start by brushing the keys, prodding the odd one here and there, making a pass over them and then he would sink into velvet, sometimes accompanying himself, his head down, in an attractive nasal voice, like a sung whisper. He gave the impression of delivering the piano of its sound, like a mother of her child. He cradled it, sang to it softly, like a rider to his horse, like a shepherd to his flock, like a thresher to his oxen.[39]

Cecilia Dunoyer, in describing a Debussy piano roll of 'Danseuses de Delphes', writes that 'the sensual chords gently envelop the simple melodic line in a homogeneous halo of harmony'.[40]

An erotic music

The evasive nature of eroticism only intensifies when considered within the realm of music. Barthes provides an intriguing point of departure. He writes, 'Were we to succeed in refining a certain "aesthetics" of musical pleasure, then doubtless we would attach less importance to the formidable break in tonality accomplished by modernity'.[41] He calls for a new type of history of music, which concentrates on Julia Kristeva's notion of the *geno-song*, incorporating 'the space where significations germinate "from within language and in its very materiality"' and 'the voluptuousness of its sounds-signifiers'.[42] The very fact that music is experienced on a different level can be erotic, precisely because that level is physical, because the experience revolves around physical sensation without analysis, and because that is not the institutionally sanctioned way to listen to music. Debussy's view of music as something to be felt, not analysed, and his rejection of accepted rules of composition in favour of losing oneself in moments of sound disable the normal modes of 'interpretation'. Debussy nudges us into the *geno-realm*, a realm in which his music resides naturally.

Even so, eroticism in music existed long before Debussy. In fact, there are conventions of eroticism in all art forms – music is no exception. The standard take on the eroticism within what Barthes calls 'the authority of the fundamental code of the West, tonality',[43] plays out as follows:

A minor increase of tension is created by the musical movement into
dissonance and followed by enjoyable tension relief as the music returns to
consonance. Thus the playful mastery of the threat of being overwhelmed
by sounds becomes an enjoyable ego activity which contributes to the total
enjoyment of the music.[44]

Susan McClary has referred to 'the metaphorical simulation of sexual activity' within music, with tonality, 'with its process of instilling expectations and subsequently withholding promised fulfillment until climax' as
'the principal means during the period from 1600 to 1900 for arousing
and channelling desire'.[45] Wagner is the master manipulator of these erotic
codes:

Wagner's music relies heavily on the traditional semiotics of desire
available in the musical styles he inherited, and listeners understand his
music in part because they too have learned the codes (the minor sixths
demanding resolution, the agony of the tritone, the expectation that a
dominant-seventh chord will proceed to its tonic, and so on) upon which
his metaphors depend.[46]

Debussy's eroticism does not often operate according to these codes. In fact,
it is the rejection of these codes that enables his own form of eroticism, an
eroticism of uncertainty, of ambiguity, of excitement, of freedom.

That Debussy thought in these terms is clear. He writes, 'For a long time
the continuous use of sixths reminded me of pretentious young ladies sitting
in a salon, sulkily doing their tapestry work and envying the scandalous
laughter of the naughty ninths.'[47] He criticises composers who claim 'to
encapsulate life in chords of the seventh'[48] and speaks of 'floating' chords,
through which one can 'travel where one wishes and leave by any door'. He
says, 'There is no theory. You merely have to listen. Pleasure is the law.'[49]
'Beauty has its own laws.'[50] Debussy is concerned not with the conscious
withholding of resolution, but with the conscious rejection of the need to
resolve at all.

Charles Minahen differentiates between the veiled eroticism of Mallarmé
and the more explicit and obscene eroticism of Verlaine.[51] Mallarmé's dis-
ruption of syntax disables the usual modes of relating to words, forcing the
reader or listener to focus on other aspects – on the sounds themselves, to
flounder a little in the uncoded, physical world of the senses. Debussy is
much like Mallarmé in this way; he disrupts the usual musical syntax. As
Claude Abravanel states, 'Debussy did not abolish the musical language of
his time; rather, he separated its elements and recombined them in different
ways.'[52] Robin Holloway calls this a 'disembodied usage of chords'[53] and
describes Debussy's instinctive methods as creating implicit deliciousness
and light, sensual pleasure.[54] When Degas complained to Mallarmé that he

was having a difficult time writing a sonnet and wondered why, as he had ideas 'coming out of his ears – too many ideas', Mallarmé replied, 'You don't make sonnets out of ideas, Degas. You make them out of words.'[55] Debussy makes music out of sonorities. His music 'engenders a sonorous trajectory whose elements . . . unfurl freely', and 'is realised in a sonorous environment like a powder of sound cast into the light'.[56] It is Mallarmé's sort of eroticism in which Debussy participates, 'embracing the shiver of music's mystery'.[57]

The desire of *The Blessed Damozel*

The death . . . of a beautiful woman is, unquestionably, the most poetical topic in the world.
EDGAR ALLAN POE

Rossetti's poem and painting, both entitled *The Blessed Damozel*, were in-spired by Poe's *The Raven*. In both paint and word Rossetti conjures a heaven that defies the usual Christian conception. His heaven is an erotic landscape populated by couples languorously entangled in intimate embraces, enjoy-ing eternal, physical, sexual fulfilment. And it does not provide perfect peace for all, for Rosetti's Damozel is hardly content there. This is a heaven where eternal unhappiness is a possibility, where God is not enough. Here death does not halt desire, neither does it diminish physical beauty. Edward Lockspeiser notes 'the melancholy of her greenish-blue eyes, the peculiar curve of her sensual protruding upper lip, her copper-coloured locks and the curvature of her swan-like neck repeated in the draperies of her celestial gown.'[58] The Damozel desires not spiritual fulfilment, but sexual fulfilment with her lover who remains on earth. Her only wish is to continue in heaven the physical love she experienced on earth.

She weaves herself a fantasy which pulls religious ideals and erotic de-sires into a blasphemous knot. For many artists and writers, especially the Pre-Raphaelites and the Symbolists, beauty and physical love constituted a religion. A young Pierre Louÿs sequestered himself in a monastery in 1890, where he sketched plans for three books modelled on the Bible, *The Imitation of Christ*, and the *Spiritual Exercises* of St Ignatius. He replaced Christian re-ligion with a cult of Beauty, and the Christian god with a goddess of Beauty, who taught that one should love only Beauty. For Louÿs, 'Beauty constituted the supreme artistic ideal, one intimately more significant than Morality or Truth.'[59] In Walter Crane's painting *Altar of Love* (1870), a beautiful young woman kneels in prayer not before a crucifix, but before 'an ideal of fleshly love', while 'the kneeler's pose, the shape and character of the altar, the pil-grim staff all draw upon Christian iconography'.[60] So too in *The Blessed Damozel*, a religious shrine has been built for Love. The religious imagery in combination with a conduct that 'smacks too severely of earth to be imaginable in even a poetic heaven'[61] creates a discomfort and an erotic tension similar to that found in Rossetti's *Venus Verticordia*, in which competing iconographical signs make reference to Venus, Cupid, Eve and the Virgin Mary,[62] or in *Beata Beatrix*, which explores the 'mystic significance of love and of female beauty', where 'the loosened hair, the yearning expression, and half-closed eyes and half-opened mouth are not without sensuous appeal'.[63] The Pre-Raphaelites 'set conventional morality at defiance, exalted beauty above duty, and used medieval subject matter specifically as a sensually liberated and liberating antidote to Victorian prudery, earnestness, and high seriousness'.[64] Debussy's choice to set Rossetti's poem reflected his aesthetic alliance with Poe, the Pre-Raphaelites and the Symbolists.

Rossetti focused on 'the sensual and quasi-spiritual nature of sexual love'.[65] He emphasised the physicality of the Damozel and challenged the reader 'to notice the warmth of the girl's bosom' claiming 'that sex may become sacred',[66] and Debussy follows suit, emphasising this ambiguity between the sacred and the profane for a piece to be in a 'mystic, slightly pagan vein.'[67] The tonally ambiguous opening, with its parallel fifths, its 'strangely ethereal registration of the chords',[68] and its 'swaying, static circularity'[69] leads us into a place without time, a place that could very well be heaven. James Hepokoski has identified this typical Debussyan modal/chordal opening as suggesting 'primeval times, ecclesiastical austerity, quasi-mystical reverie, or uncommon experience'.[70] The dominant-ninth chords that flood this piece create a feeling of lush suspension.

This is a heaven of angelic female voices, where all signs of men have been removed except within the mind of the Damozel.[71] The choir that frames her fantasy sings full, bright, major triads, and it is in this angelic mode that they describe a woman, painting a picture of a perfect virgin Pre-Raphaelite beauty, complete with unfathomable eyes, long, flowing, yellow hair and the adornment of symbols of Mary herself. But the true nature of this heaven is revealed when a full orchestral 'whoosh' leads to a climactic F♯ major as choir and orchestra share the melody which comes to represent physical bliss in heaven, the only wish of the Blessed Damozel.

> Around her, lovers, newly met
> Spoke evermore among themselves
> Their new names of ecstasy . . .

This music recurs when she speaks of the perfect strength of two prayers, hers and her lover's, with perfection harmonised with another dominant-ninth chord. 'And why would I be afraid?' she asks. Thus Debussy unites prayer, erotic union and complete faith in God.

The entrance of the Damozel is built up as if she were the Virgin herself. The choir sings of her voice, like 'the voice the stars had when they sang together', to the accompaniment of string tremolos and harp figurations. Complete silence precedes her first utterance, which is unaccompanied. This silence can be interpreted as spiritual reflection, and as Mallarmé's 'silent, reflective, libidinally-charged moment', which is for Charles Minahen 'a voluptuously exquisite one'.[72] All of *Prélude à l'après-midi d'un faune* occurs in silence, in the dreamy spaces of the faun's imagination and memory, and the love between Pelléas and Mélisande is declared in total silence. The Damozel also desires the physical, and her silences are filled with dreams, not of God, but of her lover.

While the chorus and *récitante* sing in the imperfect and simple past tenses, the Damozel is rooted firmly in the future, the tense of fantasy as hoped for reality. The references to previously heard music cease when the fantasy begins. She enacts her own erotic script in all its details, and the orchestra follows in empathy. A slightly quicker compound-duple metre and oscillating chords provide a rocking quality suggestive of a soothing lullaby as the Damozel comforts herself, imagining every detail of her lover's arrival in heaven. The open, parallel fifths in the cellos provide an archaic sense of religiosity. When she sings of the secret mystery of nature and its mystic connection to Christ, the horn plays a melody which, with the help of the string tremolos, reinforces the noble nature of Christ himself and the sincerity of the Damozel.

Her fantasy includes many sensory details, such as her pleasure in voicing the 'sweet symphonies' that are the names of Mary's handmaidens, which Debussy sets as a melodic arch, beginning with ever-rising major thirds. Later, the harps become the guitars and citoles of the angels, played with syncopated joy. The meeting with Christ is the climax of this fantasy, and it is inseparable from her physical desire for her lover. The Damozel sings in unison with the orchestra the holy motive played earlier by the horn, stating her intention to ask Christ himself 'Simply to live as once on earth in Love, – and to be forever . . . together, I and he.'

Her final words 'All this will be when he comes', again unaccompanied, sung on the same pitches as those with which she began, verify that nothing has happened except in her mind.[73] This is an artwork of frustrated desire, of fantasy unfulfilled, not very different from Debussy's *Prélude* to Mallarmé's poem. He has intensified the religious-erotic connections of the poem by musically validating the fantasy of the Damozel. Her innocence, her naive simplicity make her physical desires seem pure. Debussy emphasises this juxtaposition by intensifying both the religious and the erotic elements, and in fact does make sex sacred.

Pan and his flute; Bilitis and her memories

O Pan, the sounds of your syrinx, like a wine
Too fragrant and too sweet, have intoxicated me... GABRIEL MOUREY, *PSYCHÉ*

The erotic power of the syrinx, its ability to seduce with its floating melody, constitutes a dominating theme in the works of Debussy. *Diane au bois, Syrinx*, Bilitis and her musical descendants, including the songs, the incidental music, the *Epigraphes antiques* and 'Des pas sur la neige' tangle together into one vast erotic arabesque.

Debussy wrote *Syrinx (La flûte de Pan)*[74] for solo flute for Gabriel Mourey's play *Psyché*, which was performed on 13 December 1913. The stage directions at the beginning of act III, scene 1 read in part as follows:

> The moon spreads over the countryside... In the clearing, the nymphs dance... adorned in white... Some collect flowers... some, stretched out at the water's edge, admire themselves. At intervals they all pause, astonished, listening to the syrinx of the invisible Pan, moved by the song that escapes from the hollow reeds.[75]

The music of the syrinx sounds throughout the scene until just after the nymph's line quoted above. This is the flute of the Faun, the flute of Lykas, the flute of Pan, with its inward curling, its ornamental stasis, fluid lines leading nowhere, suspended in the air. Pan's music draws the nymphs languorously in. This is the music of seduction, a music which had long fermented in the soul of a composer by this time well-versed in the musical seduction of women. M. Croche once said, 'My favourite music is those few notes an Egyptian shepherd plays on his flute: he is part of the landscape around him, and he knows harmonies that aren't in our books.'[76] The harmonies of erotic seduction are the mysterious sounds of nature.

Debussy described Pierre Louÿs's *Chansons de Bilitis* as containing 'all that is passionate, tender and cruel about being in love, so that the most refined voluptuaries are obliged to recognise the childishness of their activities compared to the fearsome and seductive Bilitis'.[77] Bilitis was born at a time when Debussy and Louÿs were the most intimate of friends. It was just after their friendship began that Louÿs met the first inspiration for the *Chansons*, Meryem ben Ali, aged sixteen. In the fall of 1893, André Gide, who was the object of many a practical joke regarding his timidity in matters of sex, experienced, according to H. P. Clive, a 'moral transformation' as he rejected Christianity and went to Africa to pursue 'normal sexuality'.[78] Meryem had been instrumental in the success of Gide's new sexual pursuits, and his descriptions of her talents were so enthusiastic that Louÿs changed his travel plans in order to go to Biskra to meet her. He described her in a letter to Debussy:

> We met over there a young personage of sixteen, whose morals are
> extremely depraved, and whose name sounds like that of a little bird,
> Meryem ben Ali . . . She is from that Arab tribe . . . where the girls earn
> their dowry through disreputable means; nevertheless, she knows French
> so well that, at a certain moment (that I cannot, in all decency, specify
> precisely), she breathed out, 'Tararraboum!! There it is!!'[79]

Louÿs's fascination with Meryem resulted in his writing many of the Bilitis
poems and the 'Life of Bilitis' introduction while with her in Constantine,
and the first edition of the poems was dedicated to her. In the manuscript
notes for the poems he wrote that she 'was the reason that I began Bilitis
again entirely, after her image, from the day I first saw her . . . She was a
marvel of grace, delicacy and ancient poetry.'[80] Back in Algeria, in 1897, he
met Zohra ben Brahim. He also described her in a letter to Debussy:

> But it is impossible to resist a person who can perform for you the Seven
> Days of the Week with no difficulty whatsoever, when other women of her
> race play the Week of the Seven Sundays! Moreover, she is so very brown;
> and, I tell you, a chocolate-brown woman on white sheets is very
> pretty . . . We are stuck, each to the other, like two dogs in the street.[81]

He took numerous photographs of her and proudly claimed, 'I will soon have
more than 100 absolutely lifelike poses of that little savage.'[82] His adventures
with Zohra inspired more Bilitis poems and it was during this time in Biskra
that he sent 'La chevelure' to Debussy for inspiration.[83]

Louÿs then shattered the boundary between the 'pure' home and exotic
Other by bringing Zohra to Paris to live with him, so he and his friends
could enjoy *La Mauresque*, as they called her, anytime. Jean-Paul Goujon
describes how Louÿs's friends, including Debussy, were completely seduced
by her.[84] Clive explains that 'Zohra's unashamed sensuality and her freedom
from sexual hypocrisy formed . . . a pleasing contrast with the puritanical
and, in his [Louÿs's] opinion, perverse moral code which governed French
society.'[85] In fact, Louÿs was determined to reinstate Greek sensuality in
the modern world. In the introduction to his immensely popular novel,
Aphrodite, he states that 'sensuality is a condition, mysterious but necessary
and creative of the intellectual process. Those who have not felt the demands
of the flesh to their fullest . . . are incapable of comprehending the extent of
the demands of the mind.'[86] This novel epitomised the decadent mixture of
love and death, of sensual eroticism and cruelty.

Debussy shared Louÿs's interest in photography.[87] There are several extant photographs of Gaby, draped in flowing cloths, which exude a languid
eroticism that is strikingly similar to that found in Rossetti's photographs
of Jane Morris and photos of Alfons Mucha's models.[88] The friends also
shared a somewhat bawdy sense of humour. When writing the incidental

music for a recitation of some of Louÿs's poems, Debussy wrote, 'I am putting the finishing touches on *Bilitis*...if I may thus express myself.'[89] This private performance for three hundred invitees consisted of a recitation of ten of the *Chansons de Bilitis*, with miming by a group of models in various stages of undress, providing a 'brazen display of unveiled, or, at best, barely veiled pulchritude'.[90] Louÿs reported his pleasure in supervising the rehearsals: 'I'm spending all my afternoons this week with naked women.'[91] A reporter for *Le journal* wrote that these women allowed the spectators to believe themselves 'transported to the great age of pure nudity'.[92] For two flutes, two harps and celesta, this music sparkles languidly. The text of the sixth poem describes Bilitis in true Art Nouveau form, and it was followed by a wash of sound: 'Me, I would only know how to live naked. My lover, take me as I am, without robes or jewels or sandals. Here is Bilitis, bare. My hair is black with its own blackness and my lips are red with their own redness. My curls float around me, free like feathers.'[93]

Louÿs bathed his erotic fantasies in beautiful language and the protective arms of history. Venturing back to the past, especially ancient Greece, became a common artistic trend. Richard Jenkins explains: 'The Greeks... invented nudity' and 'the classical world lends respectability to what is essentially a picture of a pretty girl taking her clothes off', offering 'a way in which a dangerous subject could be broached, or forbidden fantasies indulged'.[94] The hoax behind the publication of the *Chansons de Bilitis* allowed the reader to revel in the erotic activities of Bilitis without feeling any tinges of moral guilt. This was history, not fiction, and the authenticity of Bilitis made her even more enticing.[95]

A few years after Louÿs's death a vast array of manuscripts was discovered, which revealed what Goujon calls a 'real fascination with the written expression of eroticism'[96] and an obsession with feminine sexuality, 'autonomous and independent of man'.[97] Louÿs seems to revel in the beauty and power of his women, and this attitude is reinforced by the beauty of his language. These 'secret' works emphasised lesbian scenes and sexual escapades in private boarding schools and convents. Goujon even asserts that 'Louÿs felt a certain pleasure in putting himself in the place of the women, or, more exactly, to assume a role of a woman.'[98] Louÿs described young girls 'for whom sex is second nature, their only thought and occupation, to which they yield themselves with a naturalness so perfect that it strongly eclipses the obsession that adults can have'.[99] In these writings, 'the traditional entities, God or Society, are deliberately replaced by sex, a new divinity, infinitely more tyrannical and cruel than the others, because it breaks all norms and all values, only in order to ordain excess'.[100]

Among these manuscripts were the 'Secret Songs of Bilitis', twenty-one more poems with more emphasis on children and lesbianism. In 'Les petits enfants', Bilitis watches the little children play in the river, trying to engage in sexual encounters and frustrated by bodies that are too young. She then enters the water and allows them to use her body for their (and her) pleasure. The many small comments mentioning Bilitis, the published poems and Debussy's settings all take on a new meaning when considered in light of this vast amount of erotic writing. Given the length and the nature of their friendship, it seems completely plausible that this was not a part of himself that Louÿs kept hidden from Debussy.

The non-secret poems of Bilitis are arranged in three parts, corresponding to the three phases of her life. She was born in Pamphylia, where she fell in love with a goatherd, Lykas, and had a child, whom she abandoned. This is the section from which the three poems set by Debussy are taken, and all these events take place before she turns sixteen! She then moved to Lesbos, where she fell in love with a young girl, Mnasidika, who left her after a ten-year relationship because of Bilitis's intense jealousy. The third phase of her life takes place in Cyprus, where she becomes a courtesan. The poems were a huge success: Debussy wrote to Louÿs, 'Everyone's clutching *Bilitis*.'[101]

These poems deal with erotic initiation and consecration in the Foucaultian sense. And even though Bilitis's first sexual encounter with Lykas occurs against her will, she does not lose her strong sense of self or her overwhelming desire for her lover. Throughout these poems she follows her own erotic inclinations, relating even to nature in a very sensual way. In the opening poem, 'The Tree', she strips off her clothes, climbs a tree, and takes pleasure from the branch on which she sits. And she is in love with Lykas long before their lips meet on the flute in Debussy's first song. In 'The Complaisant Friend', Bilitis's friend Selenis pretends to be Lykas, saying, 'Close your eyes, I am Lykas . . . Here are his arms, here are his hands.' Bilitis continues, 'And tenderly, in the silence, she enchanted my dream with a singular illusion.'[102] And after their first sexual encounter, her fear is very short-lived. She says, 'He did not leave me. Rather, more tenderly, he held me in his arms close to him, and I no longer saw the earth or the trees but only the gleam in his eyes.'[103] She later speaks of a delight with him from which nothing can tear her away.

It is crucial to acknowledge that these poems are memories, memories of the distant past. Louÿs writes in the 'Life of Bilitis' that 'Bilitis, in her old age, found comfort in singing about those memories of her distant childhood.'[104] Debussy too believed in the power of memory. He wrote to Louÿs, just after finishing the Bilitis songs, 'I've never been able to work at anything when my life's going through a crisis; which is, I think, why memory is a superior faculty, because you can pick from it the emotions you need.'[105]

In the first song, Bilitis describes her erotic flute lesson with Lykas. The opening ritornello evokes the music of the syrinx, followed by an oscillating succession of chords that only adds to the ambiguity already set up between G♯ minor and B major. The melody of the flute rises and falls back on itself. This harmonic and melodic swirling is beautiful and sensual, the static nature of the music mirroring the emotions of Bilitis. She does not want to leave, but would rather linger in the moment. Even her declamatory vocal line turns back on itself. Susan Youens has spoken of 'the wonderfully Symbolist tension between what is remembered and/or dreamed and the present',[106] and Debussy's music enhances this very idea. Bilitis begins the poem in the past tense: 'he gave me a flute', as if she were recounting the event. The opening bars can thus be interpreted as the melody of Lykas's flute in her mind, as she remembers it. She begins to sing and the same melody repeats under her, as if still playing within her mind. Only through memory can a person be in two different time spheres at once. Bilitis speaks in the present about the past, and the music we hear is the same music she hears – music of the past. She becomes so entangled in this memory that she cannot break from her repetitive melodic pattern, and then everything stops on the phrase 'like honey'. When the music begins again, she sings in the present tense: 'He is teaching me to play.' She has lost all sense of time as she now relives the events leading to the touching of their lips on the very flute she hears. It is memory that has brought her back to the past, and music that makes her past present. Debussy has achieved a musical time warp and revealed the power of memory through music. The repetition of the opening bars at the end signifies the drifting of her mind, of her memory, to where she wants to be. And it is the flute and its specific erotic associations that keep pulling her back. It is clear that this is a memory Bilitis treasures, a memory that empowers and comforts her.

The second song, 'La chevelure', is a memory of a memory of a dream. The entwinement of Bilitis and Lykas in Lykas's dream is matched by the entwinement of narratives. She once again becomes caught up in her own memory of the telling of the dream. The sinuous, chromatic motion on the downbeats in combination with the repeated chords on the offbeats together create an erotic tension that is 'relieved' only during the two points of climax, where the only significant rising melodic lines occur, first when the two are metaphorically joined, and second, when they are physically united. Lykas says that he becomes Bilitis and that *she* enters *him*, and Bilitis, through the very telling of the dream, becomes Lykas. Once again, Bilitis is brought back to the present, or at least up another layer towards the present, with the return of the music from the opening bars. The erotic nature of Bilitis's original experience is compounded by the retelling and rethinking of it. The past and the present mingle, for certainly her memories here are coloured by her sexual relationship with Lykas, even though it had not yet occurred at the time of this dream.

The third song has evoked comments regarding Bilitis's regret for her 'unrecoverable love',[107] and the lament for the passage of her innocence.[108] While the final poem does mark the end of a phase of her life, it is only one phase in a life that is long and certainly not ever lacking in erotic substance. She lives on and loves again, becoming a woman of power and experience.

Debussy's dedication of a score of *Prélude à l'après-midi d'un faune* for Pierre Louÿs reads, 'Some airs of the flute to charm Bilitis'.[109] The faun's music may have charmed Bilitis, but it failed to attract any nymphs; thus Minahen refers to the faun's erotic ponderings as a 'confused, unsatisfying and inadequate conception of desire'.[110] Both Mallarmé's poem and Debussy's music dwell in the hazy spaces where sexual fantasies are born, between dream and memory, the conscious and the unconscious, reverie and reality, sleep and wakefulness, and desire and music making. The ambiguous, erotic images and intangible language of the poem are mirrored in the music where tonalities are only suggested and rarely confirmed, where themes remain undeveloped. Lockspeiser writes, 'No sooner are they announced than they become merged with other themes, modulate, change their character or disappear in fragments.'[111] As the faun contemplates the erotic possibilities in a state of confused and drowsy desire, searching for evidence of his 'erotic epiphany',[112] forming various hypotheses, the flute arabesques into various musical possibilities, in the end, lulling him back into sleep. Debussy's self-referential, circular music is a musical exploration of the inner workings of the depths of the erotic mind.

A voyeur, a hair fetish, and the elusive and mysterious Mélisande

O fleece, billowing down to the neck!
O locks, O fragrance laden with languidness!
O ecstasy!   BAUDELAIRE, 'LA CHEVELURE'

Voyeurism exists 'where sexual gratification is achieved through surreptitious looking at the sexual activities or parts of others'.[113] In *Dans le jardin*,[114] Debussy depicts a happy voyeur who finds all the sexual satisfaction he needs in secretly watching a child and in the subsequent telling of his adventure to this object of his desire. The song begins with melodic stops and starts, as if portraying the tiptoeing of the voyeur and the thrill of seeing without being seen. The rhythmic pattern of this tiptoeing figure continues throughout much of the song as an indicator of his covert obsession. When he speaks of the thrill in his heart, that triplet figure trips over itself, unable to move beyond a two-note oscillation, as if time has stopped for him. Debussy tells us that the suffering of which the voyeur speaks is all a part of the same fantasy, if not the highlight of it, by continuing the same winding, rhythmic figure in the piano, this time intensified with parallel first-inversion triads in the left hand when he describes his bleeding fingers, and then essentially repeating it when he describes her face, her hair, her brow. Just like the faun, whose interest in the nymphs is 'purely physical, as is evident in the way he focuses metonymically on their bodies, not as complete entities, but as amalgamations of parts',[115] this voyeur fragments the body of his subject. The short, repeated arpeggio figures, at first outlining dominant-seventh chords, achieve a state of dreaminess that indicates he has fallen more deeply into reverie, as he draws his attention to her eyes, her eyelashes, her frail body, her voice and her gestures.

Ingres's painting *Bather of Valpinçon* (1808) ruins the pleasure of the voyeur by highlighting

> the bather's ear, tuned perfectly to the harmony of her private world. The pure sound of the falling water and its sensual reception mark this painting as an allegory of the sense of hearing. The spectator lured to the vision of the beautiful woman discovers too late that he stands before a remote entity – the untouchable realm of sound.[116]

In the tower scene of *Pelléas et Mélisande*, we eavesdrop on a similarly intimate moment, a woman at her *toilette*, experiencing, without orchestra, 'the tender voice of Mélisande, secretly overheard'.[117] But even the realm of sound brings us no closer to the mystery that is Mélisande. The voyeur sees *and* hears, but the subject remains remote. When Pelléas enters and her hair tumbles down, he experiences an erotic pleasure that is fetishistic, and another dimension is added to the voyeuristic adventure.

The term 'fetishism' was coined in 1887 by French psychologist Alfred Binet in reference to 'the myriad sensory triggers of sexual pleasure: touch, color, sound, taste, odour'.[118] Pathological fetishism, 'the adoration of things inappropriate to directly satisfying the ends of reproduction', was 'a matter of erotic synecdoche or metonymy'. Thus the part substitutes for the whole: 'the accessory becomes the principle'.[119] The most common fetish in *fin-de-siècle* Paris was the fetish for women's hair, and Debussy's women are women with Baudelairian hair – hair that seduces. Mélisande's hair is the medium through which Golaud and Pelléas attempt to relate to her. Pelléas's desire for Mélisande is in part fulfilled by her hair. In the tower scene he loses himself in her hair, unconscious of her actual conscious existence and emotional discomfort above him. He does not need her to participate in this fantasy. 'And it loves me, it loves me more than you', he says. And Golaud takes out his frustration with Mélisande through her hair in the most violent scene of the opera. Thus Mélisande's hair becomes a symbol for the close proximity between erotic desire and violence, what Catherine Clément calls 'those primitive feelings that only hair evokes bodily for men'.[120] This hair becomes a symbol for 'the eternal feminine', 'the mystery of femininity, deep and enticing as the sea',[121] a woman's sexuality.[122] It is erotic hair music that connects Bilitis to Mélisande, as Katherine Bergeron identifies the same music used in 'La Chevelure' and in the tower scene in *Pelléas*.[123] She writes, 'This timeless song of hair is desire's tune.'[124]

Debussy's portrayal of erotic love defies operatic convention, rejecting the usual externalised, emotional aria outpourings. Mélisande avoids communication where the typical operatic woman would burst into song. When Pelléas finally hears the words he has been longing for, words conveyed in orchestral silence, he does not respond with a joyous outburst, but rather his sense of awe hangs over eerie harmonics in the violins. Debussy writes:

> I tried to capture all the mystery of the night and the silence in which a blade of grass roused from its slumber makes an alarming noise. And then there's the sea nearby, telling its sorrows to the moon and Pelléas and Mélisande a little scared of talking, surrounded by so much mystery.[125]

The opera swims in mystery, ambiguity and uncertainty, and it is these very elements that intensify the erotic feel of the work.

Golaud senses that there is more to be had from Mélisande. He exclaims, 'I am so close to them that I can feel a little breeze when the eye-lashes blink, and yet I am nearer to the great secrets of the next world than I am to the smallest secrets of those eyes!' In Poe too, women are 'always lost, vanishing before they can be embraced'.[126] Ligeia's husband desperately wants to understand the expression of her eyes: 'What *was* it? I was possessed with a passion to discover. Those eyes!'[127] And the male certainty that all women are holding back something, something crucial, extends beyond the frame of fiction.[128] For even Debussy finds Mélisande elusive, writing, 'I've gone looking for music behind all the veils she wraps round herself',[129] and 'Notice that the motif which accompanies Mélisande is never altered; it comes back in the fifth act unchanged in every respect, because in fact Mélisande always remains the same and dies without anyone – only old Arkel, perhaps? – ever having understood her.'[130] Even the music refuses to deliver, and Mélisande's secret remains hidden.

From 'languorous ecstasy' to sensual nightmare

It haunts me like a beautiful nightmare D E B U S S Y[131]

'C'est l'extase' perhaps most intensely illustrates in musical terms a sensual experience of nature that is at once spiritual and erotic. The lush, falling chords in the piano glide to a classic Debussyan ninth chord, suspended in space, followed by a slow, languid descending vocal line. It is as if the speaker can barely muster the energy to even utter the first words: 'This is languorous ecstasy.' Here small, voluptuous motives are repeated, with the tiniest of variations – grass exhales, leaves murmur, breezes embrace, and the vocal line expresses its delight in these rustlings, caressing every word and every note. Every detail of nature reverberates within the soul of the speaker, as the piano and the voice weave in and out of one another, as when, under the words 'it is like the soft cry the ruffled grass exhales', the piano moves in a reverse chromatic motion that mirrors that of the voice, as if the speaker becomes a reflection of the nature in which he or she is enveloped. The vocal line is a slow, languorous arabesque, an arabesque in which every note is elongated and enjoyed. The voice moves primarily downward, with every melodic leap followed by a descent; the melody lingers on a note, moves away from it, and then returns to it, thus creating an expression of pulsating desires, of tiny waves of erotic delight. Momentary doubt leads to the only *mf* in the song, but a typical musical climax is undermined here, for the voice relaxes into a slow descent into the deeper realm of the soul, cushioned in complete harmony with nature.

The mysterious pleasure of the overwhelming, over-sensitised, erotic experience of nature that dominates Debussy's early songs is balanced by its erotic opposite – a mysterious, sensual terror. For Georges Bataille, death and violence are the only paths to erotic satisfaction. Life is discontinuous, but people desire continuity. The 'erotic impulse' is an attempt to attain that continuity, but it brings us only to 'the brink of death', 'the abyss that separates humanity from the continuity it desires'.[132] D. H. Lawrence's views on the fine line between love and death come extraordinarily close to those of Bataille. He writes,

> Love is the mysterious vital attraction which draws things together, closer, closer together. For this reason, sex is the actual crisis of love. For in sex the two blood-systems, in the male and the female, concentrate and come into contact, the merest film intervening. Yet if the intervening film breaks down, it is death.[133]

Man's problem, says Lawrence, is his desire for oneness: 'He wants his nerves to be set vibrating in the intense and exhilarating unison with the nerves of another being; and by this means he acquires an ecstasy of vision, he finds himself in glowing unison with all the universe.'[134] Man, then, wants this vibrating unison to be constant, but this violates the fundamental law of isolation of all creatures. Herein lies the fine line between pleasurable eroticism and eroticism that destroys. 'There is a limit to love', summarises Lawrence; 'To *know* a living thing is to kill it.'[135]

The sweet, sensual vibrating of the soul in harmony with nature becomes an uncontrollable, violent shaking at the mercy of this same nature, no longer sweet, but suffocating. With his work on *La chute de la maison Usher,* Debussy effected a move down the continuum of erotic sensory perception to the end where the pleasure has been seemingly left behind, where only fear remains, where things once pleasurable and profound have become a sensual threat. Even the arabesque becomes a sign of derangement in the realm of Poe. He uses the term to describe Usher's hair: 'The silken hair, too, had been suffered to grow all unheeded, and as, in its wild gossamer texture, it floated rather than fell about the face, I could not, even with effort, connect its arabesque expression with any idea of simple humanity.'[136] So too is Usher's song (Lady Madeleine's song in Debussy's text), like his 'wild improvisations' on the guitar, 'an explicit musical metaphor for derangement of intellect'.[137] Thus the creative act becomes an act of madness. In Debussy's scenario, Lady Madeleine becomes the guitar, 'on which Roderick plays cruelly'.[138] Causing her madness, here sexual and musical violation become one. Usher's paintings evoke 'an intensity of intolerable awe' in his friend, who claims, 'no shadow of which felt I ever yet in the contemplation of the certainly glowing yet too concrete reveries of Fuseli'.[139] This comparison to Fuseli's pornographic paintings makes the link between hysteria, sex and art even more explicit. It is little wonder that Debussy had a difficult time finding the right music, the very act of composing bringing him ever closer to the crimes of Usher. How does a composer who has devoted much of his music to sensory pleasure move into the realm of sensory hell? According to Poe, the line between the two is the thinnest thread.

All of *Usher* takes place in the atmosphere of the vaults of *Pelléas*, which Debussy described as being 'full of impalpable terror and mysterious enough to make the most well-balanced listener giddy.'[140] Here terror and mystery are evoked through the very depths of orchestral sound, with creeping cellos, contrabasses and bassoons. For *Usher,* he sought similar, otherworldly effects to evoke 'the secret atmosphere, the feelings, tensions, and the emotions contained in the tales of Poe [which] have not previously been translated into music'.[141] He describes one such discovery: 'The music has an attractive mustiness obtained by mixing the low notes of the oboe with harmonics of the violin.'[142]

Yet Debussy wrote that he was unable to find the right music for 'this exploration of anguish, which is what *La chute de la maison Usher* will be'[143] precisely because he was unable to escape traditional writing. 'For every bar that has some freedom about it, there are twenty that are stifled by the weight of one particular tradition; try as I may, I'm forced to recognise its hypocritical and destructive influence.'[144] But he persisted, and not without pleasure, working with his Poe operas for years and years. He tells Durand that he has been completely caught up with the Usher family, saying, 'the outside world hardly exists for me', and 'This is a delightful state of mind.'[145] He writes that he is spending his days in *La maison Usher*: 'You get into the strange habit of listening to the dialogue of the stones and expecting houses to fall down as though that were a natural, even necessary phenomenon.'[146] And he refers to the similarity between himself and Usher, thereby forging a bond between them which extends to Poe himself,[147] writing, 'We share a certain hypersensitivity.'[148] Debussy's experience of the world around him was an erotic one, and he extended this experience into his music, attempting to expand the musical language of eroticism to encompass the full erotic continuum, with all its ambiguities and discontinuities, as a part of the mystery and magic that defined for him the essence of music.

8 Debussy and nature

CAROLINE POTTER

Debussy liked to give the impression that he was a reluctant reviewer of concerts. Often, prior to giving his assessment of a particular performance, he writes of the beauty of the day on which the concert took place, unfavourably comparing his delight in nature with his unfortunate obligation to attend the concert. In an article written for *La revue blanche* in 1901, Debussy wrote of being in the countryside, far from artistic debates, the first performances of new works and everything else associated with the Parisian musical world. He wrote:

> I was alone and deliciously disinterested; perhaps I had never loved music more than at that moment, when I never heard anyone talk about it. It appeared to me complete, in all its beauty, not in overheated or stingy little symphonic or lyric fragments.[1]

Debussy often said that he disliked analytical approaches to music (in common with many composers), and he was quite naturally irritated by uninformed discussion about music. Moreover, his love of nature was coupled with a misanthropic streak. I suspect that he preferred the open spaces and silence of the countryside (a silence broken only by the sounds of wind, water and other natural phenomena) to the company of his fellow human beings.

Later in this article Debussy stresses that he believes the Prix de Rome competition is ridiculous, implying that this competitive approach to composition is unnatural. Music, for him, should be a part of nature, or something sharing its characteristics; on many occasions he expressed his distaste for academic forms and harmonic formulae. He made his feelings clear when questioned about the direction young composers should follow, replying:

> People put too much stress on the methods of writing music, on formulae and on craftsmanship! People look for ideas in themselves, whereas they should seek them outside of themselves. We don't pay enough attention to the thousand noises of nature around us; we don't listen out for this music which is so varied, which she offers us so generously . . . This, according to me, is the new path [which young composers should follow].[2]

He drew a parallel between the freedom of nature and an idealised free music, based on an imaginative transformation of nature:

> Everything which can be perceived by a fine ear in the rhythm of the surrounding world can be represented musically. Some people want most of all to conform to the rules; I, on the other hand, want only to render what I hear.[3]

The people he criticises here are surely the Conservatoire professors who taught him the traditional disciplines of writing music, and perhaps particularly the judges of the Prix de Rome, who rewarded conformity rather than imagination. He believed that music should provide instant pleasure; 'it should impose on our senses or insinuate itself into our nerves without us having to make any effort whatsoever to grasp its meaning'.[4] In the same way that the appreciation of nature should not be the sole preserve of those able to analyse it, music should not be accessible only to experts.

Debussy's preference for nature rather than nurture is clear. Debussy's view of traditional forms, such as fugue and sonata form, was that they were sterile, academic structures rather than living entities with parallels in nature. The view that form and content could be two separate things – with content tailored to a set musical form – was anathema to him, and the academic training he received at the Conservatoire could only, according to him, lead to a painting-by-numbers approach to musical composition. For him, music was a living, organic art, which only truly existed in performance rather than on paper; the audience's perception of the gradual growth of the work was a central part of the musical experience. This emphasis on the organic growth of the ideal musical work explains why Debussy so disliked 'stingy little symphonic or lyric fragments'. The performance of a complete musical work was therefore, according to him, the only valid way of experiencing it, exactly paralleling our experience of the natural world; we do not experience the landscape, weather conditions and other natural phenomena as unconnected things. Debussy's rejection of classical forms is in fact a rejection of formalism, as this formalism represents a distancing from the ideal forms of nature.

The idealisation of nature has a long and distinguished history in French literature, most notably in Jean-Jacques Rousseau, who praised the noble, uncorrupted savage. While Debussy made no explicit reference to the concept of the noble savage, many of his writings on nature reveal his essentially idealistic view of a life lived in tune with the rhythms of the natural world, an existence diametrically opposed to a modern civilisation that has grown away from nature. While this Edenic representation of humankind is a glorification of a simpler life than that lived by Debussy and his Parisian contemporaries, it is also a nostalgic evocation of a 'paradise lost' – in fact, a paradise they never knew, indeed, that never existed other than in the imagination of artists such as Debussy. A distaste for the present, which this idealisation suggests, is reinforced by Debussy's admiration for composers of the Renaissance period (whom he significantly termed 'the primitives') such as Palestrina, and for non-Western musics such as the Javanese game-lan, these musics being distant in time and space from Debussy. Debussy believed that music, of all the arts, is closest to nature. He wrote in 1913:

> Painters and sculptors can only give us a rather free and necessarily partial interpretation of the beauty of the universe. They seize on but one of its aspects, on a single moment in time; composers alone have the privilege of capturing all of the poetry of the night and day, of the earth and of the sky, to reconstitute their atmosphere and to give rhythm to the immense palpitation of nature.[5]

Therefore, music is the superior art because it exists in time and can consequently capture the movements and sounds of nature far more effectively than the plastic arts or literature. More importantly, music is not restricted to a literal depiction of natural phenomena.

Nature and imaginative reproduction

After the premiere of *Pelléas et Mélisande* (1902), Debussy explained to an interviewer why he wrote the opera. He explained that he sought a new form for the operatic genre:

> Earlier experiments in the realm of pure music led me to detest classical development, whose beauty resides solely in technique, which can only interest those academics amongst us. I wanted music to have a freedom that she perhaps has more than any other art, as it is not restricted to a more or less exact reproduction of nature, but instead deals with the mysterious correspondences between Nature and the Imagination.[6]

For Debussy, then, a musical response to, or identification with, nature could not result in a simple imitation of natural phenomena. Small wonder that he disliked Beethoven's *Pastoral* Symphony. Reviewing a performance conducted by Felix Weingartner, he wrote that the work was conducted as if 'the gentle valleys were portrayed in plush material bought for 10 francs per metre, and the hills seemed as if they were made of cheap wire'. Debussy clearly had reservations about this particular interpretation of the symphony, which made it sound like a cheap imitation of a countryside scene, and he did not identify with the methods Beethoven used to evoke a natural scene, in particular his introduction of animal and bird sounds,

Example 8.1 *Pelléas et Mélisande*, prelude to act I (bars 1–9)

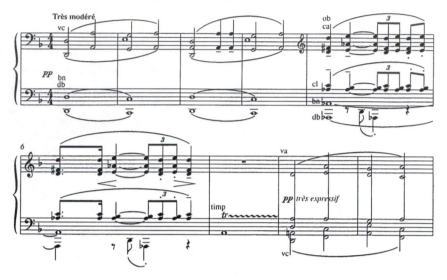

which are intended to be realistic. In his view, the musical depictions of cows drinking and cuckoos calling are 'either pointlessly imitative, or capable of evoking many and varied interpretations'.[7]

Nevertheless, his dislike of this symphony was not symptomatic of a more general allergy to Beethoven. As he wrote later in the same article:

> Some passages of the old master's music are so much more deeply expressive of the beauty of a landscape, simply because they do not imitate it directly, but are an imaginative emotional response to what is invisible in nature. Does measuring the height of the trees reveal the mystery of a forest? Isn't it actually the immeasurable depth of the forest which stimulates the imagination?[8]

Certainly the act of measuring trees cannot explain the effect a forest has on our senses; it is a separate act and one of, perhaps, limited interest. By analogy, this comparison of Debussy's could suggest that the composer was not so much against music analysis *per se*, but instead was anxious that it should not be seen as a replacement for, or the equivalent of, the musical experience itself.

We do not know which Beethoven pieces Debussy was referring to when he wrote about the composer's imaginative response to nature, but we do know that the prelude to his own *Pelléas et Mélisande* is intended to depict a forest in musical terms (Example 8.1).

How does he achieve what he terms a 'transposition sentimentale de ce qui est "invisible" dans la nature' in this prelude? There are no birdsongs

Example 8.2 *Pelléas et Mélisande*, act III, scene 1 (bars 18–24)

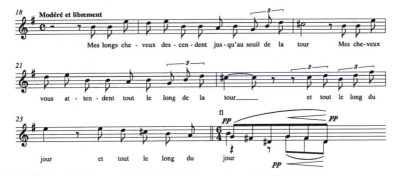

or other simple imitations of the natural world in Debussy's forest. Instead he uses musical symbols and gestures to render his vision of the forest. The low dynamic level of much of the prelude and the low-pitched instruments heard at the start are well-known symbols of mystery and darkness. This is not primarily a depiction of the forest itself, but a composer's imaginative response to the sensation of being in a forest. Also, the immediate repetition of most bars of the prelude (even if most of these repetitions are inexact) evokes the sense of an enclosed, claustrophobic world. As this symbolism of a contained world can also be applied to the place in which the opera's characters live, the prelude is as much a psychological portrait of Allemonde and its inhabitants as of the forest. Forests, like all natural phenomena, are also associated with timelessness; while individual trees may die, the forest is self-renewing and thus eternal. Debussy's use of modality and bare fifths at the start of the prelude has a parallel in, for instance, several passages in his later *Prélude* 'La cathédrale engloutie' (1909–10), which are presumably intended to evoke the medieval period. These musical devices are perhaps intended to suggest the great age of the forest and to evoke a sense of religious awe.

Maeterlinck and Debussy portray Mélisande as an ethereal, blonde woman-child. She does not answer questions directly or explain her motivation – if the passivity which is her essential characteristic can be so described. Her status as an unthinking child of nature is best demonstrated, musically speaking, at the beginning of act III, where she sings unaccompanied as she arranges her hair for the night (Example 8.2). The modal inflections of her song are evocative of an idealised folk music, and the lack of accompaniment heightens the spontaneity, in particular the song's apparent freedom from metrical constraints. It is as if Mélisande is singing 'with the naïve candour of childhood' that Debussy once stated to be his ideal.[9] The folk-like, untutored quality of her song evokes the innocence and artlessness Debussy associated with the natural world.

It is highly likely that Debussy was familiar with the writings of the mathematician Charles Henry. Henry's theories of colour and shape were based on idealised notions of harmonious or inharmonious relationships, which can be defined objectively in numerical ratios. He influenced several artists – notably Paul Signac, and also Georges Seurat, Paul Gauguin and Maurice Denis – some of whom were friends of Debussy. In his pamphlet *Introduction à une esthétique scientifique* (1885) Henry wrote:

> Science will never be able to create beauty, for in order to realise beauty, one must possess the universal formula: but to possess the universal formula, wouldn't that be to know it? And the day when the problem will be close to being solved, will not humanity have returned once again to the unconsciousness of nature?[10]

As Roy Howat puts it: 'In short, Henry sought to give simple and workable definition to the relationships between mathematics and art in ways that could also link all the arts.'[11] Debussy's identification of music and nature should therefore be viewed in the context of Henry's belief that there is a 'universal formula' governing everything.

A simple example of Henry's theory of shape is his belief that an ascending line has positive implications, and a descending line produces the opposite effect. In his words: 'the agreeable directions from low to high, down to up and from left to right are found to coincide with the tendencies of man towards the light'.[12] He goes on to connect this phenomenon with the growth of plants, which turn towards a source of light or grow upwards towards the sun. In Western European music the association of low sounds with darkness and depth and high-pitched sounds with light and altitude is commonplace. Debussy's music features several examples of this, and it is likely that Henry's giving a scientific basis for the 'agreeable directions' interested him.

Perhaps the clearest illustration in Debussy's oeuvre of a move from depth to height, and concurrently from darkness to light and from low-pitched sounds to high-pitched sounds, occurs in *Pelléas*, in act III, scene 2. Golaud tries to scare Pelléas by showing him the vaults of the castle, asking his half-brother if he can smell 'l'odeur de la mort qui monte' and threatening to hang him over a precipice. The murky depths of the castle vaults are suggested musically by low-pitched instruments, especially the lower strings. Sudden dynamic swells add to the air of menace. Pelléas, both petrified and stifled, leads the way towards ground level, and the gradual registral shift from low to high pitches depicts musically this ascent towards the light. Debussy's musical fleshing-out of the effects of darkness and light is a prime example of his adding an extra dimension to Maeterlinck's words, and the brilliant and palpitating orchestral texture representing light brings to mind 'the teeming voices of nature', which Debussy aimed to emulate in musical terms. The move from darkness to light is reinforced by a harmonic change (from the unclear whole-tone-with-added-notes mode of the music associated with darkness to the tonally less ambiguous B major for the bright music), and by the move from one character to another, Golaud being to the fore when the half-brothers descend to the vaults, and Pelléas leading the way towards the light. Of course, words point the way towards a specific interpretation of this passage; but the effects Debussy created could be reproduced by him in purely instrumental contexts and retain the same significance.

Nature and the arabesque

Henry's theories paralleled the practice of artists associated with the Art Nouveau movement, a movement close to Debussy's heart; his friend Pierre Louÿs described Debussy's flat in rue Cardinet as 'your Art Nouveau den'.[13] The line was of central importance to these artists, and the designs they produced were generally based on natural forms, especially the curved shapes of vines and tendrils. Lockspeiser writes of Debussy in the 1890s: 'We have much evidence showing that Debussy's musical and artistic sensibility at this stage was a reflection of the theories of the Art Nouveau movement. His conception of melody as an "arabesque" was the direct musical counterpart of these theories.'[14]

Debussy's critical response to another 'old master', J. S. Bach, is of particular interest because he focuses on the link he perceived between Bach's music and nature. He insists that Bach did not use the 'formules harmoniques' he detests; rather, he lived in an era 'when "the adorable arabesque" flourished, and music thus shared in laws of beauty inscribed in the general movement of nature'.[15] Debussy, of course, sees in Bach's music what interests him as a composer. Another criticism, written for *La revue blanche* in May 1901, provides more detail: he wrote that 'the primitives, Palestrina, Vittoria, Orlando di Lasso, made use of that divine "arabesque". They discovered the principle in Gregorian chant and supported its delicate intertwinings with firm counterpoint. When Bach took over the arabesque he made it more supple and fluid and, despite the severe discipline that great master imposed on Beauty, it was able to move with that free, ever fresh fantasy which still amazes us today.'[16]

The term 'arabesque' is not generally used in a historically accurate manner when applied to music. Maurice J. E. Brown, writing in the *New Grove*, defines the word as 'A term, apparently introduced into Europe during the Moorish conquest of Spain, first applied to architecture or painting to describe an ornamental frieze or border, whose elaborations, foliate and curlicued, have their counterparts in music in ornamentation and complex figuration'. The common use of the term as applied to music therefore postdates its original application in the plastic arts – in buildings such as the Alhambra Palace in Granada – by several centuries. Brown notes that an arabesque in music can be the 'contrapuntal decoration of a basic theme', the ornamentation of a melodic line, or 'a rapidly changing series of harmonies which decorate, without furthering, a point in the progress of a composition', citing Nocturnes by Field and Chopin as examples of the third category. He ends his short article by referring to 'Debussy's *Deux arabesques* . . . whose charm and delicacy reflect perfectly the conception of the arabesque as a decorative rather than emotional effect'.[17] Leaving aside the dubious notion that the perception of music as charming is not an emotional response, it seems clear that in this early work Debussy views the title as indicative of a flowing and decorative type of piano writing. His writings on Bach, cited above, tend to support the view that he associated arabesque with continuously evolving melodic lines and with music that grows organically rather than being divided into periodic phrases. The ornaments which pervade the second *Arabesque* demonstrate the essentially decorative associations of the term, and the undulating, legato melodic lines of the first piece illustrate the curved shape of the traditional arabesque. This shape has, of course, a direct parallel in the ballet position known as the arabesque. It is likely that the qualities of grace and charm associated with the term 'arabesque' spring from its use in dance, and more specifically from its association with female dancers.

Jann Pasler highlights Debussy's interest in the Javanese gamelan he first heard at the 1889 Exposition de Paris and rightly suggests that 'its roots in nature and the importance it ascribed to musical line' had particular appeal for him. She goes on to say that

> what attracted Debussy to . . . the sixteenth-century 'primitives', Bach, and Javanese music, was what results from a multiplicity of simultaneous lines . . . Rather than the emotive power of a single line, as in a melody, it was lines in relationship to other lines and in constant metamorphosis that he understood as synonymous with musical beauty.[18]

Debussy associated all of these things with the arabesque and, given his love of nature, it is unsurprising that the arabesque appealed to him.

Arabesques in Moorish art are based on natural forms – such as leaves, vines or branches – and these units are multiplied to create larger forms, the parts of which are related proportionally. They are the foundation of an art form in which the realistic representation of living beings – whether people, animals or birds – was taboo. We have already seen that Debussy did not appreciate Beethoven's attempts to introduce reproductions of animal and bird sounds in his *Pastoral* Symphony, which were, given the constraints of his musical language, as accurate as possible. His dislike of the crudely imitative passages of Richard Strauss's symphonic poems is also well documented.

Charles Henry mentions the idea of 'continual autogenesis', an idea he explicitly links with the arabesque. José Argüelles, a commentator on Henry's writings, describes this as a 'dynamically creative, or procreative, energy principle', and defines an arabesque (whether musical or visual) as a decorative motive that is 'often intricate, repetitive, self-reproductive, and, ideally, self-mutative'.[19] Used correctly the term should not simply refer to a decorative, flowing and curved line. Although arabesques had a decorative function – they did not determine the form of the architecture – they were not merely pretty patterns.

Debussy famously wrote, in the guise of Monsieur Croche: 'My favourite music is those few notes an Egyptian shepherd plays on his flute: he is part of the landscape around him, and he knows harmonies that aren't in our books. The musicians amongst us hear only music written by trained composers, never the music of nature herself. To see the sunrise does one far more good than hearing the *Pastoral* Symphony.'[20] The sunrise, of course, follows an upward trajectory – an 'agreeable direction' according to Henry – a direction traced in the first pages of 'De l'aube à midi sur la mer', the first movement of Debussy's three symphonic sketches, *La mer* (1903–5).

The composer's reference to 'an Egyptian shepherd' is loaded with meaning. This shepherd – it goes without saying that he is an idealised rather than real character – is representative of the ideal union of music and nature. Not being a professional musician (rather, his profession connects him with the soil), he is not hidebound by academic rules, but instead is a conduit for the voices of the natural world. The many arabesque-type patterns written for the flute in Debussy's works – the best known being the opening of his *Prélude à l'après-midi d'un faune* (1892–4) – leads us to imagine that the shepherd is playing a similar pattern. Indeed, the opening arabesque of this Debussy piece spans a tritone, an interval that does not usually suggest a tonal centre; this lack of specific harmonic direction of Debussy's evokes the drowsy nonchalance of the faun, an effect the composer could best create by using 'harmonies that aren't in our books'. As the shepherd is 'part of the landscape around him', there is no distinction between his music and his surroundings. Finally, Monsieur Croche's reference to the shepherd's nationality emphasises his exoticism, his 'otherness' when viewed through French eyes, and it is possible that when mentioning this idealised

Example 8.3 'Pastorale', Sonata for flute, viola and harp (bars 12–15)

shepherd's nationality, Debussy intended to stress the 'Arab' origins of the arabesque.

In his later works, Debussy's musical interpretation of the arabesque is more profound than in his early piano works of that title. The first movement, 'Pastorale', of his Sonata for flute, viola and harp (1915) has a title which explicitly links it to the natural world. It features many arabesque-type patterns, right from the flute's entry in bar 1. In bars 2 and 3 the flute line is almost exactly symmetrical, and its ambit gradually increases. These almost perfectly palindromic figures again reflect Debussy's love of the forms of nature; so many natural objects and creatures are symmetrical. The viola and harp parts in bars 14–15 (see Example 8.3) and 16-17 are an especially good example of the arabesque technique, as the two instrumental parts are related but not perfectly identical; the shape of the figures is similar, while the note lengths are different in each instrument. The flute part in bar 12 is particularly interesting. Debussy's idealised Egyptian shepherd again springs to mind, not only because of the arabesque shape of the line. At this point the time signature is 9/8, but the flute line does not fit into this mould; it is as if the flautist is improvising above the sustained viola and harp parts (which do conform to the time signature). Rather than include triplet, quintuplet and other precise rhythmic indications, which would enable the flute line to fit into the 9/8 time signature, Debussy prefers to give the performer a certain amount of freedom. It seems clear that the relative duration of each group of notes should be observed, but the composer does not seek the rhythmically rigid result a more precise notation could have created. In this bar, freedom from constraint is created by a freedom from precise rhythmic notation.

At the end of the movement the musical lines progressively contract. Bar 74 is the climax of the movement, where the two principal melodic ideas (first stated at bar 1 and at bars 14–15) are united. From this point until the end, there is a progressive liquidation of the melodic line, until only two notes remain.

Clouds, water and Debussy's musical imagination

There could easily be a conflict between Debussy's hatred of musical formulae and his desire to reproduce the natural phenomena he perceived. Music can, of course, only suggest natural phenomena (such as waves, the wind, clouds, and contrasting light effects); it cannot present them in an unambiguously pictorial form, and it can only suggest these if the composer uses musical devices that are immediately understood by the audience. This necessity to communicate the phenomena in as unambiguous a manner as possible could result in the composer using musical formulae which are recognisable because they have been tried and tested by many other composers – in short, because they are clichés.

How, then, does Debussy render natural phenomena in musical terms? First of all, we shall briefly examine 'Nuages', the first movement of the triptych *Nocturnes* (1892–9). Of course, Debussy's descriptive title points the listener towards a particular interpretation of the music. Perhaps it was relatively easy for Debussy to create an original musical response to this particular natural phenomenon, as few musical representations of clouds predate his movement. This is hardly surprising, as clouds do not produce a sound we can perceive and thus imitate; they are, arguably, things that painters can portray more easily than composers. But they move – they are blown by the wind, and they constantly change shape – and music is perhaps the only art form which can capture this essential feature of clouds.

So, Debussy's imaginative reproduction of clouds concentrates on their colour, shape and movement. Although music cannot suggest particular

Example 8.4 *Nocturnes*, 'Nuages' (bars 11–14)

colours in the absence of verbal cues, it can suggest the idea of a restricted palette of colour if listeners are prepared to accept orchestral timbres as analogies for visually perceived colours. The limited range of cloud colours is often evoked in this movement by the use of a single, uniform orchestral timbre: the string orchestra (as in Example 8.4). The generally low dynamic level of the movement enhances this deliberately monotonous colouristic range. Debussy uses shifting chords, usually in a homophonic texture, to portray the shape and movement of clouds, and, perhaps most importantly, his harmonic language is either modal and/or based on parallel triads. The use of explicitly tonal musical devices, such as cadence, was no doubt avoided because tonality is a goal-directed musical language, based on tension and resolution. As clouds do not move towards a specific goal, this choice would have been unsuitable.

The central section of 'Nuages' provides a brief colour contrast; as the timbres of the flute and of the harp in its middle or higher register are traditionally considered 'bright' colours, commentators on the movement are united in labelling this section a brief glimmer of light, before the 'cloud' material returns to close the movement. The pentatonic mode chosen for this section again lacks the goal-oriented quality of tonality. Overall, 'Nuages' could be considered a snapshot of nature in the sense that it is a composed picture in sound. At the same time, it is not a snapshot in the way that a pictorial composition would be, because this is unachievable in an art form that exists in time. Instead, it is an imaginative reproduction of a natural phenomenon in musical terms.

There are more potential pitfalls in the musical depiction of water, a subject to which Debussy turned time and time again. Not the least of these difficulties for the composer was surely the towering example of Wagner's prelude to *Das Rheingold*. That powerful and mesmerising depiction of the Rhine is entirely based on one chord: chord I in the key of E♭ major. The low notes in the opening bars of the prelude suggest the great depth of the water, and the arpeggiations of the triad, which constitute its essential musical material, convey a sense of movement and depict the wave-like currents of the water. This musical image may be powerful, but it is also an example of a traditional musical response to water imagery as it is based on the arpeggio.

In *La mer* Debussy avoids monotony by using a multitude of water figurations that could be classified as musical onomatopoeia: they evoke the sensation of the swaying movement of waves and suggest the pitter-patter of falling droplets of spray. It is interesting that the composer appears deliberately to avoid straightforwardly arpeggiated triads in his water figurations here. Every page of the score could be selected as a source of examples of water figurations; the first two bars of fig. 14 of the first movement, 'De l'aube à midi sur la mer' (Example 8.5), are an interesting, multi-layered example of the composer's technique. Each of the layers of this section is clearly distinct as each is given a different rhythm. This rhythmic density brings to mind the complex and constantly shifting movements of the sea. The quintuplet rhythm assigned to the first harp is a visual as well as musical representation of a small wave. Every individual line in this section features some kind of oscillating shape, and the dynamic swell in the second bar of Example 8.5 could again be interpreted as evocative of the movement of the sea. As in 'Nuages' the combination of specific descriptive titles and evocative musical figurations guides the listener to a particular interpretation of the music by encouraging him or her to compare the piece of music with his or her own experiences of the natural phenomenon being portrayed.

Conclusion

Debussy's approach to nature is essentially one of imaginative evocation, an evocation which centres on an idealised vision of a pure, untainted world in which living creatures either are absent or play an unimportant part. Imitations of living things were as unacceptable to Debussy as they were to artists working in the arabesque tradition of decoration; he preferred to evoke timeless natural phenomena such as the sea. Moreover, there is generally an absence of pathetic fallacy in Debussy's nature-based works, as he was a composer who saw himself as a conduit for the sounds of nature, who aimed to portray musically a 'correspondence between Nature and the Imagination' rather than use nature as a tool for the expression of human emotion. The titles of his works and individual movements that evoke natural phenomena demonstrate this. For instance, the title of the

Example 8.5 *La mer*, 'De l'aube à midi sur la mer' (fig. 14)

finale of *La mer* ('Dialogue du vent et de la mer') suggests that this is an *objective* portrayal of a storm at sea, not a Romantic vision of storm and stress reflecting the artist's state of mind. The sea, like all natural phenomena, simply *is*.

Debussy's love of music and love of nature were one and the same. He declared that he passionately loved music, 'and it is out of love for it that I try to release it from those sterile traditions which stifle it. It is a free, vibrant art, an open-air art, an art which measures up to the elements, to the wind, the sky, the sea! We must not turn it into a closed and academic art.'[21]

PART THREE

Musical techniques

9 Debussy's tonality: a formal perspective

BOYD POMEROY

Debussy as a tonal composer: reception and stylistic evolution

There are many possible ways to approach the question of Debussy's tonality, which over the last fifty years has inspired an unusually diverse range of critical and analytical viewpoints. The focus here will be on tonality's relationship with other aspects of formal process (especially thematic): how the nature of this relationship serves both to connect Debussy's music with earlier traditions of tonal composition and to set it apart from such traditions. First, though, we must consider the more fundamental issue of the music's status as *tonal* music: how Debussy adapted his inheritance of late Romantic chromatic tonality to the service of a modernist musical outlook and how the music expresses tonal function in an idiomatically Debussyan way.

As a preliminary observation we could note a striking divergence of perception between musical scholars (especially analysts) on the one hand and the listening public on the other, regarding Debussy's harmonic language or tonal practice in a general sense. While analysts have usually considered this aspect of Debussy's art to be rather problematic in the sense of abstruse, elusive or otherwise difficult to grasp (and hence to explain through analysis),[1] it would be fair to say that this perception has not been shared by concert audiences; on the contrary, Debussy remains one of the most enduringly popular composers of the post-Romantic era. Although there are many reasons for his music's evident accessibility, not least among them is surely its instantly identifiable tonal idiom or 'accent'. Debussy's tonality, while perennially new and exotic-sounding, yet retains powerful and familiar resonances from the tonal language of his predecessors; it exhibits a strong sense of tonal centre, expressed through vividly projected attributes of tonal function both melodically and harmonically.

Secondly, we might observe that Debussy's musical language always remained rooted in triadic consonance and the principle of monotonality.[2] In this respect the contrast with some other progressively oriented composers of the same period is indeed striking; one thinks, for instance, of the evolutionary paths pursued by Bartók and Skryabin (in their very different ways) from a late Romantic tonal language to their own, radically post-tonal brands of musical modernism.

In Debussy's case stylistic evolution rather entailed an ever greater refinement of principles established at a relatively early stage. The songs and piano music of what we might think of as his 'first period' (c. 1880–92) saw the consolidation of the formative elements of his tonal language: a chromatic tonality derived from late-Romantic practice, both French and Wagnerian, alongside a marked penchant for harmonic and tonal adventurism (during these years it was more pronounced in the songs *Ariettes (oubliées)*, *Cinq poèmes de Baudelaire*, and *Fêtes galantes*, series 1). Here Debussy's progressive tonal outlook is clearly evident in his fondness for juxtaposing remotely related chromatic regions with exotic-sounding uses of chromatic modality, and perhaps most of all in a characteristic penchant for certain non-diatonic pitch collections, especially the whole-tone and octatonic scales.[3]

In the works of his early maturity and subsequent 'middle period' (c. 1893, String Quartet; *Prélude à l'après-midi d'un faune* to 1909–12, *Préludes*, book 2; *Images* for orchestra), stylistic elements from the earlier period were distilled and refined towards a greater economy of means. With respect to tonal vocabulary, his middle-period music increasingly took on a certain quality of elliptical concision of tonal succession, involving both (diatonically based) tonal syntax and 'exotic', or colouristic harmonic elements. In particular, this period is characterised by a more seamless integration of symmetrical collections into the chromatic vocabulary generally.

Debussy's late music (c. 1913–17, *Jeux*, *Etudes*, chamber sonatas) shows simultaneous trends in what appear to be divergent directions: on the one hand a more refractory than ever approach to syntactical continuity of harmonic practice (as exemplified throughout *Jeux*, for instance, and movements such as 'Sérénade' from the Cello Sonata); on the other, the emergence of a new neoclassical simplicity (as in the first movement of the Violin Sonata and numerous passages throughout the *Etudes*).

Debussy's tonal practice: idiosyncratic features

Harmonic and melodic vocabulary
The tonic–dominant relation
One of the least traditional aspects of Debussy's tonal practice concerns his treatment of this fundamental harmonic relation, its radical transformation in some pieces and (real or apparent) conspicuous absence from others. For some analysts (most notably Richard S. Parks), this departure from earlier tonal norms effectively disqualifies Debussy's music from consideration as genuinely tonal.[4] While the point is well taken it is at least arguable that this represents less of a radical break with the tonal tradition than some have claimed. Historically, the I–V relation's centrality to compositional practice

had been steadily declining through much of the nineteenth century; the evolution, from Schubert to Liszt and beyond, of what eventually became a fully chromatic tonal system was distinguished (*inter alia*) precisely by its gradual shift away from fifth relations as the primary basis of composers' large-scale tonal structures in favour of an increasingly important role for third relations. Moreover, the principle of tonic–dominant polarity is arguably still operative in much of Debussy's music, albeit typically under the surface rather than as a salient feature of foreground (chord-to-chord) harmonic process. This is especially true of Debussy's longest, most elaborately developed forms, a topic to be returned to below.

Modality (diatonic)
In Debussy's mature style, while the traditional major/minor system continues to inform tonal identity on a large scale in whole pieces, or substantial, self-contained sections thereof, at the level of surface detail that system is often undermined by a prevalence of degrees of modal scales such that melodies and chord successions often resist traditional tonal classification. Some well-known instances are the oboe d'amore theme from 'Gigues' (bars 21ff. are Aeolian/Dorian; the tune's lack of a mode-defining sixth degree is characteristic), the main themes of 'Fêtes' (bars 29ff. are Mixolydian) and 'Sirènes' (bars 26ff. are Lydian), and the opening idea (*quasi guitarra*) of 'La sérénade interrompue' (Phrygian).[5]

Chromaticism
As further explored below, Debussy's music is distinguished by a highly individual fusion of fundamentally different kinds of chromaticism: tonally functional (that is, governed by the *syntactical* resolution tendencies of common-practice tonality) and non-functional (originating outside those tonal-syntactical constraints, and often collectional, e.g. whole tone and octatonic). Concerning chromaticism of the latter kind, its centrality to Debussy's tonal practice points to an important distinction of emphasis when comparing his chromatic usage to those of such post-Romantic contemporaries as Delius, Elgar, Sibelius and Strauss. Whereas collectional chromaticism is by no means uncommon with these composers – in the Strauss of *Salome* and *Elektra*, for instance, and much of the later Sibelius – it nevertheless remains a secondary, rather than primary, resource of the chromatic arsenal.

Non-functional diatonicism
In Debussy's diatonic writing the quality of harmonic goal-directedness, so crucially defining for earlier tonal styles, is often undermined through the characteristic presence of a (strictly non-functional) pentatonic patina (quite apart from its undermining by other factors, rhythmic and

phrase-structural, on which more below). For a good example of this, see the very beginning of *La mer*.

Chordal vocabulary

As often observed, Debussy's surface chord successions typically serve ends of colouristic effect rather than tonal-syntactical coherence. This is especially so with respect to the frequent presence of functionally 'superfluous' (non-resolving) chordal sevenths and ninths. In contrast to their explicitly syntactical role (that is, their stylistic and grammatical imperative to downward resolution, even if not directly realised in their immediate context) in common-practice tonal music, Debussy's chordal dissonances often (though by no means always) constitute static, colouristic embellishments of the basic triad. See, for example, bars 26ff. of 'Sirènes' (arrival of the tonic B major), where the chordal flat sevenths (A♮s), far from implying any kind of harmonic motion towards the subdominant, are strictly decorative.

Chordal syntax

In many cases Debussy's chordal successions are better understood as textural thickenings of the melodic line than as harmonic progressions in the traditionally accepted sense. This penchant for non-functional (organal) melodic doubling typically takes the form of parallel triads or open fifths. The triads can be in any position: root position, as in the opening ideas of *Préludes* 'Canope' and 'Brouillards' (cf. Example 9.2 below); first inversion, as in the opening woodwind theme of the prelude to *Le Martyre de Saint Sébastien*; or second inversion, as in the C major theme (bars 28ff.) from 'La cathédrale engloutie'. For an example of 'organal' doubling in open fifths, see the woodwind idea at bars 33–4 etc. of 'De l'aube à midi sur la mer'.

Arabesque and chord progression

Such a catalogue of unorthodox technical features can usefully point to *what* is different about Debussy's tonality, but does not go very far towards telling us *why*. To understand what makes such a tonality 'tick', the irregularities must be considered in the larger context of compositional aesthetics; specifically, Debussy's oft-expressed ideal of the kind of 'ornamental' melodic art he found in the music of Palestrina and Bach ('melodic arabesques, which create their effect through contour'[6]). In Debussy's own music, that ornamental conception finds its most characteristic form in harmonic inactivity, without the dimension of chord progression to distract from the 'curve' and 'contour' of the melodic arabesque. This harmonic inactivity typically extends to the level of the self-contained melodic phrase or thematic entity.

Several writers have observed a kinship between this aspect of Debussy's art and certain ornamental or decorative manifestations in the visual arts, particularly Art Nouveau.[7] One of the fundamental attributes of Art Nouveau is its appearance of irresistible decorative impulse to fill available space.[8] Debussy's thematic arabesques seem to obey a comparable impulse to fill registral space, in a combination of stepwise and relatively undulating disjunct motion (typically avoiding intervals larger than a fifth).[9] The pentatonic subset of the diatonic scale is inherently conducive to such registral-space filling; crucially lacking those very scale degrees ($\hat{4}$ and $\hat{7}$) indispensable to tonal definition by means of genuine harmonic progression, its true nature resides in decorative embellishment of the tonic triad.[10] For a classic example of the Debussyan pentatonic arabesque, see the above-mentioned woodwind theme from 'De l'aube à midi sur la mer' (bars 33–4).

Debussy's arabesques take many other forms besides pentatonicism: diatonic modality (cf. the modal themes cited above), including the major mode itself (as in the *sevillana* main theme of 'Par les rues et par les chemins', bars 8ff.), and chromatic. Chromatic arabesques often feature an admixture of totally chromatic scalar segments with whole-tone or octatonic elements; here, the *locus classicus* is the opening flute solo of *Prélude à l'après-midi d'un faune* (chromatic and whole tone). Pure whole-tone or octatonic arabesques are comparatively rare; for a pure octatonic example, see the long-breathed lyrical tune (oboe, solo viola) at bars 140ff. in 'Par les rues et par les chemins'. More typical is a seasoned blend of both collections, as in the horns' theme in octaves at bars 35ff. of 'De l'aube à midi sur la mer' (octatonic and whole-tone).

Debussy integrates such thematic ideas into larger formal sections via a characteristic technique whereby arabesque-like units, typically two bars in length, are combined through a chain-like process. This constructive technique is so prevalent as to constitute one of his most readily identifiable stylistic traits.[11] The units' identity as such is established by symmetrically balanced contrast and juxtaposition in factors such as motive, texture, and harmonic rhythm (also, of course, secondary parameters of instrumentation, dynamics and so forth); larger form is generated by the hierarchical chaining of units and their compounds. While such a pronounced emphasis on two-bar segments might seem unremarkable in itself, the technique's conjunction with the arabesque's characteristic quality of non-goal-directedness in the harmonic sphere adds up to a novel and distinctly twentieth-century approach to form generation.

This essentially additive approach to form building might be described as kaleidoscopic or block-like; it is possessed of a singular clarity of outline. (In this connection it is ironic that Debussy's forms have often been both criticised and praised for supposedly 'Impressionistic' or modernist tendencies to the very reverse of such clarity.) The technique enabled the construction of expansive thematic-presentational areas incorporating sufficient internal

Example 9.1(a) 'Pagodes' (bars 3–4)

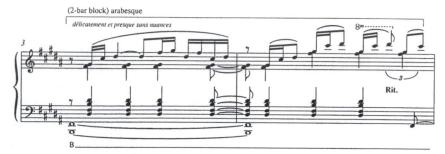

(b) 'Bruyères' (bars 8–10)

contrast without (necessarily) the component of harmonic progression. The point is well illustrated by the harmonically static D♭ major expanse in bars 31–42 of 'De l'aube à midi sur la mer', already discussed with respect to its thematic component parts.

Harmonic progression often appears as a slower-moving underlay to motivic arabesque-activity on the surface. Synchronisation of this harmonic underlay with the motivic symmetry of the 'two-bar block' technique results in a metrical (and hypermetric) regularity that again sits oddly with the notion of 'Impressionist' amorphousness. A classic example is the opening of 'Pagodes' (Example 9.1a). The size of Debussy's constructive 'blocks' is not invariably two bars; Example 9.1b shows its expansion to three in the main theme (bars 8ff.) of 'Bruyères', an expansive idea articulating a complete (I–ii^7–V^7–I, bars 8–14) progression before moving to a half-cadential dominant (this characteristic thematic type is further discussed below).

When the block technique serves an extended area of harmonic inactivity, as in the above-cited passage (bars 31–42) from 'De l'aube à midi sur la mer', harmonic progression sometimes takes the form of a distant undercurrent far beneath the surface. This is well illustrated by the same passage's larger context, a tonally open-ended formal section (bars 31–83) that eventually modulates from the movement's tonic (Db major) to the subdominant (Gb), the latter thematically articulated by the internal reprise (bar 68) of the section's opening material. Between the section's initial tonic and its long-range subdominant goal, an internal contrasting section (bars 47–67) articulates another static tonal area, the minor dominant (Ab minor).

Areas of harmonic inactivity often coexist with a highly chromatic musical surface, often of a whole-tone or octatonic orientation. Such collectional focus in the foreground attenuates harmonic-functional sense, which nevertheless still emerges at a higher level. A good illustration of this phenomenon is the extended octatonic area, over E in the bass, at bars 122ff. of 'Par les rues et par les chemins' (containing the oboe/viola theme mentioned above). On the surface harmonic function seems suspended for the duration, while the octatonic collection sustains an intricate motivic polyphony (the passage also shows how such harmonically inactive areas serve Debussy's penchant for motivic combination). But in its larger tonal context, the same passage plays a pivotal harmonic role: it relates both backwards, as a retroactively applied dominant to the preceding extended emphasis on A (= V/V, bars 90–121) and forwards in the role of supertonic relative to the following area of D (= V, bars 170ff.).

In contrast to the harmonically inert arabesque, another Debussyan thematic type is based on harmonic progression, most often of an open-ended (I–V or half-cadential) variety. Such themes invariably occupy the role of an opening or main theme, as in 'Bruyères' (bars 8–17); other examples include 'Danseuses de Delphes' (see below), 'Les collines d'Anacapri', 'Poissons d'or', 'Jeux de vagues' and 'Dialogue du vent et de la mer'. As in earlier tonal music, this thematic type is often associated with an actual or incipient antecedent-consequent period (cf. 'Les collines d'Anacapri' and 'Dialogue du vent et de la mer'). The complete I–V–I progression, as the harmonic basis of a thematic entity, is rare in Debussy; in the middle-period piano and orchestral works the nearest candidate is perhaps the dominant-key theme (bars 86ff.) in the sonata-like form of 'Fêtes'. Themes based on non-tonally-functional chromatic progressions are rarer still, a *sui generis* example being the march episode (Debussy's 'dazzling fantastic vision') that constitutes the middle section of the same piece.

Analytical approaches to Debussy's tonality: a selective survey

From a tonal perspective, existing analytical studies can be viewed as falling into two broad camps: accommodationist (of established tonal theories to

Debussy's idiosyncratic brand of tonality) and rejectionist (of the viability of any such accommodation).

Prominent in the first camp have been several attempts at a Schenkerian approach, with its emphasis on linear voice leading rather than the moment-to-moment identity of harmonic constructs. But although Schenker's influential theory of tonal music remains unrivalled in its explanatory depth and subtlety, its application or adaptation to any music outside Schenker's own select band of composers (from Bach to Brahms, more or less) – and especially to twentieth-century music – has always been highly controversial.[12] The first analysts to apply Schenkerian concepts to Debussy's music were two of Schenker's own pupils, Felix Salzer and Adele Katz. Though both are insightful and provocative, their approaches are quite different. Salzer liberally reformulates many of his teacher's basic precepts, in the process tending to blur Schenker's absolute distinction between consonance and dissonance, which Salzer justifies as reflecting twentieth-century stylistic realities.[13] Katz is, generally speaking, more reluctant to modify the original theory; as a result, her emphasis is much more on the unconventionality of Debussy's tonal practice compared to earlier composers.[14] While Katz restricts her analyses to short passages (from *Pelléas* and selected piano pieces), Salzer is more ambitious in his attempt to show the large-scale tonal coherence of whole pieces ('Bruyères') or large sections thereof (*Prélude à l'après-midi d'un faune*, bars 1–30).[15] But Katz goes further in her pursuit of a broader historical agenda, casting Debussy in the role of natural heir to Wagner in a tonal evolutionary process extending from Bach to the early twentieth century.[16]

By way of contrast, Werner Danckert approached Debussy's tonality from the perspective of harmonic function after Hugo Riemann's influential ideas on the ultimate reducibility of all chords to some form of tonic-, dominant-, or subdominant-functioned expression.[17] Danckert's analyses are less illuminating than those of Salzer and Katz, not because of any shortage of functional sense in the music itself, but rather on account of his literalistic, inflexible employment of the Riemannian apparatus in inappropriate chromatic contexts. Altogether more successful is Rudolph Réti's wide-ranging motivic study of 'La cathédrale engloutie', an ingenious analytical tour de force in the Schoenbergian tradition of thematic/motivic 'musical logic'.[18] More recently there have been a few attempts at a systematic explanatory synthesis of the music's dualistic basis in triadic tonality on the one hand and symmetrical collections on the other. Arnold Whittall, for example, explores ways in which Debussy expanded his legacy of Wagnerian tonality through absorption of a structural role for the whole-tone scale.[19]

Katz, having demonstrated a cogent post-Wagnerian tonal practice at work in some pieces, then turns to others (principally the *Préludes* 'Voiles' and 'Les tierces alternées') only to find a 'structural vagueness' resistant to her well-defined tonal criteria.[20] She concludes that Debussy, having first expanded the technical and expressive possibilities inherent in the old tonal system, ended up going beyond its natural limits. As for that perplexing 'structural vagueness', it will require nothing less than a (new) 'form of analysis to cope with the problems to which the new systems give rise'.[21]

One such 'new form of analysis' was eventually provided by pitch-class set theory, originally intended for music more obviously 'atonal' than Debussy's.[22] The most notable exponent of such an approach has been Richard S. Parks, who adapts the concept to Debussy's triadically based language by refracting it through four 'genera': diatonic, chromatic, whole-tone and octatonic.[23] The resultant analyses capture well one of Debussy's most salient compositional traits, namely his penchant for kaleidoscopic contrasts of certain kinds of diatonic and chromatic pitch resources in block-like juxtaposition. But while the set-theoretical approach can hardly be criticised for failing to address issues that lie beyond its scope, it must be said that its drastic negation of tonality results in a somewhat one-dimensional picture.

Large-scale form in Debussy's instrumental music

Most of the copious literature on this subject has been more concerned with Debussy's supposed formal radicalism than with uncovering any underlying connections to earlier traditions. Indeed, to assert their existence to any significant degree implies a substantial revisionism of much prevailing critical wisdom. The view of Debussy as a proto-avant-gardist owes much to the Darmstadt serialists of the post-war period, who in retrospect seem to have been intent on reinventing Debussy after their own image, with such concepts as 'statistical form' (Stockhausen) and 'vegetative circulation of the form' (Herbert Eimert).[24] Another commonly encountered view is that Debussy's forms somehow exemplify the antithesis of a typically 'Germanic' aesthetic of 'developmental' form. This line of argument is well represented by Edward Lockspeiser:

> Thematic or harmonic development, in the form of a musical argument ruthlessly pursued, demands a firmer, less ambiguous harmonic structure, and it was no doubt for this reason that Debussy particularly mistrusted musical development as a method of composition.[25]

(Boulez, on the other hand, speaks of Debussy's '[overthrowing of] not so much the art of development as the very concept of form itself'.[26])

Debussy's most favoured formal design, which he employed with inexhaustible variety, was ternary (A–B–A') form, whose fundamental attribute is the presence of a contrasting middle section followed by a thematic/tonal reprise of the first part. While the possibilities for varying such an elementary scheme are obviously practically limitless, the most basic distinction among sub-types is harmonic, concerning the tonal destination of the form's first part (A section): closed (first part ending in the tonic followed by a middle section in a tonally contrasting area) versus open (first part ending off-tonic, either by way of modulation to another key or simply on a non-tonic chord). Some examples of the first (closed) type are the *Préludes* 'La cathédrale engloutie', 'La puerta del vino', and 'Général Lavine – eccentric', and the *Nocturnes* 'Nuages' and 'Sirènes'. An example of the second (open) type is 'Danseuses de Delphes', further discussed below. On a larger scale some orchestral representatives of the open type feature the expansion of their (modulating) first part into a sonata-like exposition incorporating both the (I–V) tonal polarity and thematic duality characteristic of that form: see 'Fêtes', 'Jeux de vagues', and 'Par les rues et par les chemins'.

Another important Debussyan formal type is cyclic or rotational form, which involves the recurrence of an established sequence of material. An outstanding example is the *Prélude* 'Des pas sur la neige', with its obsessive duality of a three-note diatonic ostinato (D–E–F) juxtaposed with incursions into ever more distant chromatic regions. On other occasions the result is a rondo-like form, as in 'Brouillards' (see below) and 'Dialogue du vent et de la mer'.

A further category could be characterised as through-composed, broadly defined as a continuously developing form, lacking both ternary form's overriding symmetry of reprise process and cyclic form's regular alternation of material. A good example of this type is the fantasia-like form of 'Les sons et les parfums tournent dans l'air du soir', analysed below; others include 'Jardins sous la pluie', 'Ondine', 'De l'aube à midi sur la mer', and 'Les parfums de la nuit'.

Debussy's forms correspond most significantly to traditional tonal models less in the realm of their overall design, or the lower-level details of such, than in the kinds of dynamic musical *process* that constitute the life-blood of our experience of musical form: that is to say, the various kinds of *formal function* expressed by the form's constituent parts.[27] As in earlier tonal music such function is articulated through thematic and motivic processes in the context of open and closed harmonic structures; similarly, the overall form arises from large-scale harmonic tensions and contrasts. Furthermore, the radical surface novelty of Debussy's music often conceals a more fundamental (harmonic or voice-leading) structural basis remarkably reminiscent of earlier tonal music. Lower-level formal processes are likewise articulated by form-functional phenomena of a traditional nature: for example, those of cadential closure or half-cadential caesura; thematic constructs such as the antecedent–consequent period; motivic processes of development, frag-mentation and so forth. They are always creatively transformed in an id-iomatically Debussyan way.

Tonal-structural diversity in the *Préludes*

The two books of *Préludes* make excellent case studies on account of this hybrid genre's restricted dimensions and formal concision. They can serve to illustrate a diverse assortment of idiomatically Debussyan tonal and formal techniques, from those most reminiscent of traditional tonal practice to some of his furthest departures from that practice. This characteristic tonal-structural diversity could usefully be conceived in terms of a hypothetical continuum along which the relative position of individual *Préludes* would be indicative of the extent of traditional tonal practice operative in a given piece. Those least traditional would occupy the left end of such a continuum, those most traditional the right:

>   post-tonal *Préludes*
>   *Préludes* of non-functional triadic basis
>   *Préludes* with substantially developed tonal structures

Criteria for classification of *Préludes* along such lines could be defined as follows:[28]

> *Préludes* of non-triadic structural basis
> *Préludes* of triadic structural basis, exhibiting an (almost always) clearly defined tonic, but lacking in certain features traditionally associated with normative tonal forms (such as a structural dominant)[29]
> *Préludes* exhibiting fully formed tonal structures (structural tonic–dominant relations; linear and harmonic elaborative techniques reminiscent of earlier tonal music)

In fact only one *Prélude* ('Voiles') meets the criterion for inclusion in the 'left' group as defined above. In its explicit negation of tonal reference, stemming from the outer sections' drastic restriction of pitch-class content to a single transposition of the whole-tone scale, this *Prélude* is paradigmatic for Debussy's furthest extreme of post-tonal practice.[30] As a compositional experiment in pitch-class restriction it occupies a unique place in Debussy's output. More representative are the three *Préludes* analysed below, from the 'left' end of the hypothetical continuum's middle group ('Brouillards') through the 'right' end of that group ('Les sons et les parfums tournent dans l'air du soir') to the 'right' group itself ('Danseuses de Delphes').

Example 9.2 'Brouillards' (bar 1)

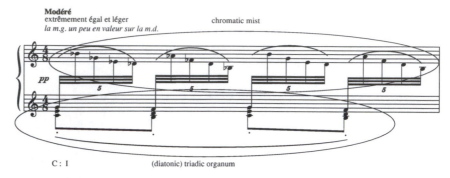

Three *Préludes*
'Brouillards'

In its triadic, albeit non-functional structural basis, 'Brouillards' is more representative of Debussy's 'modernist' practices than 'Voiles'. The identity of the *Prélude*'s tonic is not in doubt, but that identity is defined to an unusual extent by non-tonally-functional means.

The piece is a study in texture; specifically of the sonorous and textural possibilities arising from a continuous opposition of independent 'white key' and 'black key' materials: an 'organal' procession of diatonic triads circling around the tonic, set against faster-moving chromatic figuration, doggedly shadowing the triads in the same register (Example 9.2). As a result, the *Prélude*'s tonic of C major appears shrouded in a continuous chromatic haze or mist ('brouillard'). The chromatic mist obscures not only the clarity of individual diatonic triads, but also the outlines of larger-scale tonal relations, which consequently take on a somewhat unreal, disembodied quality. In addition to these more localised effects, the pervasive tonal mist has longer-range ramifications for the identity of the tonic triad itself, which motivates a process that hinges on its chromatic/common-tone transformation to other triads, thus: C major–C♯ minor (sharing E♮ as common third); C major–C minor (sharing C and G as common root and fifth).

The *Prélude*'s form is rondo-like:

A (bars 1–9)–B (10–17)–A′ (18–28)–C (29–37)–A″ (38–end)

Despite the music's largely non-functional surface, this formal process is nonetheless characterised by an alternation of tonic (A sections) and dominant (B and C sections) triadic emphasis. Furthermore, skeletal tonal processes operate internally within sections. The A section manifests an elementary skeletal harmonic basis in a I–V–I progression, the I–V motion

Example 9.3 'Brouillards' (bars 35–6)

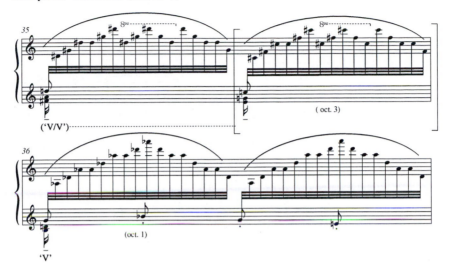

filled in by the traditional tonal gesture of a fourth-descent in the bass from tonic to dominant (bars 3–4). The C section is underpinned by a large-scale applied-dominant progression: D (= V/V, bars 32–5) to G (= V, bars 36–7); see Example 9.3. While this applied-V relation is underscored by the section's formal design of parallel phrases, its harmonic identity is drastically attenuated by the music's relentlessly dissonant surface overlay (octatonic, on which more below), illustrating the earlier point concerning the chromatic mist's 'disembodying' effect on tonal relations.[31]

As mentioned above, the form's recurring 'A' sections emphasise the tonic. The two thematic reprises of this material are prefixed by a motive in octaves (bars 18 and 38; see Example 9.4) of a mysterious character; it is tonally ambiguous at its outset as on both occasions the motive follows directly on from an extended orientation to the dominant (G), so its opening pitches C♯–D–G initially seem to relate to that context (Example 9.4). The motive expands chromatically to settle on a C♯ minor triad,[32] the effect of which is one of reorientation to a familiar object (the tonic triad) that had been lost sight of in the mist and now reappears in a strangely (chromatically) dislocated guise.

This effect of tonal dislocation is temporary, for on both occasions the 'C♯' motive gives way to the familiar, chromatically misted C major (see Example 9.2). The final C♯–C juxtaposition (bars 41–3) motivically highlights the common-tone aspect of this chromatic triad-relation: E♮, first as minor third of C♯, then as major third of C, audibly plays the role of mediator between the two triads.[33]

Example 9.4 'Brouillards' (bars 38–40)

Example 9.5 'Brouillards' (bars 46–8)

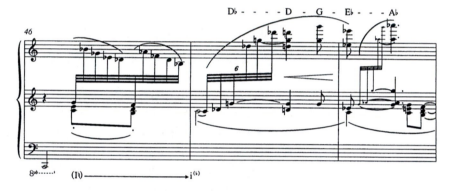

The end invokes the other triad-transformation referred to at the outset: C major–C minor (see Example 9.5). Now the relation between tonic triad and its chromatic derivatives is quite literally spelled out: bars 47–8 are an ingenious enharmonic resetting of bars 38–9 whereby chromatic alteration of triadic context (C♯–C) transforms the scale-degree referentiality of the same succession of pitches thus:

		C♯	D	G	D♯	G♯
bars 38–9	C#	$\hat{1}$	♭$\hat{2}$	♯$\hat{4}$	$\hat{2}$	$\hat{5}$
bars 47–8	C	♭$\hat{2}$	$\hat{2}$	$\hat{5}$	♭$\hat{3}$	♭$\hat{6}$
		D♭	D	G	E♭	A♭

Although traditional tonal techniques are largely (though not completely) absent from 'Brouillards', the tonic triad itself – its identity and transformations – nevertheless remains central to the piece's idiosyncratic tonal and formal process.[34]

Much of the chromaticism in 'Brouillards' invokes symmetrical collections, in this case octatonic rather than whole-tone. In the recurring A sections, octatonicism arises as a by-product of some white-key/black-key combinations (as at the very opening) but not others (bar 4, for example). The B section is not octatonic at all; the C section, on the other hand (including the spectacular *Petrushka* burst of bars 29–30), is conspicuously octatonic for its entire duration, prominently emphasising all three collections (Example 9.3 shows two of these).[35] Although octatonicism contributes much to this *Prélude*'s distinctive soundworld, its role is less tonally focused than in some other *Préludes*, where one octatonic transposition (collection) is closely identified with a specific tonal function (particularly that of tonic). We will encounter a good example of this in 'Les sons et les parfums tournent dans l'air du soir', analysed below.

'Danseuses de Delphes'

This counterpart to 'Brouillards' (as the opening *Prélude*) in Book 1 represents the 'right' end of our tonal continuum: a beautifully clear ternary form, tonally organised along traditional lines in its large-scale basis in tonic–dominant polarity:

sections   A   B   A'
        I–   V   (V–)   I   (V–I)

The A section (bars 1–5, which are repeated with some textural variation), based on a I–II–V progression, presents one of Debussy's half-cadential themes, as discussed earlier.[36] In stark contrast to 'Brouillards', the music exhibits a remarkable, almost Classical translucence of tonal syntax, both harmonic and linear (Example 9.6). Note the beautifully protracted elaboration of the tonic chord through slow chromatic lines that fill in its constituent thirds: Bb–D, inner voice (bars 1–3), which is then transferred to the bass (bars 3–4) while the inner voice doubles at the upper tenth.

Example 9.6 'Danseuses de Delphes': foreground graph (bars 1–5)

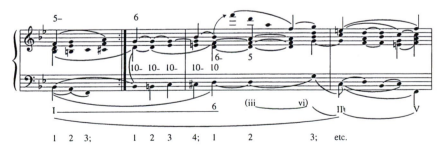

Example 9.7 'Danseuses de Delphes': B section, middleground graph (bars 5–10)

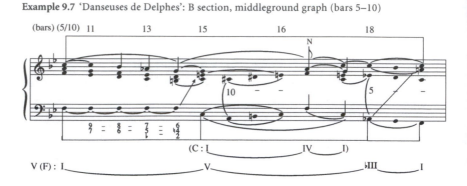

Observe, in particular, Debussy's treatment of the bass version of this motive, whose rhythmic expansion to crotchets leads to the music's temporary overspilling of its metrical confines (bar 4, where the bass D's displacement from the first to the second crotchet necessitates a temporary stretching of the metre from triple to quadruple).[37]

The B section (bars 11–20) then extends the half-cadential dominant from the end of the first part. Compared to the first part, the music here is less susceptible to a detailed tonal explanation; note, in particular, how the new pentatonic descant introduced in bar 11 serves to cast a diatonic haze over proceedings: another good example of Debussy's non-functional diatonicism as discussed above. Even so, the section coheres as a tonal whole through its middleground 'backbone' (see Example 9.7), a descending arpeggiation of the dominant chord coloured by chromatic alteration of its chordal third (Ab, bar 18) and incorporating, en route, a leisurely detour by way of its own dominant, C (= V/V, bars 15–17).

Bars 21–4 present a curious situation, a formal 'no man's land' between the end of the dominant-based middle section (bar 20) and the onset of the A′ section (bar 25). While the tonic appears to return in bar 21, it is not accompanied by a thematic reprise of the first part (rather, its motivic content continues that of the preceding dominant; cf. Example 9.8, motive 'x'); when this occurs later in bar 25, it effectively upstages the earlier tonic (in addition to the thematic return, note the imposing effect of the bass's entrance on bottom Bb). Meanwhile, a rising idea (bars 23–4) effects a form-functional gesture of 'lead-in' to the 'official' reprise – but a lead-in from what? Not the earlier tonic, whose very presence would render the gesture quite redundant; by the same token, not the preceding dominant, which the first tonic has already effectively superseded. All in all, the passage might well appear to be a prime candidate for the 'structural vagueness' that Katz found in certain other *Préludes*.

Example 9.8 'Danseuses de Delphes' (bars 21–27, beat 1)

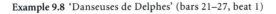

The thematic reprise itself is radically foreshortened to a mere two bars, followed by a codetta-like cadential reiteration. While such abbreviation of the ternary reprise section is quite characteristic of Debussy, this *Prélude* takes the technique to an extreme, in the process running the risk of un-balancing the formal edifice. That no such impression (of formal imbal-ance) arises is perhaps in large part due to the abbreviated reprise's tonal pre-empting in the preceding 'no man's land', the role of whose seemingly premature or redundant tonic is thus retrospectively clarified. (If the idea seems dubious, try playing or imagining the piece without bars 21–4.)

Structural closure, while implicit in the V–I progressions of bars 25–6ff., is attenuated through their non-diatonic format; instead of providing struc-tural melodic resolution (2̂–1̂; C–B♭), Debussy's retention of the chromatic second degree (C♯) produces V chords of augmented quality, whose tonic resolution (C♯–D) rather emphasises scale-degree 3̂ (see example 9.8). This melodic focus on the chordal third sustains to the end the floating or hov-ering quality that seems to permeate the entire *Prélude*, invoking a cer-tain quality of detached remoteness about the Delphic dancers' ritualised steps, as if too strong a melodic resolution would puncture that elaborately maintained distance.

Example 9.9 'Les sons et les parfums tournent dans l'air du soir' (bars 1–6)

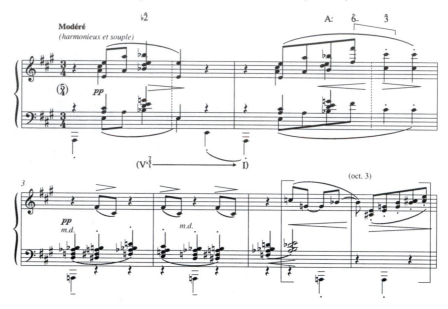

In 'Danseuses de Delphes' chromaticism is in large part, though by no means entirely, accountable to tonal function; it is characterised by its resolution-dependence on diatonic scale degrees. Although chords of whole-tone quality appear frequently, their chromatic elements nonetheless tend to resolve to consonant triad members (as in the 'augmented' V–I cadences just discussed).

In both *Préludes* analysed so far, the distinction between functional and non-functional kinds of chromaticism appears relatively clear-cut. The next analysis will focus on a more elusive and characteristically Debussyan use of chromaticism that seems to transcend such a hard-and-fast distinction by partaking of significant qualities from both categories.

'Les sons et les parfums tournent dans l'air du soir'

The *Prélude*'s main thematic idea (bars 1–2) introduces three principal motivic components in turn (see Example 9.9, which shows part of the opening section): (1) the rising melodic fourth E–A; (2) chromatic embellishment of the tonic (A major) triad by 'Phrygian' scale degree ♭2 (along with its supporting bass, E, suggestive of a heavily altered V^7); (3) the falling-fourth motive F♯–C♯ (bar 2), outlining the scale-degree succession $\hat{6}$–$\hat{3}$.

The next formal segment (bars 3–8) is highly chromatic; it is unified by its gravitation around a prevailing harmony, the seventh chord A–C♯–E–G, which in structural terms represents the addition of a dissonant seventh to the initial stable tonic triad (see Example 9.10, a reduction showing the opening section's underlying voice-leading basis). On the surface, chromaticism

Example 9.10 'Les sons et les parfums tournent dans l'air du soir': opening section, middleground graph

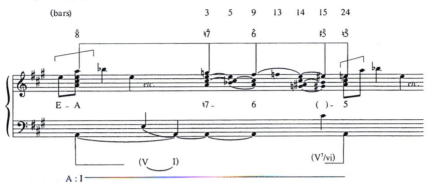

now takes on a strongly octatonic flavour using collection 3,[38] which predominates in bar 5, beat 2 to bar 8; this new chromatic perspective finds motivic expression in a new transposition (C–G) of the falling-fourth motive (see Example 9.9). Notice, though, that the octatonic collection in question – represented by the diminished seventh chord on C♯ together with C♮ and the bass pedal A – is slightly, but crucially, diluted through the presence of a 'foreign' pitch, A♭, which Debussy retains from the preceding B♭[7] chord (bar 5, beat 1).[39]

In bars 9–12 the underlying harmony changes again, to an F♯ minor 6/3 chord (which thus provides downward resolution of the preceding section's sustained emphasis on the dissonant seventh, G; see Example 9.10). While F♯ is itself embellished by its chromatic neighbours E♯ and G, the melody insists upon D♯ (see bars 9ff.), which results in another new chromatic perspective, now whole-tone. Tonal focus is tantalisingly elusive in these four bars: while the 'whole-tone' chords of bars 9, 11, etc. are clearly of embellishing status vis-à-vis the passage's triadic basis in F♯ minor, the melodic D♯s serve to undermine both that local context and the larger (A major) one.

In reaction to this passage of tonal ambiguity, the next segment (bars 13–23) effects a decisive change of tonal reference away from A to the dominant of F♯ (major, by implication). This transformation serves to assimilate those hitherto anomalous-sounding D♯s, now contextualised as the upper note of a '9–8' appoggiatura motive (bars 16ff.). As in bars 3–8, the passage's prevailing harmony (the C♯[7] chord) is octatonically enhanced, through a return of the same collection as before (i.e. collection 3; see bars 19, 21–3). This octatonic collection thus plays a mediating role between the tonal regions of A (bars 1–8) and F♯ (bars 15–23; unstated as a local tonic, but powerfully suggested by virtue of the sustained emphasis on its dominant).

Bars 24–6 return to the tonic in an internal reprise of the opening material. The return is accomplished via a sudden reorientation of the octatonic collection to its original tonal context of A major, thus graphically 'fore-grounding' the collection's mediating role (bars 24, bcats 1–2).

To summarise, the *Prélude*'s opening section chromatically elaborates a well-defined tonic (A), incorporating a modulatory excursion to a contrasting tonal region (F♯). On the surface the kaleidoscopically changing chromatic contexts cohere through their common grounding in the tonic pedal together with Debussy's exploitation of the octatonic collection's potential for double tonal meaning. At a deeper level the successive formal segments are bound together through a slowly descending line in the upper voice: A–G–F♯–E♯(F)–E (see Example 9.10; note how this chromatically filled fourth parallels on a large scale the (E–A) fourth-motive announced at the outset). Most remarkably this rather elaborate tonal edifice is built entirely without recourse to harmonic progression of any kind.

The remainder of the *Prélude* presents a highly unusual design, whose improvisatory tonal freedom is curiously reminiscent of an earlier keyboard genre, the eighteenth-century fantasia. Like many of those pieces (C. P. E. Bach, Haydn, Mozart), the form is articulated by various new settings of the opening thematic material separated by modulatory linking passages.

In bar 27 the music is suddenly plunged into flat tonal regions brought about by the falling-fourth motive's enharmonic transformation from F♯–C♯ (bar 26, in its familiar setting as $\hat{6}$–$\hat{3}$ in A major) to G♭–D♭ (see Example 9.11).[40] Initially contextualised as $\hat{4}$–$\hat{1}$ in D♭ major (bass, bar 27), the motive then migrates back to its customary upper-voice setting, where it appears transposed to scale degrees $\hat{3}$–$\hat{7}$ (F–C) in that key. D♭, however, turns out to be the subdominant of A♭ major in which key the fourth-motive's new transposition (F–C) can now revert to its more familiar diatonic-referential setting of $\hat{6}$–$\hat{3}$ (bars 28–9). A♭'s status as a temporarily stable tonic is then confirmed by means of a new cadential idea, elaborating a ii⁶–V–I progression which in turn forms the culmination of an improvisational sequence on the fourth-motive, now set against a chromatic bass (bars 29–31, Example 9.11).[41] Thus in the space of an eventful few bars we have journeyed to the region of ♭I (!); moreover, this extravagantly flat tonal realm is afforded the luxury of an elaborately prepared cadential progression, something conspicuously denied the tonic itself in the course of the long opening section.

However, no sooner is A♭ major convincingly established as a local tonic than it is unceremoniously 'corrected' back to A major in a sequential repetition that hinges on the abrupt chromatic transposition of triads on the raised seventh degrees of the respective keys (bars 35–7): G(=A♭:$\hat{7}$)–G♯(=A:$\hat{7}$).[42] But A major proves transient in turn when arrival on its mediant, C♯ (bar 42), turns downward to arpeggiate the triad of F♯ major, in which key the main

Example 9.11 'Les sons et les parfums tournent dans l'air du soir' (bars 26–31)

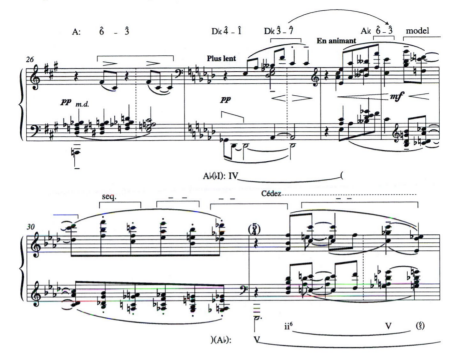

thematic idea now reappears (bar 45; see Example 9.12), thus providing long-delayed fulfilment of that key's strong suggestion in the *Prélude*'s first part (bars 15ff.; cf. Example 9.13 below).

The appearance of F♯ major provides the cue for a return of octatonicism, conspicuously absent from these intervening developments. Once again it takes the form of collection 3, the *Prélude*'s 'home' octatonic collection, now producing a new 'diminished' harmonisation of the Phrygian motive (bar 46, Example 9.12). As in the opening section, octatonicism provides the link between the tonal areas F♯ and A, this time in a modulatory sequence via a different octatonic collection (collection 1), see bars 46–7, Example 9.12. With the return of A major (this time rendered definitive by renewed conjunction with the 'home' octatonic collection), the stage is at last set for tonal resolution in the form of a reprise, in the tonic, of the (A♭ major) cadential idea from bar 31. Arrived at by way of so many delays and detours, this cadential reprise (bar 50) thus both provides long-distance tonal resolution of that earlier chromatic episode and parallels on a large formal scale the local ♭I–I resolution of bars 33–8 (Example 9.13). At the same time it finally supplies the tonal ingredient missing from the opening section, a structural harmonic progression in the tonic.

Example 9.12 'Les sons et les parfums tournent dans l'air du soir' (bars 42–51)

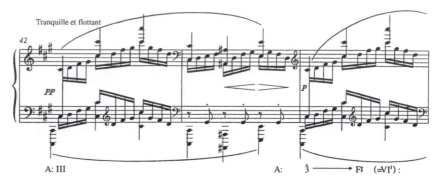

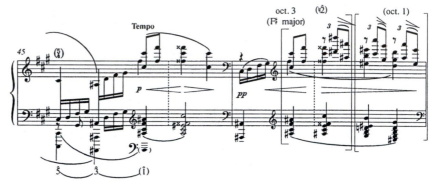

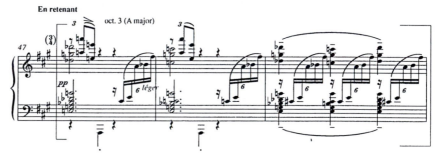

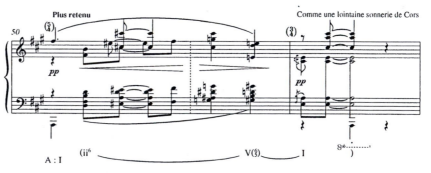

Example 9.13 'Les sons et les parfums tournent dans l'air du soir': whole piece, bass-line sketch

Formal expansion: piano triptychs, orchestral music

The above analyses have highlighted a few facets of the rich tonal-structural diversity found in these two books of *Préludes*, from tonal forms of a decidedly traditional cast ('Danseuses de Delphes') to radically modernist departures from that tradition ('Brouillards') in which the tonic triad nevertheless remains the central focus of tonal/formal process.

To conclude, a few remarks on Debussy's longer tonal forms are in order. The pieces comprising the middle-period piano triptychs, the *Estampes*, and *Images*, series 1 and 2, are typically more expansive in scale than the *Préludes*. The tonal forms encountered here constitute more elaborately developed counterparts to *Préludes* from both ends of our hypothetical continuum, from conspicuously modernistic essays, 'Mouvement', 'Cloches à travers les feuilles', 'Et la lune descend sur le temple qui fut', to pieces that feature a degree of tonal-structural elaboration far beyond that found in any of the *Préludes*: 'La soirée dans Grenade', 'Jardins sous la pluie', 'Reflets dans l'eau', 'Hommage à Rameau', 'Poissons d'or'.

In the middle-period orchestral pieces, from *Prélude à l'après-midi d'un faune* to the *Images*, we find Debussy's most elaborately developed tonal forms. To cite but one telling symptom of this greatly increased tonal-formal scope, compared to both the *Préludes* and the piano triptychs all the individual movements here (with the exceptions of 'Nuages' and 'Par les rues et par les chemins') begin off-tonic with an extended introductory section that elaborates a non-tonic chord or tonal region, from which the piece's tonic is approached circuitously – through the back door, so to speak. In 'De l'aube à midi sur la mer', for instance, the tonic eventually arrives via a large-scale progression from the flat side, formally occupying an opening section of slow-introduction function: *Très lent*: iv/IV(B)–iv(f♯) to the first main section, *Modéré, sans lenteur*, bar 31: I(D♭). For the orchestral music, the tonal-continuum concept is no longer applicable, as every movement would take a place on the extreme right.

In keeping with the progressive artistic spirit of the new century, Debussy succeeded in forging elements from the tonal practice of his predecessors into something radically new. At the same time, his tonal language, even at its least orthodox, never loses sight of the traditional principles that ultimately give it meaning. In Debussy's music, tonal and formal processes continue to interrelate in ways not so fundamentally different from the tonal masterpieces of the preceding two centuries. To the extent that so vital an engagement with the tonal tradition went hand in hand with the creation of such strange and wonderful new sound-worlds, whose vivid modernity remains undimmed at the turn of another century, his achievement was perhaps unique.

10 The Debussy sound: colour, texture, gesture

MARK DEVOTO

Everyone who knows Debussy's music recognises a distinctive 'Debussy sound' that is not a single quality but many; the sound of Debussy's style in most of his works is harmony, instrumentation, texture, timbre, all to a greater or lesser extent.

Even such wide-ranging elements as melody, rhythm, and microform affect Debussy's quality of sound. The composer Jean Barraqué, an astute analyst, spoke of Debussy's habit of repeating phrases and phrase fragments in immediate succession as 'the sole weakness that one might find in Debussy's scores',[1] without suggesting that this kind of repetition is a fundamental aspect of Debussy's sense of form; paired repetition, like breathing (which as a marker of time it somewhat resembles), is a trait of many composers from Vivaldi to Mozart to Rossini to Debussy; but in combination with others that we think of as characteristically sonorous, it is a trait that makes Debussy's style instantly recognisable even on first hearing.

Here we will discuss the sonorous rather than the temporal aspects of Debussy's music, focusing particularly on orchestral and piano style, texture, and colour, recognising that these aspects often penetrate each other as much as they are components of overall form.

Debussy's earliest instrumental style

Debussy's earliest piano pieces and songs include a variety of different piano styles and textures, but nothing that is markedly different from those of his French contemporaries or from his Parisian predecessor Chopin, for whose music he always had a special understanding and regard. Accompanimental textures in Debussy's songs of his Conservatoire years are more economical than in Fauré's of the same time, and for that reason they are often more effective. The Piano Trio of 1880, which Debussy did not publish, is the first of his works in which we can glimpse an instrumental style in addition to that already developing for the piano, but even though the ensemble always works well, again there is no notably original pianism.

The *Deux arabesques* of 1888–91 still echo Chopin's influence but reveal more imagination and skill than Debussy had shown earlier, plus a remarkable mastery of complex diatonic harmony well regulated by classical progressions and bass lines. Idiosyncratic touches also appear, of which the most important is the parallel harmony with octaves between upper and lower voices at the end of *Arabesque* No. 2; this is even more striking in the song 'Chevaux de bois', composed at about the same time. Such parallel writing was not without occasional precedent in the nineteenth century; part of the Finale of Berlioz's *Symphonie fantastique*, with melody in three octaves and lacking only parallel fifths, is a clear example that startles even today. Debussy made this kind of parallel writing a persistent trademark all the way to his last completed work, the Violin Sonata.

The Symphony in B minor for piano four hands dates from 1881, one of Debussy's summers in Russia when he was discovering the music of Tchaikovsky. Even without any indications of orchestral instruments, it is not hard to imagine functions in this piece that would reflect Tchaikovsky's music or contemporary French scores by composers such as Bizet, Delibes and Lalo that Debussy would surely have heard. A more distinctive orchestral style is perceptible in the earliest available of Debussy's orchestral scores, *L'enfant prodigue*, and we know how much Debussy revised it before publishing it in 1908. Its orientalism *à la Lakmé* has been called facile, but there is no denying its skill; Debussy would hardly have wasted his time during the composition of the required Prix de Rome cantata behind locked doors on such an extensive orchestral episode as the 'Cortège et air de danse' (nearly twenty pages of score) if the piece had not captured his imagination. In the case of *Printemps*, composed in 1887, we have an even less precise idea of Debussy's original orchestration, because the score as published (1913) was re-orchestrated by Henri Busser from Debussy's directions, the original with chorus having been lost. (Busser's re-orchestration dispenses with the wordless female chorus Debussy had included in the lost score of the earlier version. In 1913, having already demonstrated this novel tactic in 'Sirènes' of 1899, Debussy apparently had no desire to show it again.[2])

The heterophonic orchestra

La damoiselle élue, for soprano and alto soloists, female chorus and orchestra, was completed in 1889 (five years after *L'enfant prodigue*); the *Fantaisie* for piano and orchestra followed a short while later. These two neglected works of Debussy's first years independent from the constraints of the Prix de Rome are quite distinct from each other in narrative and expressive character, but one finds in both an orchestral style that is fully formed and mature – an early maturity then with a number of trademarks that were to be extensively developed and ripened in Debussy's later works. The most important of these I refer to here as the 'heterophonic orchestra'.

'Heterophony' is a term variously applied to different musical phenomena, but perhaps most often it is encountered in descriptions of non-Western instrumental music, where it means the *simultaneous* variants of a given melody, often ornamented and improvised on by two or more players. We will use the term here somewhat more freely to cover the general complexity and rapid colouristic changes of Debussy's textures, as well as his tendency to blur the melodic line, but at the same time to strengthen it with added ornamentation in mixed timbres. In Debussy's heterophonic orchestra several qualities typically stand out:

1. Primarily soft dynamics in a texture spread over a wide range; predilection for upper register of the strings in soft textures
2. Divided strings in multiple doublings from *à* 2 to *à* 6, in parallel or in maximally different rhythms, often with bowed and plucked notes at the same time; often with embellished arpeggiation of a single harmony
3. Woodwind and brass layers in harmonic doublings, with or without the strings, often in different simultaneous patterns or figurations
4. The principal melodic line doubled in one or more octaves either within or between instrumental choirs; preference for woodwind solos in the melodic line
5. Varied orchestral emphasis of the harmonic background, less often of the contrapuntal line

Divided strings, such as one encounters at the start of *La damoiselle élue* (see Example 10.1), are typical of the Debussy's heterophonic orchestra, but of course he had plenty of predecessors. The 'Forest murmurs' in *Siegfried* is perhaps the closest antecedent among Wagner's works; in this well-known episode the first and second violins are each divided in four, both layers oscillating uniformly between a single harmony and its auxiliary chord, while divided violas and cellos sustain single notes in harmonics. The Act I Prelude to *Lohengrin* uses divided and solo violins to explore ethereal upper-register sound. In the *Liebesnacht* scene in Act II of *Tristan und Isolde*, during Brangäne's call, the *pianissimo* muted strings are elaborately divided and differently textured, but melodic and registral differences in the strings are submerged in a blanket of wind sound, very rich but without much delicate coloration – not much like Debussy's heterophony.

It is possible that Debussy's image of soft *divisi* strings was inspired more by his forebears in France than by Wagner's examples in *Tristan* and *The Ring*. The 'Queen Mab' Scherzo in Berlioz's *Roméo et Juliette*, in which both first and second violins are marked *divisi* from beginning to end, seems to be an obvious model, and its remarkable use of harmonics is also one of the earliest in the standard repertory; Berlioz, for his part always

Example 10.1 *La damoiselle élue*, string parts only (bar 4)

passionate about Shakespeare, doubtless admired the elfin string textures (unmuted!) in Mendelssohn's Overture to *A Midsummer Night's Dream*. Another possible influence is Lalo's orientalist ballet *Namouna*, premiered in 1883 and cheered enthusiastically by the nineteen-year-old Debussy.[3] The Prelude to *Namouna* is marked by a complex and glittering string *divisi* clearly inspired by the Rainbow bridge scene in *Das Rheingold*, but the dreamy *dolce far niente*, with its muted strings, atmospheric pedal points, and parallel fifths with paired cors anglais adumbrates Debussy's orchestra as does no other work of its time.

The decade after *La damoiselle élue* represents Debussy's most intense period of artistic growth, marked by his primary focus on orchestral music and opera. His two years of effort (1890–2) in composing Catulle Mendès's *Rodrigue et Chimène* fizzled out, but the attempt sharpened his skills for the next one, *Pelléas et Mélisande*, which became a milestone in the history of operatic sound as well as dramatic treatment. Along with the no less remarkable String Quartet (1893) and some excellent songs, Debussy's other major accomplishments of the 1890s were orchestral, the *Prélude à l'après-midi d'un faune* after Mallarmé (1894) and the *Nocturnes* (1892–9), both recognised in popular opinion as primary emblems of musical Impressionism.[4]

Faune is unusual in Debussy's orchestral output for its textural complexity, which seems paradoxical because of the abundance of instrumental solos in the context of the relatively small orchestra. The complexity resides above all in the upper melodic line, which is full of changing motives, varied rhythms, and winding shapes, almost entirely conjunct but freely moving over a wide range, and constantly interacting with secondary lines from the interior of the texture; only in the *très soutenu* middle section does the principal line become somewhat more stable, and then only briefly, as the accompanimental patterns move to the forefront to absorb it in the only real *tutti* of the piece. The twisting vines of the melody amount to an idiosyncratic art of arabesque, which is indeed part of the very melodic essence of *Faune*, whereas in later works like *La mer* and *Jeux* they are more aspects of melodic coloration within the overall texture.

One observes, too, that *Faune* often features a diffuse orchestral counterpoint, but one that attempts to break away from the often more conventional counterpoint of *La damoiselle élue* in the direction of more rapidly changing, soloistic textures – ironically rather like some of Mahler's music of the same period, which in every other respect could not be more different from Debussy's. In *Faune*, the least heterophonic of Debussy's larger orchestral works, one is moved to compare the overall orchestral conception not to Impressionist painting (which *Faune*'s Symbolist poetic inspiration might already discourage) but to the sinuous precision of Art Nouveau. Debussy worked for a full year on this ten-minute-long work. The evidence of the *Particell* suggests that he struggled intermittently with subtle details of orchestration, details mostly in choice of solo instruments and doublings, but only seldom involving changes in textural layout.

The contrast of *Faune* with Debussy's next orchestral work, *Nocturnes*, could not be more striking, particularly in the first piece, 'Nuages', arguably his boldest single leap into the musical unknown. 'Nuages' defines a kind of tonality never heard before, based on the centricity of a *diminished* tonic triad (B–D–F♮), highlighted in turn by an extremely reduced rhythmic dimension in steady and oscillating crotchets. The recurrent call in the cor anglais is dynamically prominent even in *piano*, but most of the time the melodic line is fixed in the quietly rocking background, paired collaterally with one or two other parts but doubled in two or even three octaves at once and chiefly in the *divisi* strings spread out over a wide range. When pure triads appear, at bars 29–31, *forte*, the climactic effect is all the more dramatic, a culmination of motion tending more and more towards purely parallel (see Example 8.4, p. 148 above).

The correlation of the beginning of 'Nuages', two paired parts doubled in octaves, with Musorgsky's *Sunless* has been pointed out by numerous writers, and Debussy several times acknowledged his admiration for Musorgsky's music; it seems no less certain that Debussy was influenced, in 'Nuages' and even more in *Pelléas*, by specific aural images from *Boris Godunov* and other works by Musorgsky (such as Boris's 'My soul is sad!' in the Prologue, scene 2).

In a letter to Eugène Ysaÿe of 1894 in which he refers to *Nocturnes* (at a time when he had in mind a work for solo violin and orchestra), Debussy compared the sound he was striving for to 'different combinations that can be obtained from one colour – like a study in grey in painting',[5] which recalls what he had said much earlier in a conversation with his teacher Guiraud: 'A painting executed in grey is the ideal.'[6] 'Nuages' is an apt realisation in music of what Debussy thus described, if only because by far the greater part of the orchestral texture is the constantly and subtly changing array of divided muted strings, beginning with high first violins divided in six (bars 7–10) and eventually ending with low divided cellos and basses (bars 88–97).[7] In between these registral antipodes, every register is marked by some uniquely characteristic string texture, including alternating chords doubled in octaves with simultaneous *arco* and *pizzicato* over a pedal point (bars 43–50), and a sustained harmony reinforced with two muted horns, surmounted by a melody in violin, viola and cello solos in three octaves (bars 71–4). The tutti at bar 42, the loudest point in the piece, with oboes, clarinets, bassoons and two horns, keeps all sections of the strings (without the basses) divided in two within a two-octave span, and still muted. All of these different string textures sustain the impression that in 'Nuages' the background is the musical protagonist, the wash of cloud and sky within which a minimum of gestural events occur – the *bateau-mouche* cor anglais and its muted-horn echo, the brief change of scene in D♯ minor with flute and harp.

In 'Sirènes', the third of the *Nocturnes*, Debussy sought an even more radical orchestration than in 'Nuages', but without the ideal of a 'study in grey'. The strings are often divided (usually in two, occasionally in four) and spread colouristically over a wide range, but the rest of the orchestra, including three trumpets and a second harp, shares the stage equally. The famous women's chorus is an additional element of the orchestration; the voices, without text, become a polyphonic instrument of a single coloration. Rapid colouristic changes, with heterophonic doublings, are much more prominent in 'Sirènes' than in 'Nuages' or 'Fêtes', and indeed significantly foreshadow the brilliant timbral dimension of *La mer*; yet the heterophony is seemingly more tentative and less confident than in the later works, as we know from the multitude of changes that Debussy later made in 'Sirènes', far more than in almost any other work.[8] If there is anything less successful about the sound of 'Sirènes', it comes from the squareness of the phrase structure; nearly everything is in one-bar or two-bar units, with more paired repetitions than in any other work of Debussy's; timbral and textural successions thus tend to be block-like and abrupt. Yet these successions are so frequently bound up with characteristic parallel harmonic motion that one can only say that they sound like Debussy and no one else.

By the time Debussy set his hand to orchestrating *Pelléas*, during the year before the opera's production in 1902, he was much more certain about what he wanted. If he never did get the sounds of the sea in 'Sirènes' quite right, he had no difficulties in the grotto scene at the end of act II of *Pelléas* (Example 10.2). (In the example it is the sea behind them that Pelléas says is not happy.) The passage shows a maximum of coloration and subtle changes of doubling and textural rhythm, with only one very slight change of harmony. Note the contrast in bar 1 between wind and string sound, even while the uppermost line, in the violins, alternates C and D immediately after the C and D an octave below in the winds (cor anglais, muted horn). The C and D in the upper violins are doubled in two lower octaves, including plucked cellos. (As an absolute-pitch aural image, this becomes a subtle and sinister leitmotif in act II, scene 2, in the underground caverns, where Golaud asks Pelléas, 'Do you smell the odour of death?', and the C–D pair appears in the timpani.) Debussy later retouched this page slightly but tellingly, adding a lower octave in the tuba to the trombone notes in bars 2 and 3.

Piano sound: block chords and arpeggios

During the 1890s Debussy concentrated on opera and orchestral music and mostly neglected the piano. The one major work for piano solo he wrote during that decade comprised the three pieces entitled *Images*, unpublished except for the Sarabande, which, in a revised form, became part of *Pour le piano*, published in 1901.[9] *Pour le piano* marks a new point of departure in Debussy's productivity in piano music, which is most abundant during the decade that followed. The three pieces of *Pour le piano* show a wide range of keyboard styles. The Prélude, with its extensive pedal points, diminished seventh chords, and predominantly classical tonality with concomitant dominant–tonic relationships seems somewhat incongruously to hearken back to Bach's organ music. The third piece, Toccata, has passages that seem like a later working out of the Passepied in *Suite bergamasque*;

Example 10.2 *Pelléas et Mélisande*, act II, scene 3: short-score reduction of full score

PELLÉAS

El - le ne   sem - ble pas heur - eu - se cet - te nuit...

yet it also seems to reflect the very un-Bach-like organ styles of such composers as Widor and Vierne, notwithstanding its episodes of well-ordered and completely Debussyan parallel harmony.

Debussy's use of parallel harmony extends from pure triads with doubled root to a large variety of chordal types with dissonant intervals, which are almost always best understood less in terms of root function in one or more keys, and more in terms of specific sonorities deployed as a colouristic

Example 10.3 *Pour le piano*, Sarabande (bars 25–7)

expansion of a single melodic line. Debussy's parallel harmony employed in this way is usually the principal textural element, sometimes the only one; thus it can be differentiated from simple melodic doubling in parallel intervals, including thirds in the *Petite suite* and 'Voiles', fifths in *La mer*, and major seconds in 'Jimbo's lullaby', in all of which there is usually a significant accompanimental element.

In the Sarabande we find Debussy's parallel harmony at its most crystalline, untrammelled by arpeggios and figurations, and with minimal contrapuntal delineation; the style reappears in 'Hommage à Rameau' (another sarabande) and in several of the *Préludes*, especially 'La cathédrale engloutie'. What is most important in the Sarabande is the differentiation between chordal types: in the opening measures a major ninth chord changes position before moving to a stable triad; bars 6–8 have root-position triads and seventh chords moving in opposition to a well-defined bass; bars 11–12 include parallel dominant seventh chords moving by whole tones with a contrasting melody above; bars 23–8 feature parallel motion of chords not previously found in Debussy (Example 10.3). These can be considered sonorities of three perfect fourths plus an octave doubling, or perhaps V_3^4 chords in which the third is replaced by an appoggiatura; but the most prominent aspect of their special sound is the departure from what up to now in the Sarabande had been specifically root-position harmony. In bars 61–3 we see three characteristic types of triadic root-position harmony: stepwise parallel triads as accompaniment to a contrapuntally differentiated upper melody; anti-parallel block triads, well in opposition to the bass; and parallel root-position triads with octaves in the outer voices. Some of the latter are incomplete, with root and fifth only, a favourite sonority of Debussy's, especially when arpeggiated, as in *L'isle joyeuse*, bars 99ff.

The 'Danse sacrée' for harp and string orchestra can be mentioned here as perhaps the most intentionally austere of Debussy's exercises in parallel harmony. Except for a contrasting middle section, most of this short movement features block chords for the harp, chiefly in parallel root-position triads, often with the root doubled in the top voice. A few deviations appear: parallel triads without third, chords with seconds similar to the Sarabande type mentioned in Example 10.3 above, and sparing rhythmic-contrapuntal differentiation in the melodic line. Even the string accompaniment mostly consists of doubling the harp's melodic line singly or in octaves, with unexpectedly striking colouristic richness that is hardly suggested by the simplicity of the texture. Only once does the dynamic rise above *forte* amidst abundant *pianissimo, très doux et expressif* markings, but the strings remain unmuted until mutes are added for the beginning of the 'Danse profane' that follows without pause.

The year 1901 was a pivotal one for Debussy, as it was for Maurice Ravel as well, who at the age of twenty-six completed his *Jeux d'eau*. This was a pioneering example of new pianism that could hardly have failed to impress the older composer, already impressed by Ravel's 'Habanera' (1895, *Sites auriculaires* for two pianos, 1895–7). Whether there was direct influence or not, Debussy's interest in piano music took on new energy and he began to explore what for him were new directions. The arpeggiated pianism that in the Toccata was relatively restrained begins to be more elaborate: in 'Pagodes' (the first of the *Estampes* of 1903) and in 'Reflets dans l'eau' (the first of the first set of piano *Images*, 1905). 'Reflets dans l'eau' is a sound-study of Lisztian dimensions, complete with a sweeping *stringendo* cascade that Debussy cannot quite bring himself to call a cadenza (he labels it 'Quasi cadenza'). If Ravel's *Jeux d'eau* is inspired directly by Liszt's 'Les jeux d'eaux à la Villa d'Este' as many have claimed, then Debussy's aquatic style is surely influenced by such sonorous pieces as 'Au bord d'une source' and the *Harmonies poétiques et réligieuses*. In 'Pagodes', the slightly earlier *D'un cahier esquisses*, and 'Reflets dans l'eau' Debussy's impressionistic piano style is born, realised in a movement away from the regular phrases, steady tempos, and dance rhythms of earlier works and the elaborately digital, mechanical or *martellato* style of 'Chevaux de bois', *Pour le piano*, 'Jardins sous la pluie', and *Masques* towards a more rhapsodic style of freely changing textures and tempos, with more concentration on soft dynamics, weakly measured arpeggios and simultaneous use of high and low registers; in a sense, Debussy's *esprit* of Chopin became enlarged to include Liszt, but both remained prominent in the background of his own pianistic art all the way through the *Préludes* to *En blanc et noir* and the *Etudes*.

Harmony as sound: Debussy's characteristic sonorities

When we say that Debussy's characteristic harmony is often independent of its tonal function (at least as we define tonal function according to the

Example 10.4 *Nocturnes*, 'Fêtes': harmonic reduction (bars 12–13)

principles of common practice), we mean that he chooses a harmony first and foremost for its value as sound and sonority. There are many places in Debussy where a classical tonal progression can be perceived, with strong root motion in the bass, even as strong as dominant and tonic in imperfect or perfect cadence; but these are not what we consider to be distinctive of Debussy's harmony. It is the non-functional dominant that is an immediately recognisable signal of Debussy's harmony, especially in its most characteristic spacing. (Example 10.4). The dominant major ninth sonority Db–F–Ab–Cb–Eb in this spacing is rare in the history of music before Wagner, and when it appears it is usually functional as a dominant or as part of extended chromatic voice leading of the type encountered in, for example, *Parsifal.* In Debussy, its dominant functionality is weakened beyond the point of no return. In 'Fêtes', the strongest tone-centring element is the Ab minor scale, structurally related to the F minor that begins the movement. In 'Nuages' the subtly balanced ambiguity between B minor with F♯ and B minor with F♮ is abruptly washed away by a succession of distantly related dominant ninths; at the corresponding place later in the movement these are transformed into inverted dominant sevenths.

The distinctive interval of Debussy's dominant ninth sonority is the (compound) major ninth that spans the chord from top to bottom, that is, a major second with one or more added octaves. The major second itself, the complement of the minor seventh whose harmonic value originates in the dominant-seventh chord, historically 'the first unequivocal harmonic dissonance', is another distinctive marker in Debussy, whether as a prominent component of the French augmented-sixth chord (which maps onto the whole-tone scale), or as a contrapuntal element.

The berceuse-like sonorous seconds of 'Le jet d'eau' have a direct antecedent in Borodin's undinist song *Morskaya tsarevna* (The sea princess, 1868), which Debussy might well have heard during his early visits to Russia. The major second becomes a psychological leitmotif, a shudder of subconscious fear of discovery, as Pelléas playfully ties Mélisande's hair to the willow branches below her tower in act III, scene 1 of the opera (five bars before fig. 15). The major second here has the mildest value of dissonant tension (*aussi doux que possible* in the preceding bar), but it resolves unexpectedly by chromatic expansion to a major third in a functional dominant ninth harmony.

Elsewhere Debussy explores expanded textures of major seconds in combination with octave doublings, as in the passage at bar 112 of 'De l'aube à midi sur la mer' that later merges smoothly with a whole-tone texture. In *En blanc et noir* some of the characteristic harmony includes diatonic seconds, that is, triadic harmony with added major or minor seconds from within the scale. At one point Debussy goes so far as to mark a passage *rude* to underscore the intentionally harsh effect of adding acciaccatura-like seconds to the chorale melody 'Ein' feste Burg', but this is an extreme instance.

A favourite among Debussy's piano works, and one that most closely answers to a popular conception of musical impressionism, is No. 10 of the first book of *Préludes*, 'La cathédrale engloutie'.[10] Debussy's markings even include narrative details: *Profondément calme (Dans une brume doucement sonore)*; *Peu à peu sortant de la brume*; *Un peu moins lent (Dans une expression allant grandissant)*, etc. But above all else, 'La cathédrale engloutie', with its echoes of medieval organum, and its *quasi campana* and *organo pleno* writing, is Debussy's untrammelled exploration of chordal sound over the full range of the piano (Example 10.5). It begins with a basic midrange chordal motive, in *pp* doubled open fifths, framed by a bell chord in the top and bottom registers together; this is answered by a high-register melody in semibreves, *doux et fluide*, in three octaves, against a sustained upper pedal on E, also in three octaves, in a spare two-part counterpoint characteristic of 'Nuages' and many other places in Debussy. The open-fifth motive returns for two bars, but its colour is already changed by a left-hand harmony with a superposed additional fifth and a departure from strict paralleling (at the end of the piece, it changes once more, again for just two bars). At bar 16, 'little by little coming out of the fog', the texture and the harmonic flavour are instantly changed to one of Debussy's characteristic sonorities: a major tonic triad with added major second and major sixth degrees, in an arpeggiating pentatonic texture similar to the final bars of *Arabesque* No. 1, but here over an undulating tonic–dominant bass. This shifts to E♭ and finally C major for a climactic authentic cadence with pealing bells – with so many added major seconds one would call this pan-diatonic harmony (except that the leading-note B is present only melodically).

'La cathédrale engloutie' illustrates, as does no other piano work of Debussy in such a short frame, the variety of Debussy's inspiration in chordal textures. The sonorous bell fifths might have been inspired by Grieg's 'Klokkeklang' (*Lyric Pieces*, Op. 54, No. 6); but where since Musorgsky's 'Great Gate of Kiev' and some of Brahms's late Intermezzi have block triads sounded so well on the piano? The entire piece is dominated by chords in

Example 10.5 *Préludes*, book 1, 'La cathédrale engloutie' (bars 22–30)

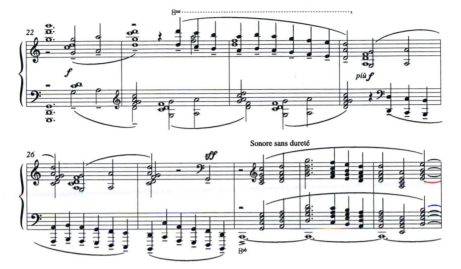

steady motion, with relatively little of pronounced rhythmic character in the melodic line; yet the narrative structure is excellently proportioned and the drama entirely successful, in large part because the tonal structure is also well planned.

Debussy's later heterophony

With *Pelléas*, which he orchestrated in 1901, Debussy acquired still fuller confidence in his orchestral skill and imagination. Four years later came *La mer*, a score which, as pure sound, is much more complex than anything he had written earlier. In 'Sirènes' he experimented with multi-rhythmic doublings and layered changes of instrumental colour, without escaping a certain squareness of phrase, but this squareness is absent in *La mer* where the phrases are more freely shaped and more smoothly blended from one to the next. Timbral and textural changes, with spare and widely spaced textures and abundant instrumental solos, occur in *La mer* more frequently than in 'Sirènes', often with dizzying rapidity. Some parts of 'Jeux de vagues' involve such quick harmonic and timbral changes that the ear follows them only with difficulty, and perhaps it was passages like bars 5–8 and 142–52 that Ravel had in mind when he told Henri Sauguet that '*La mer* is poorly orchestrated. If I had the time, I would reorchestrate *La mer*.'[11] Nevertheless, Debussy's fearless imagination in *La mer* often results in an orchestral sound like nothing ever heard before, as in the first 80 or so bars of 'De l'aube à midi sur la mer'.

The heterophony of timbre in *La mer* is heightened by Debussy's increased use of rapid ornaments – grace notes, mordents, and rapid *gruppetti*.

These are an occasional feature of Debussy's earlier piano music, as in the Prélude of the *Suite bergamasque*, but they grow to larger proportions involving chromatic turns and tirades with whole-tone or chromatic scales in *Faune* and *Nocturnes*. Especially in Debussy's writing for the strings, these ornaments are less accentual devices than colouristic, of the same stripe as high-register trills and tremolos, and more typically are applied to weak beats. In 'Gigues' and *Jeux* especially, ornaments are associated with short melodic fragments and rapid changes of timbre or dynamics; where the beat is accented, pitches are de-emphasised. The obvious ancestor of this gestural, punctuated orchestral style is Berlioz. At roughly the same time as the last orchestral works, Debussy was working on the piano *Préludes*, in which instantaneously executed ornaments are prominent and often quite tricky to play ('La danse de Puck', 'La puerta del vino'); a few years later they form the basis of the *Etude* 'Pour les agréments'.

Like the *Etudes*, composed in memory of Chopin, *En blanc et noir* is one of Debussy's last works, composed in a remarkable burst of steady inspiration that lasted only a few sunny months in 1915 when he was already ill with cancer. *En blanc et noir* exhibits a complexity of texture, including an entirely idiosyncratic non-dialogue counterpoint, that Debussy could not have achieved with one piano, and at the same time an intensification of his keyboard style that he could not have felt in the same way in his orchestral works. Yet the two instruments are perfectly combined, and not even an instant of the three pieces seems texturally overloaded or a note superfluous. Much of *En blanc et noir* explores block-chord sonorities and keyboard patterns in ways that Debussy had never tried before, let alone any other composer for the two-piano medium. Years later, in his memoirs, Igor Stravinsky wrote about when he and Debussy met in 1912 to play through the piano-duet reduction of Stravinsky's newly composed *Le sacre du printemps*:

> What most impressed me at the time and what is still most memorable
> from the occasion of the sight reading of *Le Sacre* was Debussy's brilliant
> piano playing. Recently, while listening to his *En blanc et noir* (one of which
> pieces is dedicated to me), I was struck by the way in which the
> extraordinary quality of this pianism had directed the thought of Debussy
> the composer.[12]

Some of Stravinsky's influence, particularly from *Petrushka*, can be traced in *En blanc et noir*; but like every other external influence in Debussy, it is perfectly assimilated.

Jeux, Debussy's 'tennis ballet' commissioned by Diaghilev (composed 1912, premiered 1913 with choreography by Nijinsky), is his last major orchestral work and the only one of the late works that he orchestrated himself.

Stravinsky stated in his memoirs that Debussy frequently consulted him about the orchestration of *Jeux* during 1912 (when Stravinsky himself was composing *Le sacre du printemps*).[13] *Jeux* is a 'poème dansé' only eighteen minutes long but of extreme narrative concentration, with a maximum of gestures and events. As an intensification of orchestral tendencies seen earlier in *La mer*, *Jeux* does not reveal individual instrumental writing of such whirlwind velocity as the fleetest passages in 'Jeux de vagues', but rather it involves the pace of musical ideas. These are due to the meticulous correlation of the music with the choreographic events on stage, as reflected in the brevity of melodic gestures and constant sudden shifts of tempo and texture.[14]

There are very few motives of obvious structural importance in *Jeux*, but their constant reassociation and recombination makes for a remarkable continuity of ideas: the protean flexibility of the thematic material of *Jeux* is evident on nearly every page. There is plenty of regularity of phrase and subphrase, but it is often broken up by changes of tempo, a *bricolage* of musical events. As Jean Barraqué remarked about *La mer*, the formal process is a *devenir sonore*, a 'sonorous becoming . . . a developmental process in which the very notions of exposition and development coexist in an uninterrupted burst'.[15]

Jeux calls for an orchestra of 2 flutes, 2 piccolos, 2 oboes, cor anglais, 3 clarinets, bass clarinet, 3 bassoons, sarrusophone, 4 horns, 4 trumpets, 3 trombones, tuba, timpani, tambourine, triangle, cymbals, celesta, xylophone, 2 harps, strings, which is close to the instrumentation of *Petrushka*, premiered in 1911. Except for the slightly larger complement of *Le martyre de Saint-Sébastien*, this was Debussy's largest orchestra. Much has been made of the complexity and richness of the orchestration of *Jeux*, especially by the post-war generation of European composers, who saw in Debussy's score an anticipation of Messiaen's highly detailed orchestral style. Most of all, however, one recognises in *Jeux* what Barraqué recognised in *La mer*, that the compositional and orchestral processes are completely unified.

Herbert Eimert, in a landmark article on *Jeux* first published in *Die Reihe* in 1959, speaks of the 'vegetative inexactness', the 'organic inexactness of vegetation' ('organische Ungenauigkeit des Vegetativen') in *Jeux*, by which he seems to mean the resemblance of the motivic and formal growth of *Jeux* to the budding and leafing of a developing twig or branch at unsymmetrical, unspecifiable but inevitable points. As Eimert remarks, most tellingly,

> [E]ven though the themes and groups of motives in *Jeux* are mostly in four and eight-bars, they do not comply with traditional formal claims.
> Concepts such as antecedent and consequent are no longer applicable. If one tried to apply them, one would have to say that the themes of *Jeux* are made up wholly of antecedents.[16]

This appraisal seems particularly apt when one compares *Jeux* with 'Sirènes'. Paired repetitions in *Jeux* sometimes involve short units, one bar or even less, but they are often four-bar phrases, which may be separated by entirely different gestures, even by different tempos. (Compare, for instance, bars 224–34 (from figs. 27–8) and 245–55 (figs. 29–30), each passage involving three changes of tempo and texture, with no motive longer than two bars.)

The ornamental melodic style, full of trills, graces and *gruppetti*, that characterised much of *La mer* and was carried further in the orchestral *Images* reaches its highest point of elaboration in *Jeux*. It is as though the pensive but intense decorative style of Couperin's harpsichord pieces has been transferred to all divisions of the orchestra and greatly accelerated in tempo, like a speeded-up film, with much blurring of the musical surface. It was probably this aspect more than the timbral that bothered Stravinsky when he wrote, 'I still consider *Jeux* as an *orchestral* masterpiece, though I think some of the music is "trop Lalique".'[17] Stravinsky wrote further: '*Jeux* discovers a whole new world of nuance and fluidity. These qualities are French, even peculiarly French, perhaps, but they are new.'[18] Even before *Jeux*, Stravinsky himself, an apt student of *La mer*, was inventing similar nuances and colorations in *L'oiseau de feu*, and it is not surprising that passages such as the one shown in Example 10.6 seem to echo the Firebird's first dance. This passage marks the first appearance of the two female dancers, 'timid and curious'. The melody is in the upper part, with upper second violins in *tremolando* and short staccato notes, doubled at the unison by harp and an octave below by the rest of the second violins, pizzicato; the first violins, divided in two, double these same upper notes with trills that Debussy notates in three different ways, and so fastidiously that one still wonders how, for instance, the double grace note A–B♭ on the third quaver can possibly be executed as written, with an up-bow on the beat. The melody itself is clearly perceptible, but it is coloured with a shimmer of Monet-like brushstrokes. The accompaniment to the melody is a single harmony, bitonally suggestive of the *Petrushka* chord, distributed between the lower strings, harp, three clarinets, and muted trumpet and horn. Note also the dynamic and expression markings, *très léger*, *détaché*, mutes on the brass but not the strings, *sur la touche*, *lointain*, specification of just three stands of tremolando violas, etc., all of these adding up to a degree of notational precision equal to that of Webern's most meticulously marked scores.

Even in the largest climaxes of *Jeux* (as at bars 645 and 653, marked *Violent* but only *f*) there is no full *tutti*, but instead a careful and rapidly changing separation of colouristic elements. The *fortissimo* dramatic climax, at bar 677 (fig. 78), lasts just two bars, with a big unison of the main four-note motive in three octaves, middle register to top, harmonised by a single major second.

Example 10.6 *Jeux*: short-score reduction of full score (fig. 10)

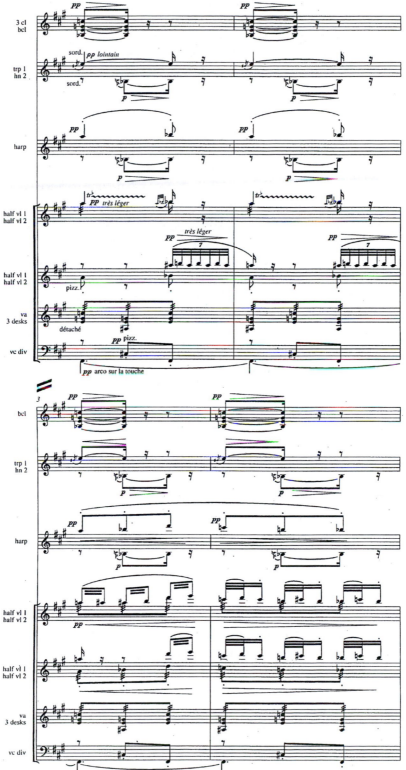

In the last sonatas Debussy achieves a remarkable refinement and re-adoption of classical chamber-music textures that he had outgrown after his student works, with some of the chordal spacing reminiscent of Schubert and Brahms's chamber works with piano; yet some of this is not widely different in texture from some of Debussy's own piano pieces, neither does he entirely avoid emulating the filigreed sound of the impressionist orchestra. The Sérénade in the Cello Sonata features some unprecedented and very effective *quasi chitarra* pizzicati, but the guitar is also imitated in the piano at the beginning of the Finale, and in most of the work a smooth cantabile dominates the writing for cello. In the Sonata for flute, viola and harp, typical gestures of the virtuoso harp style, especially glissandos and arpeggios, are mostly avoided in favour of an equal share in a balanced dialogue between melodic roles for all three instruments; 'Bruyères', in book 2 of the *Préludes*, is not a particularly striking kind of piano writing, but when the same style reappears in the first movement of the Sonata nothing could be more appropriate to the serene neo-archaic atmosphere of the piece. The Violin Sonata shows what is perhaps the most obvious Debussyan sound in its writing for both instruments; the rippling parallel harmony at the beginning of the last movement seems to go back as early as the song accompaniments of the 1890s. But the Intermède, marked *Fantasque et léger*, for all its textural simplicity, shows a new colouristic voice in its repeated notes and chords; nothing else of Debussy's prepares the listener for the strange sound of the violin's high double-stop major thirds, doubled by piano an octave lower, at bar 101.

The individual aspects of Debussy's sound are well rooted in, and logically descended from, the music of his predecessors. His great achievement was to synthesise these into a distinctive and personal style that, even as it evolved, remained consistent from the earliest works to the last. The Great War and Debussy's death in his prime marked the end of what some writers called the Impressionist period in music, but his achievement endured in full force. Although Debussy's style was manifold, in the realm of pure sound there was nothing inimitable about it; for better or worse, no other style, particularly in orchestral music, has been more widely or more successfully imitated in the twentieth century. Ravel, Stravinsky, Respighi, Casella, Holst, even composers as different as Prokofiev and Berg, as well as two or three generations of later French, British, Iberian, Soviet Russian and American composers, were all keenly influenced Debussy in their compositional makeup.

11 Music's inner dance: form, pacing and complexity in Debussy's music

RICHARD S. PARKS

Introduction

The evocative title for this essay refers to the sense that in performance music *moves* – and we with it – in complex and ever-changing ways. The word 'form' generally connotes morphological paradigms: familiar tonal schemes such as 'binary', or 'ternary', or 'sonata', or their refashioned derivatives in the twentieth-century post-tonal epoch. However, for *Syrinx*, the *Première rapsodie* and 'Sirènes' I will discuss only briefly their morphological forms.[1] Instead, this study focuses upon the fluid nature of musical materials and relations, a dynamic and rhythmic aspect of musical form that is more often remarked than examined, and for which static morphological form merely provides a framework.[2]

Among the assumptions that direct the analyses herein, two in particular warrant mention: first, that compositions consist of congeries of diverse musical events, whose concatenations over time convey impressions of vitality to us as listeners and performers; and second, that these impressions are a crucial aspect of musical experience – hence the frequent recourse in conversation about music (albeit less often in its literature) to animate metaphors in paired oppositions such as 'ebb and flow', 'rise and fall', 'intensification and relaxation', 'approaching towards and receding from', 'climax and release'.[3] Sources for this sense of vitality include the *pacing* over time of changes in musical materials, which imparts a sense of quickening or of slowing, and the varying *complexity* of musical events over time, which imparts a sense of intensification versus subsidence. Both affective domains convey impressions of tension versus repose and of motion. We can locate much of what we experience in music as invigorative either in the changing durations separating myriad changes (which occur as, from moment to moment, established musical continuities are disrupted to make way for new ones) or in the mutable complexity of musical materials (the piling up or thinning out of textures, instrumental forces, harmonies, notes sounding in succession and the like).

Pacing and complexity defined

Musical form is intrinsically rhythmic, consisting as it does of the temporal ordering and durations of a piece's musical events. What makes these rhythms dynamic are their tendencies of pacing and complexity, and the structures that arise from them and from their interactions. *Pacing* resides in durations, in particular those durations that separate musical junctures wrought by various kinds of breaks in musical continuities, such as pauses, changes and reprises. Pacing *structures* include *tendencies* (for example 'deceleration', where durations tend to lengthen progressively, versus 'acceleration', where they tend to shorten) and *patterns* (e.g. 'short–long–short').[4] Tendencies and patterns emanate from within and among all classes of musical events, including harmony, motive and form itself, as well as register, orchestration, intensity and that most multifarious of musical elements, texture. Because the temporal locations of changes reveal themselves through cues in scores, we may use simple methods to discover pacing structures: we need only decide what kinds of musical events to consider, count the changes that occur within each, and then observe the structures that emerge from the data. *Complexity* resides in the changing concentrations of elements within classes of musical events from moment to moment. We may imagine the range of complexity as spanning a continuum, from 'simpler', on one hand, to 'more complex', on the other, where 'more complex' associates itself with higher values and 'simpler' with lower ones. By this definition, higher frequencies equate with 'more complex', lower frequencies with 'simpler'; more notes in succession per beat equates with 'more complex', fewer notes with 'simpler'; more musical gestures during a particular interval of real time with 'more complex', fewer gestures with 'simpler'; a wider span of register with 'more complex', a narrower span with 'simpler', and so on. As a theoretical term, 'complex' has psychological counterparts in terms like 'intense', 'dramatic' and 'expressive', and common sense suggests that musical content in general that is more complex impresses listeners and performers alike as more intense, dramatic or expressive than simpler musical content. Like pacing, changes in complexity are rhythmic events, with series of changes exhibiting tendencies and forming patterns – structures – which are by nature dynamic. As with pacing, we may use simple analytical methods to discover these dynamic structures: we decide what kinds of events to consider, count the number of events that occur within each and observe the complexity structures that emerge.

Analytical method

In an article of 1999 I explored a single type of dynamic structure in one piece: rhythmic-pacing structures that arise from changes in instrumentation in the *Prélude à l'après midi d'un faune*.[5] But Debussy's music really is awash with dynamic structures, within and among all its musical elements, which combine to generate a highly complex counterpoint of independent rhythmic streams. For this study I have examined nine musical elements, among which the reader will discern two general types: those that unfold independently during the course of the piece versus those whose unfolding takes place in conjunction with some other dynamic structure. In the pages that follow I shall discuss each of them and demonstrate the analytical techniques employed. Of the nine elements, all but two (which I shall discuss first) belong to the second category, combining the dynamic structure of some musical element with that which arises from the durations of small formal units. I shall begin by describing each element along with the analytical technique and method of presentation I have used.

Durations of formal units

In Debussy's music the durations of formal units vary widely and frequently at all hierarchical levels, which range from large sections, to subdivisions of sections, to musical gestures (or 'phrases'). The resultant tendencies – for formal units on any level to become longer or shorter – are palpable and often dramatic in effect. In order to observe such changes precisely, it is useful to establish a constant-duration unit of the bar (hereafter 'CDU') for the object of analysis.[6] In both *Syrinx* and 'Sirènes' the crotchet serves as the CDU; for the *Première rapsodie* it is the crotchet in the *lent* tempo of the piece's opening section. To compare durations of formal units at any level we need only count the number of CDUs each contains; the counts then yield values. Across a succession of formal units, a tendency for values to decrease indicates acceleration/intensification, whereas a tendency for values to increase indicates deceleration/subsidence. In *Syrinx*, for example, where the first main formal unit is two bars long ($= 6$ CDUs) and the second is 8 ($= 24$ CDUs), the values <6–$24>$ indicate a deceleration.[7]

Harmonic materials

In Debussy's music, if we construe harmonic materials in terms of characteristic scale types, that is, if we categorise a given passage's pitch materials according to whether they match up with a diatonic, whole-tone, octatonic or chromatic scale, we have the means to identify the greatest magnitude of change in pitch materials that we will encounter.[8] Given a succession of such changes, the durations separating them form a series that we can represent in values based on a CDU such as the crotchet. Changing values form tendencies of either decrease ($=$ acceleration/intensification) or increase ($=$ deceleration/subsidence). We will examine such changes and derived values in *Syrinx*.

Repetitions

Repetition is a hallmark of Debussy's style, more pervasive in some works than others but always conspicuous. Generally, repetitions are readily distinguishable, and in music where they are especially copious their presence or absence from moment to moment is a source of complexity, either intensification or subsidence. We may measure the varying presence of repetitions by assigning values according to the following scheme: for each CDU, assign a value of '1' for each repetition present. Consider bars 1–4 of *Syrinx*, for instance, for which the CDU is a crotchet (see Example 11.1, which reproduces bars 1–8). There is no repetition at bar 1 beat 1, so the value for this CDU is '0'. Beat 2, however, repeats the rhythm of beat 1, so its value is '1'. Beat 3 is new; its value is '0'. In bar 2 there is a repeated rhythm (from bar 1) on beat 1, thus its value is '1'. As there are no repetitions on beats 2–3, their values are each '0'. The series of values for bars 1–2 is <010100>, whose changing values evince intensification–subsidence–intensification–subsidence. Bar 3 exactly repeats the material of bar 1, for which each of its beats receives a value of '1' (i.e. <111>). In addition, it exhibits the same internal scheme of repetition as bar 1 (<010>) which, when added to the '1s' for the overall repetition yields the series: <121>. Bar 4 beat 1 reiterates the rhythm heard in bars 1–3 (♩♪), for which it receives '1'; beat 2 repeats the contour of beat 1 (= 1); beat 3 begins with the same contour but slightly altered (= 1). As well, bar 4 beats 1–2 together form a longer contour (b♭1–b♮1), heard an octave higher in bar 3 beat 1, which adds '1' to each beat so that the series of values for this bar is <221>. Taken together, the series of values for bars 3–4, <121221> both mimics and extends the pattern of intensification/subsidence of bars 1–2 in the complete series: <010100–121221>.

Durations between successive attack points

An attack point is the beginning of a note, its initial moment of attack.[9] A succession of attack points generates a series of durations, whether or not the notes occur in the same voice or part. Changes in the durations between successive attack points (hereafter 'SAPs') effectively convey acceleration or deceleration, intensification or subsidence: we hear a decrease in durations (i.e. more notes per unit of time) as acceleration/intensification, an increase (i.e. fewer notes) as deceleration/subsidence. Such changes are easy to measure and observe. We can express the rate of SAPs in values based on the ratio between the number of SAPs that occur in a given passage and the number of CDUs for that passage: count the SAPs and divide by the number of CDUs. For say 9 SAPs in a space of eight crotchets (where the crotchet serves as the CDU), the value would be $9 \div 8 = 1.1$. Whereas a tendency for such values to increase indicates acceleration/intensification, a tendency to decrease indicates deceleration/subsidence. Bars 1–7 beat 1 of the *Première*

Example 11.1 Repetitions in *Syrinx* (bars 1–4)

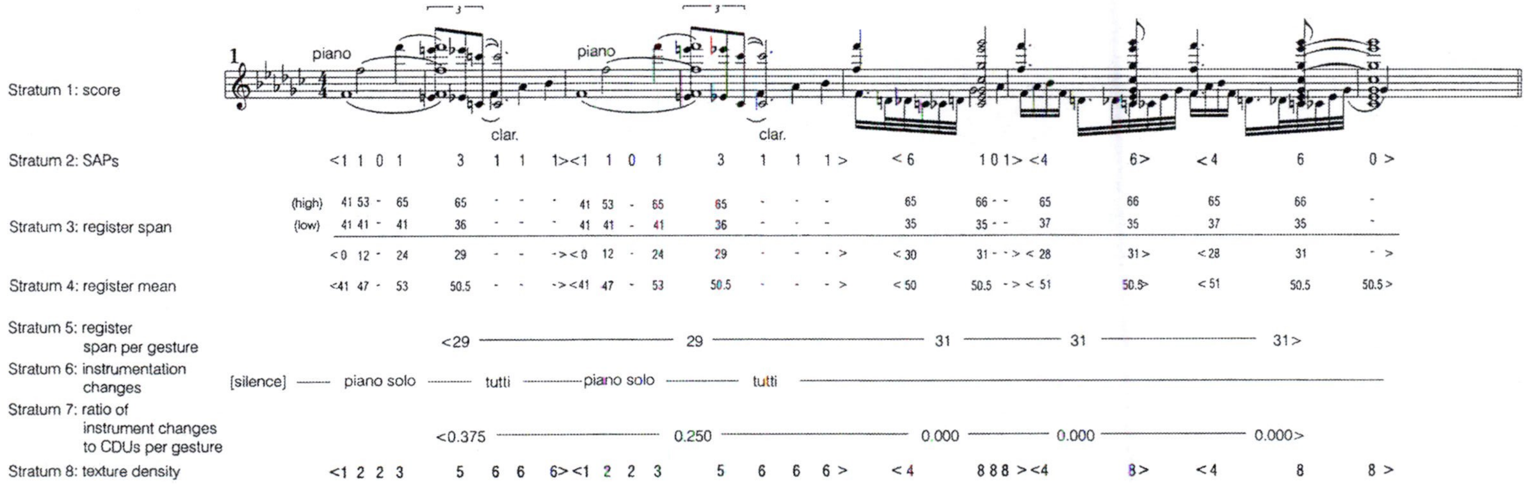

rapsodie contain forty-six SAPs spread over five musical gestures as follows: <11013111>, <11013111>, <6101>, <46>, <460> (see Example 11.2, stratum 2). The vacillating values point to accelerations within each of the first and last pairs of gestures, deceleration within the middle gesture. Calculated as explained above, the values for each gesture form a series unfolding much more slowly, <1.1–1.1–2–5–3.3>, which embodies gradual acceleration followed by deceleration.

Register span and placement

Measuring changes of register involves two essential variables: *span*, which is the amount of frequency range utilised from lowest to highest notes; and *placement*, which is the location of that frequency range, its relative overall highness or lowness. We can measure register span by counting semitones from lowest sounding note to highest within a specified duration. To observe such changes during the course of each musical gesture we need to identify the lowest and highest sounding notes that occur within each CDU and count the semitones between. The placement for each CDU will be the mean between the lowest and highest notes. Using bars 1–7 beat 1 of the *Première rapsodie* as an example, the lowest and highest notes for each CDU are shown in Example 11.2, stratum 3, together with each gesture's series of values.[10] The mean placements are shown on stratum 4. Changes in register span from one gesture to the next exhibit tendencies of increase or decrease (= intensification or subsidence, respectively); changes in placement exhibit tendencies towards ascent or descent (= intensification or subsidence). To measure changes in register from one *gesture* to the next, extract highest and lowest notes per gesture, and calculate the difference in semitones. For the five gestures of bars 1–7 beat 1, the values are <29–29–31–31–31>, a very slight intensification.

Melodic contour

Melodic contour is a prominent focus of variability in terms of complexity versus simplicity, but how may we measure and compare melodic contours, and what constitutes a 'complex' contour versus a 'simple' one? Robert D. Morris offers a solution in his concept of melodic 'primes', coupled with his contour-reduction algorithm.[11] Morris's primes are paradigms that underlie all melodic contours and to which any contour may be reduced. These paradigms range in size from one to four generalised pitch members, which are pitch-relative to each other in the following manner: lowest pitch (to which he assigns the value 0), next lowest (= 1), higher still (= 2), and highest (= 3). In most general terms, Morris's primes consist of a melodic contour's first, last, lowest and highest notes. If all four are different, then the prime will have four members (such as <1032>); if the first or last notes

Example 11.2 *Première rapsodie* (bars 1–7 beat 1)

Stratum 1: score

Stratum 2: SAPs

Stratum 3: register span

Stratum 4: register mean

Stratum 5: register span per gesture

Stratum 6: instrumentation changes

Stratum 7: ratio of instrument changes to CDUs per gesture

Stratum 8: texture density

Example 11.3 Morris's algorithm used to analyse melodic contours in *Syrinx* (bars 1, 2 and 4)

are identical to the highest or lowest notes, the number of elements will be less than four.[12] Contours with only two distinct elements are not uncommon. A simple ascending line will have the contour <01>, and so will one that ascends to a highest note and then returns to the starting pitch: <010>. The last two figures illustrate another dimension of contour primes, namely, variability in the number of 'time points' each contains. The prime <01> has two time points, meaning that the two elements in the prime occur at the beginning and end of the contour they underlie. In contrast, the prime <010> has three time points: the first, intermediate and last notes. The number of time points in a prime must be at least equal to the number of distinct elements, but primes with only one or two distinct elements may each have one additional time point. Two aspects of complexity are the numbers of elements and time points to which a given melodic contour reduces, with those reducing to primes with fewer elements or time points being 'simpler' than those with more. Another gauge of complexity is the number of steps necessary to reduce a melodic contour to its paradigmatic prime using Morris's *contour reduction algorithm.*

Morris's algorithm begins with a complete melodic gesture, such as that of bar 1 of *Syrinx* (see Example 11.3). We begin by copying the noteheads of the pitches in the melodic gesture onto the staff below, adding stems and beams as follows: add both ascending and descending stems to first and last notes (bb^2 and db^2), and connect them with beams both above and below. Next, for each note that lies at a cusp of a contour change, stem to either the beam above or below, depending upon whether the note is the goal of an ascent or a descent, respectively. For the gesture of bar 1, the first $a\natural^2$ and the gb^2 are stemmed down because both are goals of descents, while $b\natural^2$ and the second $a\natural^2$ are stemmed up because each is the goal of an ascent. The

ab^2 is not flagged, nor are gb^2, f^2 or $e\natural^2$ because all are intermediate notes of descents rather than boundary pitches. This process completes stage 1. For the second stage, omit all notes that were unstemmed in stage 1, and copy the remaining noteheads onto the staff below (labelled stage 2). To this reduced contour again add ascending and descending stems to first and last notes and connect both to upper and lower beams as before. Next, examine the contour formed by *only the notes stemmed upwards in stage 1*, and again stem up to the beam those that are higher than notes already stemmed upwards, as well as any remaining notes that lie at cusps of contour changes within the stemmed notes from stage 1. For this example, only $b\natural^2$ is stemmed since it is higher than bb^2 and there are no other upwards-stemmed notes that lie at cusps of contour changes.[13] Return now to the notes that were stemmed downwards in stage 1, and stem down to the beam those that are lower than notes already stemmed downwards, as well as any remaining notes that lie at cusps of contour changes among downwards-stemmed notes in stage 1. In this instance, for stage 2 no more notes are stemmed downwards because both $a\natural^2$ and gb^2 are lower than bb^2 but higher than db^2. For stage 3, copy as noteheads onto the staff below only the stemmed notes from stage 2, adding stems as follows: stem first and last notes in both directions to beams above and below. Next, consider only the contour of the notes stemmed upwards in stage 2, and stem up to the beam those that are higher than notes already stemmed upwards, as well as any remaining upwards-stemmed notes from stage 2 that lie at cusps of contour changes. Since $b\natural^2$ is higher than bb^2 stem it to the upper beam. This completes stage 3 for bar 1 of *Syrinx* as there are no more notes to consider; since all remaining notes are stemmed we have reduced the contour to its prime, which is <120>. Morris calls the number of stages required to reduce a contour to its prime its 'depth'. I call the value that is the sum of a prime's time points plus its distinct elements its 'density', which in this case is 6 (3 + 3). To arrive at a value representing the contour's complexity, add the number of stages required to reduce the original contour to its prime (here, 3) – in this case 9 (6 + 3). In the illustration, the value representing the contour's combined density and depth is given together with its prime, separated by a slash: 9/<120>.[14]

Instrumentation

Consider the varying rate of changes of instrumentation as they occur from one musical gesture to the next. In the *Première rapsodie*, the possible combinations are limited to three: piano and clarinet together, piano alone, and clarinet alone. In 'Sirènes' the possibilities are far more numerous. We can express such changes as ratios between the number of changes divided by the number of CDUs per gesture. In the five gestures of the *Première rapsodie* bars 1–7 beat 1, only the first two exhibit changes: from silence, to piano solo, to tutti in bars 1–2; from tutti to piano to tutti in bars 3–4; tutti throughout in bars 5–7 beat 1 (see Example 11.2, stratum 6). Here again, fluctuating values form tendencies of either increase (= acceleration/intensification) or decrease (= deceleration/subsidence), hence these five gestures evince a subsidence of tension during their course.

Texture density

Related to but different from register span and placement, texture density has to do with the number of parts or doublings sounding at once. To observe changes within musical gestures we need only count the number of parts/doublings sounding per CDU and note the tendency patterns that emerge. Across the five gestures of the *Première rapsodie*, bars 1–7 beat 1, the series of values are: <12235666>, <12235666>, <4888>, <48>, <488> (see Example 11.2, stratum 8). Observe that for all of these gestures the fluctuating values exhibit tendencies of increase (= acceleration/intensification), which is a hallmark of Debussy's style.

Complex textures formed of ostinatos

In his mature instrumental works, such as 'Sirènes', Debussy often wove complex textures by employing several ostinatos at once, each comprising several rhythmic and instrumental strands. The complexity (= intensity) of such passages is a function of both the number of ostinatos and each ostinato's complexity. Unfortunately, assigning values that take both factors into account is problematic, since we have no way of knowing how to weigh these two components relative to each other. Accordingly, I have merely added the number of ostinatos (distinguished by the durations of their cycles) to the number of parts/doublings they comprise. In 'Sirènes', bar 3, for instance, there are two ostinatos: one with a cycle of one crotchet beat (cellos, *divisi* violas and clarinet 1); the other with a cycle of two crotchet beats (flute and harp 2). The total number of parts/doublings (6) and ostinatos (2) yields a value of 8. Changing values from one bar to the next (ostinato textures never change more often than at one-bar intervals) form tendencies of either increase (= acceleration/intensification) or decrease (= deceleration/subsidence).

As an antidote to the exposition of methodology just completed we shall now turn to the three pieces that form the core of this study: *Syrinx*, the *Première rapsodie* and 'Sirènes'. For each, I have chosen several musical elements, enumerated the changes that occur within them, and identified the dynamic structures of pacing and complexity that emerge.

In *Syrinx*, whose simple monophonic texture allows us to concentrate on aspects of pacing and complexity unburdened by the complications of texture, harmony, counterpoint and instrumentation, we shall examine pacing in the domains of form, repetition and harmonic materials, and complexity in the realms of SAPs, melodic contour and register. The modest forces of the *Première rapsodie* in its original version for clarinet and piano (as distinguished from that for clarinet and orchestra[15]), present a felicitous segue from monophonic *Syrinx* to the complex textures of 'Sirènes'. In it, besides the pacing of formal units and complexity in SAPs we will consider new domains, including complexity in texture density and pacing in changes in instrumental colour. In 'Sirènes', a composition made up largely of ostinatos, we shall again focus upon both pacing and complexity in the domain of form, and we will consider textural complexity as well.

Syrinx

At a bit over two minutes' duration *Syrinx* is brief but not a miniature.[16] Despite copious repetition among its melodic constituents, in general the piece is characterised by its continual invention. I shall begin by proposing a formal plan for the piece as a useful backdrop against which to view other aspects of the music. While many of Debussy's musical forms employ simple recursive schemes, such as rondo-like alternations of material, others embody an innovative variations paradigm in which an initial musical idea is presented and then 'grows' progressively into something else, until at some point the process ceases, the initial idea is restated and the growth process begins anew.[17] This process may be repeated many times, as it is in the *Prélude à l'après-midi d'un faune*, or only a few, as in 'Des pas sur la neige' (*Préludes*, book 1). *Syrinx* employs this principle to create a form with four main sections, each consisting of one statement-and-growth cycle.

Form

Among the devices that can effectuate clear divisions within a piece, the most obvious are pauses. In *Syrinx* there are two complete cessations; they are long enough for sound to stop in a typical hall, even for the flautist to lower the instrument away from the embouchure. They occur in bars 2 and 25, each at the end of a passage marked by a note of substantially longer duration than its predecessors and stretched even further by fermatas. (See Figure 11.1, stratum 1. The figure reproduces the score amidst graphic representations of other features to be discussed shortly.) There are also two less marked pauses following bars 8 and 15 respectively, underscored by instructions to slow up (*retenu* and *cédez*). The first of these, at the end of bar 8, is only slightly less arresting than those of bars 2 and 25 because of the pronounced lengthening of note values at its approach coupled with the tempo change

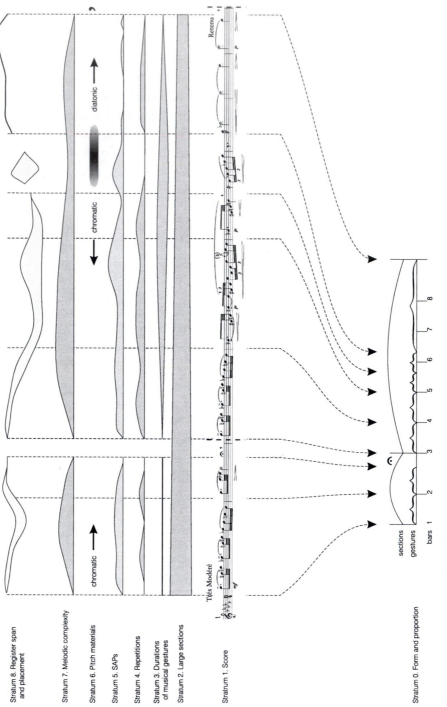

Figure 11.1 Form, pacing, and complexity in *Syrinx*

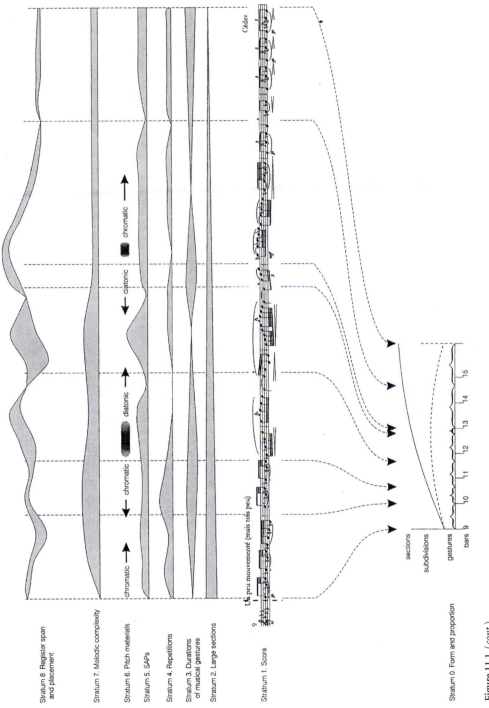

Stratum 8. Register span and placement

Stratum 7. Melodic complexity

Stratum 6. Pitch materials

Stratum 5. SAPs

Stratum 4. Repetitions

Stratum 3. Durations of musical gestures

Stratum 2. Large sections

Stratum 1. Score

Stratum 0. Form and proportion

chromatic — diatonic — chromatic

chromatic — diatonic — chromatic

Un peu mouvementé (mais très peu)

Cédez

sections
subdivisions
gestures
bars

9 10 11 12 13 14 15

Figure 11.1 (*cont.*)

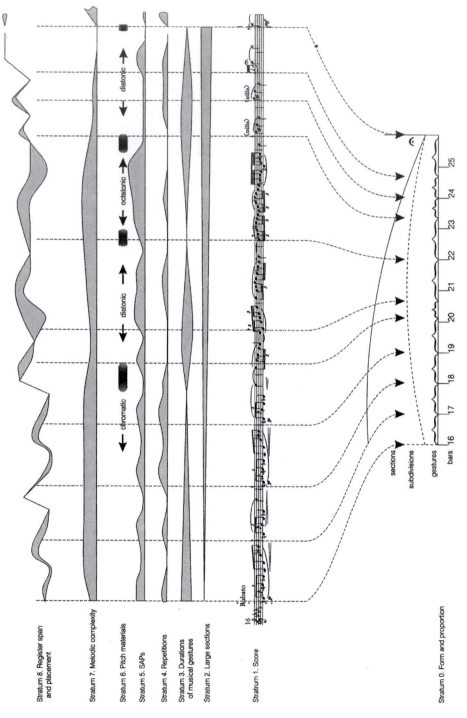

Stratum 8. Register span
and placement

Stratum 7. Melodic complexity

Stratum 6. Pitch materials

Stratum 5. SAPs

Stratum 4. Repetitions

Stratum 3. Durations
of musical gestures

Stratum 2. Large sections

Stratum 1. Score

Stratum 0. Form and proportion

Figure 11.1 (*cont.*)

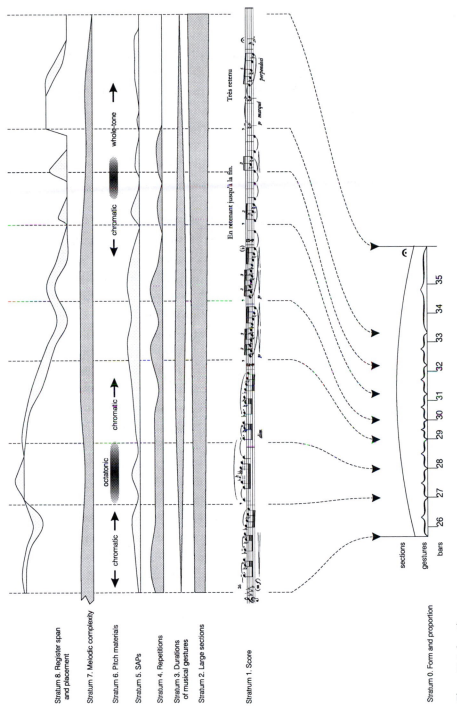

Stratum 8. Register span and placement

Stratum 7. Melodic complexity

Stratum 6. Pitch materials

Stratum 5. SAPs

Stratum 4. Repetitions

Stratum 3. Durations of musical gestures

Stratum 2. Large sections

Stratum 1. Score

Stratum 0. Form and proportion

chromatic → octatonic → chromatic → chromatic → whole-tone

sections

gestures

bars

26 27 28 29 30 31 32 33 34 35

En retenant jusqu'à la fin.

Très retenu

Figure 11.1 (cont.)

indicated in bar 9 (*un peu mouvementé (mais très peu)*), all features that conspire to underscore the sense that, however briefly, the piece has ceased. The pause at bar 15 entails merely a *cédez*, unaided by lengthened note values, though the *rubato* at the beginning of the next bar heightens the sense that one thing has ended and another begun. If the other three junctures are true pauses, the end of bar 15 is a 'near-pause', which marks off two *subdivisions*, in contrast to the larger *sections* defined by the pauses at bars 2, 8 and 25.

The result is a scheme comprising four sections with a subdivision of the third (see Figure 11.1, stratum 0, which depicts *Syrinx*'s form proportionally). Note the mingling of symmetries and asymmetries. Section 3 lies *almost* at the piece's centre and sections 1–2 together *almost* balance section 4; nonetheless, compared with the others, section 1 is extraordinarily brief and section 3 is extraordinarily long. These varying lengths combine to form a dynamic cycle of two opposing tendencies, first expanding then shrinking, which conveys a sense of gradual deceleration followed by gentle acceleration. Figure 11.1, stratum 2 graphically depicts this cycle of deceleration–acceleration in the shaded band superimposed over the formal plan (where narrower = deceleration).

At the level of detail we may further partition the five large divisions and subdivisions into series of brief musical gestures. (In Figure 11.1, stratum 0, musical gestures are depicted proportionally as curly brackets, their boundaries aligning with the score by means of the broken lines and arrows.) These gestures constitute a surface-level hierarchical formal level, whose durations form a rhythmic counterpoint to those of the higher level comprising sections and subdivisions. The gestures themselves are defined by very brief pauses (e.g. as in bar 5 beat 2 and bar 6 beat 1), by repetitions (e.g. rhythm in bar 2 beat 1, bar 4 beat 1, rhythm and contour in bar 5 beat 1) and by marked changes in melodic contour (e.g. in bar 10 beat 3, bar 11 beat 3, bar 12 beat 3.5). Here again, only more vividly, the varying durations of gestures create patterns of tendencies: of acceleration and towards complexity as durations of gestures shorten and the number of CDUs we encounter per small formal unit decreases; of deceleration and towards simplicity as gestures lengthen and the number of CDUs increases. In Figure 11.1, stratum 3, the shaded band depicts acceleration–deceleration and complexity embodied in musical gestures (where wider = acceleration/more complex). Section 1 is 'flat' insofar as both gestures are of equal length (I have not counted the pause as part of the gesture), but the durations of section 2's five gestures form a single cycle of increase followed by decrease (in the number of gestures encountered per given time interval) as <33228> (where 1 = ♩). Section 3, subdivision 1 contains $2\frac{1}{2}$ such cycles, as does subdivision 2, but because the lengths of the subdivisions themselves increase slightly over that of section 2, there is an increase in complexity. Simply stated, we hear more activity (i.e. fluctuations) in the number of CDUs per tendency cycle throughout section 3 compared with sections 1 and 2.

Repetitions

Syrinx is surfeited with motivic repetitions.[18] (See Example 11.1 and Figure 11.1, stratum 4. As previously explained, in Example 11.1 repetitions are shown above the staff indicated by brackets with arrows pointing back to their sources. Figure 11.1, stratum 4 depicts repetitions as a shaded band, where wider = more per CDU.[19]) While most repetitions are very brief, lasting only a beat or so, there are five that span a bar or more: at bars 3–4, 9–10, 18–19, 25–7 and 29–30. Four of these (at bars 3–4, 9–10, 25–7 and 29–30) share the same material and are thus repetitions of repetitions; they especially command our attention since they all follow pauses.[20] The hierarchical scheme of subdivisions within the third division reflects not only the ambiguous character of the third pause (after bar 15), but also its remove from the large repetition at bar 18 as well as the lack of connection of the latter with the other three large-scale repetitions.

In *Syrinx* very few repetitions are literal; most entail modifications. The original gesture reappears transposed (compare beat 2 of bar 1 to beat 1), its continuation altered (compare bar 10 with bar 9), its rhythm applied to a new contour (compare beat 1 of bar 2 with beat 1 of bar 1), its contour set in a new rhythm (compare bar 12 beats 1–2 with bars 10 beat 3 through 11 beat 2). Some repetitions are nearly literal (compare bars 18–19 to bars 16–17); for others, modifications almost efface the identity of the variant with its original (compare beat 1 of bar 4 with beat 1, bar 3). But whether literal or varied, repetitions are so pervasive throughout *Syrinx* that their momentary absences in bars 7–8 and 33–5 are striking. The fluctuations in concentrations of repetitions form cycles of tendencies that generally correlate with the main junctures of the formal plan: the concentration of repetitions attenuates markedly throughout bars 3–8 and again throughout bars 26–35. Thus the boundaries for two of the four sections also coincide with the boundaries of repetition *tendencies*.[21]

Repetitions in *Syrinx* are distributed unevenly. They are most concentrated in bars 3–5, 9–10, 16–19 and 26–30, hence these bars are sites of heightened complexity. We already observed that the most sparsely repetitive passages occur just prior to the pause at the end of bar 8 and just before *Syrinx*'s conclusion. Both times attenuation occurs gradually, effectively diminishing intensity through a reduction in the number of repetitions. In part then, tendencies towards attenuation in the realm of repetitions *characterise* section 2, section 4 and the second part of section 3. These characteristic tendencies help to define the formal units internally just as pauses help to define

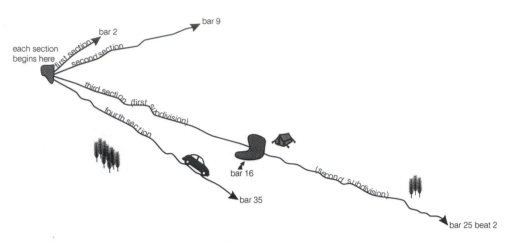

Figure 11.2 *Syrinx*'s formal plan depicted as a series of journeys

them externally, and they contribute to a sense of vitality – the impression that the piece is moving away from or towards moments of intensity.

Although Figure 11.1, stratum 0 renders the temporal proportions and divisions of *Syrinx* visible and enduring, it fails to capture the sense of vitality, the swings between activity and lassitude, animation and ennui conveyed by the counterpoint of fluctuating rhythms of repetitions versus musical gestures. Also left unexpressed is the sense of a range of varying weights in the main disjunctions themselves, variations wrought by subtleties in the length and fidelity of large-scale repetitions. Strata 2–3 of Figure 11.1 more effectively portray these things. Still, Figure 11.2's map-like visage perhaps better captures the kaleidoscopic, protean quality of *Syrinx* that is so apparent in performance. In order to call attention to the wide variance in the length of sections (ranging from two to seventeen bars) and the fecundity of invention coupled with the prevalence of variation among the copious repetitions, which generate ever-new figures and gestures, Figure 11.2 likens *Syrinx* to a series of brief journeys, each commencing from the same locale but heading in different directions, proceeding for different lengths of time, travelling over different terrain and ending in different places. Pursuant to the simile, the journey that is the long, third section includes a significant stop along the way (after bar 15). The paths are never retraced, however; instead, each trip ends at some new place after which the traveller must somehow be transported back to the starting point in order to set off again.

Successive attack points
In *Syrinx* (as in any piece) the sheer numbers of notes to be executed and the fluctuation in that number from moment to moment engenders a readily apprehensible dynamic structure. These fluctuations form tendencies of

increase and decrease that contribute to a sense of activity, of flow and ebb, of approaching towards and receding from those moments that serve as zeniths, nadirs and formal boundaries. Using the crotchet beat as the CDU, we simply need to count the number of notes initiated within the span of each beat and observe the rhythmic patterns that emerge. Figure 11.1, stratum 5 models the results by means of the shaded grey area above the staff in which 'narrower' means fewer SAPs per CDU and 'wider' means more. Section 1 (bars 1–2) reveals a brief cycle of intensification followed by attenuation. There are several similar cycles in section 2 and, indeed, throughout the piece.

Within sections opposing tendencies combine to create cycles of increase followed by decrease. These cycles themselves increase and decrease in their overall durations, often in tandem with the cycles of SAPs. In section 2, for example, the crest of SAPs (seven within a crotchet) occurs at bar 4 beat 3 while the nadir (zero notes) occurs twice towards the end (bars 6–8); the crest lasts for only one beat while the nadir is spread over three bars; the crest is approached and left by a relatively large magnitude of change (from three SAPs, to seven, to three) while the nadir is approached by a relatively small magnitude of change (from one to zero SAPs). Here all three possible variables – the number of SAPs per beat, the magnitude of change in value, and the number of beats *at* a given value – move together to reinforce and intensify each other's effects and contribute to this section's distinct dynamic character. In similar fashion, each section evinces its own character. The first section's single cycle of intensification followed by relaxation unfolds within a similar cycle of durations of changes; the music hurries into the first section and dallies on the way out. Section 3 is the most varied – appropriate for the longest section – and contains the culmination of intensity for the piece as a whole (9 SAPs at bar 12 beat 1).[22]

Harmonic language

Syrinx's generic harmonic language can be described in terms of four familiar common or exotic scales: chromatic, diatonic, octatonic and whole-tone. The pitch materials for passages characterised as *diatonic* will map onto one or another of the twelve distinct major scales;[23] those for passages characterised as *octatonic* will map onto one of three transpositions of the symmetrical, eight-note scale alternating semitones and tones; those characterised as *whole-tone* will map onto one of the two whole-tone scales; and those characterised as *chromatic* include notes that do not map onto any of the other three scalar constructs but which do include chromatically variant pairs of pitch-classes (e.g. A and Ab).

Identifying changes in harmonic language is not difficult; we need merely note where the combinations of pitch classes characteristic of particular generic scales occur. The pitch content of bars 20–1, for instance, is *diatonic* (the C♭ major scale will account for all of the notes in these bars) whereas that of bars 32–5 is *whole–tone* (the whole-tone scale on D♭ encompasses all pitches). Similarly, we can classify the pitch material of bars 1–4 as *chromatic* because its pitch contents can be rearranged to form a contiguous ten-note segment of the chromatic scale. The octatonic scale spelled from D♭ accounts for the pitch content of bar 22 beats 1–2, and also for bar 27.[24] What is less clear is exactly when the changes occur from one genus to another. Figure 11.1, stratum 6 identifies the source scales for pitch materials throughout *Syrinx*. The loci of mutations from one scale type to another are identified by shaded bands whose spans indicate passages where notes could be heard as aligned with either of the abutting scale types. Consider bars 1–8, whose pitch materials change from 'chromatic' to 'diatonic'. The change could occur as early as bar 5 beat 3, because all four of those pitch-classes (A♭, C♭, D♭, F♭) can be found in the same major-scale collection that encompasses bars 6–8 (C♭ major), *and* there are no chromatic-variant pairs after this juncture. The B♮ on beat 2 could be construed as a pivotal note between the two collections since it is part of a chromatic-variant pair, B♭/B♮, but it is also enharmonically equivalent to C♭ (indeed, notated parenthetically as C♭ in all editions). Then again, all of the pitches of bar 5 beat 3 through bar 6 beat 1 occur within the chromatic scale segment that serves as resource for bars 1 through 5 beat 2, and so the listener may not immediately notice the sudden sparsity of pitch-class content that distinguishes the diatonic passage from the chromatic.

Figure 11.1, stratum 6 shows there is no change of harmonic language in the briefest section (section 1), and that the largest number of changes (and in quickest succession) occur in the second subdivision of section 3, which is also the longest section. Hence, whereas section 1 is least active with respect to harmonic language, section 3 is most active and most varied, particularly in its second subdivision.[25]

Melodic contour

Earlier we used Morris's method of contour analysis to reduce the first melodic gesture of *Syrinx* to a moderately complex value of 9/<120> (see Example 11.3). Figure 11.1, stratum 7 traces the varied contours of musical gestures throughout *Syrinx*, and depicts changes in complexity by means of a shaded band of varying width (wider = more complex). The second melodic gesture (Example 11.3, bar 2) is much simpler than the first. Although it embodies three time points, its prime comprises only two elements and the reduction requires only two stages. Its density is 5, its depth is 2, its prime is <010>, and so it is designated 7/<010>. The contour of bar 3 is identical to that of bar 1, i.e. 9/<120>. The melodic gesture of bar 4 (Example 11.3), which is the most complex so far, reduces in three stages to a prime consisting of four time points and four elements: 11/<1032>.

Figure 11.1, stratum 7 confirms that complexity attenuates slightly across the two gestures of section 1, consistent with trends already observed in other parameters. Section 2 begins with an increase in density from the first gesture to the second, followed by a gradual attenuation of density and depth through the penultimate gesture, before the slight increase that heralds the end of the section. The first subdivision of section 3 reveals two cycles of complexity-towards-simplicity tendency pairs. The second subdivision resembles the first in its one and one-half pairs of tendency cycles but ends in a long, gradual reduction of complexity. The last section mimics the second subdivision of section 3, except that both its nadir and its peak of intensity occur somewhat sooner. Within each section there is a tendency for changes in contour to occur at first slowly, then more rapidly, then more slowly again as the end of the section approaches. These tendencies of pacing heighten the sense of plunging into each section only to emerge at the other end more slowly, like diving into a pool, a sense reinforced by tendencies in the realm of SAPs, but mitigated by that of repetitions.[26]

Register

The last dynamic structure I will discuss for *Syrinx* resides in the domain of *register*. Of course, fluctuations in the use of register in a monophonic piece entail only one characteristic element that can be measured note by note: pitch placement. The other characteristic element – the span or range of pitches utilised – can only be considered in accounting for groups of notes.[27] In order to examine fluctuations in placement and span I have again used the crotchet beat as the CDU, identifying the highest and lowest pitches that occur within each beat throughout the piece (see Figure 11.1, stratum 8).[28] I have depicted these fluctuations visually by means of shaded areas of varying sizes and heights (where 'up' = higher frequency and 'down' = lower frequency).

Section 1, bars 1–2, for example, evinces two cycles of complementary tendencies. On one hand, the register extremes first span a major second ($a\natural^2$–$b\natural^2$ on beat 1 bar 1 followed by $g\natural^2$–$a\natural^2$ on beat 2), then widen to encompass a perfect fourth (db^2–gb^2 on beat 3 bar 1), then narrow again to a major second (bb^2–c^2 on beat 1 bar 2) followed by a unison (bb^2 on beats 2–3 bar 2). On the other hand at the same time there is another, complementary cycle of tendencies to be seen in fluctuations in placement: a descent from bb^2 (the mean between $a\natural^2$–$b\natural^2$) at bar 1 beat 1 to ab^2 (the mean between $g\natural^2$–$a\natural^2$) at bar 1 beat 2, to between e^2 and eb^2 (the mean between $d\flat^2$–$g\flat^2$) at bar 1 beat 3, followed at bar 2 beat 1 by an ascent to $c\flat^2$ (the mean between $b\flat^2$–c^2), before alighting again on $b\flat^2$ (which is its own mean) for bar 2 beats 2–3. In a general fashion both tendency cycles recur in section 2, but greatly elongated. Like section 1, the widest register spans occur in the interior of section 2, reached through a series of expansions (in bars 3–4) and followed by a dramatic narrowing to unisons (in bars 6–8). Also like section 1, the register placement descends, but further (by a perfect fifth) than in section 1, before ascending gradually to $e\flat^2$ in bar 8.

If wider register spans entail a sense of more complexity than narrower spans, the effect of the tendency cycles in register span is intensification followed by subsidence. This effect is opposed, however, by register placement, where the tendency is to descend and then ascend. Again, the opposing trends manifest by the two kinds of values embodied in register changes contributes as well to section 2's distinct character. Moreover, the greater variety and complexity of these features compared with section 1 appropriately utilises section 2's much greater length and capitalises on its later temporal position, where a modicum of familiarity with the material of bars 1–2 just heard invites a more leisurely pace, expansion of musical ideas and greater complexity. In a similar manner sections 3 and 4 evince their own, unique profiles, and, as we might expect, the longest section exhibits the most complex fluctuations and tendencies.[29]

Form and dynamic structures

Figure 11.1 allows us to observe in their entirety the trends and tendencies in all of the domains discussed. Even in the first, brief section (bars 1–2) the juxtapositions let us see a complicated counterpoint of myriad tendencies unfolding together, in which trends within some strata support and thereby intensify each other's effects, while opposite tendencies in other strata counteract and thus mitigate each other. In section 1 both pitch materials and the durations of the two musical gestures are static, which allows our attention to focus upon other, actively evolving domains such as repetition and melodic contour, which proceed in tandem, reinforcing each other's impression of attenuated complexity. At the same time, register and SAPs together undergo a cycle of increase followed by decrease, for which the peak occurs towards the end of bar 1.

The cycle of expansion/descent followed by contraction/ascent that characterised register in section 1 repeats in expanded form across lengthier section 2. Again, trends in SAPs roughly parallel those in register, as do those in musical gesture lengths. In all three areas, complexity increases towards a locus of peaks roughly centred about bars 4–6 (note the symmetrical exchange between SAPs and register span) and culminating in a harmonic change, after which everything attenuates except melodic contour. Sections 3 and 4 each evince similar overall patterns of increase followed by decrease, but with many local convolutions, sometimes mutually supportive, at others conflicting. Once our sensitivity to the subtle counterpoint engendered by diverse musical elements in *Syrinx* is heightened, we may more readily hear such rhythms throughout Debussy's oeuvre.

Première rapsodie

Form

Unlike *Syrinx*, whose evocative dramatic function (in Mourey's play) placed no constraints on its form other than brevity, the formal plan for the *Première rapsodie* is dictated at least in part by practical exigencies attending all the Paris Conservatoire's *concours* pieces, which are designed to challenge and display both the technical and the lyrical aspects of playing.[30] But whereas most *concours* pieces employ a bipartite plan with a single distinct division, in which a second, fast-paced virtuosic section follows a slow lyrical first section, Debussy's *Première rapsodie* alternates lyrical passages with those demanding velocity in a meandering, rondo-like scheme rotating among four distinct thematic entities (see Example 11.4 and Figure 11.3). Each has its own tempo, ranging from very slow (*rêveusement lent*), to moderately slow (*poco mosso*), to moderately rapid (*modérément animé*), to quite rapid (*scherzando*). Hence, to the customary demands of lyricism and velocity, Debussy added subtle mastery over frequent tempo and mood changes as

Example 11.4 Four themes in the *Première rapsodie*

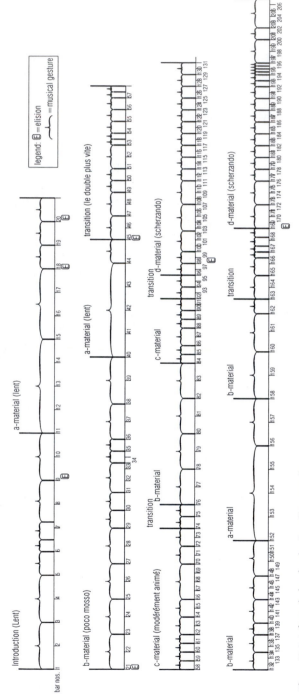

Figure 11.3 A formal plan for the *Première rapsodie*

Table 11.1. Première rapsodie, *bipartite overall formal plan*

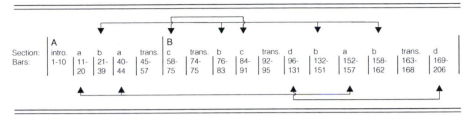

Table 11.2. Première rapsodie, *tripartite overall formal plan*

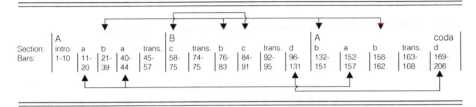

well as the attendant complications of ensemble. While the first forty-four bars of the piece are devoted exclusively to the lyrical, the virtuosic material that dominates the second half is leavened by four prominent passages devoted to material first presented earlier. If we posit two main sections, as in Table 11.1, the overall scheme resembles what has come to be a formulaic bipartite plan for Conservatoire jury pieces. However, this division ignores the reprises of early material, which commence as soon as bar 76, and dominate thirty-one of the last seventy-five bars. Table 11.2 posits an alternative plan of large-scale groupings, which is at least as plausible (or implausible) as that of Table 11.1.

The numerous changes of tempo, which themselves impart by turns a sense of acceleration or deceleration, are enhanced by frequent changes in the durations both of musical gestures and of the larger sections which comprise them. (Figure 11.4, which is constructed in a similar way to Figure 11.1, depicts portions of dynamic structures for four elements: durations of surface-level formal units, changes in instrumentation and texture density, and SAPs, all aligned and superimposed in strata above a formal plan.) The languidness of the theme with which the piece begins is enhanced on one hand by the relatively long durations of the musical gestures throughout the first twenty bars (Figure 11.4, stratum 2), and on the other by the relatively long durations of the tendencies themselves, which are towards shorter durations in bars 1–6 of the introduction, then towards longer ones in the remainder of the introduction, bars 7–10, and again towards shorter durations throughout the next section, bars 11–20. Faster sections

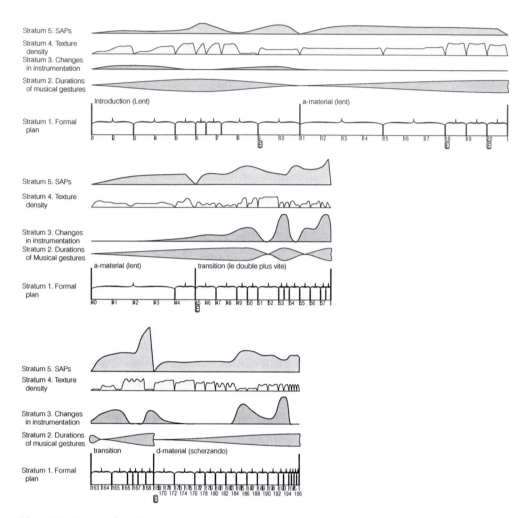

Figure 11.4 Form and pacing structures in passages from the *Première rapsodie*

are accompanied by shorter durations of tendencies: five tendencies in transitional bars 45–57, compared with three in expository bars 1–20, where the overall duration of the latter is more than twice the former. The relatively lengthy transition is crucial because it signals a turning away from the main lyrical portion of the piece and into the composition's first virtuosic material. This characteristically volatile material is further intensified by the very short durations of tendencies towards shortening or lengthening of musical gestures.

A singular passage occurs at bars 76–83 (not shown), where there are no changes at all in the durations of musical gestures. Here the relative absence of changes in other features complements the static succession of formal durations (there is, for instance, only one change in figuration and no change in density of texture).

Instrument changes

As observed earlier, for the *Première rapsodie* the instrumentation permits only three possibilities: solo piano, solo clarinet and tutti. Changes in instrumentation occur when one instrument joins the other after resting and when both play by turns. Figure 11.4, stratum 3 depicts the fluctuating structure of instrumental changes for three passages (wider band = more changes). In contrast to the very active transitional passages of bars 45–57 and 163–8, where changes occur rapidly, the passage containing the initial presentation of a-material (bars 11–20) is entirely tutti, hence devoid of any changes at all. This passage is typical of those devoted to the lyrical first and second themes, including reprises, all of which are almost wholly tutti throughout, and the inertia in instrumental colour contributes to the languorous character of both themes. In contrast, the transitional passages exhibit frequent changes, usually in the form of antiphonal exchanges between piano and clarinet, which imparts a sense of instability that contributes to the transitional character. Despite its essentially tranquil quality, even the introduction (bars 1–10) is more active than the passages devoted to a- and b-material that follow in bars 11–44, which helps heighten the sense of anticipation introductions typically encourage. The *scherzando* sections (such as bars 169–96) also evince frequent changes in instrumental colour comparable to the transitional sections. Like them, the *scherzando* changes heighten the sense of excitement and thereby increase the listener's attentiveness. Surely the changes serve a didactic purpose as well, since they display the performers' ensemble skills, in particular their ability to seamlessly coordinate very rapid changes.

Texture density

Texture density in the *Première rapsodie* is most interesting when viewed in terms of sounding parts or doublings per CDU within each musical gesture. These numbers fluctuate constantly. By far the most pervasive tendency is for the texture to thicken or intensify as the gesture proceeds. Figure 11.4, stratum 4 depicts such fluctuations graphically, with more parts or doublings represented by wider shaded areas. The first (repeated) gesture is that which opens the work, bars 1–2 (and 3–4). Each time, the number of parts or doublings per crotchet CDU yields the series that expands, wedge-like: <12235666>. The next two gestures are similar: <4888> for bar 5, and <48> for bar 6 beats 1–2 (which is also repeated). Not until the sixth and seventh gestures do we encounter reductions in parts or doublings: <8881111> for bar 7 beats 2–8, and <54444444> for bars 9–10. In order, the seven gestures of the introduction (including the two repetitions) yield the scheme shown in Table 11.3. Similarly, the gestures of transitional bars 45–57 and *scherzando* bars 169–82 fluctuate greatly and most often evince

Table 11.3. *Texture-density fluctuations in the Première rapsodie (bars 1–20)*

bar numbers by gesture:	1–2	3–4	5	6, beats 1–2	6, beat 3–7 beat 1	7, beat 2–8	9–10
parts/doublings per CDU:	<12235666>	<12235666>	<4888>	<48>	<488>	<8881111>	<54444444>

Table 11.4. *Texture-density fluctuations in the Première rapsodie (bars 45–57)*

bar numbers by gesture:	45–46	47–48	49	50	51–52	53, beats 1–2	53, beats 3–4	54	55	56	57, beat 1	57, beat 2
parts/doublings per CDU:	<34223233>	<23223233>	<3377>	<3377>	<77888888>	<34>	<34>	<4522>	<2335>	<2335>	<41>	<41>

Table 11.5. *Texture-density fluctuations in the Première rapsodie (bars 169–82)*

bar numbers by gesture:	169–72	173–76	177–78	179–80	181–82	183–84	185–86	187–88	189–90	191–92	193	194	195 beat 1	195 beat 2	196 beat 1	196 beat 2
parts/doublings per CDU:	<6677888>	<66778888>	<6667>	<6667>	<6363>	<6363>	<1222>	<2222>	<5455>	<5455>	<55>	<45>	<54>	<54>	<54>	<54>

wedge patterns (see Tables 11.4–5). Such rapid fluctuations are another hallmark of Debussy's style, contributing to a constant sense of flux in rapid cycles of intensification-subsidence.

Successive attack points (SAPs)

There is a general correlation among fluctuations in the numbers of SAPs, frequency of instrumental changes and the durations of musical gestures. While the contrasting characters of the languid a- and b-theme materials evince fewer changes and dissipating tendencies, the agitated c- and d-theme materials exhibit more changes and intensifying tendencies. For the three passages depicted in Figure 11.4, stratum 5, SAPs in the introductory bars 1–10 proceed from relatively little activity to rather a lot in bars 6–7, then subside in bar 8 before intensifying again in bars 9–10; expository bars 11–20 employ an active figuration throughout, but one that is quickly established and nearly devoid of changes thereafter (and therefore static); like all such passages, transitional bars 45–57 are both active and fluctuant. Bars 163–195, which encompass another transition and the last *scherzando* section, are quite active and fluctuant throughout.

'Sirènes' from *Nocturnes*

Form

For the purpose of this analysis I have divided 'Sirènes' into five sections, all similar in length (though not identical), partitioned not so much by changes in thematic material as by significant disruptions in the otherwise smooth flow of material (see Figure 11.5).[31] The overall form is more or less continuous, alternating between two important and related motto themes that are stated and repeated, over and over, separately and together (see Example 11.5A and B). From time to time a clear winding down of activity disrupts the formal continuity, often reinforced by a temporary slowing of tempo. A thinning of forces, dramatic reduction in ostinato complexity, and a clear attenuation of intensity (indicated by *p e dim. molto* in the strings) spanning four bars signals the end of what I have called section 1. A similar winding down, enhanced by a *retenu*, precedes the end of section 2, again spanning the last four bars, and the appearance of a new theme at bar 58, just two bars after the restoration of tempo, heightens the sense that a significant juncture has just passed. The last four bars of section 3 are marked, once again, by reductions in both forces and dynamic level, reinforced this time by a conspicuous slowing of tempo; they are also the site of the first of several whole-tone trumpet calls (see Example 11.5C). Moreover, bar 87 is marked by a return to the previous tempo as well as its instrumental forces and

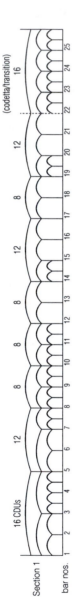
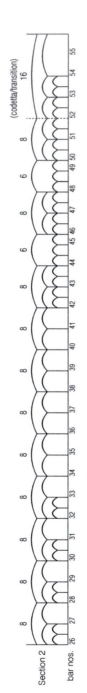
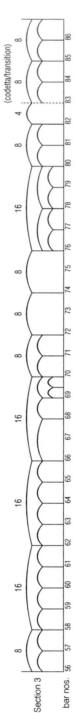
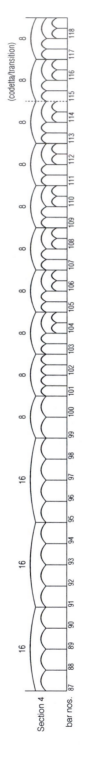
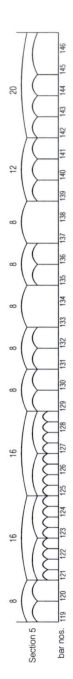

Figure 11.5 A formal plan for 'Sirènes'

Example 11.5 Themes and a motive in 'Sirènes'

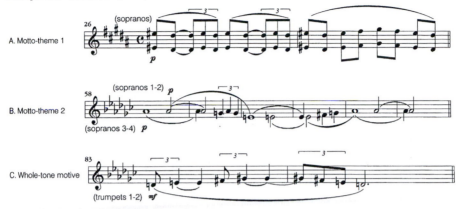

complex ostinatos. At the end of section 4, instead of a reduction of forces there is a lengthening in the durations of ostinato cycles (in the last four bars the three superimposed ostinatos are two beats, four beats and eight beats long respectively). The whole-tone motive sounds again here (first in the cor anglais, then in the trumpet). Immediately after, whole-tone scales in contrary motion accompanying a whole-tone version of the first theme suggest the commencement of a new section, and two bars later there is a reprise of the second motto-theme.

Each of the five sections divides into many brief, coherent musical gestures (comparable to 'phrases'); most are from two to four bars long. In turn, we may further subdivide many of these gestures into fragments (comparable to 'figures') consisting of a distinct component of a musical gesture usually accompanied by a complex of repeated ostinatos. Finally, many of the gesture fragments can themselves be partitioned into the individual presentations of ostinatos which they comprise. The mosaic appearance of the hierarchical formal plan as depicted in Figure 11.5 mimics this intricate nesting of formal components that gives rise in performance to the heterophonic and labyrinthine soundscape of 'Sirènes'.

As in *Syrinx* and the *Première rapsodie*, one source of vitality in 'Sirènes' is the tendency patterns formed by series of changes in the durations of the formal units themselves. Figure 11.6, stratum 3 shows these tendencies formed of sequential shortening and lengthening the durations of gestures, and depicts their assumed effects of intensification or subsidence by means of the variable shaded band. Note in this regard that whereas the odd-numbered sections are quite active – that is, they contain several cycles of tendencies – the even-numbered ones are more quiescent. Note also that over the course of the first four sections the overall durations lengthen,

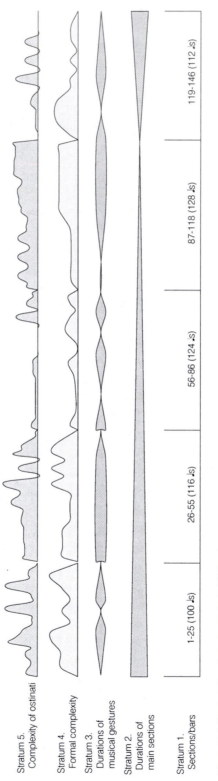

Stratum 5.
Complexity of ostinati

Stratum 4.
Formal complexity

Stratum 3.
Durations of
musical gestures

Stratum 2.
Durations of
main sections

Stratum 1.
Sections/bars

| 1-25 (100 ♩s) | 26-55 (116 ♩s) | 56-86 (124 ♩s) | 87-118 (128 ♩s) | 119-146 (112 ♩s) |

Figure 11.6 Form and pacing structures in 'Sirènes'

before shortening somewhat in section 5. Figure 11.6, stratum 2 throws into relief the overall decelerative–accelerative tendency of the section-durations against the varying tendencies of the musical gestures (depicted in stratum 3).

The presence and varying durations of divisions and subdivisions within musical gestures creates changing patterns of complexity: while more formal units and formal levels within a given number of beats (i.e. per CDU) engenders greater complexity, fewer units or levels engenders less. Figure 11.6, stratum 4 depicts formal complexity. Here we see a different overall structure: while the middle section of the five evinces the least complexity, the fourth section evinces the least variability; the first, second and fifth sections evince the greatest complexity as well as considerable variability.

Ostinatos
'Sirènes' is almost wholly constituted of ostinatos. Only in the exact centre of the piece (bars 72–9), and for a few other brief moments (e.g. bars 44 and 48) are ostinatos absent. Most are dense, consisting of many parts or doublings, and often several ostinatos unfold simultaneously. At bars 42–3, for example, we may identify three different ostinatos comprising twenty-eight parts or doublings: one consists of ten parts and doublings and repeats at crotchet intervals (violins I–II and double basses, *divisi*); another comprises seven parts and repeats at crotchet intervals, but syncopated, beginning on the second quaver of bar 42 (violas and cellos, *divisi*); the third comprises eleven parts and doublings and repeats at minim intervals (harp II, horns II–IV, clarinets I–II, flute I). Another complex passage occurs at bars 115–18, again consisting of three distinct ostinatos, this time comprising fifteen parts or doublings: an ostinato in the strings consists of seven parts or doublings that repeats at minim intervals (*divisi* violins I–II and violas); a second ostinato has four parts repeating at semibreve intervals (clarinets I–II, harps I–II); a third that repeats every two bars comprises four more parts (horns I–IV). In contrast, a much simpler texture appears in bars 121–4, where a single ostinato comprising only two parts repeats at crotchet intervals and accompanies the women's chorus (*divisi* violas in bars 121–2, violins II in bars 123–4).

I have measured the complexity of ostinatos in the following manner: for each successive ostinato passage I have counted the number of parts and added to it the number of ostinatos distinguished by the durations of their cycles.[32] The result is a series of values that I have converted to graphic format as a shaded band in the manner of previous illustrations (see Figure 11.6, stratum 5). Note the many parallels between textural and formal complexity. To some extent (but not wholly) these parallels derive from the fact that often the lowest-level formal units are defined at least in

part by the boundaries of ostinato cycles. Note also that vacillations in ostinatos occur frequently and vary across a wide range of magnitude through
most of the piece, but are conspicuously absent about the composition's
centre.

Conclusions: the performers' dance

I think you would have enjoyed their voluptuous rhythms[33]

In the end, what does all this counting mean, all these values transformed
into graphic images in Figures 11.1, 11.4 and 11.6? It reflects, on one hand,
the fact that change – of all magnitudes, in all manner of musical domains,
and in myriad combinations – is a pervasive feature of Debussy's music, that
within any musical domain the changes evinced are remarkably diverse,
and that because these changes unfold across time they form a veritable
counterpoint of changes, whose patterns in combination are astonishingly
multifarious and which never, ever repeat exactly. What could be more vis-
cerally Debussyan? On the other hand there is another point to be made
about these rhythmic complexes of changes, found in all of his mature
works (certainly from *Prélude à l'après midi d'un faune* onwards), which the
graphic images help to reify: they capture music's sub-surface rhythms that
mirror those seen in natural phenomena like atmosphere and water, like
clouds and the sea – except that the graphic images arrest the motion, like
a painting. It would be better to imagine the shapes of Figures 11.1, 11.4,
and 11.6 moving slowly, gracefully, from left to right – better still in three
dimensions.

The last point I wish to make has everything to do with the *experience*
of music. Listeners hear the tendencies and vacillations discussed above
as intensifications or diffusions eliciting heightened or reduced attention.
Performers, however, experience these things even more acutely because
the aforementioned musical effects are effectuated by physical action. If
'music's inner dance' is found in the play of fluctuations in pacing and
complexity within and among various musical elements, the complementary *performers' dance* resides in the myriad, multifarious bodily motions
required to execute the music. All of these pieces imply the various fin-
gering patterns necessary to execute the scalar types embedded in their
unfolding musical gestures. Some scale types, such as the octatonic, require more intricate, less comfortable manoeuvres than others, such as the
diatonic, which execution in turn requires of the player different degrees
of deliberation. In the matter of velocity, passages of rapid notes require

more digital exertion and heightened concentration than their opposite. Different register spans and placements make different demands of the embouchure. In short, the act of performing involves an intricate choreography of arms, hands, fingers, embouchure, tongue, breath, eye movement, stance, etc., and the acts of musical ensemble engage the additional choreography of physical ensemble. In the light of the relation between musical pacing structures and performance, the term *harmony* takes on an added dimension, as the harmonious coordination of the performers' dance with the inner dance of the music. Ideally, the gradation and concatenation of changes in musical values will unfold in harness with their physical counterparts.

12 Debussy's 'rhythmicised time'

SIMON TREZISE

Introduction

We love Debussy's music intimately and yet detailed knowledge of it often seems remote and elusive.[1] Doubtless Debussy would have been delighted, for the realisation that he had denied analysts and theorists their quarry and encouraged some writers to assert, metaphorically at least, the unknowable intangibility of his music would have suited him very well, as we know from his dismissive comments about harmonic analysis and so on. One can imagine his pleasure growing at the recognition that one of the most successful pieces of Debussy scholarship – in the analysis of his music – to come in the post-war years is Roy Howat's *Debussy in Proportion*, a brilliant study that, in revealing a crucial aspect of Debussy's compositional process, raises an inescapable question of what it means for our perception of the music: he takes us into a mysterious domain. *Debussy in Proportion* proves beyond doubt that Debussy used Golden Section and other ancient proportional devices in his music,[2] for the examples Howat adduces, and others that have come to light since, are too compelling to be coincidence or the result of dark, subcutaneous forces. For example, in 'Reflets dans l'eau' the music reaches its loudest level in bar 58; bar 58 out of 94 bars is 0.62 of the piece, which is very close to Golden Section (the golden proportion is 1 : 1.618).[3] Having established this, however, we then have to ask, as Howat and many others have done, how we listen to proportion in music. We have a fairly good notion of how we experience pulse, metre, phrase, and such associated elements in the rhythmic cosmos as Cone's 'structural downbeat', and we can extrapolate from our experience theoretical systems of some complexity, but how do we respond at a deeper, more analytical level to proportion and ratios? After all, we do not know that we have been subject to Golden Section until the end of a movement or work, so the benefits are in one sense retrospective. On the other hand, we are willing to say that we feel a work is well proportioned, which indeed reflects a retrospective analytical decision. Architects use the same Golden Section proportions in buildings and rooms in buildings – the inner spaces – when there is no possibility that the eye could embrace the full effect simultaneously. Time and space cohabit in the world of proportion. Debussy would, I am sure, have enjoyed the mystery he had created in his musical universe for posterity.[4]

The mystery deepens when we look around at the complex problems Debussy's pursuit of pleasure have posed in the domain of harmonic and tonal theory. His refutation of the unified cosmos he inherited from his predecessors (Boyd Pomeroy would debate, to some extent at least, the scope of this unity in the nineteenth century; see chapter 9) has led to the partitioning of his pitch world into genera, which freely alternate and intertwine, inspiring David Lewin's view, cited by Arnold Whittall in chapter 14, that we comprehend such music no longer through a 'hierarchically stratified context', but rather through '"transformational networks", which treat the musical material as a mixture of motivic and harmonic components in a logically evolving...context'. So the music, or rather our theoretical grasp of it, 'splinters into fragments';[5] it can no longer offer the theorist and consumer of theory the reassuring notion of unity and organic form that Schenker bestows on Mozart and Beethoven, and Allen Forte on Schoenberg and Webern.

Even if we consider the ternary forms Debussy was so devoted to, the *sense* of reprise that is vital in an ABA form – and here we have only to think of the significance form takes on in the writings of Carl Dahlhaus and other German writers – often seems to evaporate or get compromised, though perhaps not in the 'anti-reprise' manner of Varèse, who undermines recapitulation even as he engages with repetition in a closing section. Debussy takes us a step or two closer to 'moment forms', which

> verticalize one's sense of time within sections, render every moment a present, avoid functional implications between moments, and avoid climaxes, they are not beginning–middle–end forms. In contrast to the possibly displaced beginnings and endings and multiply-directed time...a composition in moment time has neither functional beginning nor ending.[6]

In one area there is still the prospect of a coherent explanation of Debussy's music, if this is what we still aspire to. Debussy talked of his idea of music as 'colours and rhythmicised time', albeit in the context of rebutting formal stereotypes.[7] He did not leave us many clues as to the technical nature of his music, but this is one of the few comments that has come down to us, and it is a valuable one. It has done little to alter the pitch-centredness of much writing on Debussy, which in any case faithfully reflects the traditions and interests of generations of theorists and analysts, and has been very successful; rhythm is still the ugly duckling of theory, in spite of corrective publications in the past couple of decades. Unfortunately, the study of rhythm carries with it a great deal of unresolved baggage, the exposition of which, let alone its resolution, would take several volumes the size of this Companion. Nevertheless, there are a small number of places to look for a suggestive treatment of rhythm in Debussy.[8] That this number is small may be worrying, but our concerns should be tempered by the knowledge that Debussy's treatment of rhythm shows many more congruities with the nineteenth century than, for example, his treatment of harmony: the flattening out of climaxes implicit in moment form and the destruction of the 'beginning–middle–end logic of the dramatic curve'[9] in some modernistic art and music does not pertain in Debussy; the reverse is true (except in isolated instances, especially in the late works). For this chapter a few topics are explored without inappropriate – in this context – grappling with the knotty theoretical issues behind them. The conclusion at each stage is that rhythm can receive independent consideration, and its analysis provides a rich base from which to explore and explain the music. Effectively pursued it answers structural questions. As to how we choose to analyse the 'colours' of Debussy's letter, that is another, even more elusive question.

A temporal dichotomy

Julian Epstein offers us a fundamental temporal dichotomy between 'chronometric' and 'integral' (sometimes referred to as 'experiential') time.[10] The one is more 'purely mechanistic': 'emphasis within this domain is metrical accent, largely mechanical and virtually automatic, associated mainly with those beats of a measure (or larger dimensional levels) that are strong'.[11] Integral time is unique to each work, being formed from the experience of each work: since its elements are not predetermined in the manner of chronometric time, 'the strong pulses of rhythmic patters arise contextually. Because temporal phenomena cannot demarcate themselves, rhythmic strengths and weaknesses . . . are effected by events in other domains such as harmony (in its progression, tension and relaxation, stability and instability), melodic contour, cadence.'[12] There is a sense that while chronometric time belongs to music in its notated form, with its bar lines denoting metre, performed music, the individual work alive in real time, often with the bar lines dissolved in a 'performative' sense, inhabits the domain of integral time. These are the two polarities of rhythmic analysis or the study of time in music. It is predicated on the existence of two worlds, which might also be conveniently labelled 'metre and rhythm', as if the vocabulary were not already sufficiently compromised; they both imply hierarchical organisation, but metre-centred theory allows a higher level of abstraction in the sense that it is 'all about regularity of duration . . . meter arises from series of equal durations separating accents, with non-metrically-accented material filling the intervals between'.[13] In contrast, 'rhythmic analysis' founds its hierarchical structure upon the differentiation of accented and unaccented events in the manner advocated by, for example, Walter Berry.[14]

Perhaps in an ideal world, a world in which the performance is the 'real music' and the score a necessary abstraction, we would merge the two; it would be preferable, perhaps, to ignoring one or the other as so often happens. On the other hand, since phrases, melodies, sections often begin at the point of metrical accent, and melodies often climax and cadence at the point of rhythmic accent, there is not necessarily an undesirable level of abstraction in the one or arbitrariness in the other: if one accepts the duality, they can coexist very nicely. One of the two poles is encountered separately in Parks's chapter 'Meter' in *The Music of Claude Debussy* in which accent is permitted to be the determinant of metrical hierarchy (in a rhythmic sense) – see below; in Kramer's *The Time of Music* the emphasis is on metre and greater metrical groupings (hypermeasure and hypermetre[15]); rhythmic analysis here is considered a somewhat irritating and limited mode of enquiry.[16] A rapprochement between them is undertaken in Christopher Hasty's book *Meter as Rhythm*,[17] which spawned the separate analytical riposte to a review by Justin London; it culminates in a penetrating analysis of the opening of Debussy's Violin Sonata.[18] I hope that the metrical and rhythmic analyses that follow are sufficiently transparent to stand without a great deal of independent theoretical preparation.

Pulse/beat

Pulse is an aspect of how we hear time passing in music. It is the smallest denominator, but it is neither the smallest rhythmic element in a composition nor the largest; it is usually something in the middle. Even when it is not literally present, one senses its existence, but the composer has to establish it in some way: in the performance of music we do not usually 'see' the score. Pulse is regular in much music of the common-practice period. Each manifestation of it may not be precisely the same length as the previous pulse or the next (we know this well from measuring performance practice), but there is a common thread that usually runs the length and breadth of a composition uniting them within a common framework, which is why we still experience it when the sound marking the timepoint of its initiation has been suspended, as in the oft-encountered hemiola.

Varèse was influenced by Debussy in many ways: alongside Stravinsky he is close to him in history and style, but he quickly moved away from

Debussy's treatment of rhythm. For long stretches in his music ties over the bar line and changing time signatures not only obscure a regular pulse, they often prevent one being established at all; witness, for example, the opening of *Octandre*. Debussy, on the other hand, makes conspicuous use of a regular pulse in almost all of his music. Even when he opens a work with ties over the bar line and irregularly placed rhythmic events, he usually issues a corrective within a few bars, thereby establishing regular pulse and with it a yardstick against which to measure subsequent musical events. From its establishment as a near-universal background feature in most of Debussy's music, pulse is sometimes foregrounded as a gestural feature: the stakes are raised and in extreme cases Debussy might even take a step closer to the post-war avant garde and Eimert's espousal of *Jeux* as 'the vegetative circulation of form' (see the discussion of 'Gigues' below).[19]

From the analyses that follow it is apparent that Debussy sometimes challenged the hegemony of regular, unitary pulse, perhaps by setting two conflicting metres against each other, but there is usually a common thread against which one is heard as a disruptive element, and one metre is usually firmly established by the end.

Metre

The next level up from pulse and beat is metre and motive, as Epstein designates them.[20] It is useful to make this distinction, because not all music reflects the notated metre, which is the manifestation of time signature and bar line. Waltzes sail along nicely reiterating metre as they circulate, but motivic combinations often contradict the notated metrical patterning in other types of music. Curiously for our study, Debussy was very fond of dance music, especially in his early works. His later music contains numerous references to dances and marches – albeit subsumed into grander designs. All of which is highly suggestive. Even a cursory rhythmic analysis of his music quickly discloses a deep-seated and extensive adherence to regular metre, which in many works is often contradicted by nothing more radical than a hemiola in the manner of a waltz.

We mean by this that the patterns established in the melody or accompaniment are a direct reflection of the metre indicated in the time signature. Most banally this is the low–high–high, i.e. strong–weak–weak, accompaniment to a waltz theme, which does the two most elementary things required to confirm metre: provide a downbeat accent and then the one or two (in a waltz) continuing, evenly spaced temporal events to constitute a pattern.[21] When this process is repeated the satisfying hierarchical integrity of the marking of time passing in music is realised: the beginning of each

Example 12.1 'Voiles': metrical ambiguities (bars 1–9)

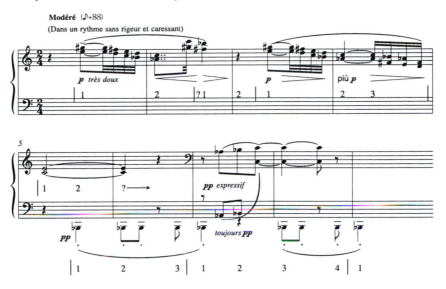

bar (in this instance) forms a second level of pulse, which rises then to the next level, which is hypermeasure or phrase (the rhythmic equivalent).[22]

A brief survey of the first book of *Préludes* gives a rounded view of Debussy's treatment of metre. These works accurately reflect many aspects of Debussy's music and so constitute an excellent starting point for this investigation.

No. 1, 'Danseuses de Delphes', presents a straightforward and immediate agreement between motive and meter, which is analogous to the relative simplicity of its diatonic pitch organisation. The rising three-note motive in crotchets is completed on the third crotchet of the 3/4 bar and the metrical conclusions we reach on this evidence are confirmed in the slightly varied repetition of bar 2. Less common in Debussy's music in general are the changes of time signature (to 4/4 in bars 4 and 9).

No. 2, 'Voiles', is the polar opposite in its tonal and rhythmic structure. Its famously exclusive whole-tone pitch organisation (apart from the pentatonic B section) is mirrored by the many accentual ambiguities that obscure its notated metrical structure of 2/4. The *Prélude* starts on the second beat of the bar. When the right hand begins to establish a duple metre, a left-hand ostinato begins in the bass, again on the second beat. Its grouping resembles 3/4 in bars 3–4 and 4/4 in bars 7–8. Regular metrical groupings are finally assured in the B′ section when the left-hand ostinato is transmuted into a regular ♩. ♪ figure (Example 12.1).

No. 3, 'La vent dans la plaine', immediately establishes a strong pulse through regular iterations of a sextuplet figure and left-hand B♭. In common

Example 12.2 'La vent dans la plaine' (bars 3–5, beat 1)

x 12.2

with many other works by Debussy, the two bars of essentially undifferentiated crotchet events establish the hypermetric unit (two bars) in advance of the metre, which arrives in an ambiguous form in bar 3 with the accent falling on beat 2 and then defining a 4/4 grouping across the bar for a two-bar span (Example 12.2).[23] This sets the first metrical unit (bars 1–2) and the metrical unit defined by the melody out of synchronisation with each other. Not until bar 9 is there agreement between left and right hands. The second-beat accent continues to feature, as in bar 34.

No. 4, 'Les sons et les parfums tournent dans l'air du soir', is a specimen of Debussy's rare use of an irregular time signature, 5/4. In passages of greater flow and longer-breathed ideas, the *Prélude* nevertheless falls predominantly into a regular 3/4, which begins in bar 3. In other words, the reticent irregularities of the first bars are soon superseded by bars of metrical regularity.

In No. 5, 'Les collines d'Anacapri', the hypermetric unit of two bars is established first without making any clear commitment to the dual metrical schemes indicated in the time signature (12/16 and 2/4), which are to intertwine throughout the piece. In bar 8 we first hear the duple division of the bar (2/4) and finally in bar 14 we encounter the 12/16 metre, albeit with the accent on the second quaver. Cross rhythms are avoided in the A and A′ sections of this ternary composition by the simultaneous use of mainly quaver patterns in the 2/4 metre against triplet-semiquaver patterns of the 12/16. The opening of the *Prélude* (Example 12.3a) hints ambivalently at another organisation, triplet quavers (one might hear the quavers in pairs or triplets), which are taken up in the B section. Although Debussy does not indicate a change of time signature in the score, this section is effectively 6/8 superimposed upon 3/4 (Example 12.3b), but the resemblance to bar 1 indicates that the quaver pattern is directly derived from the A section's opening – a derivation that is confirmed in bar 63 when the bar 1 figure is restated in 6/8 metre (Example 12.3c). Even so, the conjunction of 3/4 and 6/8 was a favourite of Debussy's and produced some of his most characteristic cross rhythms and polyrhythms.

Example 12.3(a) 'Les collines d'Anacapri' (bar 1)

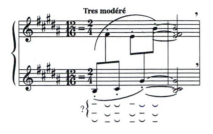

(b) 'Les collines d'Anacapri' (bar 49)

(c) 'Les collines d'Anacapri' (bar 63)

Passing over *Prélude* No. 6, 'Des pas sur la neige', which is discussed in more detail below, we come to the Lisztian turbulence of No. 7, 'Ce qu'a vu le vent d'Ouest'. There are metrical complexities aplenty, but the basic metre is established by bar 3 after two bars in which beats 1 and 3 are accented; in bar 3 beats 2 and 4 receive secondary accents that consolidate the 4/4 metre.

No. 8, 'La fille aux cheveux de lin', starts serenely with a monodic figure of the sort established as a Debussy archetype in *Prélude à l'après midi d'un faune*. In bars 1–2 'La fille' glides languorously across the bar line without creating a clear strong–weak pattern in accord with the notated metre of 3/4. In the light of bars 1–2's repetition scheme the obvious reading would be of a three-minim group in 3/2. Emphasis shifts away from this with the tie across the bar line in bar 7, which breaks up the hitherto regular hypermetric unit as well as initiating an unambiguous transition to 3/4, which is completed in bar 14.

No. 9, 'La sérénade interrompue', sounds like an *étude* for Debussy's Spanish triptych 'Ibéria'. Played in a suitably accurate, neutral manner

Example 12.4 'La cathédrale engloutie' (bars 1–2)

(in other words without gratuitous accents at the start of bars 2, 6, 8, etc.), the opening two bars might as easily be interpreted in duple as in triple time. Not until bar 9, where a falling offbeat figure is played, can we be sure of the 3/8 time signature.

Writ large, No. 10, 'La cathédrale engloutie', expands the 3/4–6/8 dichotomy of 'Les collines d'Anacapri' in a broad 6/4–3/2 juxtaposition (expressed in the time signature itself). One might wonder where the binary division of the bar implied by 6/4 occurs, however, for much of the writing is unambiguously in three minims to the bar. In bar 1, where the minim is not in control, one imagines that the intention is to persuade the pianist to allow the B to flow up to the syncopated E, if not the whole crotchet melody, thus avoiding even the slightest hint of an accentual pairing of E–B and D–E (Example 12.4). In bar 16 this inference is confirmed in the varied B major repetition of the opening, for the left hand is clearly presented with a 6/4 grouping, encapsulated in the left hand's change of direction at the midway point of the bar.

No. 11, 'La danse de Puck', clarifies its duple metre (the time signature is 2/4) early on, though the accentual pattern often emphasises the quaver (4/8). The 3/4 section sports some of the most complex cross rhythms in the first book of *Préludes*, particularly in bar 41.

No. 12, 'Minstrels', is unambiguous in its correlation of motive and notated metre: a regular 2/4 pattern is established from bar 1.

By the time of Debussy's last creative flowering, most of which took place in the glorious summer of 1915, there are sporadic hints that regular metre is beginning to lose its grip. There are more changes of time signature and longer stretches in which either pulse or metre is obscured. Nevertheless, as Aysegul Durakoglu has shown (see below, pp. 252ff.), in the *Etudes*, one of the most considerable products of this most productive summer, regular metre is still a central resource. Perhaps if Debussy had been granted a few more years we would have seen him moving closer to the rhythmic changes apparent in the music of Stravinsky and Varèse.

Metrical units/hypermeasure and beyond

As we ascend the hierarchy, the compromises and contrivances of rhythmic analysis can be more irksome. Nonetheless, the principle remains constant: the tendency of pulses to accumulate into groups of two or three (and multiples thereof) continues so that single metrical groupings (bars) now form themselves into units of two or three. This next level can be subsumed under the general heading of phrase and then period, for which a substantial study exists in William Rothstein's *Phrase Rhythm in Tonal Music*.[24] His focus is music of tonal common practice, a point that alerts us to the weakening of aspects of phrase structure that Debussy's at least partial denial of tonal grammar and voice leading entailed.

Without the 'rhythm' of recurring harmonic events in the tonic–dominant grouping, other factors have to take their place, which necessarily challenge Rothstein's definition of phrase, or at least encourage us to develop it further:

> [Definitions by Roger Sessions and Peter Westergaard] describe a motion with a beginning, middle, and end; but Westergaard's describes a *tonal* motion with a rhythmic component . . . rather than a rhythmic motion with an unspecified tonal component.[25]

As we move further up the hierarchy to phrase groupings ('periods'), which produce formal sections, the expanses of music have become such that one might cynically argue that we are now in the domain of formal analysis. Edward T. Cone and others have again shown how rhythm operates at these high levels. Notions of cadential arrival and departure have been grouped around Cone's seductive heading 'structural downbeat'.[26] After all, music moves through time, so if we do divide a piece into five sections, say ABACA, as in a rondo, one still expects other parameters to be the agents of that formal grouping. In sonata form the development section, or a significant part of it, takes on the role of an extended upbeat to the moment of tonal and thematic return, the structural downbeat. In Classical music, harmony, voice leading, texture and other elements all contribute to a unified manifestation of a greater rhythmic movement that, in Kramer's evocative description, gathers hypermetric elements into a single linear process:

> The temporal form of a tonal piece typically consists of a move towards a point of greatest tension that is usually remote from the tonic, followed by a drive back towards the tonic. The return of the tonic is an event of rhythmic importance, a structural downbeat, a point of resolution, the goal.[27]

Applying this to Debussy, we at once miss the defining power of I–IV–V–I progressions and their many associates. Even in the early and in some

Example 12.5 Nocturne: harmonic reduction (bars 6–14)

ways atypical Nocturne (1892), the opening bass line tips us off to Debussy's early exaltation of his pleasure and the concomitant displeasure of his professors of theory. This bass line runs Bb–Eb–A♮–Db(bar 1), all crotchets (the last one suspended over the bar where there is a I$_3^6$ arpeggiation), which denies the tonal association of leading note (A♮) and provisional tonic (Bb). The main theme, beginning in bar 6, arranges itself in four-bar phrases based on two-bar subphrases (much of Debussy's music takes the two-bar unit as its starting point) with the promise of Romantic harmonic phraseology in the sense that the phrase begins partway through a tonal progression on iv of Bb minor (the piece is in Db major but there is a strong, Chopinesque Bb minor lean at the start; cf. the Scherzo in Bb minor/Db) and would then, if this were Chopin, move through to the dominant–tonic parts of the harmonic phrase (see Example 12.5). Debussy blunts this, indeed pulls a veil over it, by allowing the V^9 of Bb minor in bar 7 to progress to a Bb^7 chord with a prominent Ab in the tenor voice. The phrase ends in bar 9 on an even blunter chord, that of Ab^7 (there has been no suggestion as yet of a tonic Db major triad).[28] Nevertheless, thanks to this dominant seventh, and the preceding dominant minor ninth on F, there is a strong dominant 'charge' in this phrase, which needs to find release (or 'discharge', to use Daniel Harrison's useful term[29]); this becomes significant in a few bars' time, but even in the Romantic context of this Nocturne, Debussy's harmonies are not going to respect conventional tonal voice leading. The next four-bar phrase might be more properly described as comprising four separate one-bar phrases (or we might follow Hasty's example and relinquish this all-too-loaded vocabulary); these one-bar units progress in parallel dominant ninths rooted on Db (so the V^7 is released to the tonic, but with its seventh flattened), G, Eb (bars 10–12). The bass line connecting the Eb minor chord in bar 12 to the reprise of the main theme on bass C in bar 14 travels in a chromatic descent E♭–D♮–D♭–C. This bass line seems to carry the 'dominant charge' mentioned above in bars 6–9: if we take the harmonies away and consider the bass, we see the residue of a tonal progression in A♭ (dominant of D♭) as the bass descends through what might have been the grammatically 'correct' dominant-of-the-dominant on D♮ (it would be the chord B♭^{7}), to D♭ (part of a V$^6_4$ of A♭), to C, the first inversion of A♭ (at this point I part from Harrison, for 'dominant charge' would not apply to a descending line in his dualist system, but in the voice-leading sense intended here the descending line would be paired with rising semitones as leading notes resolve upwards, which is a crucial aspect of the linearity of the tonal system and therefore of phrase rhythm). At this juncture Debussy could have boarded the tonal gravy train and modified the chords to support the implications of the bass, but instead we hear a minor-seventh chord on C (C–E♭–G♭–B♭) as the endpoint of a series of harmonies that subvert tonal progression, not least in bars 10–12 where there is a sense of weightlessness or disconnection. All this illustrates an interim stage in Debussy's departure from the Conservatoire textbooks and inhalation of air as fresh and as inter-galactic as Schoenberg was to experience a full decade-and-a-half later.

My aim in pointing out so much detail is also to show that even this early on in Debussy's career, and in a work that looks back as much as this, the harmonic phrase is not quite the driving rhythmic force in the linear sense required by Rothstein. Rhythmic momentum comes from other factors such as the *crescendo* at the end of the second phrase (bars 12–13), and the extended reprise of the opening bass line (a kind of recitative) in bars 51–4, which generates the 'unaccent' needed for the rhythmic articulation of the return of the main theme in A′ (of this ternary form).[30] (Even when there appears to be a linear, rhythmic harmonic movement, as in the V–I succession from bars 11 to 12, Debussy uses various blunting techniques to deflect us from the harmonic upbeat–downbeat inference that might otherwise have been drawn.) Later he generates harmonic tension by changing the tonal genus, e.g. from a diatonic collection to a whole-tone one.

Shaping of the melody, dynamics, texture, agogic accent, dynamic accent, the number of voices playing, repetition of themes, recurring harmonies and other factors shape one's perception of 'phrase' and hypermeasure in Debussy and articulate the tension–release schemes essential to the definition of a rhythmic structure (at least the sort of rhythmic structure Debussy apparently sought). Without the defining properties of the tonal phrase some familiarities have been removed, and one should be prepared for a little flexibility in recognising and analysing Debussy's alternative structures. Pursued in this way the Nocturne poses few obstacles to the extension of the style of hypermetric analysis undertaken by Kramer.

Pursuing the argument that there is a rational connection between ideas in Debussy's music, which no longer depends upon tonal voice leading, we should consider the many passages in his music that are devoted to escalation – the generation of climactic moments that articulate the broader rhythmic structure. Such passages follow a pattern that can, even at risk of over-generalisation, be categorised as follows:

interruption–alienation–preparation–escalation–confirmation

These passages often begin with a breaking off from an established idea; 'alienation' often takes the form of substituting a new pitch grouping, such as the whole-tone scale; 'preparation' might entail the institution of an ostinato; escalation sometimes deploys a great deal of repetition, often sequential, heightening dynamics and related devices; 'confirmation' may involve a return to, or renewed use of, triadic material, a loud dynamic, and other, related devices. Such passages take on great prominence in Debussy's music (see below).

Parks cites the climax of the slow movement of the String Quartet in bar 76 as an example of Debussy's use of Golden Section.[31] It is the point of greatest affirmation, featuring a return to the triadic genus from whole-tone collections with a *forte* restatement of the central section's main theme after a succession of whole-tone harmonies. It is approached by a rising tide of sequential repetitions beginning in bar 62 (fig. 13), *piano*. Debussy characteristically marks a return to *piano* at each new beginning in the escalation (a marking more honoured in the breach than in the observance by performers). Clearly bar 76 is a point of maximum rhythmic stress: Parks marks it thus (level 3 – the highest value in his three-level hierarchy for the movement), and we have to remember that Parks is employing an 'experiential' scheme for his analysis founded on 'successive-attack activity . . . loudness, sonorous density, and placement of the theme in the extreme upper register'.[32] If we now stand back from accent as the main agent of division and consider the more 'neutral' claims of hypermetre, we find the slow movement's climax following a logical ordering of the metrical hierarchy: as elsewhere there is a tendency towards irregularity in the sense that groupings of two are often followed by a grouping of three, but since this recurs it becomes a regularity; at the highest level such irregularities are subsumed into larger regularities (Example 12.6). In Table 12.1 we find a structure rising up from a consistently maintained pulse, through regular metrical groupings, to a clear hypermetric outcome. The notations of the table rise from the metre (bars) in the bottom row; the duple and occasionally triple groupings of bars in row a; row b shows how larger groups are

Example 12.6 String Quartet, slow movement: melody line (bars 62–79)

Table 12.1. *String Quartet, slow movement: hypermetric analysis of central climax (bars 62–84)*

	62	63	64	65	66	67	68	69	70	71	72	73	74	75	76	77	78	79	80	81	82	83	84
d															|								
c	|														|								
b	|					|				|					|				|		|		
a	|		|		|		|		|		|		|		|		|		|		|	|	
	|	|	|	|	|	|	|	|	|	|	|	|	|	|	|	|	|	|	|	|	|	|	|

arrived at as we rise through the metrical structure. In row c, the second-highest level analysed here, we see how the aggregated groupings articulate the linear progressions towards the structural downbeat of bar 76, the *forte* restatement of the main theme of the central section, on row d. (The largest number of vertical strokes indicates the strongest metrical accent; Parks uses similar notation but his accents are based on rhythmic properties of the music, which do not always coincide with metric accents, though in bar 76 metrical and rhythmic accent do coincide.)

Returning now to the pattern advocated above for the articulation of this rhythmic structure through escalation, we find many aspects of it confirmed: all rhythmic activity stops in bar 61 and the patterns obtaining in bar 61 are dropped (interruption); the triadic genus of bar 61 is replaced by the whole-tone scale (alienation); a new ostinato is established (preparation); tempo and dynamic are gradually heightened, and tension is further increased by sequential restatements of the theme (escalation); the apex is reached with the triad of G♯ minor, *forte* dynamic, expressive intensification and an expanded, definitive restatement of the main motive (confirmation).

In voice-leading terms there is a profound disjunction between bars 61 and 62 that Schenkerian analysis would, to put it mildly, find uncomfortable. In rhythmic terms the passage is comprehensible within a broad, congruent scheme.

Examples of rhythmic structure

'Jardins sous la pluie'

Having considered the concept of metrical and rhythmic levels, we now take some examples that cover different aspects of rhythmic structure. We begin with 'Jardins sous la pluie' (*Estampes*, 1903) in which we encounter Debussy following principles reminiscent of those of the String Quartet in a characteristic, toccata-like context. It is in a sort of rondo form with a lyrical interlude (not quite central section). The rondo theme is nothing more than a brief snatch of a popular lullaby 'Do, do, l'enfant do' that Debussy was evidently strongly attracted to. It's the sort of snippet of melody that runs around and around in one's head on the way to work; the only way to be free of it, if you're Debussy, is to 'compose it out'.

Pulse is based on a minim and the notated metre is 2/2. Note grouping establishes pulse and metre in bar 1, as it does a four-semiquaver subdivision of the main unit of pulse. The duple grouping of the pulse is mirrored on the next level by metric units founded on two bars, though as in the String Quartet example above, there are extensions to three bars, beginning in bars 3–5. The point of departure for the piece, the first downbeat, is the opening, which gives us the most cursory statement of the 'Do, do, l'enfant do' fragment. The piece now proceeds to inhale and exhale excitedly through a series of escalations and confirmations, culminating in the triumphant E major cadence in the last three bars. Tonally its points of arrival are marked by returns to the triadic genera of F♯ minor/major, C minor, D♭ major, F♯ major, B minor (not fully established) and E major. All are accompanied by the 'Do, do, l'enfant do' fragment. In between these triadic points of arrival (characterised by different levels of certainty and emphasis), alternative genera are employed, including the ubiquitous whole-tone and octatonic collections. The paradigm adumbrated above (from interruption to confirmation) consistently applies.

In terms of metrical units the first phase of the process is probably capable of several interpretations, but if Table 12.2 effects a successful interpretation of the hypermetric structure, it is apparent that the opening two-bar–three-bar unit has reverberations at a higher level, which indicates the efficacy of this type of analysis in unveiling parallelisms at different structural levels in the best Schenkerian manner. Table 12.2 follows the same notational principles as Table 12.1 with the greatest number of vertical

Table 12.2. 'Jardins sous la pluie': hypermetric analysis (bars 1–32) strokes indicating the strongest metrical accent, the hierarchy rising logically through duple and ternary groupings to the first point of release in the repeated As in bar 25 that preface the return of the lullaby theme in bar 27.

Even more striking than this relatively neutral level of working is the more distinctively gestural or motivic character of the rhythmic play of this composition. The opening five bars accommodate a playful gesture that reverberates throughout the piece both in the microcosm and in the macrocosm. The particularity of this gesture is the manner in which the first statement so rapidly degenerates: in bars 1–2 we get a strong exposition of motive, tonality and metre, with the promise of resumption and affirmation in bar 3, hence the 'Do, do, l'enfant do' rhythmic unit used in these bars. Instead of the proposed affirmation, tonal and motivic focus rapidly decays from bar 3, and we soon begin a long period of escalation towards the delayed affirmation (in other words, the 'downbeat' aspect of the temporal structure is prematurely subsumed into a long afterbeat, from which Debussy extricates himself in a variety of ways in pursuit of the upbeat and consequent recycling of the gesture in new guises). Much of the playfulness of this composition stems from this gesture, not least the manner in which several of the main stress points – the structural downbeats – are not re-statements of the theme but prefatory, thematically neutral gestures, such as the *ff* D♭ major arpeggiations in bar 47 and G♯–F♯ trill in bar 126, both of which lead to the theme being treated as a consequent. On the other hand, the theme itself does occupy the arrival or antecedent point in bar 43, the C minor passage, but it is superseded in terms of accent within just a few bars by the D♭ major arpeggiations (Example 12.7).

This and other factors ensure that 'Jardins sous la pluie' engages us first and foremost as an exercise in rhythmic play. As a tonal exercise it is puzzling and disparate. Formally we have no very great desire to hear this tiresome snippet of melody arrayed in rondo or any other form (lest this be misunderstood, the original song is delightful, but most of the notes are omitted and its character wholly transformed by Debussy), for form is the great exponent of reprise, and the form of this work seems to be at the disposal of stretching and retarding the moments of upbeat preparation: stretching in the vastly long preparation for the G♯–F♯ trill (bars 100–25) and retardation in the ravishing lyrical episode that precedes bars 100–25 with its limpid, non-escalatory phrases of seven and eight bars framing a more characteristically short-breathed central part, distantly based on 'Nous n'irons plus au bois' (the whole section is from bars 75–99).

'Des pas sur la neige'
The subject of some of the most celebrated writing on Debussy's tonal structures, 'Des pas sur la neige' is a triumph of harmonic disjunction.[33] No two

Example 12.7(a) 'Jardins sous la pluie' (bars 1–5)

(b) 'Jardins sous la pluie' (bars 43–8)

sections employ the same tonal materials, though there are intersecting elements and a clear tonic note. Both the title and the instructions to the performer connote mental and physical movement. The subject is undefined, but we know that at some point in the piece the subject experiences a 'tendre et triste regret', which affirms and closes the many currents of the work and presents a stark juxtaposition of two related genera in the closing parts, namely Gb major (bars 29–31) and D harmonic minor (32–end). The various other harmonic genera encountered earlier on, including the whole-tone scale, are discarded. The juxtaposition in the last two sections is also between a tendency in favour of the ostinato established at the beginning and against it (it is first suspended in bar 7). In the penultimate section (bars 29–31) the ostinato is entirely discarded and then ritually incorporated into the first two bars of the closing section (bars 32–3).

In terms of texture, mood and pitch centricity the work *sounds* unified, but there is another connecting thread that meshes every part of the work

Example 12.8(a) 'Des pas sur la neige' (bars 2–3)

(b) 'Des pas sur la neige' (bars 28–30)

together: the polarisation of two metrical poles, one implied by the time signature of four crotchets in a bar (4/4), which opposes the duple time implications of the ostinato (2/2). As the ostinato continues in bar 2, melody springs up awkwardly against it, limping in a syncopated, incomplete way and emphasising the crotchet beat; it stumbles on to the end of bar 3 where it is held over. Like the ice and snow, the scene is frigid, but as we progress through this remarkable piece memories melt through the ice, and with them the two disparate metrical organisations also melt into each other until there is a period of the greatest freedom when the left and right hands coordinate in two liberating bars of quadruple time, first in the fulfilled liberation of the melodic impulse (bars 28–9) from the limping version of bars 2–3 (Example 12.8), and then in the ritualised restatement of the ostinato in the right hand with a new, ostinato-like figure in the left. The *Prélude*'s rhythmic premise is consistently explored in the piece, resulting in pauses, interruptions, diversions and so on.

'Gigues'

The orchestral *Images* (1905–12) deserve to be considered the pinnacle of Debussy's achievement as a composer for orchestra rather more than the oft-cited *Jeux*. Their extraordinary richness is manifested in almost every aspect of composition, from the orchestral sound itself to the breathtaking beauty of the sectional transitions in 'Ibéria' (a sublime response to Wagner's art of transition?). It was in a letter of 1907 to his publisher about work on *Images* that Debussy spoke of his new, 'immaterial' music, which he could no longer handle like a 'robust symphony, walking on all four feet (sometimes three)', an oblique reference perhaps to his three-movement and somewhat symphonic *La mer*.[34] He continued with the intriguing claim that his music 'consists of colours and rhythmicised time'.[35] There are five movements in this extensive work, three of which belong to 'Ibéria'; they are flanked by the single-movement 'Gigues' and 'Rondes de printemps' (some conductors have rearranged the order in performance so that the set ends with the more extrovert 'Ibéria', including Eduard van Beinum, whose live recording with the Concertgebouw of 1948 presents the work in this revised order[36]).

As Robin Holloway has shown, Wagner is rarely entirely absent for long as a presence in Debussy's music; even when the musical detail of his voice is absent, other aspects of Debussy's demon seem to emerge, as here in 'Gigues' where the tempo markings allow the interpreter a high level of freedom. The only specific marking is the *Modéré* at the start, after which there are a series of qualifiers and reversions. The same situation prevails in the vast Prologue (and much of Act I) of *Götterdämmerung*, where the conductor has to look back to the start of the Three Norns scene, bar 1 of the opera, to find a definitive tempo marking by which to gauge the appropriate tempo for the love duet; and Wagner, like Debussy, had little trust in metronome markings. On the other hand, Debussy also had little patience for very subjective interpreters who used his music as a springboard for their own ruminations on life, so 'Gigues' requires a great deal of empathy if it is to be realised with the precision and sense of what is right that its creator presumably wanted. At least one can say that the intention is to have the temporal structure rooted in one central tempo with perhaps the first twenty bars slightly slower than much that ensues (subsequent *a tempo* markings appear to apply to the *plus allant* of the oboe d'amore's theme).[37]

Metrically the work consistently combines and interleaves 2/4 and 6/8, the first heard at the beginning with the flute motive and the second first and most strongly defined by the oboe d'amore. Debussy follows his favoured procedure of introducing the rhythmic world of the piece in the order hypermetric unit followed by metre. The duple metre is in fact only hazily outlined by the harp in the introductory section; the oboe d'amore then plainly establishes the duple division of the bar in its melancholy 6/8; a fresh, more nervous metrical element is then introduced at figure 3, the motivic basis of which resides in the introduction and which might, in another context, be notated as 4/8. These three elements are joined later by various other ingredients, such as the *Le sacre du printemps*-like ostinato figure at fig. 11 ('Gigues' came first), closely followed by a sensual

Example 12.9(a) 'Gigues' 'slow music' (bars 3–9)

(b) 'Gigues' '*moderato* music' (bars 21–4)

(c) 'Gigues' 'fast music' (bars 43–4)

flute theme that is extensively developed and forms the basis of the main climax.

As 'Gigues' is a moderately paced movement, unified in tempo (though subject to various speedings up and slowings down), one might not expect from it such a diverse temporal experience as it invariably yields. The sensation is of listening to a combination of slow, moderate and fast music – a superimposition of three movement characters in one (Example 12.9). The polyrhythmic character is omnipresent, and can be categorised into the three elements of (a) the hypermetric unit, (b) the 6/8 duple division of the bar, and (c) the nervous 4/8 motives. They overlap, fade in and out, play together, and in the closing pages their coalescence dims in favour of the two-bar hypermetric unit with which the piece began. The climax at around fig. 18 (bar 182) has the voluptuous flute melody outlining the duple division of the bar superimposed on 4/8 material; like so many of Debussy's climaxes, the apex or structural downbeat is short-lived and collapses into a *Jeux*-like chromatic descent for piccolo, flute and solo violin, which reinstates movement founded on the hypermetric unit – an abrupt reduction in activity.

'Gigues' is a study in rhythm, Debussy's *Pacific 231*, but infinitely more subtle and variegated than Honegger's metrical *tour de force*.

Etude No. 3, 'Pour les quartes'
In his highly detailed doctoral investigation of four of the piano *Etudes*, Aysegul Durakoglu posits these general points about rhythm in Debussy: Debussy's piano music makes extensive use of 'contrapuntal lines [in the]

stratification of piano sound in layers. . . . At the source of his conception lies Debussy's treatment of rhythm in each line.'[38] He argues that Debussy took much from the past, including the use of

> rhythmic modes deriving from . . . ancient Greek theory; the repetition of the rhythmic patterns in different lines reflecting . . . isorhythmic technique in Renaissance polyphony; the idea of arabesque and ornament lying at the essence of all art according to Debussy, and the use of ties over bar lines giving a sense of measureless time [such as] one can find in the long melodies of . . . Gregorian Chant.[39]

Durakoglu describes the sense of 'freedom and flexibility' encountered in 'Pour les quartes' and notes the collage-like effect created by 'abrupt changes in the regular flow of music'.[40] These are characteristic features of Debussy's late music and suggest that he was moving ever closer to modernist constructions of musical structure. The sheer diversity and range of metrical arrangement is illustrated by Durakoglu's list of rhythmic patterns in the piece: their rhythmic modes encompass the trochaic, dactylic, iambic, anapaestic, tribraic and amphibraic, a list that does justice to the flexibility of the music, but not to Durakoglu's view that Debussy used ancient Greek modes in a systematic way redolent, for instance, of the isorhythmic motet.[41]

Debussy makes little attempt at the start of 'Pourles Quartes' to establish regularity of pulse or metre (Example 12.10a).[42] If account is taken of the contrapuntal interlocking of the organum-like lines traced by the left and right hands, the six beats of the metre have been accounted for by the end of bar 2, but only via a multiplicity of accentual patterns. Moreover, the need for confirmation through repetition upon which rhythmic theory is often founded is denied us, for the flowing lines manifest constant renewal and change prior to the regularisation of accent and, as the *stretto* indicates, change of pace in bar 7, which is also short-lived. Ties and a reduction of contrapuntal activity in bars 4–6 weaken what little definition there has yet been of the 6/8 metre, and with it the harmony loses its token F major focus in favour of chromatic collections in bars 6 and 7. A 3/4 metre is more effectively asserted, as indicated above, in bars 7–11, but abrupt changes of pattern and pace deny us confirmation, and the music returns to a hesitant espousal of 6/8 in bars 13–19. The extremely assertive F major cadence in bars 18–19 is surprising in context, sounding somewhat gratuitous, or at the very least premature in a harmonic and rhythmic sense.

In this opening section Debussy fully explores the potential of withholding temporal certainties from us, and the assertion of this strategy in the premature cadence drives the point home. Elements of this section invade the next, which reinforces Durakoglu's use of the term 'collage'. However,

Example 12.10(a) *Etude* 'Pour les quartes' (bars 1–2)

(b) *Etude* 'Pour les quartes' (bars 68–70)

the temporal character of the music is slowly mutating, for in bars 29ff. a diatonic genus is predominant and with it comes growing metrical regularity, especially with the downbeat C struck in bar 30 (the downbeat having been withheld in the previous bar). Repetition and regularity also clarify the hypermetric structure: the reiteration of the 3/4 stretto bars (10–12) in the new section (bars 37–42) changes their character entirely, making them a point of rhythmic release rather than tension-building.

The *Etude* falls into four sections, the third of which begins in bar 43 followed by a change of key signature to A major in bar 46 (the triadic connotations of this are not present). Rhythmicised motives, repeated, begin a passage of escalation, which changes the rhythmic character of the piece from localised effect to broad upbeat–downbeat patterning. From bar 53 the pulse is dramatically foregrounded with a striking bass figure on Db–Ab which survives in a regular, metrical form for three bars minus a beat. Its new form in bar 56 is potentially destabilising, for it shifts the accent away from the beginning of the bar to beat 2, but regular rhythmic patterning in the right hand continues in bars 56–7. After one bar both left- and right-hand patterns are resumed (in bar 59), but the accent has shifted to beat 2 in the right hand, beat 3 in the left, which reflects the increasing urgency of the music (the rhythmic sequence implied here matches the melodic one). This climactic section is almost strident in its rhythmic character, but it is not an isolated phenomenon of the sort that would encourage avant-gardists of the 1950s to squirrel this *Etude* away as a clairvoyant essay in moment form: great metrical clarity was imminent in section 2, and in the final section (the fourth) a chorale-like simplification of texture and music gesture sings confidently of the newly won triple metre (see Example 12.10b). The incorporation of material from earlier sections (reprise is too strong a word) confirms the synthetic workings of this music and the rejection of the inherently unstable 6/8 metre with which the work began. There is, in short, a sturdy underpinning of rhythmic process here.

It seems that as our understanding of Debussy's tonal language takes a leap forward through the realisation that alternate approaches to the old organicist one are the order of the day, rhythm must surely take its place as a vital element in the Debussyan analytical cosmos. It is an area rich in potential and yet scantily explored so far. Moreover, Debussy himself gave us clues as to the importance of time in his music, not least in his careful proportioning of so many works.

PART FOUR

Performance and assessment

13 Debussy in performance

CHARLES TIMBRELL

How did Debussy and the musicians in his circle perform his works? What did he listen for when he coached performers? Were his performance expectations similar for pianists, singers and conductors? Through a rich array of contemporary recordings, memoirs, letters and reviews Debussy is the first composer for whom we can answer such questions in a definitive way. This chapter begins with a consideration of Debussy's own piano playing and the advice he gave to various pianists, some of whom later recorded his works. Subsequent sections are devoted to the singers and conductors who came in contact with him, and to their recordings.

'I have never heard more beautiful pianoforte playing'

So thought Louise Liebich, Debussy's first biographer, when she heard him play 'Danseuses de Delphes'.[1] Certainly his piano playing was very different from the dry, highly articulated style of many of his French contemporaries. It is likely that his tone-sensible approach was fostered by his early teacher Mme Mauté de Fleurville, who claimed to have studied with Chopin. It was she who prepared him for admission to the Paris Conservatoire, where he studied with Antoine Marmontel, a highly regarded teacher. Marmontel's comments on Debussy's performances at the Conservatoire's year-end competitions ranged from 'charming musical nature' (1874, for a piece by Moscheles) and 'true artistic temperament' (1875, for Chopin's Rondo, Op. 16) to 'careless and inaccurate, could do much better' (1876, for the scherzo from Heller's Sonata, Op. 88).[2] Other repertoire that Debussy studied during his seven years with Marmontel included Bach's Toccata in G minor, Beethoven's Piano Sonata in C minor, Op. 111, Weber's Piano Sonata in A♭, Thalberg's Sonata in C minor, Mendelssohn's Piano Concerto No. 2 in D minor, Chopin's Piano Concerto No. 2 in F minor, Fantaisie, Ballade No. 1 in G minor and *Allegro de concert*.[3] According to recollections of his classmates, Debussy's student playing was sometimes marred by exaggerated rhythms, heavy breathing and impulsive gestures.[4] The Parisian press, however, chose to emphasise his positive qualities during this period, including his 'surprising security and power' (in the Chopin concerto) and his 'promise as an exceptional future virtuoso' (in the Chopin

Ballade).[5] Although he won a second prize in 1877 playing the first movement of Schumann's Sonata in G minor, he failed to win a first prize during his next attempts – a circumstance that put an end to his hopes for a solo career. In 1880, however, he was awarded a first prize in Auguste Bazille's class in accompanying and practical harmony. After this he entered the composition class of Ernest Guiraud – and the rest is history. We may never be able to explain the metamorphosis of his pianism during the period between his student years and the emergence of his mature style around 1903.

Once established as a composer, Debussy confined his public performances mainly to his own music. As a soloist he played twenty-three of his pieces: 'La soirée dans Grenade', 'Jardins sous la pluie', 'Reflets dans l'eau', 'Hommage à Rameau', the six pieces of *Children's Corner*, and thirteen of the *Préludes*.[6] As a collaborating artist he gave performances of his works with singers Jane Bathori, Claire Croiza, Rose Féart, Jean Périer, Maggie Teyte and Ninon Vallin; violinists Arthur Hartmann and Gaston Poulet; cellist Joseph Salmon; and pianists Jean Roger-Ducasse and Ricardo Viñes. After a performance of four of the *Préludes* in 1910 the critic Auguste Mangeot wrote, 'Is there a pianist who has a more beautiful sound than Debussy on an Erard? I don't think so.'[7] And Paul Landormy wrote of the same concert: 'One can't imagine the sweetness of his caressing playing, the sublimity of his singing touch – which said so many things at half voice, as it were – and how his smallest intentions came across.'[8] One might add here that in small halls Debussy usually preferred to play with the piano lid down.[9] It should also be noted that he preferred rich-sounding German pianos to the thin-sounding French ones of the period. From around 1904 he had a small Blüthner grand in his salon; it was a special model with an extra set of strings placed over the others, permitting an enriched sound through sympathetic vibrations. From about 1907 he had a Pleyel upright in his study, and by 1913 he had also acquired a Bechstein upright.

Two further descriptions of Debussy's playing offer insights. One comes from a review of a concert in Brussels in 1914 on which he played 'La soirée dans Grenade', 'Jardins sous la pluie', 'Hommage à Rameau', 'Reflets dans l'eau', and three of the *Préludes*:

> Debussy's interpretation is free of every mannerism and it surprises one by its simplicity. There is never any underlining of harmonic subtleties. The melodic lines are designed in thin strokes and the rhythmic alterations don't vainly declare themselves. This great simplicity, which at first is disconcerting, soon seduces one.[10]

Another description was provided by the Italian pianist and composer Alfredo Casella, who knew Debussy from 1910 to 1914 and played two-piano scores with him:

No words can give an idea of the way in which he played certain of his own *Préludes*. Not that he had actual virtuosity, but his sensibility of touch was incomparable; he made the impression of playing directly on the strings of the instrument with no intermediate mechanism; the effect was a miracle of poetry. Moreover, he used the pedals in a way all his own. He played, in a word, like no other living composer or pianist.[11]

Many of the above-mentioned aspects of Debussy's playing are captured on the piano rolls he made for the Welte-Mignon company probably in 1912. These are heard to best advantage on Kenneth Caswell's recent transfers to compact disc, which correct the distortions that marred previous transfers. The rolls contain fourteen pieces: *D'un cahier d'esquisses*, *La plus que lente*, 'La soirée dans Grenade', the six pieces of *Children's Corner* and five of the *Préludes*: 'Danseuses de Delphes', 'Le vent dans la plaine', 'La cathédrale engloutie', 'La danse de Puck' and 'Minstrels'.[12]

A detailed consideration of these rolls is not possible here, but a few observations are in order. Although Debussy's playing is not always technically perfect, the rolls confirm his reputed control of touch, imaginative pedalling and powers of evocation. This is especially true in the case of 'La soirée dans Grenade', which Debussy's stepdaughter Mme de Tinan considered the only roll that came close to the subtlety she recalled from hearing him play often in her youth.[13] The opening is quite slow and truly 'dans un rythme nonchalamment gracieux', with a sense of suspended time and a loose approach to the dotted rhythms. Interestingly, the sections marked *tempo giusto* are played with some rubato, and a number of the later triplets seem to be inexact for expressive reasons. Two-bar pedalling clouds up the harmonies in bars 100–7 and a number of rests and staccatos are similarly pedalled through. This recording enables one to appreciate the words of pianist Marguerite Long: 'When he played [this piece] there was nothing but profundity, allurement, envelopment, inexplicable "magic charms".'[14] In 'Danseuses de Delphes' the weightless chords seem to float in the air, and we hear the purposely blurred pedalling that some of his contemporaries described as characteristic. 'Le vent dans la plaine' and 'The Snow is Dancing' display quite a different aspect of his pianism, with fine control of the rapid, quiet semiquavers throughout. 'La danse de Puck' shows a similar command of fast, light figures together with surprisingly long pedals. The playing of some of the other pieces is less polished, but even in these Debussy often conveys a real sense of improvisation, a quality we know he valued in performance.[15]

We should remember that piano rolls do not necessarily preserve a performer's tempos. This is clear from a comparison of two transfers of Debussy's roll of 'Doctor Gradus ad Parnassum' from *Children's Corner*. One, produced by Caswell, has a duration of 1 minute 46 seconds, with a maximum tempo on the final page of crotchet = 207. The other, issued on Columbia, has a duration of 1 minute 32 seconds, with a maximum tempo on the final page of crotchet = 245. Yet both transfers were made from copies of the original 1913 roll. Further suspicion is cast on the rolls of *Children's Corner* by the fact that the tempos on the 'Licencee' version (produced around 1921 from a copy of the original roll) are approximately 30 per cent slower than the ones on the original rolls – a circumstance that suits the four fast pieces but not the two slow ones. For these reasons Roy Howat has concluded that the lost master roll of *Children's Corner* was tampered with before any rolls were produced and that the tempos we now hear from these rolls should not be assumed to be Debussy's.[16]

On the other hand, the rolls preserve the relationships of tempos within a recorded performance. The roll of 'La cathédrale engloutie' has therefore attracted considerable attention over the years, for in bars 7–12 and 22–83 Debussy doubles the tempo. This interpretation, which was followed by some but not all of the pianists he coached, is still questioned by some performers.[17]

Unlike the piano rolls, the four acoustic recordings that Debussy made with soprano Mary Garden in 1904 allow us to hear him in 'real' time. Details are faint, but it is interesting to note that the tempos are all on the fast side by today's standards, with no lingering or agogic point making. The first *ritardando* is ignored in 'Green', as is the one at the end of 'Il pleure dans mon cœur', while the *stringendo* is greatly exaggerated in 'L'ombre des arbres'. Also worth noting is the fact that Debussy never anticipates a written tempo change – a characteristic not always found in the piano rolls. Taken together, these characteristics suggest that the performers may have been anxious not to exceed the time limit available on 78-rpm recordings of the time.

'One must forget that the piano has hammers'

Debussy's admonition must have been heard by many of the pianists he coached.[18] Before considering the recordings and recollections of these musicians, it is important to identify the pianists who were his most active champions during his lifetime, for some of them, of course, did not receive his coaching. A tabulation of the Debussy repertoire of pianists mentioned in the leading French, British and American music periodicals from 1900 to 1918 indicates that the English-American pianist Walter Rummel performed the largest number of Debussy's works during his lifetime, followed by the American George Copeland and the Spaniard Ricardo Viñes. Other leading advocates were Harold Bauer, Norah Drewett and Franz Liebich (all English); Theodore Szántó (Hungarian); Richard Buhlig, Felix

Fox and Heinrich Gebhardt (American); Rudolf Ganz (Swiss); Alfredo Casella (Italian); Marie Panthès (Russian); and Jane Mortier, Edouard Risler, E. Robert Schmitz, Victor Staub and Ennemond Trillat (French).[19]

One of the most famous of these pianists was Ricardo Viñes (1875–1943), who studied in Barcelona with Juan Pujol and in Paris with Charles de Bériot (who was also Ravel's teacher). He had a very large and wide-ranging repertoire of standard literature as well as new music by French and Russian composers. According to his diary he met Debussy in late 1901 and thereafter played *Pour le piano* for him. Debussy was pleased and Viñes premiered the work a few weeks later.[20] From then until 1913 Viñes was practically Debussy's official pianist, premiering *Estampes, L'isle joyeuse, Masques*, both books of *Images* and six of the *Préludes*. His Debussy performances were typically praised for their 'marvellous spirit and suppleness' as well as their 'intelligence, subtlety, brilliance and richness'.[21] Despite Viñes's skill and devotion, however, Debussy began to complain about his playing in 1908, when (in a conversation with Victor Segalen) he accused him to being 'too dry', and (in a letter to Georges Jean-Aubry) of 'distorting the expression' of the *Images*, series 2.[22] Finally, in 1913, after he and Viñes had given a public performance of André Caplet's two-piano arrangement of 'Ibéria', Debussy wrote to Caplet: 'I missed you every moment – I know the careful balance of each sound so well and every time I felt as though I'd sat on a gas lamp! . . . And those tremolos sounding like the rumble of so many dead pebbles.'[23] This was the last time that Debussy asked Viñes to play his music. In 1930 Viñes recorded two of Debussy's pieces. 'La soirée dans Grenade' is played rather quickly, and though the performance contains some subtle rubato it lacks the rarefied atmosphere that Debussy prescribes in the score and conveys on his piano roll. (It is interesting that in 1912 Viñes commented in his diary that Debussy 'never finds [this piece] played as he likes it'.[24]) 'Poissons d'or', however, is a complete success: fast, light, elegant and full of the sort of colouristic pedal effects for which he was always praised, it could well serve as a model for Debussy performers today. Nothing here seems distorted, so perhaps Debussy's displeasure with Viñes's *Images* had to do with the two slower pieces from this book.

Maurice Dumesnil (1884–1974), a student of Isidor Philipp, had a successful performing and teaching career in his native France and later in the United States. He played the premiere of 'Hommage à Rameau' in Paris in 1905, heard Debussy perform in public, and received some coaching from him. He later published a booklet about Debussy performance problems that was endorsed by Debussy's widow. It includes exercises for obtaining control in quiet playing, for half-pedalling, bringing out different notes in large chords, and achieving a caressing touch by dropping and sliding the hand with outstretched fingers. For quiet chords he advocated keeping the fingers in contact with the surface of the keys, quoting one of Debussy's chief instructions: 'Play chords as if the keys were being attracted to your finger tips and rose to your hand as to a magnet.'[25] Also of interest is Dumesnil's article on the specific advice Debussy offered him for 'Hommage à Rameau', 'Clair de lune', 'Reflets dans l'eau', 'Poissons d'or', *Children's Corner* and *Pour le piano*. Here he speaks of Debussy's admonitions to observe exact dynamics, to pedal according to one's ears, to keep the textures clear, and to play in a straightforward manner without romantic affectations.[26]

The noted English pianist Harold Bauer (1873–1951) was largely self-taught, though he received some tuition from Ignacy Jan Paderewski. He played *L'isle joyeuse*, 'La soirée dans Grenade', and 'La puerta del vino' in London in 1906 and gave the premiere of *Children's Corner* in Paris in 1908. Debussy coached him in *Children's Corner*, although no details are provided in the pianist's autobiography. At the premiere Debussy was so nervous that he remained outside the hall. After the performance he asked Bauer, 'How did they take it?', and he was relieved when Bauer replied that the audience had appreciated the humour. According to Debussy's friend Léon Vallas, who attended the concert, Bauer 'interpreted it with all his usual skill but in a rather romantic style, indulging in uncalled-for contrasts and effects'.[27] This style is evident in Bauer's two Debussy recordings. *Rêverie* includes some altered dynamics, 'expressive' non-synchronisation of the hands and occasional rewriting of notes, while 'Clair de lune' features frequent arpeggiations of the chords on the first two pages. However, the recordings also reveal the subtle pedalling and colourism for which Bauer was frequently praised. He became an active champion of Debussy's music, playing all of the above works as well as *Estampes*, 'La cathédrale engloutie', and 'Les collines d'Anacapri' in major halls in Europe and the United States even during Debussy's lifetime.

Bauer's student George Copeland (1882–1971) gave the first known performance of Debussy's piano music in the United States, playing the *Deux arabesques* on 15 January 1904 in Boston. In 1909 he played the first of his many all-Debussy recitals, and in 1911 he played ten of Debussy's pieces for the composer. According to Copeland, Debussy was greatly pleased and replied, 'I never dreamed that I would hear my music played like that in my lifetime.' At one point, however, Debussy asked him why he interpreted certain bars in 'Reflets dans l'eau' the way he did. When Copeland replied that he just 'felt it that way', Debussy said that he felt it differently – but that Copeland should continue to do it his way.[28] Debussy particularly praised the quality of Copeland's *pianissimo*, saying that he 'let air get in under the notes'.[29] During the next fifty years Copeland included Debussy's music on every programme he performed in the United States, Canada and Europe, and in New York on 21 November 1916 he played the world premieres of two of the *Etudes* – 'Pour les sonorités opposées' and 'Pour les arpèges composés'. Although his recordings of more than twenty of Debussy's pieces are uneven, the best of them verify what a critic once wrote: '[Copeland's assets include] his touch of crystalline clearness; his exquisite sense of rhythm; his intimate variety of tonal colours; and a musical nature that delights in bitter-sweet dissonances . . . twilight effects, and exotic and vaguely sensuous melody.'[30] His most successful recordings from the 1930s evince an improvisatory sense and a control of touch that are reminiscent of Debussy's. Although the repertoire is not identical, one hears these qualities especially in Copeland's accounts of 'Voiles', the 'Sarabande' from *Pour le piano*, the Menuet from *Suite bergamasque* and his own beautifully evocative transcription of the *Prélude à l'après-midi d'un faune*. It would be unfair to compare Copeland's brisk account of 'La soirée dans Grenade', which at 4 minutes, 36 seconds approaches the time limit of the 78-rpm recording, with Debussy's much more leisurely piano roll.

A fascinating personality in Debussy's circle was the pianist and composer Walter Rummel (1887–1953), who studied with Leopold Godowsky in Berlin and moved to Paris around 1910. He and Debussy had become friends by 1912 and remained close until Debussy's death. This unusual friendship is documented in ten extant letters, including one that gives an important new reading for one of the *Etudes*.[31] In 1913 Rummel played both books of *Images* on his Paris debut recital and the second book of *Préludes* at the Aeolian Hall in London. During the war he performed on some of the same charity programmes as Debussy, and he was often invited to the composer's home for dinner and to play for guests afterwards. His Debussy repertoire included twenty-nine pieces, of which he had premiered ten, including some unidentified *Etudes* and the suite *En blanc et noir*. Critics praised his Debussy playing for its 'great delicacy and sympathy' and its 'lightness, ease, and remarkable understanding of the half tints'.[32] Because Debussy's letters clearly indicate that he thought highly of Rummel's playing, it is a great pity that Rummel made no Debussy recordings. Interestingly, his recordings of Chopin and Liszt feature the kind of exaggerated rubato that Debussy disliked, at least in his own music.

Elie Robert Schmitz (1889–1949) studied with Louis Diémer (the teacher of Alfred Cortot and Robert Casadesus) and launched a promising career before his hand was injured while serving in the artillery during World War I. He settled in the United States during the 1920s and was active as a pianist, teacher, conductor and concert promoter. He knew Debussy from 1908 to 1915, serving as accompanist for his coaching sessions with singers and receiving his occasional pianistic advice in the solo music. In his book *The Piano Works of Claude Debussy* Schmitz makes valuable comments on the artistic and literary influences on the music and provides rather detailed formal analysis for each work. His comments on interpretation are quite dry, however, and his technical advice is often extremely idiosyncratic. Schmitz had to rework his technique extensively after his wartime hand injury, and this fact may account for the inelegant and erratic playing heard on many of his Debussy recordings. More worth recommending is his article, 'A Plea for the Real Debussy', in which he stresses the importance of touch and the avoidance of exaggeration.[33]

Marcel Ciampi (1891–1980) also studied with Diémer, although his playing was indebted mostly to Marie Perez de Brambilla, a former student of Anton Rubinstein. Around 1915 he was coached by Debussy in *Pour le piano*, *Children's Corner* and many of the *Préludes*, seven of which he later recorded. His playing of 'Les collines d'Anacapri' is fast and clean, with careful balances of the texture, a wide dynamic range and a sensuously free middle section. In 'La sérénade interrompue' he projects true spontaneity without ever violating indications in the text. In 'La cathédrale engloutie' he finds a wide variety of touches and sonorities and his changes of tempo are similar to those on Debussy's recording. In his teaching Ciampi emphasised a number of qualities that we know Debussy also valued, including careful differentiation of sound levels, subtle pedalling and a caressing or sliding touch.[34] Some of Ciampi's recollections of his coaching with Debussy have been incorporated in the new *Œuvres complètes* edition.

One of the last pianists to receive Debussy's coaching was Marguerite Long (1874–1966), who studied with Henri Fissot and Antonin Marmontel (the son of Debussy's teacher). An early reviewer summed up her best qualities admirably: 'One could not play with better fingers, with more clarity and good taste, with a more charming and natural simplicity.'[35] At first Long resisted Debussy's music, finding its style enigmatic. In May 1914, however, she organised a concert in which she and Debussy both performed, and a few weeks later she played *L'isle joyeuse* for him. This was the beginning of their plan to work together regularly, but the war and the death of her husband intervened. It was not until the summer of 1917 that she was able to play a large repertoire for Debussy: *Estampes*, *Pour le piano*, *Images*, series 1 and several of the *Préludes* and *Etudes*. Unfortunately, Long's book *Au piano avec Claude Debussy*, written more than forty years after the composer's death, is uneven and self-aggrandising. Although the pages on *L'isle joyeuse* and *Pour le piano* are insightful, the ones on the *Préludes* and *Estampes* are banal. It is worth noting, however, that her playing of the *Etude* 'Pour les huit doigts' apparently convinced Debussy of the legitimacy of using thumbs – contrary to his instruction in the printed score.[36] Long's only performance of Debussy's music during his lifetime was at a concert of the Société Nationale in November 1917, when she played two of the *Etudes*, 'Pour les arpèges composés' and 'Pour les cinq doigts'.[37] She later recorded four of

Debussy's pieces, the *Deux arabesques*, *La plus que lente* and 'Jardins sous la pluie'. The first three are full of grace, tonal subtlety and charm, but 'Jardins', at 2 minutes 57 seconds, is inappropriately fast and superficial-sounding.

In 1917 Debussy heard recitals by the great French pianist Francis Planté (1839–1934). In a letter to Jacques Durand he reported: 'He's prodigious. He played – very well – the Toccata (from *Pour le piano* by C. Debussy) and was marvellous too in Liszt's *Feux follets*.'[38] Amazingly, these few words of praise are the most extravagant Debussy ever used in any of his letters about a pianist. He also mentions that Planté had sought his advice prior to performing 'Reflets dans l'eau' and 'Mouvement', but unfortunately no details have survived; nor did Planté record any of Debussy's works other than his transcription of Schumann's 'Am Springbrunnen'.

After Debussy's death a number of pianists performed privately for his widow Emma, who was a trained musician and former singer. These included Alfred Cortot, Denyse Molié and Marius-François Gaillard (who in 1920 became the first to perform Debussy's complete piano works in public). Emma also heard Arthur Rubinstein play 'Ondine' and declared that 'it was better than anyone'.[39] After hearing Walter Gieseking both she and her daughter Dolly (Debussy's stepdaughter) felt that his playing resembled Debussy's 'as faithfully as could be'.[40]

It is fitting to conclude this section with another observation from Emma: 'It is so rare to hear a faithful interpretation. Many pianists should bear in mind that if they play Claude's music and someone tells them how wonderful their technique is, then they are not playing Debussy.'[41]

'Forget, I pray you, that you are singers!'

This instruction to the singers who premiered *Pelléas et Mélisande* must have been puzzling.[42] What Debussy seems to have meant was that he wanted intelligent musicians who were 'singing actors' rather than 'opera stars'. In his subsequent advice to a half-dozen singers he often emphasised that vocal and verbal values should be in perfect balance.

The most renowned of these singers was the Scottish soprano Mary Garden (1874–1967), who created the role of Mélisande and later sang it in Brussels and New York. At the time of the Paris premiere Debussy wrote, 'I can't imagine a gentler or more insinuating timbre. It's tyrannical in its hold on one – impossible to forget.'[43] One hears something of this quality even in her 1904 recording of 'L'ombre des arbres' (*Ariettes* (*oubliées*), published in 1903), but it comes across more strongly in her later account of *Beau soir*, although here one wonders if Debussy would have approved of the very slow tempo, the stretched rhythms and the prolonged notes (especially in bars 9 and 34). Garden studied the *Ariettes (oubliées)* and the *Chansons de Bilitis* with Debussy and premiered *La damoiselle élue* in its revised version. Although her autobiography includes nothing about Debussy's advice, she must have passed it on when she coached Irène Joachim in 1940 for her performances (and subsequent recording) as Mélisande.[44]

The French soprano Ninon Vallin (1886–1961) was a soloist in the premiere of *Le martyre de Saint-Sébastien* and was accompanied by Debussy in the first performance of *Trois poèmes de Stéphane Mallarmé*. After hearing her sing the *Proses lyriques* and *Le promenoir des deux amants* in 1913, Debussy wrote: 'It was enough to make one weep . . . I don't know where she finds that voice. It understands the curves which the music describes through the words . . . but it's utterly beautiful and very simple.'[45] Vallin recalled her lessons with Debussy:

> Nuances, accents, pauses, changes of tempo, sudden 'pianos', all the things which are so characteristic of Debussy's writing, none of them could be glossed over . . . The duplets and triplets which . . . are nearly always opposed to the rhythmical movement of the accompaniment, had to be perfectly balanced.[46]

In all these respects her recording of 'Green' is a model.

Another of Debussy's favourite singers was the mezzo-soprano Claire Croiza (1882–1946), who was accompanied by him at several concerts. In her masterclasses she passed on advice similar to Vallin's recollections, constantly admonishing students to follow Debussy's notation and expression marks precisely. 'We can never sing Debussy's music "exactly" enough. . . . He has marked his words and music so clearly, we must just try and sing what he has written!'[47] In her recording of 'Il pleure dans mon cœur' she (like Vallin in 'Green') follows the score closely but at a slower tempo than Garden. (The conspicuous *ritardando* added in bars 45–6 was perhaps the idea of Croiza's pianist Francis Poulenc.) In her recording of 'Le jet d'eau' Croiza sets a sensible *Andantino tranquillo* tempo of crotchet = 68 and is careful to return to it each time it is marked. In the opening of the same song Maggie Teyte achieves Debussy's requested *languide* character by choosing a tempo of crotchet = 50, but she never returns to it in the later sections, which she sings faster. Teyte also indulges in a *portamento* in bars 4–5 that Croiza carefully avoids. Interestingly, both singers pick up the tempo at bar 35 – where the marking is *meno mosso tempo rubato* – and both add an early *ritardando* at bar 32. In 1915 Debussy coached Croiza for the role of Geneviève in *Pelléas et Mélisande*. Although the performance never took place, she sings the letter-reading scene (act I, scene 2) on a 1928 recording of excerpts conducted by Georges Truc. Here her recitative style is somewhat more restrained and less 'sung' than that heard from others in the role.

The English soprano Maggie Teyte (1888–1976) took over the role of Mélisande from Garden in 1908. At first Debussy praised her 'charming voice' and 'true feeling for the character of Mélisande', but during later rehearsals he became somewhat disenchanted, noting that she showed 'barely as much emotion as a prison door'. He changed his mind again, however, and accompanied her in the second set of *Fêtes galantes* in 1911 and 1912 and in six songs in London in 1914. Teyte recalled that Debussy's comments and corrections consisted of 'just small details now and then'. She accredited this to her careful observance of exact note values in her study of Mozart with Jean de Reszke and Reynaldo Hahn. 'Perhaps Debussy had not heard his music sung like this before.'[48] A critic summed up her strengths in 1911, especially praising her Debussy interpretations: 'She is a singer of exceeding intelligence, of fine taste and musical feeling ... In phrasing and in finish of style her best is of remarkable excellence.'[49]

Unlike the above-mentioned singers, who were all active in opera, the French soprano Jane Bathori (1877–1970) confined herself largely to championing contemporary French song. By 1908 she had sung for Debussy several times and he praised her 'fine talent and excellent musicianship'.[50] The following year she sang twenty-one of his songs at a single recital in Paris, and in 1911 she premiered *Le promenoir des deux amants*. Her recordings of *Chansons de Bilitis* and *Fêtes galantes*, series 2, made toward the end of her career, reveal a small, vibrato-less voice that is almost the opposite of Teyte's in these same songs. Still, one can admire Bathori's care with the text, including her marked changes of timbre for the questions and responses in 'Le tombeau des Naïades'. In her book on the interpretation of Debussy's songs, Bathori stresses that singers must study Debussy's notes and dynamics scrupulously, just as a pianist would study the details of a solo piece before arriving at an interpretation: 'Why allow changes of time, tempo, or expression in a song simply because there are words and because one believes that one feels them otherwise and better than the way indicated by the composer?'[51] Bathori knew this from experience, for she was an accomplished pianist who often, as on these recordings, accompanied herself.

As a group, these five singers are naturally quite diverse. Yet in their recordings we find that they share certain attributes when it comes to singing Debussy: careful attention to diction, dynamics and notated rhythms; a light and sometimes vibrato-less sound; restrained dynamic contrasts; occasional *portamenti* common to the period; and a tendency towards tempos that are on the fast side.[52]

Two male singers should be mentioned briefly here. Although their contacts with Debussy were limited, they performed leading roles in the first productions of *Pelléas et Mélisande*. Vanni Marcoux (1877–1962), who sang

Arkel in the London premiere in 1909, recorded some excerpts as Golaud in a 1927 recording conducted by Piero Coppola; and Hector Dufranne (1871–1951), the original Golaud in 1902, recorded excerpts from this role in a 1928 recording conducted by Georges Truc. In act IV, scene 1 ('Une grande innocence!'), Marcoux projects the drama better than the music. Some of his notes and rhythms are approximate and he often runs out of breath in the climactic last moments of the excerpt. He is heard to better effect in the first two prolonged solos of act II, scene 2 (they are joined together with Mélisande's contributions omitted). His voice communicates intimacy and warmth, especially in the second solo, where the tempos and dynamics are less strenuous. Dufranne is lighter, more accurate and younger sounding in the same scene (Mélisande's exchanges are retained). Debussy praised both singers, but wished they would project more character through their acting.[53]

'When I have to conduct I am ill before, during and after!'

Debussy's admission to Casella reflected his real sense of inadequacy as a conductor.[54] His first appearance, leading the Orchestre Colonne in *La mer* in 1908, was actually a success, but this was partly due to the fact that Edouard Colonne had rehearsed the orchestra beforehand. Henry Wood later did the same for Debussy in England, as did Vittorio Gui in Turin and Gustave Doret in Amsterdam. On these and other occasions Debussy was known to drop beats during page turns, to indicate tempos and entrances only approximately, to have his head buried in the score, and to almost cause a performance to come to a stop.[55]

If he lacked technique, Debussy nonetheless had a clear notion of what he wanted from an orchestra and which conductors could best provide it. He greatly admired André Messager (1853–1929), praising him for the insights he brought to the premiere of *Pelléas* in 1902 and especially for his evocation of the work's 'interior rhythm', with 'everything in its place'.[56] He also thought highly of Arturo Toscanini (1867–1957), Piero Coppola (1888–1971), Serge Koussevitzky (1874–1951) and Ernest Ansermet (1883–1969) – all of whom he knew personally, though we should remember that he never heard any of them perform his works. Toscanini conducted the Italian premiere of *Pelléas* at La Scala in 1908, reportedly from memory, and he later became a leading Debussy champion in the United States. Coppola heard Debussy conduct 'Ibéria' and the *Prélude à l'après-midi d'un faune* in Turin in 1911 and the experience had a decisive influence on his career. Koussevitzky invited Debussy to conduct in Moscow and St Petersburg in 1913 and heard his interpretations of *La mer*, *Nocturnes* and the *Prélude*. Ansermet, who led the Swiss premiere of the *Nocturnes* in 1914, related a telling story of his meeting with Debussy three years later when they discussed the tempos of many of his works. After examining Debussy's score of the *Nocturnes*, with its revisions indicated in red, blue and green pencil, Ansermet asked which of them were correct. Debussy replied, 'I don't know. Take the score with you and bring it back in a few days and choose what seems to you good.'[57]

Besides Messager Debussy is known to have heard and valued six conductors of his works: André Caplet (1878–1925), Gustave Doret (1866–1943), Vittorio Gui (1885–1975), Désiré-Emile Inghelbrecht (1880–1965), Pierre Monteux (1875–1964) and Gabriel Pierné (1863–1937). All but Caplet and Doret recorded the *Prélude à l'après-midi d'un faune*, a circumstance that begs for a comparison.

Pierné's recording is particularly disappointing in light of his long association with Debussy and the fact that the composer entrusted the premieres of 'Ibéria' and *Jeux* to him. The flautist mars the opening solo by taking a deep breath in bar 3 after the e^2. Although this is sanctioned by a pencil marking in Debussy's corrected score of c. 1908,[58] flautists generally try to play the four bars in one breath, as in the six other recordings compared here. Pierné's supporting winds are too loud in bars 4–16 and he imposes a considerable *accelerando* in bars 17–19 and an equally considerable *rallentando* in bar 25. Although his opening tempo is quaver = 90 (Debussy's corrected score indicates dotted crotchet = 44), Pierné changes the tempo to quaver = 130 for bars 21ff. and bars 26ff. The tempo variations (indicated and otherwise) are not handled very convincingly and they detract from the natural flow of rhythms and ideas. In short, this interpretation might be criticised for the same reason that Debussy criticised Pierné's premiere of *Jeux*: it lacks 'homogeneity'.[59] The performance sounds stitched together, and the wind playing is at times sour and inexpressive. Pierné's recording, at 8 minutes 28 seconds, is the fastest known to me.

The fine accounts by Inghelbrecht and Monteux are perfectly paced, even when the tempos are generally slower than the ones indicated in the corrected score, and the balances and solos are handled with much subtlety. Monteux's recording seems to me the most successful of all, with an airy texture and a fluidity of movement that are ideal. The atmospheric quality seems to result not from an imposed interpretation but simply from careful attention to every detail. A case in point is the wonderful *subito pianissimo* at bar 63, which no other conductor seems to manage as well. (In this connection it is worth remembering the occasion when Monteux was rehearsing this work and Debussy leaned over and told him, 'Monteux, that is a *forte*, play *forte!*'[60]) Monteux's ties with Debussy's music went back to 1902 when he played viola in the orchestra at the premiere of *Pelléas*. In 1913 he conducted the first performance of *Jeux* by the Ballets Russes. Inghelbrecht's connections date from 1911, when he was chorus master for the premiere of *Le martyre de Saint-Sébastien*, and include a close working friendship with Debussy from 1912 until his death.

The recording by Vittorio Gui holds together quite well even though it is the slowest of all, at 9 minutes 35 seconds. The interpretation is straightforward and the playing quite polished, though it lacks the kind of transparency that only a really superior orchestra can achieve. Bars 63–5 may not be exactly *pianissimo*, but they lead to a thrilling climax at bar 70 that is truly *fortissimo* and *animé*. The recording is of special value because it was Gui who, in Turin in 1911, saved the day when Debussy's attempts to rehearse the *Prélude* and 'Ibéria' proved disastrous. Gui rehearsed the orchestra for several days with Debussy at his side, and his sympathetic understanding and appreciation of these works earned him Debussy's lasting admiration.[61]

Other early Debussystes who recorded the *Prélude* were Piero Coppola and Ernest Ansermet. Coppola's fluid and expressive interpretation compares well with Pierné's of the same year, and the winds seem to be less obtrusive. Although his basic tempo is slower than Pierné's, his interpretation seems more flowing because his tempo changes are fewer and less radical. Ansermet, of course, benefits from more modern sound, and his balances always seem ideal. He never exaggerates the changes in tempo, but he does add a *rallentando* in bar 85 that makes sense. Debussy clearly trusted Ansermet's judgement in matters of tempo, as when he told him 'You will know' when Ansermet asked him how fast a passage marked *modéré* should go.[62] (This is perhaps the appropriate place to mention Debussy's reluctance to specify metronome markings. His publishers often coerced him into doing so, but as he told Jacques Durand, 'they're right for a single bar, like "roses, with a morning's life".[63])

An additional early recording of *Faune* should be mentioned, that by Walther Straram (1876–1933). Straram was never a member of Debussy's circle, but he was a violinist in the Orchestre Lamoureux in 1892 and later *chef de chant* at the Paris Opéra and Opéra-Comique. Most importantly he became the assistant of Debussy's student, collaborator and amenuensis André Caplet for five years during the latter's tenure as conductor of the Boston Opera. Thus Straram gained an intimate knowledge of Debussy's works through Caplet. He returned to Paris in 1914 and eventually put together an orchestra that by the late 1920s was considered by many to be the finest in all of France. During its first season (1926) the Concerts Straram played *La mer* and the complete *Images*.[64] Marcel Moyse was the orchestra's principal flautist at the time of Straram's recording of the *Prélude*, and his stunning opening solo has been studied by flautists around the world ever since. Straram's orchestra plays the work impeccably, realising the letter and spirit of the score in a manner that is truly astonishing. All of Debussy's indications for tempo, balance and nuance are observed with an unstudied ease that was exceptional for the time. In 1931 this recording won the Prix Candide, the first prize ever awarded for a recording.

Had Straram and his orchestra survived longer his recordings of Debussy's major works might well have been equal in quantity and quality to those by Ansermet, Coppola, Inghelbrecht and Monteux. As it is, however, these four conductors who knew Debussy have rightly been considered his most faithful champions, with Inghelbrecht's interpretations having perhaps the greatest overall authority. This last conclusion is supported in James Briscoe's overview of Debussy conductors.[65]

Space does not permit comparisons of historic recordings of other orchestral works, but mention should be made of outstanding individual ones by the above-mentioned conductors. Inghelbrecht's best recordings include a live account of *Pelléas et Mélisande* (1962, with a strong cast headed by Jacques Jansen and Micheline Grancher) and studio recordings of the *Nocturnes* and *Le martyre de Saint-Sébastien* (a work he first conducted in 1912). Monteux has left subtly nuanced recordings of the *Prélude à l'après-midi d'un faune*, *La mer* and *Images*. Ansermet's finest achievements as a Debussyste include *Jeux, La mer* and his two accounts of *Pelléas et Mélisande* (1952, with Pierre Mollet and Suzanne Danco; and 1964, with Camille Maurane and Erna Spoorenberg). Coppola is heard to best advantage in 'Ibéria' (which he heard Debussy conduct in 1911) and the *Nocturnes*. The best performances are generally the ones in which, in Debussy's words, 'the orchestra sounds like crystal, as light as a woman's hand'.[66]

'Don't change anything . . .'

It is interesting to note that Debussy, who could at times be strict and short-tempered with some interpreters, is on record as having told some others – including Copeland, Dumesnil, Paderewski, Teyte and the pianist Léon Delafosse – that they shouldn't change their interpretations even though he disagreed with them. So when members of the Poulet Quartet asked Debussy if their interpretation of his Quartet corresponded with his intentions he replied: 'Not in the least. But on second thought . . . don't change anything; it would spoil the coherence, and the sincerity of your playing would lose its eloquence and its original colour.'[67] To some degree, then, he accepted interpretative leeway, as is also suggested by his negative remarks about metronome markings and his reluctance to include fingerings and pedalling in his music. Like Beethoven, however, his middle and late works are loaded with verbal prescriptions for mood and tempo as well as an ever-increasing number of indications for touch and dynamics. In the very first bar of the *Etude* 'Pour les agréments', for example, we find four *tenuto* strokes, three legato slurs, two dynamic signs, a fermata, an accent and a *portato* marking – a total of twelve indications, in addition to the heading *lento, rubato e leggiero*. But a performer would be in error, just as he would be in Beethoven, if he dwelled on these nuances at the expense of line. This point is crucial in Debussy interpretation. As Briscoe has reminded us, Debussy's works tend to emphasise colour through *Nocturnes* to *Pelléas*, but from *La mer* onwards there is an increased emphasis on structural line.[68]

Simon Trezise has noted that 'an "authentic" *La mer* is an unthinkable, unobtainable concept, especially if by "authentic" we mean an attempt to recreate the first performances as closely as possible'.[69] Not only were many of those early performances unsatisfactory, but the very sound of orchestras – especially French ones – has changed dramatically since 1920, thus affecting the balances that Debussy so carefully sought. Some of today's best singers of *mélodies* seem to have ideals that are quite different from those of Croiza or Bathori, just as some of our finest pianists perform on concert-grand Steinways with the lid fully open, making frequent use of a middle pedal that did not exist in Debussy's time.

Performers are always challenged to interpret the past, but for Debussy we have more guidance than for any previous composer. A consideration of these historic recordings and memoirs allows us to interpret him more faithfully and with greater discernment.

Select discography

Recordings are listed by performer in the order of discussion in this chapter. All recordings are on compact disc unless otherwise noted. This discography identifies only those recordings mentioned in this chapter.[70]

Claude Debussy

'Danseuses de Delphes', 'La cathédrale engloutie', 'La danse de Puck', 'Minstrels', 'Le vent dans la plaine', *La plus que lente*, 'La soirée dans Grenade', *D'un cahier d'esquisses* and *Children's Corner* (probably recorded in 1912), issued on Pierian CD 0001 (earlier transfers of the five *Préludes* and *Children's Corner* issued on Columbia ML 4291 (LP); the five *Préludes* alone issued on Telefunken GMA 65 and GMA 79 (LP)).

As pianist with soprano Mary Garden: 'Mes longs cheveux' (*Pelléas*), 'Green', 'L'ombre des arbres' and 'Il pleure dans mon cœur' (recorded in 1904), reissued on Pierian CD 0001 and EMI CHS 7 61038 2.

Ricardo Viñes
'La soirée dans Grenade' and 'Poissons d'or' (recorded in 1930), reissued on Pearl Opal 9857.

Harold Bauer
'Clair de lune' (recorded in 1929) and *Rêverie* (recorded in 1939), reissued on Biddulph LHW 009.

George Copeland
Prélude à l'après-midi d'un faune (transcribed by Copeland), Menuet, 'Clair de lune', 'Sarabande', 'La soirée dans Grenade', 'Voiles', 'La cathédrale engloutie', 'La puerta del vino', 'Bruyères', 'General Lavine – eccentric', 'La terrasse des audiences du clair de lune', 'Ondine' and 'Canope' (recorded 1933 and 1936), reissued on Pearl GEMS 0001.

Walter Rummel
Thirteen works by Bach, Liszt, Chopin and Brahms (recorded 1930–43), reissued on Dante HPC027.

Marguerite Long
Deux arabesques, 'La plus que lente' and 'Jardins sous la pluie' (recorded 1929–30), reissued on Pearl GEMM CD 9927.

E. Robert Schmitz
Préludes, book 1 (recorded in 1947), reissued on RCA Camden CAL 179 (LP); *Préludes*, book 2 (recorded in 1947), reissued on RCA Camden CAL 180 (LP).

Marcel Ciampi
'Les collines d'Anacapri' and 'La sérénade interrompue' (recorded in 1929), Columbia D 13075 (78-rpm); 'La cathédrale engloutie' (recorded in 1927), reissued on Malibran-Music CDRG 115.

Mary Garden
Beau soir (recorded in 1929), reissued on Romophone 81008-2; four other songs (see under Debussy, above).

Ninon Vallin
'Green' and 'Air de Lia', *L'enfant prodigue* (both recorded c. 1930), reissued on Pearl GEMM CD 9948.

Maggie Teyte
Fêtes galantes, series 1 and 2; *Trois chansons de Bilitis*; *Le promenoir des deux amants*; *Proses lyriques*; 'Le jet d'eau' (recorded 1936–40), reissued on Pearl GEMM CD 9134.

Claire Croiza
Romance (recorded in 1927), 'Il pleure dans mon cœur' (recorded in 1928), 'Le jet d'eau' (recorded c. 1930), 'Les cloches' (published in 1936), *Les angélus* (published in 1936), 'Ballade que Villon feit à la requeste de sa mère' (published in 1936), reissued on Marston 52018-2; excerpt from *Pelléas et Mélisande* (conducted by Georges Truc, recorded in 1928), reissued on VAIA 1093.

Jane Bathori
Chansons de Bilitis, Fêtes galantes, series 2, 'C'est l'extase' (recorded 1929–30), reissued on Marston 51009-2.

Hector Dufranne
Three excerpts from *Pelléas et Mélisande* (conducted by Georges Truc, recorded in 1928), reissued on VAIA 1093.

Vanni Marcoux
Two excerpts from *Pelléas et Mélisande* (conducted by Piero Coppola, recorded in 1927), reissued on VAIA 1093.

Gabriel Pierné
Prélude à l'après-midi d'un faune (conducting the Orchestre des Concerts Colonne, recorded in 1930), reissued on Malibran-Music CDRG 140.

Désiré-Emile Inghelbrecht
Prélude à l'après-midi d'un faune (conducting the Orchestre National de France, recorded 1955–62), EMI C 153-12137/8 (LP); *Pelléas et Mélisande* (conducting the Orchestre National de France, live, 1962), Disques Montaigne TCE 8710 (3 discs); *Nocturnes* (conducting the Orchestre National de France, 1955–62), EMI C 153-12137/38 (LP); *Le martyre de Saint-Sébastien* (conducting the Orchestre du Théâtre des Champs-Elysées, recorded live, 1960), Ducretet 320 C 155 (LP).

Pierre Monteux
Prélude à l'après-midi d'un faune (conducting the London Symphony Orchestra, recorded in 1962), Decca SXL 2312 (LP); *La mer* (conducting

the Boston Symphony Orchestra, recorded in 1954), RCA 61893-2; *Images* (conducting the London Symphony Orchestra, 1963), Philips 442 595-2.

Vittorio Gui

Prélude à l'après-midi d'un faune (conducting the Florence Symphony Orchestra, recorded c. 1960), Camelot CMTS 104 (LP).

Piero Coppola

Prélude à l'après-midi d'un faune (conducting the Orchestre Symphonique de Paris, recorded in 1930); *Nocturnes* (conducting the Orchestre de la Société des Concerts du Conservatoire, recorded in 1938); 'Ibéria' (conducting the Orchestre de la Société des Concerts du Conservatoire, recorded in 1935). All reissued on Lys 295–297 (3 discs).

Ernest Ansermet

Prélude à l'après-midi d'un faune (conducting the Orchestre de la Suisse Romande, recorded in 1957), reissued on Decca 440 499-2; *Pelléas et Mélisande* (conducting the Orchestre de la Suisse Romande, recorded in 1952), reissued on Decca 425 965-2 (2 discs); *Pelléas et Mélisande* (conducting the Orchestre de la Suisse Romande, recorded in 1964), Decca 277/9 (LP); *La mer* (conducting the Orchestre de la Suisse Romande, recorded in 1964), reissued on Decca 425 781–2; *Jeux* (conducting the Orchestre de la Suisse Romande, recorded 1958), Decca 433 711–2.

Walther Straram

Prélude à l'après-midi d'un faune (conducting the Orchestre des Concerts Straram, recorded in 1930), reissued on VAIA 1074.

14 Debussy now

ARNOLD WHITTALL

The process of interpreting any great composer from the past whose music remains a vital force on the contemporary scene is, inevitably, multivalent: performers, scholars and composers all make their contributions to preserving that vitality, that presence. Moreover, the activities of scholars and composers, the prime concern of this essay, proliferate to offer further, diverse levels of discourse and response. In the case of scholarship – informed writing about music – there is a whole range of distinct though interacting theories and techniques, from matters of performance practice and the 'genetic' studies basic to historical musicology to various, often radically contrasted, types of technical analysis and hermeneutic commentary. The focus of my discussion here is the current state of Debussy interpretation from the formal and hermeneutic perspectives of theory and analysis as well as of composition, for, as will soon be evident, these points on the interpretative chain cannot easily be separated, especially when the thorny topics of Debussy's influence on, or affinity with, other composers become involved.

This is not the place for an account of the thinking and terminology that informed the analytical interpretation of Debussy during the first half of the twentieth century. But it is clear that the issues present-day musicology often addresses – how 'tonal' was Debussy's musical language, given its use of whole-tone, pentatonic and octatonic modal elements? how traditional, or organicist, was his attitude to form? how innovative was the expressive 'tone' of his music? – can all be found, however informally defined, in earlier years: for example, in Constant Lambert's *Music Ho!*, first published in 1934. Like many later commentators, Lambert was acutely aware of the difficulty of determining exactly how 'old' or 'new' the various components of Debussy's music were:

> there are very few actual harmonic combinations in Debussy that cannot be found in Liszt; the novelty of Debussy's harmonic method consists in his using a chord as such, and not as a unit in a form of emotional and musical argument . . . [1]
>
> Debussy's real revolution in harmony consists far more in the way he uses chords, than in the chords he uses. It is a development more far-reaching than any of Liszt's or Wagner's developments of harmonic vocabulary. [2]

Lambert identifies that ambivalent, unstable balance between the traditional and the innovatory which remains an abiding theme of analytical interpretation of Debussy to this day; and despite more sophisticated concern with line and interval pattern, not simply 'chord', developments in Debussy analysis since Lambert have not succeeded in proving beyond all doubt or dispute either that Debussy's musical language was *essentially* traditional – that is, tonal – rather than fundamentally 'post-tonal', or that his most characteristic structures were radically new, rejecting traditional ideals of cumulative formal continuity. Rather, these discussions have tended to point up the interactive aspect and to highlight the corresponding richness of the Debussyan musical fabric.

From a compositional perspective, the mid-1940s were years when a new disparity between the conservative and the avant-garde began to make its presence felt, and those years also saw particularly significant developments in the spheres of tonal and post-tonal music theory. It was at this time that the twentieth century's most radical and influential theory of tonality – Schenker's – was first brought to bear on Debussy, and the reverberations of that conjunction have been felt ever since.[3] Well aware that Schenker himself regarded Debussy's music as unworthy of serious consideration, Adèle T. Katz chose to underline the contrast, as she found it, between tradition and innovation, and without indulging in Schenker's own heated rhetoric, she soberly concluded her study as follows:

> He achieved an originality of expression within the realm of tonality which, despite differences in treatment and style, is based on the artistic methods of the past. In severing his connections with the past, in his experiments with new techniques, he instituted practices that were to influence the future.[4]

Katz's Schenker-inspired mistrust of those 'new techniques' came through in her comment that

> the tendency to reproduce in music effects similar to those gained by poets and painters led Debussy to stylistic innovations which in many instances were a definite negation of the principles of tonality. In fact, the more personal his idiom became, the more devastating was its impact on the tonal stronghold.[5]

But later theorists, practised in the need to value and develop Schenkerian modes of thought while rejecting Schenker's prejudices against more progressive, disruptive aspects of chromaticism, have refused to equate the 'negation' of tonality with the negation of music. In particular, they have implicitly set aside Katz's assessment that Debussy severed all meaningful connections with the past in favour of a more nuanced examination of how tradition and innovation interact in music that never entirely loses sight of either triadic harmony or tonal structure.[6]

What many recent studies of Debussy's musical language have in common is the conviction that post-tonal voice leading evolves coherently from tonal voice leading and is not in principle incompatible with it. Nevertheless, the fact that Debussyan voice leading occupies ambiguous regions of tension and interaction between diatonic and chromatic, tonal and modal, makes analytical attempts to interpret most of his compositions in these terms problematic given the difficulties of demonstrating a single, fundamental structure for complete movements or works, and also of tracing similar voice-leading procedures from work to work. It is no coincidence that the most elaborate recent analysis of pitch processes in Debussy – David Lewin's study of 'Feux d'artifice' – has focused not on voice leading as an all-embracing, goal-directed phenomenon, but on 'transformational networks', which treat the musical material as a mixture of motivic and harmonic components in a logically evolving rather than hierarchically stratified context.[7] At the moment, the density and intricacy of such analyses make them accessible to adepts only. But the prospect of a wider application of the network concept, from within the perspective of neo-Riemannian harmonic theory, as a 'response to analytical problems posed by chromatic music that is triadic but not altogether tonally unified',[8] indicates that many of Debussy's most individual works might one day be illuminated from within the parameters of such a theory.

Transformational networks help to determine musical structures by charting a process in which continuity and change interact. They therefore draw attention to concepts of form which can complement traditional generic models – ternary, sonata, rondo and the like – and are well placed to do justice to the special formal flexibility which has been another core concept of twentieth-century Debussy analysis. This concept, like Katz's, became particularly salient soon after the Second World War in the avant-garde appropriation of that 'Debussyan essence' which, in Boulez's famous words, 'precludes all academicism'. It is 'incompatible with any stereotyped order, with any dispensation not created on the instant', and rejects 'any hierarchy outside the musical moment itself', so that 'the fluid and the instantaneous irrupt[s] into music', with 'relations between objects . . . established by context, according to variable functions'.[9] Such grand generalisations make a fine rhetorical effect, but they are ripe for critique, and it can only be respect for their relevance to Boulez's own compositions, and those of other avant-garde composers of the post-war decades, that has muted this critique – see for example Laurence Berman's discussion of *Jeux*.[10] While there has been acute analytical consideration of works like 'La terrasse des audiences du clair de lune', which is 'characterized by perpetual metamorphosis from one relatively self-contained idea to another',[11] and of the extent to which *La boîte à joujoux* has the character of a collage,[12] and while such discussions have often emphasised the innovative significance of Debussy's appropriation of musical images of the Orient (the musical 'Other'),[13] it is obvious that his formal discontinuities and harmonic juxtapositions are quite different in character from the dramatically disorienting shifts of textural and emotional perspective which are the essence of twentieth-century expressionism. As will emerge below, there is no absolute incompatibility between Debussy's approach to form and an aesthetic attitude which is more 'modern classical' than modernist. But in order to treat this important topic adequately it is necessary to address the subject of modernism itself.

At the level of general aesthetic and analytical evaluation, the later decades of the twentieth century were notable for arguments about the nature of modernism, and, in particular, about whether the increasing pluralism evident in a musical landscape that, after 1970, sustained 'complexity' along with minimalism, and allowed the conservative to flourish alongside the experimental, was best defined as 'late modern' or 'post-modern'.[14] A topic which at first sight appears aridly semantic is crucial to contextualising perceptions about the extent to which composers active in those later twentieth-century decades embodied either the intensification of modernism's most essential technical and aesthetic qualities or the rejection of those qualities. My own preference is for the argument that the post-Ivesian juxtaposition of different styles – as in Peter Maxwell Davies's *Eight Songs for a Mad King* (1969) and Alfred Schnittke's String Quartet No. 3 (1983) – represents a late-modern intensification of the concern with discontinuity, and the balance (rather than synthesis) of opposites in which modernism's own opposition to classicism is rooted. Yet, as already suggested, such dramatic – often expressionistic – demonstrations of conflict, stemming in essence from the Germanic late Romanticism of Mahler, early Schoenberg and Berg, offer a very different kind of instability and contingency from that which Boulez had in mind when he celebrated Debussy's 'flexibility', that 'certain immediacy of invention, and precisely the local indiscipline in relation to the overall discipline'.[15]

Although often used in defence of the argument that Debussy (no less than Satie) foreshadowed the experimental modernism of 'indeterminacy' in general and the Cage school in particular, Boulez's comment can also serve to justify the observation that a contrast between 'local' and 'overall' implies not abandoning 'overall discipline', but rather throwing it into doubt. The way in which 'Des pas sur la neige' is radical enough to call the rootedness of D minor harmony into question but in the end allows the overall discipline of such rootedness to reassert itself, and cast the whole structure retrospectively in its light, can encapsulate Debussy's position within the framework of musical processes governed by modernism at one extreme and classicism at the other.[16] However progressive Debussy's way with harmony and texture, his resistance to expressionistic fragmentation of the kind that found its way into *Petrushka* and *Le sacre du printemps* during the years immediately before 1914, and his preference for the subtleties of gradual transition and ultimate rootedness, show him remaining faithful to the Wagnerian essence of modernism's first, Romantic phase – a phase in which the prospect of the positive rediscovery of classical virtues of integration and synthesis was always more immediate than it could ever be during modernism's later, post-tonal period.

Nevertheless, as Robin Holloway has demonstrated, to refer to Debussy in this manner is not to deny that he 'can never be called the heir to Wagner in any traditional sense by which influences are understood to be passed on. Rather than a follower who continues his line, Debussy is Wagnerian in a unique way, standing at an angle to him.'[17] The sense in which the obliqueness of that angle enables Debussy to be Wagnerian in technique and anti-Wagnerian – or at any rate non-Wagnerian, for the most part – in style is a topic well beyond the confines of the present study, although it provides the essence of a 'theory of influence' that has immediate relevance. Notions of modernism and post-modernism were not part of Holloway's critical armoury in 1978, but an argument building on Holloway's foundations can still conclude that a genuine post-modernism will be one that rediscovers classical virtues, preferring connection to disconnection, and a spirit which excludes expressionistic exaggerations. This classicism will be 'modern', or 'new', rather than 'neo', not least because in its most vital, Stravinskian form, neoclassicism offers a fractured modernism as potent as anything in post-tonal expressionism. Even the spiritual serenity reached in the final stages of *Symphony of Psalms* is far from dominant throughout that work, and the work has too many striking discontinuities for its neoclassicism to be equivalent to anti-modernism. So new or modern, classicism of the kind emerging ever more strongly at the turn of the millennium, in composers like John Adams and Thomas Adès, can arguably be connected more directly (and certainly more positively) with the early-twentieth-century resistance to expressionistic modernism such as we find in Debussy than with late-twentieth-century conservatism.[18]

At the same time, however, it is desirable to avoid the worst consequences of that sorry situation, consequent on the application of what Craig Ayrey has termed 'modern analytical techniques' which 'relegate Debussy to the status of a predecessor'.[19] For Ayrey, Debussy is a 'deconstructive' rather than modernist or even post-modern composer, and if analysis of his work is to 'escape from closed systems on the one hand, and flabby pluralism on the other', a 'radical middle way' is needed, 'a method that offers systematic procedures but is predicated on ambiguity'. This is not the place to consider Ayrey's in-depth exploration of the way in which Debussy analysis might 'replace "structure" with "discourse"'.[20] But his claim that 'music theory is often oblivious to the fact that opposition itself is a relation, a mode of connection between disparate units',[21] made in the context of discussing the nature of Debussy's role in music since 1918, can usefully be kept in mind when considering how later composers and theorists alike have explained the importance of Debussy to them.

Many twentieth-century aestheticians and musicologists were sensitive to the Debussyan balance of ambiguities, as in Roger Scruton's claim that an absence of traditional types of harmonic logic does not prevent, and even promotes, a situation like that at the start of the *Pelléas* Prelude in which 'there is a smooth musical transition from bar 4 to bar 5, as well as a contrast',[22] or Richard S. Parks's consideration of the interaction between 'kinetic' and 'morphological' types of form, the former creating a sense of motion 'from the organization of discontinuities', whereas in the latter 'stability engenders continuity'.[23] Nevertheless, Debussy can still be cast as the 'classic' upholder of an overriding continuity. For Robert P. Morgan, who clearly has the Boulez thesis in mind, 'the structure of Debussy's music often resembles a mosaic'. Yet because 'seemingly separate and self-enclosed units combine into larger configurations, the individual discontinuities' are 'thereby dissolved into a continuous, unbroken flow'. For Morgan,

> the music never degenerates into a series of pleasant yet unrelated effects, a succession of isolated musical moments; everything is held together by a tight network of melodic, rhythmic, and harmonic associations . . . [nevertheless] the type of musical form he developed is more loosely connected and more 'permeable' . . . than that of traditional tonal music. His conception of form as essentially 'open' in character was to have an important influence on much later twentieth-century music.[24]

Here, although the separation and self-enclosure of units within a form are allegedly more apparent than real, the 'continuous, unbroken flow' is nevertheless 'more loosely connected', and more '"open" in character' than in 'traditional tonal music'. With Morgan, the interaction between 'open' and 'closed' formal features neatly matches the interaction between tonal and post-tonal elements.

Morgan's attempt to square the Debussyan circle (in the tradition of Lambert's 'old but in new ways' interpretation) is clearly intended to underpin his final assertion about the importance of his influence. For a related viewpoint we can turn to Roger Nichols's eloquent declaration that 'On many fronts, [Debussy] was a deeply divided composer.'[25] But the dichotomies Nichols underlines are matters of life as well as work – for example, 'the pull between privacy and publicity is mirrored in his struggles to balance the claims of solitude and friendship, and of simplicity and complication'. Nichols also identifies a basic compositional duality in the opposition between 'the delightful surfaces of his music' and 'its rough, dangerous, even cruel undercurrents'. Nichols therefore offers particularly persuasive arguments, to do with the music's 'moral dimension' as well as its dedication to 'a feeling of transience', for Debussy's importance in his own time.[26]

Ultimately, of course, this importance is primarily to do with the perceptions of later composers, and testimonies to the power of Debussy's example for later times are legion. Among those offered by composers active at the end of the twentieth century, I would give pride of place – even over Boulez's various encomia – to Elliott Carter's claim, first made back in 1959, 'that Debussy's music, perhaps more than any other composer's of the time, has settled the technical direction of contemporary music, if not its emotional tone'.[27] Carter went on to argue that 'for its power, for its attempt to solve the problem of what is often called "musical logic" in terms of new musical situations and in terms that bear some analogy to contemporary views on the operation of human thought and feeling, Debussy's music is especially significant'.[28] For Carter this new 'logic' evidently had something to do with the balance between extreme contrast and subtle connectivity, enabling him to affirm (not unpolemically) that 'like all the best works of twentieth-century music, [Debussy's late sonatas] have an inimitably special character in which all the various novel features are brought together in an harmonious whole'.[29] Elsewhere, in an essay from 1976, Carter noted Debussy's

> dissatisfaction with the conventional methods of 'thematic development' of his time. This led him to explore static as opposed to sequential repetition and so reduce thematic material, especially in his last works, to elemental forms containing motives that formed the basis for a spinning out of coherent, ever changing continuities.[30]

Put this way, Carter could almost be claiming Debussy as the progenitor of minimalism, by way of that exploration of the 'ostinato machine' that Derrick Puffett and Jonathan Cross have discussed.[31] More saliently, however, Carter is describing Debussy's role in 'settling the technical direction' to be found in the essential technical attributes of his own later works – as an ultimate acknowledgement of the centrality of the kind of 'Gallic' (not simply neoclassical) thinking that Carter found so attractive when studying with Nadia Boulanger.

That Carter, since reaching the most extreme point of his expressionistic middle period in the early 1970s, developed a more mellow species of modernism, alongside (but not, *pace* David Schiff, replaced by) some of the features of a 'new classicism', can serve to underline the significance of Debussy for music which sounds very different, not least because of the atonality of Carter's 'elemental' motive forms and chordal vocabulary, which provide the basis for his own elaborate yet unfailingly coherent compositional 'spinning out'.[32] If this shows Carter relegating Debussy to – in Ayrey's phrase – 'the status of a predecessor', that is no more than the inevitable outcome of the passing of time and the evolution of compositional processes. It is in any case a quite different kind of 'influence' from the more explicit surface similarities that enabled Paul Griffiths to characterise Debussy's 'Feux d'artifice' as 'one of the most Ligetian pieces composed before Ligeti was born',[33] and Jonathan Cross does something similar in claiming that Ligeti's piano study 'Désordre' (1986) has 'striking parallels' with Debussy ('Brouillards', for example), as well as with the player-piano studies of Conlon Nancarrow.[34]

In noting that Debussy's music is 'particularly evoked' by Ligeti's 'more diatonic pieces',[35] Griffiths reinforces the distinction between what we might define as the transformational Debussyism of Carter and the recreative Debussyism of composers whose music can actually *sound* Debussyan. Where these distinct categories begin to overlap is in music that is in some ways rooted and repetitive, but more radical or heterogeneous in its treatment of mode or even tonality, elements Debussy never abandoned, even in his most forward-looking 'static' or 'block-form' structures. There is no need to claim, defensively, that Debussy is the sole and single source for such qualities in order to regard his continuing presence in music at the turn of the millennium as crucial. For example, it is probably right and proper that, in the case of Toru Takemitsu (1930–96), it should prove unprofitable to try to separate echoes of Debussy (or Ravel) from echoes of Messiaen, but, given that the latter are inconceivable without the former, they combine in history and theory to provide a continuum running along the spine of twentieth-century pluralism. Yet whereas Takemitsu is a fine example of a composer able to do new things with that 'flexibility' and 'intimate sensitivity' which George Benjamin defines as special for him in Debussy,[36] there are others who turn the 'ostinato machine', and the synthesising power of ultimately rooted harmony, to much more abrasive and, on occasion, genial effect – that different 'emotional tone' sensed by Carter. From Giacinto Scelsi to Louis Andriessen and on to Magnus Lindberg, as well as 'spectralists'

like Gérard Grisey and Tristan Murail, the rooted yet vibrant role of resonance has provided a gripping alternative to latter-day transformations of
early-twentieth-century expressionistic modernism. But perhaps the most
persuasive evidence of all for the continuing importance of Debussy within
the evolution of twentieth-century French composition is that of a composer in many ways Boulez's polar opposite, Henri Dutilleux (b. 1916), who
has spoken wryly of 'my excessive admiration for Debussy'.[37] At the same
time, it would be pointless to declare that Debussy is a stronger, more profound influence on Dutilleux than Bartók, or even Berg. No composer of
substance can be confined in this way; but that is not to deny the vital role
of Debussy's example in affecting the general course of twentieth-century
developments in composition.

When it came to considering the fraught question of 'Debussy's relationship with his successors', Roger Nichols referred to remarks by Boulez
which link Debussy's avoidance of formal stereotypes with similar inventiveness in Varèse and Webern, and which also hail *Pelléas* as belonging
in that 'highest class' of works 'that serve as a kind of mirror in which a
whole culture can see itself'.[38] Is that the culture of Debussy's own time,
or the culture that has evolved and flourished since Debussy? The ambiguity indicates the nature of the problem. Do Satie, Stravinsky, Varèse,
Messiaen, Carter, Dutilleux, Ligeti and Takemitsu all preserve and trans-
mit a 'Debussyan essence', encouraging the conclusion that only after the
end of the twentieth century can the true nature of Debussy's 'presence' be
determined? – as opposed, that is, to the presence of Ravel, or Skryabin,
or whoever? Or is it better to set this type of narrative aside and declare
that, simply because of the problems attendant on concepts of influence
and allusion in an age unprecedentedly conscious of the past, it is Debussy's
own works, and their ability to survive as commodities in a uniquely competitive cultural environment, that matter now, not the possible strengths
of his contribution to the music of other composers? The true pluralism
of twentieth-century culture resides in the individual identities of those
composers we continue to value. Can we confidently predict that in 2018,
the centenary of his death, Debussy will still be a strong presence on the
musical scene? If we can, should not the ultimately unprofitable attempt
to determine importance in terms of degrees of influence be definitively
abandoned? As Jonathan Dunsby has observed, 'most critics take Debussy
as some sort of modernist starting point . . . and to see what Debussy did and
thought as inevitable props in the act of writing the history of subsequent
music is simple enough, in fact a welcome, culturally reassuring mark of his
pre-eminent influences'.[39] But Dunsby's remarks are the merest preface to a
penetrating analysis of *En blanc et noir*, in which the nature and richness of

that work (and the other works with which it can be associated, of course) are the focus, not its effect on others. Now, and in the future, Debussy demands no less; and because penetrating analyses of many major works by him still remain to be undertaken, it is possible that the full potential of his relevance for new composition has still to be realised in the era of modern classicism. The story of 'Debussy now' is, above all, a story of unfinished business.

Endnotes

Introduction

1 *A Survey of Contemporary Music* (London: Oxford University Press, 2/1927), 98–9.

2 Ibid., 105.

3 *100 Years of Music* (London: Duckworth, 1974), 230.

4 Interview with *Excelsior* (18 January 1911); reprinted in Lesure, *Monsieur Croche et autres écrits*, 318.

5 Briscoe (ed.), *Debussy in Performance*, 85. This quotation concludes chapter 8, 'Debussy and nature'.

6 I invited all contributors to say a few words about their chapters and have, with their permission, freely incorporated what they have to say into the following descriptions alongside my own observations.

1 Debussy the man

1 Roger Nichols, *The Life of Debussy*, 1. This perceptive study is recommended to anyone seeking a fuller picture of Debussy the man than there is space to present here.

2 'L'âme d'autrui est une forêt obscure où il faut marcher avec précaution.' I am using Nichols's superior translation, ibid., 3. Unfortunately, Liebich does not give her source for this, though it predates the citing by Pasteur Valléry-Radot, who only knew Debussy at the end of his life (see Nichols, *Debussy Remembered*, 151).

3 As Debussy described himself to André Poniatowski in February 1893, quoting a phrase ('maniaque de bonheur') from Jules Laforgue's poem 'Solo de lune'. See *Debussy Letters*, 40.

4 *Correspondance*, 67.

5 Ibid., 267.

6 Ibid., 179 ('un vieux maniaque d'affection').

7 See Lesure, *Claude Debussy avant 'Pelléas'*, 24–5 for full reviews of this concert at Chauny on 16 January 1876.

8 Given in full in *Debussy Letters*, 3.

9 Letter of 12 July 1884 as translated in Nichols, *Debussy Remembered*, 24.

10 As recalled by Mme Gérard de Romilly, his pupil from 1898 to 1908, in 'Debussy professeur', *Cahiers Debussy* 2 (1978), 5.

11 Cited in Nichols, *Debussy Remembered*, 196.

12 As translated in *Debussy Letters*, 40.

13 From Laloy, *La musique retrouvée*, 258–9.

14 This letter, formerly in the Durand archives, Paris, is now in the Bibliothèque Gustav Mahler, Paris (like all Debussy's letters to his publisher).

15 See *Debussy Letters*, 199–201.

16 See Orledge, *Debussy and the Theatre*, 128–48 for fuller details about this ill-fated ballet, which Debussy *did* take on for money. (Also see chapter 4, 'Debussy on stage'. Ed.)

17 Letter of 12 September 1912.

18 Letter to Durand of 18 September 1913.

19 From Arthur Hartmann, 'Claude Debussy as I Knew Him', *Musical Courier* 39/19 (23 May 1918), 7.

20 Ibid., 8.

21 From René Peter, *Claude Debussy* (Paris, 1931) as translated in Nichols, *Debussy Remembered*, 135.

22 Ibid., 4.

23 From Casella, 'Claude Debussy', 1.

24 In Erik Satie, 'A table' from *L'Almanach de Cocagne pour l'an 1922*, 169, also cited in Erik Satie, *Ecrits*, ed. Ornella Volta (Paris, Editions Champ Libre, 2/1988), 51. According to Dolly Bardac, Emma banned Debussy from the kitchen after they moved into the Avenue du Bois de Boulogne in 1905.

25 According to his stepson Raoul Bardac's recollection 'Dans l'intimité de Claude Debussy', 73.

26 From a radio broadcast of 1938, as translated in Nichols, *Debussy Remembered*, 194.

27 From Durand, *Quelques souvenirs d'un éditeur de musique*, vol. II, 30. Debussy apparently had no knowledge of the workings of the parallel French copyright society.

28 See Nichols, *Debussy Remembered*, 193.

29 In Hartmann, 'Claude Debussy as I Knew Him', 8.

30 In de Romilly, 'Debussy professeur', *Cahiers Debussy* 2 (1978), 7. By all accounts, Debussy was an impatient, erratic and reluctant teacher too.

31 From Bardac, 'Dans l'intimité de Claude Debussy', 73. Emma Debussy called his special whisky 'a secret of the house' (see Nichols, *Debussy Remembered*, 204).

32 Mme Gaston de Tinan, 'Memories of Debussy and his circle', *Journal of the British Institute of Recorded Sound*, 50–1 (April–July 1973), 158. His stepdaughter Dolly lived in

the Debussy household from 1904 until her marriage in 1910.

33 Durand, *Quelques souvenirs d'un éditeur de musique*, vol. II, 92.

34 Cited in Nichols, *Debussy Remembered*, 169 and 181. The first is recalled by the pianist E. Robert Schmitz in 1937 and may be synonymous with the second, which comes from Teyte herself in 1962.

35 As translated in Nichols, *Debussy Remembered*, 132.

36 From Bardac, 'Dans l'intimité de Claude Debussy', 72.

37 From Nichols, *Debussy Remembered*, 6.

38 Ibid., 10.

39 Ibid., 49.

40 Ibid., 110.

41 In Jean-Aubry, 'Some Recollections of Debussy', 205.

42 He tore up one such photograph taken by Pierre Louÿs in May 1894, as we can see from Lesure, *Claude Debussy: iconographie musicale*, 54, plate 31.

43 See Nichols, *Debussy Remembered*, 223 (Arnold Bax) and 121 (Georges Jean-Aubry).

44 In a radio broadcast of 1938, translated in ibid., 194.

45 In Copeland, 'Debussy, the Man I Knew', *The Atlantic Monthly* (January 1955), 35.

46 From Erik Satie, 'Notes sur la musique moderne', *L'humanité* (11 October 1919), 2.

47 As translated in Nichols, *Debussy Remembered*, 137.

48 From Casella, 'Claude Debussy', 2.

49 As translated in Nichols, *Debussy Remembered*, 98.

50 Letter of 28 December 1915 cited in Lesure, *Claude Debussy avant 'Pelléas'*, 200.

51 In a letter to Henriette Fuchs of 12 July 1884, as translated in Nichols, *Debussy Remembered*, 25.

52 Cited in Nichols, *The Life of Debussy*, 44.

53 Cited in François Lesure, 'Achille à la Villa (1885–7)', *Cahiers Debussy* 12–13 (1988–9), 22. The original is in English.

54 In Lesure, *Claude Debussy, biographie critique*, 85.

55 From Lesure, *Claude Debussy avant 'Pelléas'*, 149.

56 Letter of 9 February 1897 from *Correspondance de Claude Debussy et Pierre Louÿs (1893–1904)*, 87.

57 For fuller details on this play see Orledge, *Debussy and the Theatre*, 241–3.

58 The full text of this palliative letter can be found in *Debussy Letters*, 147–8.

59 In a letter written from Dieppe on 11 August 1904, in the Beinecke Library, Yale

University (Frederick R. Koch Foundation deposit).

60 One such period was over Christmas and New Year 1909–10, as the dates on the manuscripts of the first book of *Préludes* show (now in the Pierpont Morgan Library).

61 *Correspondance*, 294.

62 From Mary Garden and Louis Biancolli, *Mary Garden's Story* (London: Michael Joseph, 1952), 80.

63 This was carefully erased from the last page of the orchestral sketch dated 'Dimanche 5 Mars 1905' in the Eastman School of Music, Rochester, NY.

64 From a letter to André Messager sent from Dieppe on 19 September 1904. See *Correspondance*, 196.

65 As in his letters to Raymond Bonheur of 9 August 1895 and Georges Hartmann of 14 July 1898. See *Debussy Letters*, 80 and 97–8.

66 From a letter of 15 July 1913. See *Correspondance*, 324.

67 In a letter of 19 July 1904, in the Beinecke Library, Yale University (Frederick R. Koch Foundation deposit).

68 Cited in Nichols, *Debussy Remembered*, 114.

69 In a letter of 25 February 1910 referring to Gabriel Pierné's conducting of 'Ibéria'. *Debussy Letters*, 217.

70 In [unnamed interviewer], 'The New Music Cult in France and Its Leader. Claude Achille Debussy Tells of His Present and Future Works', *New York Times* (16 May 1909), part 5, 9.

71 Lesure, 'Une interview romaine de Debussy [with Alberto Gasco]', *Cahiers Debussy* 11 (1987), 6.

72 In Nichols, *The Life of Debussy*, 165.

73 From [unnamed interviewer], 'Debussy Discusses Music and His Work', *New York Times* (26 June 1910), parts 3–4, 5.

2 Debussy's Parisian affiliations

1 Gabriel Astruc, 'Le Monument de "Claude de France"', typescript, *Fonds Montpensier*: Debussy, BN, Musique, Paris.

2 Letter from Debussy to Jacques Durand, 8 August 1914, *Correspondance*, 343.

3 Theodore Zeldin, *A History of French Passions* (Oxford: Clarendon Press, 1993), vol. I, 633–6.

4 Henri Rivière, *Trente-six vues de la Tour Eiffel* (Paris: Verneau, 1888–1902); see new edition, ed. Aya Louisa Macdonald (Paris: Philippe Sers, 1989).

5 By contrast the London underground opened in 1863 and the New York underground in 1868. See Jean-Claude

Demory, *Le métro chez nous* (Paris: Editions M.D.M., 1997) 5.

6 Lesure concludes a brief discussion of Debussy's ancestry with the comment: 'The origin of the family reveals no mystery: they came from the purest peasantry'. Lesure, *Claude Debussy avant Pelléas*, 9.

7 Nichols, *The Life of Debussy*, 13.

8 See Glen Watkins, *Pyramids at the Louvre: Music, Culture, and Collage from Stravinsky to the Postmodernists* (Cambridge, Mass.: Harvard University Press, 1994); Lawrence Kramer, 'Consuming the Exotic: Ravel's *Daphnis and Chloé*', in *Classical Music and Post-Modern Knowledge* (Berkeley: California University Press, 1995). Parallels can be drawn with Ravel's imaginative excursions to other cultures, such as ancient Greece, Spain to some extent and American jazz. He tended to visit the country in question *after* he had written a work evoking that culture.

9 Lockspeiser, *Debussy*, 97.

10 I am grateful to Nichols for drawing my attention to these works in a personal communication, July 2001.

11 Theodore Zeldin, *A History of French Passions* (Oxford: Clarendon, 1993), vol. II, 6.

12 Ibid., 33.

13 Ibid., 30.

14 See also Eugen Weber, 'France, One and Indivisible' (part 1, chapter 7), in *Peasants into Frenchmen: The Modernization of Rural France, 1870–1914* (Stanford: Stanford University Press, 1976).

15 Nichols, *Debussy Remembered*, 22.

16 Lockspeiser, *Debussy: His Life and Mind*, vol. I, 70–1.

17 X.M. (Danish interview), 'Maurice Ravel's Arrival', *Berlingske Tidende* (30 January 1926), in Arbie Orenstein (ed.), *A Ravel Reader* (New York: Columbia University Press, 1990), 440; see Barbara L. Kelly, 'History and Homage', in D. Mawer (ed.), *The Cambridge Companion to Ravel* (Cambridge: Cambridge University Press, 2000), 7–9.

18 'Les impressions d'un Prix de Rome', *Gil Blas* (10 June 1903) in *Monsieur Croche et autre écrits*, 188.

19 Debussy to Antoine Marmontel, 1 January 1886, *Correspondance*, 42.

20 Ibid., 33.

21 Ibid., 36 and 57.

22 Ibid., 34, 36 and 38.

23 Ibid., 38.

24 Robert Brussel, 'Claude Debussy et Paul Dukas', *La revue musicale* (1 May 1926), 101.

25 *Correspondance*, 39.

26 Baudelaire, *Petit poèmes en prose, le spleen de Paris* (Paris: Garnier frères, 1958), 26.

27 Jarocinski, *Debussy: Impressionism and Symbolism*, 81.

28 *Correspondance*, 49.

29 Charles Baudelaire, *Richard Wagner et Tannhäuser à Paris*, ed. Robert Kopp (Paris: Les Belles Lettres, 1994), 8.

30 See Ravel's idea of translating from literature to music regarding *Histoires naturelles*; Roger Nichols, *Ravel Remembered* (London: Faber, 1987), 78; see also Kelly, 'History and Homage', 17.

31 Letter from Debussy to Emile Baron, *Correspondance*, 49.

32 Letter from Debussy to Ernest Chausson, ibid., 57.

33 Baudelaire, *Richard Wagner et Tannhäuser à Paris*, 13.

34 See Baudelaire, 'Correspondances' from *The Flowers of Evil (Les fleurs du mal)* (Oxford: Oxford University Press, 1993); Baudelaire, 'De la couleur', *Le Salon de 1846*, in *Œuvres complètes*, vol. II (Paris: NRF Gallimard, 1976), 425.

35 Baudelaire, 'De la couleur', 423.

36 Letter from Debussy to Emile Baron, *Correspondance*, 49.

37 Ibid.

38 Baudelaire, *Richard Wagner et Tannhäuser à Paris*, xxx.

39 Ibid., xxi.

40 See Poe, *The Oval Portrait* and Wilde, *The Picture of Dorian Gray*.

41 Ravel was critical of Debussy's technically 'mediocre' orchestration of *La Mer* in terms of 'architectural power', Arbie Orenstein (ed.), *Lettres, écrits, entretiens* (Paris: Flammarion, 1989), 36.

42 Debussy also acknowledges 'the marvellous effects in *Parsifal*' in this letter to André Caplet, 25 August 1912. *Correspondance*, 311; and *Debussy Letters*, 262.

43 See Marie Rolf, 'Orchestral Manuscripts of Claude Debussy, 1892–1905', *The Musical Quarterly* 70/4 (Fall 1984), 538–66 and Myriam Chimènes, 'The Definition of Timbre in the Process of Composition of *Jeux*', in Smith, *Debussy Studies*, 1–25.

44 Debussy's interest in timbre and spatial organisation of sound was further stimulated by the exotic sounds of the gamelan, which he encountered at the 1889 Paris exhibition. Roy Howat reveals the impact of this on Debussy's piano writing in Howat, 'Debussy and the Orient'.

45 Letter from Debussy to Durand, *Debussy Letters*, 184.

46 Holloway, *Debussy and Wagner*, 42; Nichols, *The Life of Debussy*, 56.

47 Lockspeiser, *Debussy: His Life and Mind*, vol. I, 90.

48 *Correspondance*, 56.

49 Nichols, *The Life of Debussy*, 28.

50 Jean-Jaques Eigeldinger, 'Debussy et l'idée d'arabesque musicale', *Cahiers Debussy* 12–13 (1988–9), 6–7.

51 Théodore de Banville, *Nocturne, La revue contemporaine* (1885), 6. Banville was also the author of the article on Baudelaire, ibid., 379–90. His final adulatory comments, moreover, are reserved for Baudelaire's *Les fleurs du mal*, from which Debussy's *Cinq poèmes* are taken.

52 Dante Gabriel Rossetti, *La damoiselle élue*, trans. Gabriel Sarrazin, *La revue contemporaine* (1885), 373–8.

53 Smith, 'Debussy and the Pre-Raphaelites', 98–9; see also Debussy's letter to Henri Vasnier, 24 November 1885, *Correspondance*, 40–1.

54 Jean Moréas quoted in Paul Adam, 'Le symbolisme', *La vogue* 2 (4–11 October 1886), 398–9.

55 Ibid., 398–401.

56 Theodor de Wyzewa, 'M. Mallarmé: Notes', *La vogue* (5–12 July and 12–19 July 1886), 375; see also Wyzewa's discussion of the same work in *La revue indépendante* (January 1887).

57 See Jarocinski, *Debussy: Impressionism and Symbolism*, 86–90.

58 Lesure, *Claude Debussy avant Pelléas*, 98–9; and Nichols, *The Life of Debussy*, 61.

59 Lesure, *Claude Debussy avant Pelléas*, 94.

60 Ibid., 98.

61 Lockspeiser, *Debussy: His Life and Mind*, vol. I, 152.

62 Lloyd Austin, *Poetic Principles and Practice* (Cambridge: Cambridge University Press, 1987), 58.

63 Ibid.

64 Debussy, *Prelude to 'The Afternoon of a Faun'*, Norton Critical Score, 24.

65 Stéphane Mallarmé, 'Mystery in Letters', in Austin, *Poetic Principles*, 59.

66 Ibid., 62.

67 Nichols, *The Life of Debussy*, 82–3.

68 Debussy also gave this name to two piano works (1888–91).

69 Eigeldinger, 'Debussy et l'idée d'arabesque musicale', 7.

70 *Correspondance*, 38.

71 Jarocinski, *Debussy: Impressionism and Symbolism*, 146.

72 (For further discussion of the *Faune*, Mallarmé and a connection with *Jeux*, see Berman, '*Prelude to the Afternoon of a Faun* and *Jeux*: Debussy's Summer Rites'. Ed.)

73 *Correspondance*, 43.

74 Lockspeiser, *Debussy: His Life and Mind*, vol. I, 152.

75 Debussy, *Prelude to 'The Afternoon of a Faun'*, Norton Critical Score, 29.

76 See for example, Lockspeiser, *Debussy: His Life and Mind*, vol. I, chapters 9–11; and Howat, 'Debussy and the Orient', 45–57.

77 Lockspeiser, *Debussy: His Life and Mind*, vol. I, 50.

78 Viñes notes in his diary that he and Ravel played the piano duet version in 1897. Ricardo Viñes, Nina Gubisch, 'Le journal inédit de Ricardo Viñes', *Revue internationale de musique française* 1/2 (June 1980), 183–95; quoted in Nichols, *Ravel Remembered*, 7.

79 I am grateful to Jeremy Drake for pointing out possible connections between these works.

80 Pierre Boulez, *Notes of an Apprenticeship*, trans. Herbert Weinstock (New York: Alfred Knopf, 1968), 344–5; Debussy, *Prelude to 'The Afternoon of a Faun'*, Norton Critical Score, 161.

81 Lockspeiser, *Debussy*, 41.

82 Letter from Debussy to Chausson, 7 March 1889, *Correspondance*, 57.

83 Archives de l'Académie des Beaux Arts, 2 E 17; quoted in Lesure, *Claude Debussy avant Pelléas*, 83.

84 Ibid., 84.

85 *Correspondance*, 60.

86 Debussy to Ernest Hébert, 17 March 1887, *Correspondance*, 55; quoted in Nichols, *The Life of Debussy*, 45–6.

87 *Monsieur Croche et autres écrits*, 40.

88 See, for example, Arbie Orenstein, *Ravel: Man and Musician* (New York: Columbia University Press, 1975), 28; Léon Paul Fargue in Nichols, *Ravel Remembered*, 149.

89 Jann Pasler, 'Pelléas and Power: Forces behind the Reception of Debussy's Opera', *19th-Century Music* 10/3 (Spring 1987), 255. See also Pasler's table showing the political persuasions of particular critics and papers/journals and their response to *Pelléas*, ibid., 247–9.

90 Gaston Carraud, *La Liberté* (2 May 1902); Jean Marnold, *Mercure de France* (June), 810.

91 Henri de Curzon, *Gazette de France* (3 May 1902).

92 See Jane Fulcher, *French Cultural Politics and Music* (New York: Oxford University Press, 1999), 178.

93 See Pasler, 'Pelléas and Power', 263.

94 André Suarès, 'Debussy', *La Revue musicale*, special issue (November 1920), 112.

95 *La revue bleue* (2 April, 1904), 122.
96 *Monsieur Croche et autres écrits*, 207.
97 Scott Messing, *Neoclassicism in Music* (Ann Arbor: UMI Press, 1988), 45–9.
98 Owing to his illness and death, he only wrote three of them.
99 Ravel's own Sonata for Violin and Cello (1920–22), the first movement of which was included in the 'Tombeau de Claude Debussy' (*La Revue musicale* supplement, December 1920), goes further in emphasising new elements of bare sonorities, bitonality and jazz and can be seen as a post-war tribute.
100 Debussy, 'Enfin, seuls! . . . ', *L'intransigeant* (11 March 1915); see reproduction in *Monsieur Croche et autres écrits*, 265–6.
101 Debussy to Nicolas Coronio, September 1914, *Debussy Letters*, 293.
102 Debussy to Durand, 18 August 1914, ibid., 292.
103 Alfred Mortier, *Le courrier musical* (1 April 1918) 148–9.
104 Julien Tiersot, *Le courrier musical* (15 April 1918) 173.
105 Camille Bellaigue, *Revue des deux mondes* (15 May 1918); see his review of *Pelléas*, *Revue des deux mondes* (15 May 1902).
106 In reality neither death was heroic in a military sense.
107 Vuillermoz, *Le ménéstrel* (11 June), 241.
108 See Pierre Leroi's review of Debussy's Quartet: 'Debussy moves us in the purest and noblest ways. One cannot overstate the extent to which he is one of the greatest musical geniuses and that his name embellishes the history of our country with a glorious halo'. Leroi, *Le courrier musical* (15 February 1923, 69); for examples of war discourse see Louis Vuillemin, 'Musique et nationalisme', *Le courrier musical* (15 February 1923), 65.

3 Debussy as musician and critic
1 *Gil blas* (16 February 1903), 96; *La revue blanche* (1 June 1901), 45; *La revue bleue* (2 April 1904), 278; *Gil blas* (23 February 1903), 101; *La revue blanche* (1 July 1901), 52. All are taken from *Monsieur Croche et autres écrits* (to which page numbers apply); 'ibid.' is used *passim* in nn. 10–56 below to refer to that volume.
2 Henry Gauthier-Villars, 'Lettre de l'Ouvreuse', *L'écho de Paris* (28 October 1901), 4.
3 Gustave Doret, *Musique et musiciens* (Lausanne: Edition Foetisch, 1915), 21.
4 *Gil blas* (30 March 1903), *Monsieur Croche et autres écrits*, 137.
5 Those articles in which Monsieur Croche features are: *La revue blanche* (1 July 1901); *La*

revue blanche (15 November 1901); *Gil blas* (16 February 1903); *Gil blas* (16 March 1903); *Gil blas* (23 March 1903); and *Les annales politiques et littéraires* (25 May 1913).
6 Debussy insisted on this point in his opening article in *La revue blanche* on 1 April 1901. He repeated it in his introductory article for *Gil blas* on 12 January 1903 and again, as late as June 1914, in an interview with the critic Michel-Dimitri Calvocoressi for the American publication *The Etude*.
7 *La revue blanche* (1 July 1901), *Monsieur Croche et autres écrits*, 53. It is perhaps no coincidence that the Société des Concerts du Conservatoire was somewhat tardy in performing Debussy's music. It was not until 17 December 1905 that the *Prélude à l'après-midi d'un faune* (1894), by then regularly featured on the programmes of most concert societies, was admitted to its repertoire.
8 See, for example, the article by Pierre Lalo in *Le temps* of 25 March 1902, 3.
9 *Excelsior* (18 January 1911), *Monsieur Croche et autres écrits*, 318.
10 *La revue blanche* (1 July 1901), ibid., 51, 49.
11 *La revue blanche* (15 May 1901), ibid., 39.
12 *Le mercure de France* (January 1903), ibid., 67.
13 See *La revue blanche* (15 May 1901), ibid., 39.
14 Paul Flat, 'Théâtres', *La revue bleue* (10 May 1902), 592.
15 Alfred Bruneau, 'La Musique dramatique', *La grande revue* (1 July 1902), 219; Pierre Lalo, 'La Musique', *Le temps* (20 May 1902), 2–3.
16 *La revue musicale (d'histoire et de critique musicale)* (April 1902), *Monsieur Croche et autres écrits*, 271–4.
17 *La revue blanche* (15 May 1901), ibid., 41.
18 See *La revue blanche* (15 May 1901), ibid., 41–2.
19 See *La revue blanche* (1 December 1901), ibid., 60–1.
20 *La revue blanche* (1 April 1901), ibid., 24.
21 *Les annales politiques et littéraires* (25 May 1913), ibid., 244.
22 Letter dated 25 August 1912, *Correspondance*, 311.
23 *La liberté* (13 October 1908), 1.
24 Louis Schneider, 'M. Claude Debussy', *La revue musicale (d'histoire et critique musicale)* (April 1902), *Monsieur Croche et autres écrits*, 273.
25 *Gil blas* (16 February 1903), ibid., 96.
26 *La revue blanche* (1 April 1901), ibid., 25.
27 *La revue blanche* (1 April 1901), ibid., 27.
28 *Gil blas* (13 April 1903), ibid., 148–50.
29 *La revue blanche* (15 April 1901), ibid., 29.

30 *La revue blanche* (15 April 1901), ibid., 31.
31 *La revue blanche* (1 May 1901), ibid., 34.
32 *La revue musicale S.I.M.* (15 February 1913), ibid., 229.
33 *Gil blas* (19 January 1903), ibid., 76.
34 René Lénormand, *Etude sur l'harmonie moderne* (Paris: Le monde musical, 1913), 6.
35 Letter of 20 September 1905, *Lettres à Auguste Sérieyx [par] Vincent d'Indy, Henri Duparc [et] Albert Roussel*, ed. M.-L. Sérieyx (Paris: Librairie Ploix, 1961), 16.
36 Pierre Lalo, 'La Musique – concert officiel de musique française au Trocadéro', *Le temps* (28 August 1900), 3. Lalo supported Debussy at the time of the premiere of *Pelléas* but, in reality, he had reservations about Debussy's music and later became one of his most powerful and virulent opponents.
37 Claude Debussy, 'Déclaration à un journaliste Autrichien' (December 1910), *Monsieur Croche et autres écrits*, 308.
38 *Excelsior* (18 January 1911), ibid., 318–19.
39 Letter of 3 April 1904 to Louis Laloy, *Correspondance*, 188.
40 *Comoedia* (17 December 1910), *Monsieur Croche et autres écrits*, 312–13. Vuillemin was, in fact, a committed supporter of Debussy. As a music critic he was unswervingly positive in his reviews and as a singer he frequently included Debussy's music in his programmes.
41 Paul-Jean Toulet, 'Une intervioue de M. Claude Debussy', *Les marges* (1 October 1912), 158.
42 *Excelsior* (18 January 1911), *Monsieur Croche et autres écrits*, 318.
43 Letter to Robert Godet of 18 January 1913, Robert Godet and Georges Jean-Aubry (eds.), *Lettres à deux amis* (Paris: Librairie José Corti, 1942), 134. Debussy's first article for *La revue musicale S.I.M.* appeared in the November 1912 edition.
44 The Schola Cantorum had been founded in 1894 with the aim of training young composers in the areas of counterpoint, analysis and music history, which were marginalised at the Conservatoire. D'Indy had been involved from the start and in 1900 became director of the Schola.
45 Throughout his career d'Indy maintained that advances in French music were, to a large extent, attributable to Wagner's beneficial influence. He argued this point of view in his *Richard Wagner et son influence sur l'art musical français* (Paris: Librairie Delagrave, 1930), 65.
46 Claude Debussy, 'A la Schola Cantorum', *Gil blas* (2 February 1903), *Monsieur Croche et autres écrits*, 90.

47 See 'A la Schola Cantorum' of 2 February 1903 and 'Lettre ouverte à Monsieur le Chevalier C.W. Gluck' of 23 February 1903, both in *Monsieur Croche et autres écrits*, 89–93 and 100–3. His acquaintance with the music of Rameau was strengthened by Debussy's participation in the preparation of a complete edition of Rameau's works by the Durand publishing house. Debussy's contribution, *Les fêtes de Polymnie*, appeared in 1908.
48 D'Indy, 'A propos de *Pelléas et Mélisande*', *L'occident* (June 1902), 378.
49 *La revue musicale S.I.M.* (15 May 1913), *Monsieur Croche et autres écrits*, 240.
50 *La revue musicale S.I.M.* (1 November 1913), ibid., 245.
51 See, for example, *La revue musicale S.I.M.* (December 1912), ibid., 218.
52 See *La revue musicale S.I.M.* (November 1912), ibid., 213.
53 *La revue musicale S.I.M.* (November 1912), ibid., 214.
54 *La revue musicale S.I.M.* (December 1912), ibid., 218.
55 See *La revue musicale S.I.M.* (15 May 1913), ibid., 240.
56 *La revue musicale S.I.M.* (1 November 1913), ibid., 247.
57 This animosity even extended to Wagner, whose music was seldom performed in Paris during the war. On the other hand, Beethoven's *Eroica* Symphony enjoyed a spate of popularity among wartime audiences.
58 See Claude Debussy, 'Enfin seuls', *L'intransigeant* (11 March 1915), *Monsieur Croche et autres écrits*, 267.
59 Joseph Vallery-Radot, *Tel était Claude Debussy* (Paris: René Juilliard, 1958), 139–40.
60 Most notably, despite his advocacy of Wagner in his youth, Saint-Saëns launched a scathing and ill-judged attack on Wagner's domination of French music, which was serialised in *L'écho de Paris* from 19 September 1914 onwards and published in book form as *Germanophilie* in 1916.
61 Preface to Paul Huvelin's *Pour la musique française* in *Monsieur Croche et autres écrits*, 267.
62 Letter of 9 October 1914, *Lettres de Claude Debussy à son éditeur* (Paris: Durand, 1927), 128–9.
63 Ibid., 126.
64 At the end of the war Saint-Saëns also wrote his *Cyprès et lauriers* for organ and orchestra as a celebration of allied victory.
65 *Correspondance*, 345.
66 Jacques des Gachons, 'Depuis deux ans avez-vous pu travailler?' *Le figaro* (16 October 1916), 3.

4 Debussy on stage

1 Orledge, *Debussy and the Theatre*, 82. (This
is the most thorough study of Debussy's many
theatrical projects and interests.)

2 Claude Debussy, 'Considérations sur
le Prix de Rome au point de vue musical',
originally published in *Musica* (May 1903),
and reprinted in *Monsieur Croche et autres
écrits*, 175–9; translated in *Debussy on
Music*, 198.

3 Debussy, 'Les impressions d'un Prix de
Rome', *Gil blas* (10 June 1903); reprinted in
Monsieur Croche et autres écrits, 188–91;
translated in *Debussy on Music*, 211.

4 For documents pertaining to the Prix de
Rome, see Constant Pierre, *Le Conservatoire
national de musique et de déclamation:
documents historiques et administratifs,
recueillis ou reconstitués* (Paris: Imprimerie
nationale, 1900). On the Prix de Rome, see
also Eugene Bozza, 'The History of the
"Prix de Rome"', and Hilda Colucci, 'The
Winners of the "Premier Grand Prix de
Rome" (Music)', *Hinrichsen's Musical
Year Book* 7 (1952), 487–94; and Lesley
A. Wright, 'Bias, Influence, and Bizet's
Prix de Rome', *19th-Century Music* 15
(1992), 215–28.

5 The scenes were for solo voice from 1803
through 1830, and between 1831 and 1838 for
either one or two voices. For the balance of
the nineteenth century, three voices was the
norm. Pierre, *Le Conservatoire national*, 528–9.

6 *Debussy on Music*, 199.

7 Ibid., 200.

8 Ibid., 199–200.

9 For details regarding extant sources for
Debussy's works, see Lesure, *Catalogue de
l'œuvre de Claude Debussy*. Pending publication
of the promised revised edition of this
indispensable reference tool, also see the
catalogues included in Briscoe, *Claude
Debussy: A Guide to Research*, 17–82; and for
the early works, Briscoe, 'The Compositions
of Claude Debussy's Formative Years
(1879–1887)', 389–433, which includes some
incipits and even manuscript facsimiles not
available elsewhere. Yves A. Lado-Bordowsky's
study of Debussy's handwriting was the basis
for his revised chronology of the composer's
early works; see his 'La chronologie des
œuvres de jeunesse de Claude Debussy
(1879–1884)', *Cahiers Debussy* 14 (1990),
3–22. For a brief description of a
manuscript of *Daniel*, see Julien Tiersot,
'Œuvres de première jeunesse de Berlioz et de
Debussy', *Le ménestrel* 95 (6 January 1933),
1–4.

10 On *Le gladiateur*, see Vallas, *Claude Debussy:
His Life and Works*, 23–5 (including facsimile
reproductions of pages 58–9 of the score
between 24 and 25; the 1958 French-language
second edition of this work, *Claude Debussy et
son temps*, 52–5, incorporates some revisions
but lacks the facsimiles); Lesure, *Claude
Debussy: biographie critique*, 61–2; and John
R. Clevenger, 'Debussy's First "Masterpiece",
Le Gladiateur', *Cahiers Debussy* 23 (1999),
3–34.

11 'Nature musicale généreuse mais ardente
parfois jusqu'à l'intempérance; quelques
accents dramatiques saisissants.' Dietschy,
A Portrait of Claude Debussy, 35.

12 Guinand's texts had also been used for the
competitions in 1878 (*La fille de Jephté*), 1881
(*Geneviève*) and 1882 (*Edith*). On Debussy's
L'enfant prodigue, see especially Lesure, *Claude
Debussy: biographie critique*, 68–70; Vallas,
Claude Debussy et son temps, 56–60; and Wenk,
Claude Debussy and Twentieth-Century Music,
21–6.

13 Letter of early February 1885, in *Debussy
Letters*, 5.

14 Laloy, *Claude Debussy*, 14.

15 Maurice Emmanuel, 'Les ambitions de
Claude-Achille' (1926), translated in Nichols,
Debussy Remembered, 22.

16 'Sens poétique très marqué, coloris brillant
et chaud, musique vivante et dramatique.'
Dietschy, *A Portrait of Claude Debussy*, 37.

17 'Opéras', originally published in *La revue
blanche* (15 May 1901), and reprinted in
Monsieur Croche et autres écrits, 38–43;
translated in *Debussy on Music*, 34.

18 The score's most 'exotic' (and progressive)
harmonic effect, the use of whole-tone
harmonies to prepare the harmonic/thematic
return of the opening theme of the 'air de
danse', was not present in the original score
but was added years later when Debussy
revised the orchestration.

19 See his letter of 21 November 1910 to
André Caplet, in *Debussy Letters*, 224–5.

20 Letter of 20 March 1906, in *Debussy Letters*,
168.

21 According to Claus Røllum-Larsen, 'The
Early Reception of Claude Debussy and His
Works in Copenhagen', *Cahiers Debussy* 24
(2000), 52, Joachim Andersen conducted the
'Cortège et air de danse' in 1906 in the concert
hall of the Tivoli Gardens in Copenhagen.

22 Letter of 17 July 1907 to Jacques Durand,
in *Debussy Letters*, 179.

23 Letter of 5 August 1907 to Jacques Durand,
in *Debussy Letters*, 181–2. He was also amused
to find 'some most surprising things in the

early orchestration', notably, in the very opening bars, 'a cor anglais which quite blatantly plays fifths . . . and even thirds . . . it's really a pity such a cor anglais remains to be invented'.

24 A hand other than the composer's was responsible for the final portion of the score, from the middle of the duo (at 'Au nom de mes remords') to the end. The nature of the revision, which even involves prominent motivic alterations, suggests that it must surely have been accomplished under the composer's supervision.

25 The cantata was sung in French, which was unusual for Sheffield, and the soloists were Agnes Nicholls, Felix Senius and Frederic Austin. See Henry J. Wood, *My Life in Music* (London: Victor Gollancz, 1938), 279–80.

26 See Orledge, *Debussy and the Theatre*, 41 (and illustration on 42).

27 Paul Vidal, 'Souvenirs d'Achille Debussy', *Revue musicale* 7 (1 May 1926), 16.

28 *Journal officiel* (31 December 1886), reproduced in Guy Cogeval and François Lesure, *Debussy e il simbolismo* (Rome: Fratelli Palombi Editori, 1984), 50.

29 *Debussy on Music*, 77–8.

30 *Correspondance*, 36.

31 *Debussy Letters*, 13.

32 Cogeval and Lesure, *Debussy e il simbolismo*, 50.

33 David Weir, *Decadence and the Making of Modernism* (Amherst, Mass.: University of Massachusetts Press, 1995), 22–42.

34 *Debussy Letters*, 13.

35 Reyer's *Salammbô*, with a libretto by Camille du Locle, would have its premiere in Brussels on 10 February 1890. Notwithstanding Reyer's rights, between 1863 and 1866 Musorgsky wrote his own libretto for *Salammbô* and composed music for six of its scenes, and in 1886 a *Salammbô* with music by Nicolò Massa to a libretto by Engelo Zanardini was performed at La Scala. On musical (and cinematic) adaptations of *Salammbô*, see Gustave Flaubert, *Salammbô*, ed. René Dumesnil, 2 vols. (Paris: Société les Belles Lettres, 1944), vol. I, cxxxvi–cxlii and vol. II, 212–16. The most famous operatic *Salammbô*, of course, is the excerpt that Bernard Herrmann composed for Orson Welles's classic 1941 film *Citizen Kane*.

36 On *Diane au bois*, see Eileen Souffrin, 'Debussy lecteur de Banville', *Revue de musicologie* 46 (1960), 200–22; Lockspeiser, *Debussy: His Life and Mind*, vol. I, 75–81; Langham Smith, 'Debussy and the Pre-Raphaelites', 95–109; and James R.

Briscoe, '"To Invent New Forms": Debussy's *Diane au bois*', *Musical Quarterly* 74 (1990), 131–69.

37 Debussy set portions of scenes 1, 2 and 7 at least. The extant fragments include Hymnis's 'Il dort encore' from scene 1, published in Debussy, *Sept poèmes de Banville*, ed. James R. Briscoe (Paris: Jobert, 1984), 22–5, and 'Ode bachique' from scene 7, a duet for Hymnis and Anacréon.

38 Raymond Bonheur, 'Souvenirs et impressions d'un compagnon de jeunesse' (1926), translated (in part) in Nichols, *Debussy Remembered*, 10.

39 Alvin Harms, *Théodore de Banville* (Boston: Twayne Publishers, 1983), 163–4.

40 How else to explain the plural 'fragments' when only one item is listed, and that a duo from the latter part of the work is item number one?

41 *Debussy Letters*, 8.

42 Laloy, *Claude Debussy*, 14.

43 Undated letter of late June 1885, in *Correspondance*, 36.

44 Letter of 19 October 1895, in *Debussy Letters*, 13.

45 Letter of 23 December 1886, ibid., 18.

46 Letter of 24 November 1885, ibid., 14–15.

47 Letter of 29 January 1886, ibid., 16.

48 Letter of 8/9 September 1892, ibid., 38.

49 Vallas, *Claude Debussy et son temps*, 140.

50 On *Rodrigue et Chimène* see Abbate, 'Tristan in the Composition of *Pelléas*'; Richard Langham Smith, '*Rodrigue et Chimène*: genèse, histoire, problèmes d'édition', *Cahiers Debussy* 12–13 (1988–9), 67–81; Langham Smith, '"La jeunesse du Cid": A Mislaid Act in *Rodrigue et Chimène*', in *Debussy Studies*, 201–28; and François Lesure, 'Massenet, Debussy et la compétition des Cid', *L'avant-scène opéra* 161 (1994), 120–5.

51 *Debussy Letters*, 34.

52 Vallas, *Claude Debussy: His Life and Works*, 78; Smith, '"La jeunesse du Cid": A Mislaid Act in *Rodrigue et Chimène*', 210.

53 Paul Dukas, *Correspondance de Paul Dukas*, ed. Georges Favre (Paris: Durand, 1971), 21.

54 Smith, '"La jeunesse du Cid": A Mislaid Act in *Rodrigue et Chimène*', 202.

55 For detailed accounts of Mendès's sources, see Orledge, *Debussy and the Theatre*, 19–27; and Smith, '"La jeunesse du Cid": A Mislaid Act in *Rodrigue et Chimène*', especially 211–28.

56 Claude Debussy, *Rodrigue et Chimène*, Orchestra and Chorus of the Opéra de Lyon, conducted by Kent Nagano (Paris: Erato/Radio France 4509-98508-2, 1995). The score was reconstructed by Richard Langham

Smith, missing text was provided by Georges
Beck, and Edison Denisov did the
orchestration.

57 Raymond Bonheur, 'Souvenirs et
impressions d'un compagnon de jeunesse', *La
revue musicale* 7 (1 May 1926), 5.

58 Vallas, *Claude Debussy et son temps*, 143.
Xavier Carlier and Maurice Lefèvre were
among the composers who had approached
Maeterlinck regarding *La Princesse Maleine*. At
the time of her death, in 1918, Lili Boulanger
was working on an opera based on the play.

59 Lesure, *Claude Debussy: biographie critique*,
123.

60 The literature on *Pelléas* is enormous. See
Grayson, *The Genesis of Debussy's* Pelléas et
Mélisande; Grayson, 'The Interludes of
Pelléas et Mélisande', *Cahiers Debussy* 12–13
(1988–9), 100–22; Abbate, '*Tristan* in the
Composition of *Pelléas*'; Nichols and
Smith, *Claude Debussy: Pelléas et Mélisande*;
François Lesure, 'La longue attente de *Pelléas*
(1895–1898)', *Cahiers Debussy* 15 (1991), 3–12;
Margit Schumann, 'Une esquisse pour *Pelléas
et Mélisande*: la "Scène des moutons"', *Cahiers
Debussy* 17–18 (1993–4), 35–56; and
Grayson, 'Waiting for Golaud: The Concept
of Time in *Pelléas*', in Smith (ed.), *Debussy
Studies*, 26–50.

61 *Debussy Letters*, 54 and 56.

62 Wagnerian influences on Debussy are
discussed in Holloway, *Debussy and Wagner*,
and Abbate, '*Tristan* in the Composition of
Pelléas'.

63 The visit was reported in *L'art moderne* 13
(12 November 1893), 367.

64 Undated letter of early December 1893 to
Ernest Chausson, in *Debussy Letters*, 60.

65 On Debussy's adaptation of the play, see
Grayson, *The Genesis of Debussy's* Pelléas et
Mélisande, 113–32; and Grayson, 'The
Libretto of Debussy's "Pelléas et Mélisande"',
Music and Letters 66 (1985), 34–50.

66 *Le temps* (22 May 1893), cited in W. D.
Halls, *Maurice Maeterlinck: A Study of His Life
and Thought* (Oxford: Clarendon Press, 1960),
37–8.

67 Undated letter to Lugné-Poe, in
Lugné-Poe, *Le sot du tremplin* (Paris:
Gallimard, 1930), 237. Maeterlinck identified
these centuries as his suggestion for the style
of the costumes.

68 The circularity of the play is discussed in
Grayson, 'Waiting for Golaud: The Concept of
Time in *Pelléas*'.

69 In a letter of 1907 to Maurice Kufferath,
co-director of the Théâtre de la Monnaie in
Brussels, Debussy confided that he thought it
would have been better to 'compress' the five

acts of *Pelléas* into three (Lesure, *Claude
Debussy: biographie critique*, 287). Today, *Pelléas*
is typically done in 'three' acts, with
intermissions after acts II and III. It is even
done in 'two', with intermission after act III
(or act II).

70 In his review of the play's premiere, Sarcey
reported that some disrespectful laughter was
directed at this scene, which he judged totally
incomprehensible, not only to 'outsiders', but
to the initiates and even to the symbolist
(Maeterlinck) himself.

71 Yniold's golden ball invites comparison
with Mélisande's two golden 'circles': her
crown and her wedding ring, neither of which
she holds onto.

72 See René Terrasson, '*Pelléas et Mélisande*' ou
l'initiation (Paris: Editions EDIMAF, 1982),
for an analysis of the opera's musical and
literary symbols. The discussion of act IV,
scene 3 and some of the following remarks
on the play are indebted to this book and to
Aimé Israel-Pelletier, '*Pelléas et Mélisande*:
drame lyrique en cinq actes, musique de
Claude Debussy', unpublished paper read
at 'Festival *Pelléas et Mélisande*', Eastman
School of Music, Rochester, 5–6 May
1987.

73 Halls, *Maurice Maeterlinck: A Study of His
Life and Thought*, 38.

74 Letter of January 1894? to Ernest
Chausson, and of 28 August 1894 and 17
August 1895 to Henri Lerolle, in *Debussy
Letters*, 62, 73 and 80.

75 Letter of 9 August 1895 to Raymond
Bonheur, in *Debussy Letters*, 80.

76 The most obvious instrumental
associations are the horn with the hunter
Golaud, the oboe (and English horn) with the
sad Mélisande, the flute with the naive Pelléas,
and the cellos with the wise and
compassionate Arkel. Pedal points often
connote immobility, and whole-tone
harmonies are connected with confusion,
disorientation, incomprehension and dread.
For further discussion of these and other
'symbols' see Wenk, *Claude Debussy and
Twentieth-Century Music*, 37–50; Nichols and
Smith, *Claude Debussy: Pelléas et Mélisande*,
78–139; and Parks, *The Music of Claude
Debussy*, 163–86.

77 Letter of 3 September 1893 (with
postscript of 6 September) to Chausson, in
Debussy Letters, 52.

78 See Lesure, 'La longue attente de *Pelléas*
(1895–1898)'.

79 This is exactly what happened for a
performance of Maeterlinck's *Pelléas* at the
Croat National Theatre in Zagreb on

10 March 1908: portions of Debussy's opera, among them the interludes, were arranged as incidental music by Andro Mitrović. See Zdenka Weber , 'La diffusion de la musique de Debussy en Croatie', *Cahiers Debussy* 16 (1992), 49–50.

80 The proceedings of the arbitration meetings are reproduced in Lesure, *Claude Debussy avant* Pelléas *ou les années symbolistes*, 253–5.

81 See David Grayson, 'Debussy in the Opera House: An Unpublished Letter concerning Yniold and Mélisande', *Cahiers Debussy* 9 (1985), 17–28.

82 A baritone voice that extends into the tenor range and is named after Jean-Blaise Martin (1768–1837), who possessed such a voice, and for whom a number of roles were tailored.

83 See Grayson, 'The Interludes of *Pelléas et Mélisande*'. The original, short interludes appear in the first edition of the vocal score, published in 1902 by Fromont, and are reproduced in Howard Ferguson, 'Debussy's Emendations to "Pelléas"', *Musical Times* 129 (1988), 387–8.

84 See Grayson, *The Genesis of Debussy's* Pelléas et Mélisande, 85–6 and 129–31. The two cut passages that are absent from the full score may be found in the original vocal score (Fromont, 1902) and also in Nichols and Smith, *Claude Debussy: Pelléas et Mélisande*, 56–8; and in Ferguson, 'Debussy's Emendations to "Pelléas"' (though Golaud's 'line' has been omitted from the latter excerpt).

85 'Debussy Discusses Music and His Work', *New York Times* (26 June 1910), reproduced in David Grayson, 'Claude Debussy Addresses the English-speaking World: Two Interviews, an Article, and *The Blessed Damozel*', *Cahiers Debussy* 16 (1992), 27.

86 See Orledge, *Debussy and the Theatre*, 261–2 and 312–13.

87 Ibid., 262.

88 Ibid., 206–16, 251–3, 257–60, 264, 268–72 and 359.

89 Letter of 26 November 1903, in *Debussy Letters*, 142–4.

90 Debussy, 'Berlioz et M. Gunsbourg', *Gil blas*, 8 May 1903; reprinted in *Monsieur Croche et autres écrits*, 168–72; translated in *Debussy on Music*, 192.

91 See Lockspeiser (ed.), *Debussy et Edgar Poe: manuscrits et documents inédits*; Orledge, *Debussy and the Theatre*, 102–27; Juan Allende-Blin, 'Debussy und Poe. Eine Dokumentation', *Musik-Konzepte* 1/2 (1981), 3–9; and Antoine Goléa, 'Des cathédrales englouties', in André Boucourechliev et al., *Debussy* (Paris: Hachette, 1972), 137–53. Trezise, *Debussy: La mer*, 41–4, finds intriguing parallels between *Usher* and *La mer*.

92 The scenario is reproduced in Lockspeiser, *Debussy et Edgar Poe*, 60–3.

93 Debussy, *Correspondance*, 186.

94 *Debussy Letters*, 171.

95 Lockspeiser (ed.), *Debussy et Edgar Poe*, esquisses inédites en fac-similé, Part III; Debussy, *Morceau de concours*, ed. Roy Howat (Paris: Durand, 1980). Additional manuscript materials for *Le diable* (a description of the décor and a chanson for the opening scene, plus a further page of music) were auctioned by Debussy's widow in 1933.

96 Henri Busser, *De Pelléas aux Indes Galantes* (Paris: Librairie Arthème Fayard, 1955), 185.

97 Gino G. Zuccala, 'En parlant avec Debussy', *Musica* (12 February 1910), reprinted in *Monsieur Croche et autres écrits*, 301.

98 Letter of 18 June 1908 to Jacques Durand, in *Debussy Letters*, 192.

99 Ibid., 194. An addendum to the 5 July 1908 contract acknowledging receipt of a 2,000-franc advance is in Debussy, *Correspondance*, 240.

100 Allende-Blin's compilation, transcription and orchestration of the *Usher* materials was published by Jobert (Paris), first performed in concert in 1977 by the orchestra of the Hessischer Rundfunk (cond. Eliahu Inbal) in Frankfurt, first staged at the Berlin Opera (cond. Jésus López-Cobos) in 1979 and recorded by the Orchestre Philharmonique de Monte-Carlo (cond. Georges Prêtre) for Pathé Marconi EMI (1984; the 1993 CD reissue is EMI CDM 764687 2). Uncredited, Debussy's music was also used in 'The Fall of the House of Usher' by Eric Woolfson, Alan Parsons and Andrew Powell, which appeared on The Alan Parsons Project album, *Tales of Mystery and Imagination: Edgar Allan Poe* (Los Angeles: 20th Century Records, 1976).

101 Zuccala, 'En parlant avec Debussy', in *Monsieur Croche et autres écrits*, 300–1.

102 Letter of 18 June 1908 to Jacques Durand, in *Debussy Letters*, 192.

103 Jean Lépine, *La vie de Claude Debussy* (Paris: Albin Michel, 1930), 18.

104 See Orledge, *Debussy and the Theatre*, 296–300, for 'some reasons for Debussy's lack of theatrical "productivity"'.

5 The prosaic Debussy

1 Hugh Macdonald, 'The Prose Libretto', *Cambridge Opera Journal* 1/2 (1989), 156.

2 Ibid., 155; the Preface is published in *Autobiographie de Charles Gounod* (London: 1875), 88–93.

3 André Germain, 'Avant le rideau, Gwendoline', *L'écho de Paris* (27 December 1893); quoted in Roger Delage, *Emmanuel Chabrier* (Paris: Fayard, 1999), 299.

4 The four *Proses lyriques* (1892–3) to his own poems; the three *Chansons de Bilitis* (1897–8), prose 'songs' by Pierre Louÿs; the two *Nuits blanches* (1898) to his own poems.

5 See Denis Herlin, 'Une œuvre inachevée: La saulaie', *Cahiers Debussy* 20 (1996), 3–23.

6 'Sous la musique que faut-il mettre? De beaux vers, de mauvais, des vers libres, de la prose?' in *Monsieur Croche et autres écrits*, 206–7.

7 Peter Ruschenberg, *Stilkritische Untersuchungen zu den Liedern Claude Debussys*, especially chapter 3, 'Die Melodik und Prosodie der Gesangstimme'.

8 See Marie Rolf, 'Semantic and Structural Issues in Debussy's Mallarmé Songs', in Smith, *Debussy Studies*, 179–200.

9 I have adopted James R. Briscoe's emendation of the lower right-hand part in bars 2 and 3: *Songs of Claude Debussy*, vol. II, 9 and 44.

10 See my article 'Debussy's Two Settings of "Clair de lune"'.

11 'Du respect dans l'art', S.I.M. (December 1912) in *Monsieur Croche et autres écrits*, 217–18.

12 Debussy here omitted a fourth line, 'De vent, de froidure et de pluye', following some editions of the poem. See Cobb (ed.), *The Poetic Debussy*, 169.

13 The fourteen are: 'Souhait', 'Fleur des eaux', 'Eglogue', 'Musique', 'Paysage sentimental', 'Voici que le printemps', 'Apparition'; 'Green' from *Ariettes oubliées*; 'Le balcon', 'Harmonie du soir' and 'Recueillement' from *Cinq poèmes de Baudelaire*; 'Les ingénus' from the second set of *Fêtes galantes*; and 'Soupir' and 'Placet futile' from *Trois poèmes de Stéphane Mallarmé*. The four partly alexandrine ones are 'Aimons-nous', 'Beau soir'; 'L'ombre des arbres' from *Ariettes oubliées*; and 'Noël des enfants qui n'ont plus de maisons'.

14 *Richard Strauss et Romain Rolland, Correspondance, fragments de journal*, ed G. Samazeuilh (Paris: Albin Michel, 1951), 41.

15 Ruschenberg, *Stilkritische Untersuchungen zu den Liedern Claude Debussys*, 95.

16 Wenk, *Claude Debussy and the Poets*, 180.

17 Wenk notes the 'spiraling reflexives' here, ibid.

18 'Sous la musique que faut-il mettre? De beaux vers, de mauvais, des vers libres, de la prose?' in *Monsieur Croche et autres écrits*, 206–7.

6 Debussy and expression

1 Debussy, from a letter to Jacques Durand, 3 September 1907, *Debussy Letters*, 184.

2 Ibid., 20–1.

3 Letter to Joachim Gasquet, quoted in P. Smith, *Impressionism: Beneath the Surface* (London: Weidenfeld and Nicolson, 1995), 155.

4 Ibid., 163.

5 J. Laforgue, *Mélanges posthumes* (Paris, 1903), 136–8, quoted in T. J. Clark, *The Painting of Modern Life* (London: Thames and Hudson, 1985), 16.

6 See, for example, the critical reactions to the first Impressionist exhibition of 1874, quoted in B. Denvir, *The Chronicle of Impressionism* (London: Thames and Hudson, 1993), 88–9.

7 Report by the Permanent Secretary of the Académie des Beaux-Arts, 1887, originally printed in *Les arts français* 16 (1918), 92, quoted in *Debussy on Music*, 50.

8 *Debussy Letters*, 21, n. 1.

9 Ibid., 188.

10 Ibid., 313.

11 Ibid., 203.

12 Ibid., 38.

13 Ibid., 42.

14 Ibid., 73.

15 Ibid., 75. There is an interesting echo of this remark in a much later letter (4 February 1916) to Robert Godet about *En blanc et noir*: 'These pieces draw their colour, their emotion, simply from the piano, like the "greys" of Velázquez', *Debussy Letters*, 314.

16 Ibid., 87.

17 Ibid., 93.

18 Ibid., 100.

19 Quoted in Lockspeiser, *Debussy*, 189.

20 *Théâtre des Champs-Elysées, 17 juin 1932 . . . Festival . . . Claude Debussy à l'occasion de l'érection de ses deux monuments à Paris et à Saint-Germain-en-Laye. Programme et livre d'or des souscripteurs* (Paris, 1932).

21 Dietschy, *A Portrait of Claude Debussy*, 104.

22 *Les écrits de Paul Dukas sur la musique* (Paris: Société d'éditions françaises et internationales, 1948), 529–33.

23 *Debussy Letters*, 117.

24 R. Howat, 'En Route for *L'isle joyeuse*: the Restoration of a Triptych', *Cahiers Debussy* 19 (1995), 37–52.

25 *D'un cahier d'esquisses* has particularly striking musical links: '*D'un cahier d'esquisses* is in D♭, the tonic of *La mer*, and makes

extensive use of a rhythmic figure that dominates the cello theme of the second principal section (first movement)'. Trezise, *Debussy: La mer*, 9.

26 Debussy, *Lettres à son éditeur*, 21–2.

27 For example Debussy's reported insistence that his music be played 'Au métronome!' Long, *Au piano avec Claude Debussy*, 42.

28 *Debussy Letters*, 222.

29 Ibid., 305.

30 *Œuvres complètes de Claude Debussy*, vol. V/5: *La mer*, ed. Marie Rolf (Paris: Durand, 1997), xvii.

31 See, for instance, the list of 'water' pieces in Trezise, *Debussy: La mer*, 1.

32 *Debussy Letters*, 141.

33 Ibid., 148.

34 Letter dated 26 July 1905, ibid., 153.

35 Ibid., 164, n. 1.

36 Ibid., 163–4.

37 Laloy, *La musique retrouvée*, 146–7, quoted in Trezise, *Debussy: La mer*, 21.

38 Lockspeiser, *Debussy: His Life and Mind*, vol. II, 29.

39 Guy de Maupassant, 'La vie d'un paysagiste (Etretat, septembre)', *Gil Blas* (28 April 1886), quoted in Daniel Wildenstein, *Monet, or the Triumph of Impressionism* (Cologne: Taschen, 1996), 209. The specific painting to which Maupassant refers at the start of the extract is *Etretat, la pluie* in Wildenstein, *Monet: Catalogue raisonné*, no.1044 (Cologne: Taschen, 1996), now in the National Gallery, Oslo.

40 *Debussy Letters*, 166.

41 Carla Rachman, *Monet* (London: Phaidon, 1997), 268.

42 Sadly this is no longer a realistic aspiration as many paintings from the series are now in private collections. Fourteen of them were exhibited by George Petit in 1898. See Wildenstein, *Monet: Catalogue raisonné*, nos. 1472–89.

43 Quoted in D. Wildenstein, *Monet, or the Triumph of Impressionism*, 321.

44 See N. Savy, 'Charles Baudelaire ou l'espoir d'autre chose', *Regards d'écrivains au Musée d'Orsay* (Paris, 1992), 43–75.

45 See Denvir, *Chronicle of Impressionism*, 221.

46 *Art Monthly Review*, 30 September 1876, quoted in Denvir, *Chronicle of Impressionism*, 99.

47 Jarocinski, *Debussy: Impressionism and Symbolism*.

48 *Debussy on Music*, 295.

49 *Lettres à son éditeur*, 70.

50 *Debussy Letters*, 171.

51 *Lettres à son éditeur*, 45.

52 Ibid., 63.

53 Boulez, *Orientations: Collected Writings*, ed. Jean-Jacques Nattiez, trans. M. Cooper (London: Faber, 1986), 319–20.

54 *Debussy Letters*, 217–18.

55 *Debussy on Music*, 40–1.

56 Ibid., 92–4.

57 Ibid., 244–6.

58 Falla was about to give a performance of a piano version of the *Danses*, *Debussy Letters*, 176.

59 Ibid., 140.

60 Ibid., 249–51.

7 Exploring the erotic in Debussy's music

1 Letter to André Poniatowski, February 1893, in *Debussy Letters*, 40.

2 Robert J. Stoller, *Observing the Erotic Imagination* (New Haven and London: Yale University Press, 1985), 33.

3 John L. Connolly, Jr, 'Ingres and the Erotic Intellect', in Thomas B. Hess and Linda Nochlin (eds.), *Woman as Sex Object: Studies in Erotic Art, 1730–1970* (London: Allen Lane, 1973), 17.

4 Stoller, *Observing the Erotic Imagination*, 44.

5 Marcia Allentuck, 'Henry Fuseli's "Nightmare": Eroticism or Pornography?', in Hess and Nochlin (eds.), *Woman as Sex Object*, 37.

6 Linda Hutcheon and Michael Hutcheon, M.D., 'Syphilis, Sin and the Social Order: Richard Wagner's *Parsifal*', *Cambridge Opera Journal* 7 (1995), 261.

7 Ibid., 268.

8 Ibid., 261.

9 See Joshua H. Cole, ' "There Are Only Good Mothers": The Ideological Work of Women's Fertility in France before World War I', *French Historical Studies* 19 (Spring 1996), 639–72. Cole explains that beginning in the 1860s, population experts began to address the issue of natality, thereby providing an unprecedented amount of data to be utilised.

10 See Karen Offen, 'Depopulation, Nationalism, and Feminism in Fin-de-siècle France', *American Historical Review* 89 (June 1984), 648–76.

11 Antony Copley, *Sexual Moralities in France, 1780–1980: New Ideas on the Family, Divorce and Homosexuality* (London and New York: Routledge, 1992), 124.

12 Ibid., 82. See also Alain Corbin, *Women for Hire: Prostitution and Sexuality in France after 1850* (Cambridge and London: Harvard University Press, 1990).

13 Charles Rearick, *Pleasures of the Belle Epoque: Entertainment and Festivity in Turn-of-the-Century France* (New Haven and London: Yale University Press, 1985), 30.

14 Roger Shattuck, *The Banquet Years: The Arts in France, 1885–1918* (New York: Harcourt, Brace and Company, 1955), 32.

15 Cole, '"There Are Only Good Mothers"', 640.

16 Corbin, *Women for Hire*, 7.

17 Ibid., xv (my italics).

18 Michel Foucault, *The History of Sexuality* (New York: Vintage Books, 1990), vol. I, 66–9.

19 Ibid., 65.

20 Ibid., 58.

21 Ibid., 61.

22 An example of this form of repression and the power of the confessor may be found in William C. Carter's biography of Marcel Proust. Proust 'began what appeared to be a genuine flirtation with Mlle Germaine Giraudeau ... Marcel had obtained Germaine's photograph and described it in such heated terms in her autograph book that the girl's confessor ordered her to tear out the page and destroy the passage, thereby denying herself – and anyone else – the opportunity to read it again.' *Marcel Proust: A Life* (New Haven and London: Yale University Press, 2000), 150.

23 Foucault, *The History of Sexuality*, vol. I, 62.

24 Rosario refers to the nineteenth-century medical literature on sexual perversions as 'Latinised pornography'. Vernon A. Rosario, *The Erotic Imagination: French Histories of Perversity* (New York and Oxford: Oxford University Press, 1997), 96.

25 Ibid., 130.

26 Ibid., 4–5.

27 Linda Nochlin, 'Eroticism and Female Imagery in Nineteenth-Century Art', in Hess and Nochlin (eds.), *Woman as Sex Object*, 9–16.

28 *Debussy Remembered*, 95.

29 Mary Garden and Louis Biancolli, *Mary Garden's Story* (London, 1952), in ibid., 68.

30 Dietschy, *A Portrait of Claude Debussy*, 129.

31 Letter to Emma Debussy, 8 December 1913, in *Debussy Letters*, 282.

32 Roland Barthes, *Image – Music – Text* (New York: Hill and Wang, 1977), 149.

33 Ibid., 150.

34 Ibid., 188.

35 George Copeland, 'Debussy, the Man I Knew', *The Atlantic Monthly* (January 1955), in Nichols, *Debussy Remembered*, 167.

36 Claude Debussy, 'The Orientation of Music', *Musica* (October 1902), in *Debussy on Music*, 85.

37 Raymond Bonheur and Gabriel Pierné quoted in Cecilia Dunoyer, 'Debussy and Early Debussystes at the Piano' in Briscoe (ed.), *Debussy in Performance*, 93.

38 Karl Lahm, 'Erinnerungen an Claude Debussy', *Melos* 21 (November 1954), in Nichols, *Debussy Remembered*, 123.

39 Auguste Martin, *Claude Debussy* (Paris, 1942), in Nichols, *Debussy Remembered*, 49–50.

40 Dunoyer, 'Debussy and Early Debussystes at the Piano', in Briscoe (ed.), *Debussy in Performance*, 94.

41 Barthes, *Image – Music – Text*, 189.

42 Kristeva's *pheno-song* refers to everything related to 'communication, representation, expression, everything which it is customary to talk about, which forms the tissue of cultural values (the matter of acknowledged tastes, of fashions, of critical commentaries)', ibid., 182.

43 Ibid., 152.

44 H. Kohut, 'Observations on the Psychological Function of Music', *JAPA* 5 (1957), quoted in Stoller, *Observing the Erotic Imagination*, 67.

45 Susan McClary, *Feminine Endings* (Minneapolis and Oxford: University of Minnesota Press, 1991), 12.

46 Ibid., 25.

47 Letter to Jacques Durand, 28 August 1915, in *Debussy Letters*, 300.

48 Letter to Pierre Louÿs, 9 March 1897, ibid., 92.

49 Lockspeiser, *Debussy: His Life and Mind*, vol. I, 206–7.

50 Debussy, 'For the People', *Gil blas* (2 March 1903), in *Debussy on Music*, 132.

51 Charles Minahen, 'Eroticism and the Poetics of Sublime Evasion in a Prose Poem and Poem of Mallarmé', *L'Esprit Créateur* 39 (Spring 1999), 51. He is referring to Verlaine's *Hombres*.

52 Claude Abravanel, 'Symbolism and Performance', in Briscoe (ed.), *Debussy in Performance*, 33.

53 Holloway, *Debussy and Wagner*, 125.

54 Ibid., 223.

55 This anecdote is relayed in Roger Shattuck, *Candor and Perversion* (New York and London: W. W. Norton, 1999), 189.

56 Abravanel, 'Symbolism and Performance', 40. Abravanel's article is concerned with the erotic aspects of Debussy's music, though he never mentions the word. He writes of cultivating a more intimate relationship with this music through an understanding of the Symbolist aesthetic. This very concept is an erotic one.

57 Hepokoski, 'Formulaic Openings in Debussy', 53.

58 Lockspeiser, *Debussy: His Life and Mind*, vol. I, 120.

59 H. P. Clive, *Pierre Louÿs (1870–1925): A Biography* (Oxford: Clarendon Press, 1978), 9–10.
60 Richard Jenkins, *Dignity and Decadence: Victorian Art and the Classical Inheritance* (Cambridge, Mass.: Harvard University Press, 1992), 262–3.
61 John Dixon Hunt, *The Pre-Raphaelite Imagination 1848–1900* (London: Routledge and Kegan Paul, 1968), 79.
62 Griselda Pollock, *Vision and Difference: Feminity, Feminism and the Histories of Art* (London and New York: Routledge, 1988), 137.
63 David G. Riede, *Dante Gabriel Rossetti Revisited* (New York: Twayne Publishers, 1992), 84.
64 Ibid., 55.
65 Ibid., 78.
66 Joan Rees, *The Poetry of Dante Gabriel Rossetti: Modes of Self-Expression* (Cambridge: Cambridge University Press, 1981), 113.
67 Letter to Poniatowski, 8–9 September 1892, in *Debussy Letters*, 38.
68 Smith, 'Debussy and the Pre-Raphaelites', 102.
69 Hepokoski, 'Formulaic Openings', 48.
70 Ibid.
71 The French translation of Rossetti's poem by Sarrazin did not include those stanzas of Rossetti in which the lover on earth had a voice.
72 Minahen, 'Eroticism and the Poetics of Sublime Evasion', 50.
73 Debussy praised Blanche Marot for her performance of this piece, which he called 'other-worldly', and he wrote that her delivery of these words was 'one of the most profound musical experiences' of his life. Letter to Blanche Marot, 24 August 1900, in *Debussy Letters*, 114.
74 It was given the title *Syrinx* by the publisher Jobert.
75 Gabriel Mourey, *Psyché* (Paris: Mercure de France, 1913), 79.
76 Debussy, 'Conversation with Mr Croche', *La revue blanche* (1 July 1901), in *Debussy on Music*, 48.
77 Letter to Louÿs, 16 October 1898, in *Debussy Letters*, 101.
78 Clive, *Pierre Louÿs*, 95. According to Jean-Paul Goujon, Debussy was also known to partake in these 'jokes'. He writes, 'But who would be able to believe that the very serious Debussy also enjoyed such jokes at the expense of Gide?' *Pierre Louÿs: un vie secrète (1870–1925)* (Paris: Seghers, 1988), 66.

79 Unpublished letter, 31 July 1894, quoted in Goujon, *Pierre Louÿs*, 131.
80 Fathi Ghlamallah, *Pierre Louÿs: 'Arabe' et amoureux* (Paris: Librairie A.-G. Nizet, 1992), 30.
81 Unpublished letter, 15 April 1897, quoted in Goujon, *Pierre Louÿs*, 191.
82 Ibid., 193. Louÿs collected photographs of women, mostly nudes, and approximately seven hundred were taken by Louÿs himself. His models were mostly adolescents and working-class women. Paul-Ursin Dumont, *Pierre Louÿs: L'Ermite du Hameau* (Vendôme: Libraidisque, 1985), 130. During this four-month stay in Algeria he kept a meticulous index of the prostitutes he slept with during his frequent visits to the brothels, complete with photographs. There is an album devoted solely to Zohra, with eighty photos. Ghlamallah, '*Arabe*' et amoureux, 41.
83 Letter to Debussy, 30 May 1897, in Debussy and Louÿs, *Correspondance*, 95. Louÿs sent this poem to Debussy for inspiration in response to Debussy's letter in which he lamented that he couldn't compose. In a letter to his brother (22 April 1897) he writes that Zohra is sleeping and that he has just written two Bilitis songs, so moved is he by the evening. Ghlamallah, '*Arabe*' et amoureux, 47.
84 Jean-Paul Goujon (ed.), *Journal de Meryem; Lettres inédites à Zohra bent Brahim* (Paris: Librairie A.-G. Nizet, 1992), 69.
85 Clive, *Pierre Louÿs*, 142.
86 Louÿs, *Two Erotic Tales*, translated by Mary Hanson Harrison (Evanston, Ill.: Evanston Publishing, 1995), 27.
87 He wrote on 4 July 1897 (regarding a lunch invitation): 'If you were nice, you would bring your Kodak. Bilitis and I are at your feet.' Debussy and Louÿs, *Correspondance*, 97.
88 Photos of Gaby may be found in *Claude Debussy: Lettres 1884–1918* (Paris: Hermann, 1980); photos of Jane Morris in Andrea Rose, *The Pre-Raphaelites* (Oxford: Phaidon, 1981); and Mucha's models in Jürgen Döring and Susanne Kähler, *Alfons Mucha: Triumph des Jugendstils* (Heidelberg: Edition Braus, 1997).
89 Letter to Louÿs, 15 January 1901, in Debussy and Louÿs, *Correspondance*, 156.
90 Clive, *Pierre Louÿs*, 170.
91 Letter to Georges Louis, 23 January 1901, ibid.
92 *Le journal* (8 February 1901), ibid., 171.
93 Louÿs, *Two Erotic Tales*, 258. Here she is speaking to Lykas.
94 Jenkins, *Dignity and Decadence*, 241 and 256.
95 For the details behind the hoax – Louÿs first published the poems as actual

translations of poems found on Bilitis's tomb – see Clive, *Pierre Louÿs*, 110–12.

96 Louÿs, *L'œuvre érotique*, ed. and introduced by Jean-Paul Goujon (Paris: Sortilèges, 1994), xi.

97 Ibid., xxx.

98 Ibid., xxix.

99 Ibid., xxx.

100 Ibid., xxxi.

101 22 January 1895, in *Debussy Letters*, 76.

102 Louÿs, *Two Erotic Tales*, 252.

103 Ibid., 257.

104 Ibid., 236.

105 27 March 1998, in *Debussy Letters*, 94.

106 Susan Youens, 'Music, Verse, and "Prose Poetry": Debussy's *Trois Chansons de Bilitis*', *Journal of Musicological Research* 7 (1986), 86.

107 Nicholas Routley, '*Des pas sur la neige*: Debussy in Bilitis's Footsteps', *Musicology Australia* 16 (1993), 23.

108 Stephen Rumph, 'Debussy's *Trois Chansons de Bilitis*: Song, Opera, and the Death of the Subject', *Journal of Musicology* 12 (Fall 1994), 478.

109 Debussy and Louÿs, *Correspondance*, 63.

110 Minahen, 'Eroticism and the Poetics of Sublime Evasion', 58.

111 Lockspeiser, *Debussy: His Life and Mind*, vol. I, 158.

112 Minahen, 'Eroticism and the Poetics of Sublime Evasion', 49.

113 Tamar Garb, 'Gender and Representation', in Francis Frascina et al. (eds.), *Modernity and Modernism: French Painting in the Nineteenth Century* (New Haven: Yale University Press, 1993), 222.

114 This song was commissioned by the poet Paul Gravollet.

115 Minahen, 'Eroticism and the Poetics of Sublime Evasion', 50. Minahen claims that this tendency to objectify is typical of the male erotic imagination.

116 Connolly, 'Ingres and the Erotic Intellect', 19.

117 Debussy quoted in Dietschy, *A Portrait of Claude Debussy*, 116.

118 This broad definition 'captured everyone who experienced an erotic sensation or fantasy into the diagnostic dragnet of sexual perversity'. Rosario, *The Erotic Imagination*, 114–15.

119 Ibid., 129.

120 Catherine Clément, *Opera, or the Undoing of Women*, trans. Betsy Wing (Minneapolis: University of Minnesota Press, 1988), 112.

121 Jankélévitch, *Debussy et le mystère*, 18.

122 Pollock, *Vision and Difference*, 133.

123 Katherine Bergeron, 'Mélisande's Hair, or the Trouble in Allemonde – a Postmodern

Allegory at the Opéra-Comique', in Mary Ann Smart (ed.), *Siren Songs* (Princeton: Princeton University Press, 2000), 176.

124 Ibid., 174.

125 Letter to Henri Lerolle (regarding act II, scene 3), 17 August 1895, in *Debussy Letters*, 80.

126 T. S. Eliot, 'From Poe to Valéry', in Morton Darwen Zabel (ed.), *Literary Opinion in America* (New York and Evanston: Harper and Row, 1962), vol. II, 632.

127 Poe, *Seven Tales*, ed. W. T. Bandy (New York: Schocken Books, 1971), 107. This edition includes Baudelaire's French translation side by side with the English.

128 Emily Apter, *Feminising the Fetish: Psychoanalysis and Narrative Obsession in Turn-of-the-Century France* (Ithaca and London: Cornell University Press, 1991), 89.

129 Letter to Ernest Chausson, 2 October 1893, in *Debussy Letters*, 56.

130 Letter to Edwin Evans, 18 April 1909, in Nichols and Smith, *Claude Debussy: Pelléas et Mélisande* (Cambridge: Cambridge University Press, 1989), 186.

131 Letter to Igor Stravinsky (in reference to *Le sacre du printemps*), 5 November 1912, in *Debussy Letters*, 265.

132 Georges Bataille, *Death and Sensuality: A Study of Eroticism and the Taboo* (New York: Walker and Co., 1962). Bataille's ideas are concisely summarised in Charles D. Minahen, 'Homosexual Erotic Scripting in Verlaine's *Hombres*', in Dominique D. Fisher and Lawrence R. Schehr (eds.), *Articulations of Difference: Gender Studies and Writing in French* (Stanford: Stanford University Press, 1997), 119–35.

133 D. H. Lawrence, *Studies in Classic American Literature* (Garden City, NY: Doubleday, 1923), 74.

134 Ibid., 76.

135 Ibid., 79.

136 Poe, *Seven Tales*, 173.

137 Darrel Abel, 'A Key to the House of Usher', in Charles Feiderlson, Jr and Paul Brodthorb, Jr (eds.), *Interpretations of American Literature* (New York: Oxford University Press, 1959), 60.

138 André Schaeffner, *Debussy et Edgar Poe* (Monaco: Rocher, 1961), 11.

139 Poe, *Seven Tales*, 179.

140 Letter to Lerolle, 28 August 1894, in *Debussy Letters*, 73.

141 Interview with Debussy, *Azest* (Budapest), 6 December 1910, in *Debussy on Music*, 242.

142 Letter to Durand, 26 June 1909, quoted in Lockspeiser, *Debussy: His Life and Mind*, vol. II, 143.

143 Letter to Durand, 8 July 1910, in *Debussy Letters*, 220–1.

144 Letter to André Caplet, 22 December 1911, ibid., 252.
145 Letter to Durand, 18 June 1908, quoted in Lockspeiser, *Debussy: His Life and Mind*, vol. II, 142.
146 Letter to Caplet, 25 August 1909, in *Debussy Letters*, 212.
147 The decadence of des Esseintes in Huysmans's *A Rebours* is strikingly similar to that of Roderick Usher. Both are recluses, the degenerate offspring of intermarrying families, whose artistic and sensual endeavours become signs of decay and derangement, and both are strongly and irreversibly corrupted by their surroundings.
148 Letter to Robert Godet, 4 September 1916, in *Debussy Letters*, 317. George Copeland wrote, 'Musically, Debussy felt himself to be a kind of auditory "sensitive".' 'Debussy, the Man I Knew', *The Atlantic Monthly* (January 1955), in Nichols, *Debussy Remembered*, 167.

8 Debussy and nature
1 Article 'De quelques superstitions et d'un opéra' (15 January 1901) reprinted in *Monsieur Croche et autres écrits*, 54; 'ibid.' is used *passim* in nn. 2–21 below to refer to that volume.
2 Interview with *Comoedia*, 'La musique d'aujourd'hui et celle de demain' (4 November 1909), ibid., 296.
3 December 1910, ibid., 308.
4 Interview with *La revue bleue* (2 April 1904), ibid., 279.
5 Review for the S.I.M. (1 November 1913), ibid., 246.
6 'Pourquoi j'ai écrit *Pelléas*' (April 1902), ibid., 62.
7 Review 'Monsieur F. Weingartner', *Gil blas* (16 February 1903), ibid., 95–6.
8 Ibid., 96.
9 In an interview with *Excelsior* (11 February 1911), ibid., 325.
10 Cited in José A. Argüelles, *Charles Henry and the Formation of a Psychophysical Aesthetic* (Chicago: University of Chicago Press, 1972), 100.
11 Howat, *Debussy in Proportion*, 165.
12 *Monsieur Croche et autres écrits*, 101.
13 Cited in Lockspeiser, *Debussy: His Life and Mind*, vol. I, 119.
14 Ibid., 118.
15 Article 'L'orientation musicale', written for *Musica* (October 1902), *Monsieur Croche et autres écrits*, 65–6.
16 Cited in Nichols, *The Life of Debussy*, 101.
17 Maurice J. E. Brown, 'Arabesque', in *The New Grove Dictionary of Music and Musicians*, ed. Stanley Sadie (London: Macmillan, 1980), vol. I, 512–13.

18 Jann Pasler, 'Timbre, Voice-leading, Musical Arabesque', in Briscoe (ed.), *Debussy in Performance*, 226.
19 Cited in Argüelles, *Charles Henry and the Formation of a Psychophysical Aesthetic*, 131.
20 'L'entretien avec Monsieur Croche', published in *La revue blanche* (1 July 1901); reprinted in *Monsieur Croche et autres écrits*, 52.
21 Interview with *Excelsior* (18 January 1911), ibid., 318.

9 Debussy's tonality: a formal perspective
1 This is not a recent phenomenon; it dates back to Debussy's lifetime, notably in René Lenormand's *Etude sur l'harmonie moderne* (Paris: Monde musical, 1913). Debussy was not impressed, expressing concern to the author over 'the untrained hands that are going to fumble their way carelessly through your book, using it only to finish off all those beautiful butterflies that are already a little bruised by analysis.' See *Debussy Letters*, 260.
2 That is, the tonal-structural unity of individual pieces through the presence of a single controlling tonic. The alternative is 'directional' (or 'progressive') tonality, whereby a piece begins in one key and ends in another. Debussy used this device occasionally, notably in the orchestral pieces 'Gigues', 'Le matin d'un jour de fête', and the second movement of *Printemps*; the Prélude 'Canope' and the song 'De rêve . . .' (*Proses lyriques*).
3 From a theoretical standpoint the most significant property of both scales is their propensity for equal, hence symmetrical, octave-division, the antithesis of the diatonic scale's unequal division into perfect fifth and fourth. This symmetry of internal makeup results in a high degree of transpositional redundancy, yielding respectively three (octatonic) and two (whole-tone) chromatic transpositions (compared to the diatonic scale's twelve) before duplicating their original pitch content. The octatonic scale (or collection)'s arrangement as a continuous alternation of tones and semitones also generates distinctive chromatic chord progressions, most characteristically through a complete minor-thirds cycle. While the importance of the whole-tone scale to Debussy's music (along with the associated factor of Russian influence) has long been acknowledged, the equally central role of octatonicism has been recognised only comparatively recently: see Allen Forte, 'Debussy and the Octatonic', *Music Analysis* 10

(1991), 125–69, and Parks, *The Music of Claude Debussy*.

4 See Parks, *The Music of Claude Debussy*, chapter 1.

5 Here and elsewhere the discussion assumes the reader's access to scores of the major piano and orchestral works.

6 Cited in Josiah Fisk (ed.), *Composers on Music: Eight Centuries of Writing* (Boston: Northeastern University Press, 1997), 200.

7 Françoise Gervais compares Debussy's decorative aesthetic to that of Islamic art in 'La notion d'arabesque chez Debussy', *Revue musicale* 241 (1958), 17–20. For a good recent study of Debussy's aesthetic in a wide-ranging artistic context see Roberts, *Images: The Piano Music of Claude Debussy*, especially chapters 1–6.

8 Roberts compares the 'wealth of free fantasy' that Debussy found in Bach's melodic lines to a similar spirit of fantasy in art nouveau, whose 'florid lines, based on curving vines and reed stems, or snaking tresses of hair, take on a life of their own'. Roberts, *Images*, 67.

9 It is in precisely this restrained economy of line that Debussy's self-invoked, and at first sight seemingly far-fetched, comparison with Palestrina becomes meaningful. In this respect one might observe in Debussy's (instrumental) writing a 'vocal' quality rare in twentieth-century music. See also Gervais, 'La notion d'arabesque', 11–13.

10 On the subject of pentatonic typologies in Debussy's music, see Constantin Brailoiu, 'Pentatonisme chez Debussy', in Benjamin Rajeczky (ed.), *Studia Belae Bartok Memoriae Sacra* (London: Boosey and Hawkes, 1958), 351–98; and David Kopp, 'Pentatonic Organization in Two Piano Pieces of Debussy', *Journal of Music Theory* 41 (1997), 261–87.

11 See Nicholas Ruwet, 'Notes sur les duplications dans l'œuvre de Claude Debussy', *Revue belge de musicologie* 16 (1962), 57–70. Debussy's penchant for additive *duplication* (Ruwet's term) of cell-like units was of course highly conducive to the 'distributional' or 'paradigmatic' analytical method, as practised by several French and Canadian analysts over the following two decades. For an interesting gloss on this tradition of Debussy analysis, characterised as it was by a curious obsession with the prelude to *Pelléas*, see Ayrey, 'Debussy's Significant Connections: Metaphor and Metonymy in Analytical Method', in *Theory, Analysis and Meaning in Music*.

12 Given his notoriously low opinion of twentieth-century music in general (and certainly not excepting Debussy's), Schenker himself would hardly have countenanced any extension of his theory in this direction. On the general issues raised by such an adaptation see James Baker, 'Schenkerian Analysis and Post-tonal Music', in David Beach (ed.), *Aspects of Schenkerian Theory* (New Haven: Yale University Press, 1983), 153–86. In the specific case of Debussy, some analysts would hold that the Schenkerian approach is, at best, valid only for the early (c. pre-1890) works; see, for example, Parks, *The Music of Claude Debussy*, 4–21.

To a limited extent the analyses below will draw on the Schenkerian concepts of *chord prolongation* (by which a formal section is conceived as unified by, and ultimately representing, a tonally stable consonant triad, 'composed out' through certain contrapuntal techniques) and *structural levels* from background (the harmonic-contrapuntal 'skeleton' representing the whole piece or substantial sub-section thereof) to foreground (the actual notes in the score). Two useful introductions to the broad subject of Schenkerian analysis can be found in Nicholas Cook, *A Guide to Musical Analysis* (London: Dent, 1987), 27–66, and Jonathan Dunsby and Arnold Whittall, *Music Analysis in Theory and Practice* (London: Faber & Faber, 1988), 23–61.

13 Felix Salzer, *Structural Hearing: Tonal Coherence in Music* (New York: Boni, 1952; reprint New York: Dover, 1962).

14 Adele Katz, *Challenge to Musical Tradition* (New York: Knopf, 1945; reprint New York: Da Capo, 1972), chapter 7.

15 Salzer, *Structural Hearing*, Examples 455 (*Prélude à l'après-midi d'un faune*) and 478 ('Bruyères').

16 This view of Debussy's historical significance was shared by Schenker's contemporary Ernst Kurth; see his *Romantische Harmonik und ihre Krise in Wagners 'Tristan'* (Bern: Haupt, 1920), chapter 6.

Space precludes discussion of more recent Schenkerian studies of Debussy's music, which include James Baker, 'Post-Tonal Voice Leading', in Jonathan Dunsby (ed.), *Models of Music Analysis: Early Twentieth-Century Music* (Oxford: Blackwell, 1993), 20–41 (on bitonality in 'Canope'); Matthew Brown, 'Tonality and Form in Debussy's *Prélude à l'après-midi d'un faune*', *Music Theory Spectrum* 15 (1993), 127–43; and Pomeroy, 'Toward a New Tonal Practice: Chromaticism and Form in Debussy's Orchestral Music' (on large-scale tonal forms in the orchestral triptychs).

17 Werner Danckert, *Claude Debussy* (Berlin: de Gruyter, 1950).

18 Rudolph Réti, *The Thematic Process in Music* (London: Faber & Faber, 1961), 194–206.

19 Arnold Whittall, 'Tonality and the Whole-tone Scale in the Music of Debussy', *Music Review* 36 (1975), 261–71.

20 Katz, *Challenge to Musical Tradition*, 279–93.

21 Ibid., 293.

22 See Allen Forte, *The Stucture of Atonal Music* (New Haven: Yale University Press, 1973).

23 Parks, *The Music of Claude Debussy*.

24 Karlheinz Stockhausen, 'Von Webern zu Debussy: Bemerkungen zur statistischen Form', in *Texte zur Musik*, 4 vols. (Cologne: Du Mont Schauberg, 1963–78), vol. I, *Zur elektronischen und instrumentalen Musik*, ed. Dieter Schnebel, 75–85; Eimert, 'Debussy's *Jeux*'; see also Dieter Schnebel, '"Brouillards": Tendencies in Debussy', trans. Margaret Schenfield, in *Die Reihe* 6 (Bryn Mawr: Presser, 1964), 33–9. In this connection it is notable that the Darmstadt composers' iconic Debussy piece was *Jeux*, a stage work whose highly original freely evolving form arose at least partly in response to the demands of a dramatic scenario.

25 Lockspeiser, *Debussy: His Life and Mind*, vol. II, 231.

26 Pierre Boulez, *Notes of an Apprenticeship*, trans. Herbert Weinstock (New York: Knopf, 1968), 344–5. For a useful overview of the tradition of critical reception of Debussy as a formal radical, see Trezise, *Debussy: La mer*, 51–3.

27 The concept of formal function in this sense comes from the (tonal-) formal theories of Schoenberg and his (theoretical, not compositional) followers, especially Erwin Ratz. Schoenberg's ideas on this subject are most fully elaborated in his *Fundamentals of Musical Composition*, ed. Gerald Strang and Leonard Stein (London: Faber & Faber, 1967).

28 Clearly the definitions are somewhat informal, with a fair amount of overlap between the 'middle' and 'right' groups. This admittedly greatly simplified schema will nevertheless serve to clarify some important technical distinctions.

29 And thus selectively conforming to Richard Parks's above-mentioned generalisation as to the lack of this feature in Debussy's mature music: Parks, *The Music of Claude Debussy*, 4.

30 It might be noted that even here some commentators hear a dominant-like quality in the B♭ pedal of the outer sections, which then finds resolution in the pentatonic E♭ minor of the middle section; see, for example, Jim Samson, *Music in Transition: A Study of*

Tonal Expansion and Atonality, 1900–1920 (London: Dent, 1977), 40.

31 For another good example of such 'disembodied' tonal effects, see 'Feuilles mortes', where slow-moving bass pedals on scale degrees $\hat{1}, \hat{4}$ and $\hat{5}$ produce the effect of a distant tonal undercurrent to the music's surface of kaleidoscopic (largely octatonic) chromaticism.

32 On its first appearance (not shown), a second statement of the motive (bars 22–4) continues the chromatic expansion to a C♯ augmented triad. When the motive returns (bars 38ff.), both statements (the second now rhythmically speeded up) conform to the C♯ minor model.

33 Two well-known Classical precedents for this chromatic triad-transformation are Beethoven, Symphony No. 8, fourth movement (F♯ minor, bars 386ff. – F major, bars 393ff.), and Schubert, Sonata in B♭, D. 960, second movement (C♯ minor, bars 90ff. – C major, bars 103ff.).

34 For other analyses of this *Prélude*, see Roland Nadeau, '"Brouillards": A Tonal Music', *Cahiers Debussy*, new series 4–5 (1980–1), 38–50; Richard Parks, 'Pitch Organization in Debussy: Unordered Sets in "Brouillards"', *Music Theory Spectrum* 2 (1980), 119–34; Schnebel, 'Brouillards'. Both Schnebel and Parks view the piece as atonal: Schnebel derives Debussy's 'chromatic mists' from the harmonic series via compression of fundamental, lower and upper partials into the same register; Parks finds unity in unordered set-content. Nadeau attempts, not altogether successfully, to explain the chromatic juxtapositions in tonal-functional terms.

35 For present purposes the three octatonic-scale transpositions are identified as collections 1 (C♯, D, E, F . . .), 2 (D, E♭, F, G♭ . . .), and 3 (D♯, E, F♯, G . . .), following Pieter van den Toorn's influential study of octatonicism in Stravinsky, *The Music of Igor Stravinsky* (New Haven: Yale University Press, 1983). Likewise, the two whole-tone transpositions will be labelled collections A (whole-tone scale on C) and B (on C♯). In Example 9.3 and elsewhere, the descriptive apparatus is abbreviated thus: 'oct. 1' (octatonic collection 1), 'w-t A' (whole-tone collection A), etc.

36 See also Katz's analysis of this passage (*Challenge to Musical Tradition*, 265–6, Example 85).

37 Since the effect of the rhythmic adjustment is a (retrospectively understood) relocation of the downbeat to the second crotchet, one wonders why Debussy did not

notate the 4/4 bar (see Example 9.6) in bar 3 rather than bar 4.

38 See note 35 above.

39 Such slight modification of an otherwise 'pure' octatonic context is highly characteristic of Debussy. For more on octatonic emphasis generally in this *Prélude*, see Forte, 'Debussy and the Octatonic', 147–8.

40 As noted by Paul Roberts (*Images*, 323), the transformation is symptomatic of a 'general downward tendency' permeating the *Prélude* as a whole.

41 Notice how artfully Debussy varies this stock cadential progression. Most unusually, the entire thing is actually enclosed in a larger, unharmonised V–I bass motion in the piano's lowest depths (bars 31–2). In the progression itself (starting in bar 31, second crotchet) Debussy then avoids the obvious root-position dominant by having the bass chromatically climb to the chordal third of a dominant 6/5 (bar 31, fifth crotchet; compare Example 9.11 with Example 9.13 below, which 'normalises' the chord to a root-position V in the interests of clarifying the larger harmonic picture). Melodically, too, Debussy sidesteps the obvious in his treatment of the upper-voice suspended C (bar 31, second–fourth crotchets) which, rather than resolve conventionally by step (C–B♭), now swoops down to E♭ in an expansion to a sixth of the omnipresent descending-fourth motive.

42 Debussy evidently enjoyed the effect of such (thematically or motivically dramatised) 'chromatic corrections', which feature conspicuously in several other pieces; see, for example, 'Minstrels', bars 45–57 (F♯–G/A♭–A) and 'Le matin d'un jour de fête', bars 100–6 (G♭–G).

10 The Debussy sound: colour, texture, sonority, gesture

1 Jean Barraqué, '*La Mer* de Debussy, ou la naissance des formes ouvertes: essai de méthodologie comparative: la forme musicale considérée non plus comme un archétype mains comme un devenir', *Analyse musicale* 12/3 (June 1988), 28.

2 (A reconstruction of the original score by Christopher Palmer based on the extant arrangement for piano duet and chorus was given its premiere at a BBC Prom concert in London on 29 July 2001. Ed.)

3 On 27 August 1900 Debussy recalled his early enthusiasm for *Namouna* in a letter to the composer's son Pierre Lalo: 'Many years ago now I was forcibly removed from the Opéra for being too energetic in demonstrating my admiration for that charming masterpiece *Namouna*.' *Debussy Letters*, 116.

4 'Impressionism' is a term I use loosely in reference to music, but in applying it to Debussy's art I think especially of his heterophonic orchestra of multiple short melodic details, rhythmically varied but with more harmonic than contrapuntal value, and preference for soft textures with blended instruments in the background. In the piano music the operative characteristics are rapid arpeggios, extremes of register, pedal effects and strategic rather than formal use of themes and motives. Added to these are a lack of thematic assertiveness and the psycho-literary impact of provocative but often non-specific or even obscure titles that go far beyond the familiar outlines of the Schumannesque character pieces. All of these traits are anti-classical and 'Romantic' only insofar as they appeal to the visual and auditory senses rather than to concrete structures of logical design.

5 Quoted in Lockspeiser, *Debussy: His Life and Mind*, vol. I, 128.

6 As recorded by Maurice Emmanuel; see ibid., appendix B, 205.

7 In the same letter to Ysaÿe Debussy states that the first movement is to be given to strings, the second to flutes, four horns, three trumpets and two harps and in the third one both groups came together. *Debussy Letters*, 75.

8 Debussy acknowledged this apparent uncertainty when, not long before his death, he showed Ansermet a printed score of *Nocturnes*, marked up in several different colours of pencil and ink, and invited him to choose the revisions that he thought best! See Denis Herlin, 'Sirens in the Labyrinth: Amendments in Debussy's *Nocturnes*', in Smith, *Debussy Studies*, 51–77.

9 They were finally published in 1977 under the title of *Images oubliées* (Philadelphia: Elkan-Vogel).

10 '"La cathédrale engloutie" was inspired by an old Breton myth according to which the sunken cathedral of Ys rises to view on certain clear mornings from a translucent sea; bells chime, priests chant, until the mirage disappears again below the waters.' See Ernest Hutcheson, *The Literature of the Piano*, revised Rudolph Ganz (New York: Knopf, 1964), 314.

11 Quoted by Arbie Orenstein, *Ravel: Man and Musician* (New York: Columbia University Press, 1975), 127.

12 Igor Stravinsky and Robert Craft, *Conversations with Igor Stravinsky* (Garden City: Doubleday & Company, 1959), 52.

13 Ibid., 53.

14 For some reason, the text of Nijinsky's scenario is omitted from the orchestral score, while in the piano score all such details are included at the appropriate places; unlike the orchestral score, the piano score also includes a page listing the normal information about the premiere of the ballet, but omits rehearsal numbers.

15 Jean Barraqué, 'La Mer de Debussy', 28.

16 Herbert Eimert, 'Debussy's "Jeux", 3–20.

17 Stravinsky and Craft, Conversations With Igor Stravinsky, 53. The reference is to the Art Nouveau jeweller René Lalique (1860–1945), whose fantastically curved insectiform brooches and necklaces were very popular in the first decade of the twentieth century.

18 Igor Stravinsky and Robert Craft, Memories and Commentaries (Garden City: Doubleday, 1960), 117.

11 Music's inner dance: form, pacing and complexity in Debussy's music

1 By 'morphological forms' I mean those based on the disposition of musical materials into patterns that we may liken to static, spatial arrangements, such as we associate with traditional tonal period forms, part forms and large homophonic forms. For a detailed discussion of such forms in Debussy's music see Parks, The Music of Claude Debussy, especially chapter 10, 'Morphological Forms and Proportion', 211–32.

2 The concept of musical form as dynamic rather than static infused much of the work of Wallace Berry. In particular see his Structural Functions in Music (Englewood Cliffs, NJ: Prentice-Hall, Inc., 1976); 'Rhythmic Accelerations in Beethoven', Journal of Music Theory 22/2 (Fall 1978), 177–240; 'Formal Process and Performance in the Eroica Introductions', Music Theory Spectrum 10 (1988), 3–18; and Musical Structure and Performance (New Haven: Yale University Press, 1989). See also Parks, The Music of Claude Debussy, chapter 11, 'Kinetic Forms', 233–55. In addition, the conception permeated the work of the nineteenth-century theorist Ernst Kurth. For an introduction to his ideas see Jan L. Tripe, 'Ernst Kurth's Dynamic Formal Process and Sonata Design in Bruckner's Sixth Symphony' (London, Ontario: master's thesis, The University of Western Ontario, 1997), 10–47.

3 For examples see: Lewis Rowell, Thinking about Music (Amherst, Mass.: The University of Massachusetts Press, 1983), chapter 8, 'Values', 150–89; also Hugo Leichtentritt, Musical Form (Cambridge, Mass.: Harvard University Press, 1967), 222.

4 I use the terms 'acceleration' and 'deceleration' in the same sense as Berry, who coined the term and explicated the concept in his article 'Rhythmic Accelerations in Beethoven'.

5 Richard S. Parks, 'A Viennese Arrangement of Debussy's Prélude à l'après midi d'un faune: Orchestration and Musical Structure', Music and Letters 80/1 (February 1999), 50–73.

6 Of course, tempo changes and rubato vary significantly from one performance to the next, and equivalences that would exactly match slower passages to faster ones are often unattainable; hence, the 'constant unit' is always an approximation. Nonetheless, an 'approximately constant' CDU provides a useful approximation of the effect of varying durations across passages set in different tempos or metres.

7 Hairpin brackets ('<>') always indicate an ordered series. Here I must insert a nota bene lest the quantitative appearance of the data presented mislead: values represented by integers in the data presented throughout this study are seldom if ever quantitative, although they are always represented quantitatively. In fact most data are qualitative, and any interpretation of them is always qualitative. Thus the values just given for the first two main formal sections of Syrinx, <6–24>, indicate a deceleration because the second is longer than the first; however, simply because the second value is four times greater than the first we cannot say the deceleration is therefore four-fold: we can only say there is deceleration – dramatic for me perhaps, possibly for you as well, then again maybe not. In other words, higher values should be understood as meaning 'more than' lower values, with intermediate values falling between, but values must not be construed as meaning 'twice as much as' or 'one-third as much as'.

8 Readers interested in exploring Debussy's generic pitch resources further should see Parks, The Music of Claude Debussy, 47–160; also Parks, 'Pitch-class Set Genera: My Theory, Allen Forte's Theory', Music Analysis 17/2 (July 1998), 206–26.

9 Notes articulated simultaneously share the same attack point and are not considered here.

10 Where $0 = C_1$, lowest C on the piano, and $36 = c^1$ or 'middle C'. When referring to specific pitches I use the system of register designation where the ascending octave beginning on C two octaves below middle C = C, D, ... B; the octave below middle C = c, d, ... b; the octave ascending from middle C = c^1, d^1 ... b^1; the octave above middle C = c^2, d^2, ... b^2, etc.

11 Robert D. Morris, 'New Directions in the Theory and Analysis of Musical Contour', *Music Theory Spectrum* 15/2 (Fall 1993), 205–28. Morris's conception of contour, which includes group theoretic aspects, is richer than its application here. I discuss only what is relevant for this study.

12 If, for example, the first note is also the highest, there will be no more than three elements, as in <201>.

13 Note that unstemmed a♮^{2} lies between b♭^{2} and d♭^{2}.

14 Readers may practise Morris's algorithm on the other two contours in Example 11.3, to which we shall return.

15 While music lovers are probably more likely to have heard the *Première rapsodie* in its orchestral version, music scholars associated with music schools and conservatoires are more likely to have encountered it in its original version for clarinet and piano.

16 *Syrinx* was composed in 1913 as incidental music for *Psyché*, a dramatic poem by Gabriel Mourey, and first performed by Louis Fleury, a famous flautist of his day. For information regarding the piece's origin see Ernst-Günter Heinemann's Preface to the Henle edition (Munich: G. Henle Verlag, 1994); Orledge, *Debussy and the Theatre*, 253–4; and Lesure, *Catalogue de l'œuvre de Claude Debussy*, 138. Orledge also analyses the piece (254–6), as does William Austin, *Music in the 20th Century* (New York: W. W. Norton & Company, Inc., 1966), 7–14.

17 In a nutshell Debussy's forms tend to be simple and straightforward, largely free of the convolutions of hierarchy and subtle gradations of interdependence among sections and subsections, cadence types and thematic constructions conspicuous in the music of his tonal antecedents. It would be wrongheaded, however, to conclude that in matters of form Debussy was indifferent or unsophisticated. On the contrary, I believe the evidence encourages us to infer that his prosaic tendencies in building large forms may stem from the necessity to provide simple formal frameworks within which other kinds of formal subtleties can operate without distraction.

18 Motivic saturation as described here is common in Debussy's music, its treatment a characteristic style trait. Other conspicuously audible examples include: 'Des pas sur la neige' (*Préludes*, book 1); 'Pour les degrés chromatiques' (*Études*, book 2); Sonata for flute, viola and harp, first movement; and 'Sirènes' from the *Nocturnes* (discussed below).

19 Although Example 11.1 is incomplete, Figure 11.1 presents the results of a complete analysis of repetitions in *Syrinx*.

20 Moreover, their proximity to pauses supports the quinquepartite formal plan in which the third section is subdivided into two subdivisions about the juncture between bars 15 and 16.

21 The third and largest section (with its bipartite subdivision) exhibits a different scheme: repetitions abound at its beginning in bar 9 but gradually dissipate through the end of bar 12, proliferate once more in bars 13–19, abate in bars 20–2, and then increase slightly from bar 23 to the fermata that marks the end of the section. The overlap of the third tendency with the juncture at bar 16 further weakens that partition and reinforces a sense that this juncture is of a lesser order than the others.

22 While we may find many counterexamples, increase–decrease cycles of SAPs are the norm for Debussy. For examples, listen to: the four flourishes that begin the first movement of the Sonata for flute, viola and harp, bars 1–3; the flute solo of the *Prélude à l'après-midi d'un faune*; the initial gesture of 'Pour les Agréments' (*Études*, book 2); the long opening gesture of 'Fêtes' (bars 1–8) from *Nocturnes*; the winds' theme of bars 9–12 of the third movement of *La mer* (and the low strings' motto figure that precedes it). Even as early a work as the first of the *Deux arabesques* exhibits this acceleration–deceleration tendency cycle in most of its gestures.

23 Or their relative-minor-scale counterparts. I do not wish to imply that diatonic passages are 'in the keys of' those major scales onto which their contents map, but rather that these scales serve as convenient referents for their overall pitch contents.

24 The scale consists of pitch-classes D♭–D–E–F–G–A♭–B♭–B♮.

25 Three other pieces in which changes of pitch-class genera are really easy to hear include 'Voiles' (*Préludes*, Book 1), 'Jimbo's Lullaby' (*Children's Corner*), and 'Feuilles mortes' (*Préludes*, Book 1). In 'Voiles' the brief middle section (bars 42–7) is diatonic-pentatonic, and it shares three pitch classes with the whole-tone outer sections: G♭–A♭–B♭. 'Jimbo's Lullaby' also alternates diatonic with whole-tone passages (e.g. contrast bars 19–28 with 39–46). In 'Feuilles mortes' it is quite easy to distinguish diatonic from whole-tone or octatonic passages (e.g. bars 8–9 versus bars 21–4 and 25–8 respectively).

26 I have not yet analysed melodic contours in this fashion in much of Debussy's music but I would be surprised if the features uncovered here turned out to be other than characteristic. Certainly some of his music evinces predominantly simpler contours (much of the vocal music, for example), which would yield a narrower range of values than *Syrinx*. But exquisitely convoluted melodies occur in many pieces. Listen, for example, to the opening gesture of 'Bruyères' (*Préludes*, book 2), whose pitch-class content matches the spartan anhematonic pentatonic scale on E♭, but whose contrastingly complex contour yields a value of 9/<201>. Other pieces that come to mind include the Violin Sonata (e.g. see bars 26–7, first movement, whose contour embodies a motive used throughout), the *Première rapsodie*, discussed below, and several *mélodies*, including two very early ones: *Aimons nous et dormons* and *Rondel Chinois*.

27 Overall, *Syrinx* employs a total register span of twenty-eight semitones (two octaves plus a major third), placed about d^2 and ranging from c^1 to $f\flat^3$, thereby exploiting the lower three-quarters of the flute compass. (Modern professional flautists will have a B-foot that extends the range downward by a semitone, and can play effectively as high as e^4.)

28 Here again I have employed a kind of averaging in order to render more graspable something that is normally both intangible and ephemeral. The register span as depicted in *Syrinx* is always artificial since the highest and lowest pitches can never sound at the same time.

29 Elsewhere in similar terms I discuss Debussy's use of register in 'Des pas sur la neige', 'La fille aux cheveux de lin' (both from *Préludes*, book 1), and *Prélude à l'après-midi d'un faune*. See Parks, *The Music of Claude Debussy*, 308–13.

30 The *Première rapsodie* was composed in 1909–10 for the Conservatoire examinations that spring. In 1911 Debussy orchestrated the accompaniment.

31 In an earlier published analysis (and using different criteria) I divided the piece into three large sections. See Parks, *The Music of Claude Debussy*, 250–3. The question of which edition to use for analysis poses refractory problems. Most readers will have access to the original Fromont edition of 1900, but most recorded performances of the work employ the 1930 Jobert edition, with or without emendations emerging from a long performance tradition among conductors. Such recordings will vary slightly from one

another in various details, but substantially from the original edition. Recordings will not differ so radically from Herlin's critical edition, however, and over time we may expect conductors of new recordings to employ this edition. Hence rather than either the omnipresent original (in its published photo reproductions) or the Jobert revision, I have used Herlin's edition as my reference for this work: Claude Debussy, 'Sirènes' from *Nocturnes*, *Œuvres complétes de Claude Debussy*, series 5, vol. III, ed. Denis Herlin (Paris: Durand-Costallet, 1999), 86–137. I did make a close comparison of the Fromont edition with Herlin's, which latter represents the editor's best judgement regarding the many changes that appear in extant autographs and may reasonably be regarded as reflecting Debussy's desired revisions. The issue of sources is especially pertinent since much of my analysis consists of counting things, and insofar as possible it is important to count those things that Debussy intended to be present, and which readers will hear in performances. Regarding these emendations we should note that Herlin's edition shows the composer pruning forces more often than grafting on new ones, a tendency apparent for other pieces as well. For instance, we may regard the second movement of the Sarabande from *Pour le piano* as a 'recomposition' of the 'Souvenir du Louvre' from the *Images (oubliées)*, which it postdates. In its reduction both of doublings and chromaticism the Sarabande shows the same tendency to prune and consolidate – as does the final version of 'La fille aux cheveux de lin' (*Préludes*, book 1) compared with an early sketch. (See Parks, *The Music of Claude Debussy*, 54–6.) For more information about sources for and changes to *Nocturnes*, see Denis Herlin, 'Sirens in the Labyrinth: Amendments in Debussy's *Nocturnes*', in Smith (ed.), *Debussy Studies*, 51–77.

32 For weighing changes in the complexity of ostinatos from one passage to the next, it would be desirable to be able to factor together both the number of parts or doublings and the number of ostinatos themselves. This desideratum poses refractory problems for two reasons that can be expressed as questions: (1) what criteria should we use to distinguish one ostinato from another; and (2) how do we weigh the complexity wrought by the number of elements that constitute each ostinato versus the number of ostinatos? To answer the first, perhaps the most unambiguous way to distinguish the number of ostinatos is by the duration required for each cycle: different

durations denote different ostinatos. (Alternatively, we could distinguish ostinatos by rhythmic, motivic or instrumental colour contents, but deciding what contents cohere to form an ostinato is fraught with arbitrariness.) The second issue engages the problem, discussed early in this essay, of the qualitative nature of the data. While we may reasonably assume that a passage made up of several ostinatos is more complex than one with fewer, and that more parts or doublings engender greater complexity than fewer, we cannot say how much each factor contributes to complexity. Perhaps the number of ostinatos is less a factor in complexity than the number of parts/doublings or vice versa. In the absence of experimental data to settle the issue I can only beg this question in favour of a practical decision to assign a series of values as I have described earlier in this essay.

33 Quoted from a letter to Paul-Jean Toulet dated 7 November 1901 in reference to a performance of *Nocturnes*, *Debussy Letters*, 123.

12 Debussy's 'rhythmicised time'
1 I should like to thank Roy Howat for reading this chapter and making suggestions for its improvement.
2 Ron Knott's extensive and well-illustrated website devoted to Golden Section and other proportional systems is strongly recommended: 'The Golden Section in Art, Architecture and Music', http://www.mcs.surrey.ac.uk/Personal/R.Knott/Fibonacci/fibInArt.html.
3 Howat, *Debussy in Proportion*, 2–3
4 For discussion of the effect of Golden Section in Debussy see Howat, *Debussy in Proportion*, 25; Jonathan Kramer, *The Time of Music* (New York and London: Schirmer Books, 1988), 308–10.
5 See chapter 14, p. 280 and n. 5.
6 Kramer, *The Time of Music*, 202–3.
7 *Debussy Letters*, 184.
8 One should begin with Howat, *Debussy in Proportion*. Other rhythmic analyses of Debussy's music may be found in: Parks, *The Music of Claude Debussy*; Parks, 'Structure and Performance: Metric and Phrase Ambiguities in the Three Chamber Sonatas', in Briscoe (ed.), *Debussy in Performance*; Kramer, *The Time of Music*; Christopher Hasty, 'Just in Time for More Dichotomies: A Hasty Response', *Music Theory Spectrum* 21/2 (1999), 275–93.
9 Kramer, *The Time of Music*, 202.
10 Julian Epstein, *Beyond Orpheus* (Cambridge, Mass.: MIT, 1979), 56.

11 Ibid., 58.
12 Ibid., 59.
13 I am most grateful to Richard Parks for this elegant phrase, supplied in a private e-mail.
14 Walter Berry, *Structural Functions in Music* (Englewood Cliffs, NJ: Prentice-Hall, 1976).
15 Kramer defines the terms thus: 'hypermeasure: group of measures that functions on a deep hierarchic level much as does a measure on the surface' and 'hypermeter: the hierarchy of measures', Kramer, Glossary, *The Time of Music*, 453.
16 Ibid., 110–12.
17 Hasty writes: 'It is a central tenet of the theory presented in this book that the metrical is inextricably tied to all those aspects of music that together form the elusive and endlessly fascinating creature we call "rhythm". Because meter is here defined as a creative process in which the emerging definiteness or particularity of duration is shaped by a great range of qualitative and quantitative distinctions, we will have no reason to oppose meter to other domains or to rhythm.' *Meter as Rhythm* (New York and Oxford: OUP, 1997), xi.
18 Hasty, 'Just in Time for More Dichotomies: A Hasty Response', 289–93.
19 I am thinking here of Stockhausen's writings on time, among others. See '... how time passes ...', *Die Reihe* 3 (1959), 10–41.
20 He provides the following dualities between chronometric (metric) and integral (rhythmic) time: beat/pulse; measure/motive (or motive group); hypermeasure/phrase; macroperiodisations of hypermeasure groups/macroperiodisations of phrase groups, *Beyond Orpheus*, 61. The hierarchy outlined here is observed in my Tables 12.1 and 12.2.
21 Readers with a broader interest in the subject of rhythmic analysis will be familiar with Fred Lerdahl and Ray Jackendoff's grouping strategies in *A Generative Theory of Tonal Music* (Cambridge, Mass. and London: MIT Press, 1983). Their chapter 2, 'Introduction to Rhythmic Structure', elucidates many of the primary considerations underlying grouping strategies and rhythmic hierarchies, 13–35; chapter 3 introduces 'Grouping well-formedness rules', 36–67; chapter 4 introduces 'Metrical well-formedness rules'. A lively critique of their theory may be found in Kramer, *The Time of Music*, 110–12. Also see Hasty's evaluation of three post-war American systems of rhythmic and metrical analysis, including Lerdahl and Jackendoff's, in *Meter as Rhythm*, 48–58.

22 These terms are confusing, for while 'rhythm' is often used as the umbrella term for all temporal manifestations in music, it also designates the sphere of temporal analysis concerned with Epstein's integral time.

23 This carefully filtered reading of metrical unit and metre finds a valuable corrective in Hasty's work, which takes a good deal less for granted at the outset, thereby avoiding some of the pitfalls of rhythmic analysis hitherto.

24 William Rothstein, *Phrase Rhythm in Tonal Music* (New York and London: Schirmer Books, 1989).

25 Ibid., 5.

26 Edward T. Cone, *Musical Form and Musical Performance* (New York: Norton, 1968), 23–7. I am not alone in making a rather free use of Cone's term. See, for instance, Kramer, *The Time of Music*, 25–32.

27 Ibid., 25.

28 By 'blunt' I mean denying the voice-leading tensions in the harmony, such as the third and seventh in a dominant seventh, whose downward progression in semitonal progression (in the major mode) is a *sine qua non* of the diatonic tonal system. In a C major dominant seventh chord F would lead to E and B to C. Without these operands functioning at local and deep levels of the voice leading, common-practice tonality eventually withers and dies.

29 Daniel Harrison, *Harmonic Function in Chromatic Music: A Renewed Dualist Theory and an Account of Its Precedents* (Chicago: University of Chicago Press, 1994).

30 'An unaccent . . . *may be* a timespan. An entire timespan may be unaccented, relative to its context, because it can be an extended upbeat (a rhythmic group leading to a subsequent downbeat or rhythmic accent) or afterbeat (a rhythmic group leading away from a preceding downbeat or rhythmic accent).' Kramer, *The Time of Music*, 89.

31 Parks, *The Music of Claude Debussy*, 285.

32 Ibid.

33 Arnold Whittall, 'Tonality and the Whole-tone Scale in the Music of Debussy'.

34 See Trezise, *Debussy: La mer*.

35 Letter to Jacques Durand, 3 September 1907, *Debussy Letters*, 184. For further discussion of this letter see chapter 6.

36 'The Radio Recordings', Q Disc 97015.

37 See chapter 13, 'Debussy in Performance'.

38 Aysegul Durakoglu, 'Contrapuntal Lines and Rhythmic Organization in Selected Debussy Piano *Etudes*: A Structural Analysis with Performance Implications' (Ph.D. dissertation, New York University 1997), ix.

39 Ibid., x.

40 Ibid., 193 and 195.

41 Ibid., 201. A few of the comments that follow are partly in the spirit of, but not taken from, this dissertation; the rest is my own.

42 For a discussion of some of the problems encountered in performing this *Étude*, plus consideration of Debussy's first thoughts on aspects of its rhythmic notation, see Howat, 'Debussy's Piano Studies', in Smith (ed.), *Debussy Studies*, 105–7.

13 Debussy in performance

1 Louise Liebich, 'An Englishwoman's Memories of Debussy', *The Musical Times* (1 June 1918), 250.

2 Léon Vallas, 'Achille Debussy jugé par ses professeurs du Conservatoire', *Revue de musicologie* 34/101–2 (July 1952), 47–8.

3 John R. Clevenger, 'Achille at the Conservatoire, 1872–1884', *Cahiers Debussy* 19 (1995), 16–17.

4 Several accounts are found in *Revue musicale* 7 (1 May 1926), 3–16.

5 Léon Vallas, 'Achille Debussy, élève du Conservatoire, devant la Critique', *Revue Pleyel* 48 (September 1927), 372.

6 Debussy performed the following *Préludes* in public: 'Danseuses de Delphes', 'Voiles', 'Le vent dans la plaine', 'Les sons et les parfums tournent dans l'air du soir', 'Des pas sur la neige', 'La fille aux cheveux de lin', 'La cathédrale engloutie', 'La danse de Puck', 'Minstrels', 'Brouillards', 'Feuilles mortes', 'La puerta del vino' and 'General Lavine – eccentric'.

7 *Monde musical* (31 May 1910).

8 Paul Landormy, *La musique française de Franck à Debussy* (Paris: Gallimard, 1948), 231.

9 Maurice Dumesnil, 'Debussy's Principles in Pianoforte Playing', *The Etude* 56/3 (March 1938), 154.

10 *Guide musical*, 60/19–20 (10 and 17 May 1914), 410.

11 Casella, 'Claude Debussy', 1.

12 According to the booklet accompanying Pierian CD 0001, Caswell benefited from technical advice that his colleague Richard Simonton received in 1948 and 1952 directly from Edwin Welte and Karl Bockisch, the co-inventors of the Welte–Mignon mechanism. This included instructions on how to make 'critical fine adjustments to mate the Welte mechanism to the individual tone and voicing of the piano on which it was played'. Caswell's Pierian disc was made after a detailed comparison of all available rolls for accurate dynamics, pedalling and note

placement. His recording was done with a restored 1923 Feurich Welte piano that closely matches the mechanism of the original recording instrument.

13 Roy Howat, 'Debussy and Welte', *The Pianola Journal* 7 (1994), 16.

14 Long, *Au piano avec Debussy*, 124.

15 For further discussions of Debussy's piano rolls, see the critical notes in *Œuvres complètes de Claude Debussy*, series 5, vol. I, ed. Roy Howat and Claude Helffer (Paris, 1985) and Series 1, vol. II, ed. Roy Howat (Paris, 1998); Howat, 'Debussy and Welte', 3–18; Paul Carlson, 'Early Interpretation of Debussy's Piano Music' (Doctor of Music dissertation, Boston University 1998), 134–259 passim; and Cecilia Dunoyer, 'Early Debussystes at the Piano', in Briscoe (ed.), *Debussy in Performance*, 93–7.

16 See Debussy, *Œuvres complètes*, Series 1, vol. II, 95; and Roy Howat, 'Debussy's Piano Music: Sources and Performance', in Smith (ed.), *Debussy Studies*, 103–4.

17 For a summary of arguments in favour of Debussy's interpretation, see Howat, 'Debussy and Welte', 10–14; and Charles Burkhart, 'Debussy Plays "La cathédrale engloutie" and Solves Metrical Mystery', *The Piano Quarterly* 65 (Fall 1968), 14–16. Debussy's interpretation has not been followed on recent recordings by Philippe Cassard, Catherine Collard, Patricia Pagny and Jean-Yves Thibaudet. These pianists favour a tempo of minim = c. 42 until the section marked *un peu moins lent*. Pianist Noël Lee agrees, and he has stated that 'the grand, noble, full sonorous section beginning at bar 28 should be the passage that establishes the basic tempo of the work' (letter to this author dated 29 April 2000). (There is further discussion of Debussy's Duo-Arte piano rolls by Richard Langham Smith, 'Debussy on Performance: Sound and Unsound Ideals', in Briscoe (ed.), *Debussy in Performance*, 21ff. Ed.)

18 Long, *Au piano avec Claude Debussy*, 26.

19 For an overview of pianists active in North America, see Charles Timbrell, 'Performances of Debussy's Piano Music in the United States (1904–1918)', *Cahiers Debussy* 21 (1997), 63–79.

20 *Revue internationale de musique française* 1/2 (June 1980), 224.

21 *Revue musicale* 5/7 (1 April 1905), 216; *Courier musical* 13/6 (15 March 1910), 230.

22 *Debussy Letters*, 222 n. 2.

23 Letter to André Caplet, 23 June 1913, ibid., 274.

24 *Revue internationale de musique française* 1/2 (June 1980), 233.

25 Maurice Dumesnil, *How to Play and Teach Debussy* (New York: Schroeder and Gunther, 1932), 9.

26 Maurice Dumesnil, 'Coaching with Debussy', *The Piano Teacher* 5 (September/October 1962), 10–13. See also Dumesnil, 'Interpreting Debussy', *Handbook for Piano Teachers* (Evanston, Ill.: Summy-Birchard, 1958), 74–8. Dumesnil's only Debussy recording is a piano roll of *La plus que lent* on Ampico 65501 G, never issued in any other format.

27 See Harold Bauer, *Harold Bauer: His Book* (New York: Norton, 1948), 141–2; and Vallas, *Claude Debussy: His Life and Works*, 183.

28 Copeland, 'Debussy, the Man I Knew', 34–8; and Copeland 'The First – and Last – Times I Saw Debussy', *Musica* (November 1944), 6–9.

29 From a taped interview with Copeland by Gregor Benko (1969).

30 *Boston Herald* (25 November 1908), 7.

31 Charles Timbrell, 'Claude Debussy and Walter Rummel: Chronicle of a Friendship, with New Correspondence', *Music & Letters* 73/3 (August 1992), 399–406; and 'Walter Morse Rummel, Debussy's "Prince of Virtuosos"', *Cahiers Debussy* 11 (1987), 24–33.

32 See *The Times* (13 June 1913), 8; and *Monde musical* (15 February 1914), 49.

33 Elie Robert Schmitz, 'A Plea for the Real Debussy', *The Etude* 55 (December 1937), 781–2.

34 From the author's interview with Ciampi's student Julia Hennig (November 1998). See also John-Paul Bracey, *A Biography of French Pianist Marcel Ciampi* (Lewiston, NY: Edwin Mellen Press, 1996), 53–85 passim; and Charles Timbrell, *French Pianism* (Portland: Amadeus Press, 1999), 131–5.

35 Cecilia Dunoyer, *Marguerite Long: A Life in French Music* (Bloomington: Indiana University, 1993), 24; see also 57–79 passim.

36 Long, *Au piano avec Claude Debussy*, 75.

37 Dunoyer, *Marguerite Long*, 71–2.

38 Letter to Jacques Durand of 27 September 1917, *Debussy Letters*, 331.

39 Arthur Rubinstein, *My Many Years* (New York: Alfred A. Knopf, 1980), 132.

40 Mme Gaston de Tinan [Dolly Bardac], 'Memories of Debussy and His Circle', *Journal of the British Institute of Recorded Sound* 50–1 (April–July 1973), 159.

41 Dumesnil, 'Coaching with Debussy', 13. Mention should be made of several instrumentalists who were associated with Debussy and who made recordings, although not of Debussy's music. These include the

harpist Pierre Jamet and violinists Eugène
Ysaÿe and Gaston Poulet.
42 Mary Garden and Louis Biancolli, *Mary
Garden's Story* (London: Joseph, 1952), 62.
43 Letter to André Messager of 9 July 1902,
Debussy Letters, 130.
44 Brigitte Massin, *Les Joachim: une famille de
musiciens* (Paris: Fayard, 1999), 248–50, 389
and 394. The first complete recording (1941)
of *Pelléas et Mélisande*, sung by Irène Joachim
and Jacques Jansen and conducted by Roger
Désormière, retains its classic status today.
The cast, entirely French, benefited not only
from the advice of Garden but also from that
of the *répétiteur* for the 1902 premiere,
Georges Viseur.
45 Letter to André Caplet of 23 June 1913,
Debussy Letters, 274.
46 Nichols, *Debussy Remembered*, 182.
47 *The Singer as Interpreter: Claire Croiza's
Master Classes*, ed. and trans. Betty
Bannerman [from Hélène Abraham's *Un art
de l'interprétation* (Paris, 1954)] (London:
Gollancz, 1989), 117 and 158.
48 Garry O'Connor, *The Pursuit of Perfection:
A Life of Maggie Teyte* (London: Gollancz,
1979), 88–9.
49 Ibid., 130–1.
50 Letter to Jane Bathori of April 1908,
Debussy Letters, 191.
51 Jane Bathori, *Sur l'interprétation des
mélodies de Claude Debussy* (Paris: Les Éditions
Ouvrières, 1953), 11–12.
52 One would like to know more about the
French soprano Rose Féart, who often
performed with Debussy and was the
Mélisande at Covent Garden in 1909. Debussy
even chose her to sing on what was his last
public appearance in Paris, on 5 May 1917. Of
the male singers in *Pelléas*, Debussy had praise
for the Belgian baritone Hector Dufranne
(1871–1951), who was the first Golaud, and
the French bass Vanni Marcoux (1877–1962),
who originally sang Arkel and later Golaud. He
was less enthusiastic about the French baritone
Jean Périer (1869–1954), the original Pelléas.
See *Debussy Letters*, 126, 173, 192, 200 and 269.
53 Letter to Hector Dufranne of 26 October
1906; letter to Vanni Marcoux of 22 May
1909, ibid., 173 and 200.
54 Casella, 'Claude Debussy', 1.
55 See, for example, Lockspeiser, *Debussy: His
Life and Mind*, vol. II, 122, 129 and 134;
Lesure, *Claude Debussy: biographic critique*,
380.
56 Letter to André Messager of 9 May 1902,
Debussy Letters, 126.
57 Quoted from a BBC interview in 1969 in
Nichols, *Debussy Remembered*, 244.

58 Debussy's corrected score, including six
metronome markings, is located in the
Bibliothèque François Lang, Royaumont.
It is used as a source for the Norton Critical
Score, *Debussy: Prelude to 'The Afternoon of a
Faun'*.
59 Letter to Gabriel Pierné of 5 March 1914,
Debussy Letters, 288.
60 Quoted from a BBC interview in 1961 in
Nichols, *Debussy Remembered*, 186.
61 Vittorio Gui, 'Debussy in Italy', *Musical
Opinion* 62/736 (January 1939), 305–6; 62/737
(February 1939), 404–5; and 62/738 (March
1939), 498–9. See also *Debussy Letters*, 256.
62 Quoted in Harold C. Schonberg, *The Great
Conductors* (New York: Simon and Schuster,
1967), 333.
63 Letter to Jacques Durand of 9 October
1915, *Debussy Letters*, 305.
64 Trezise, *Debussy: La mer*, 24.
65 See Briscoe (ed.), 'Debussy and Orchestral
Performance', 80–1 and 85.
66 Letter to André Caplet of 25 February
1910, *Debussy Letters*, 217.
67 Gérard Poulet, quoting the recollections of
his father, violinist Gaston Poulet, in an essay
for the booklet that accompanies the compact
disc Arion ARN 68228.
68 Briscoe (ed.), 'Debussy and Orchestral
Performance', 77–80.
69 Trezise, *Debussy: La mer*, 26.
70 (A complete discography of 78-rpm
recordings of Debussy's music may be found
in Margaret Cobb, *Discographie de l'œuvre de
Claude Debussy* (Geneva: Minkoff, 1975). Ed.)

14 Debussy now

1 Constant Lambert, *Music Ho!*
(Harmondsworth: Penguin Books, 1948), 16.
2 Ibid., 17.
3 Adele T. Katz, *Challenge to Musical Tradition*
(New York: Alfred A. Knopf, 1945). See also
Boyd Pomeroy's chapter in this volume, and
Matthew Brown's discussion (see n. 6 below
for full citation) in *Music Theory Spectrum*
15/2 (1993), 129–30.
4 Ibid., 293.
5 Ibid., 279–80.
6 Some of the most important contributions
since 1990 are as follows: Allen Forte,
'Debussy and the Octatonic', *Music Analysis*
10/1–2 (1991), 125–69; James M. Baker,
'Post-tonal Voice Leading', in Jonathan
Dunsby (ed.), *Models of Musical Analysis: Early
Twentieth-Century Music* (Oxford: Blackwell,
1993), 20–41; Matthew Brown, 'Tonality and
Form in Debussy's *Prélude à "L'Après–midi d'un
faune"* ', *Music Theory Spectrum* 15/2 (1993),
127–43; Avo Somer, 'Chromatic

Third-relations and Tonal Structure in the Songs of Debussy', *Music Theory Spectrum* 17/2 (1995), 215–41; David Kopp, 'Pentatonic Organization in Two Piano Pieces of Debussy', *Journal of Music Theory* 41/2 (1997), 261–87; Marie Rolf, 'Semantic and Structural Issues in Debussy's Mallarmé Songs', in Smith (ed.), *Debussy Studies*, 177–200; Jann Pasler, 'Timbre, Voice-leading, Musical Arabesque', in Briscoe (ed.), *Debussy in Performance*, 225–83. See also Boyd Pomeroy's chapter in this volume.

7 David Lewin, *Musical Form and Transformation. 4 Analytic Essays* (New Haven: Yale University Press, 1993), 97–159.

8 Richard Cohn, 'Introduction to Neo–Riemannian Theory: A Survey and Historical Perspective', *Journal of Music Theory* 42/2 (1998), 167.

9 Pierre Boulez, *Stocktakings from an Apprenticeship*, trans. Stephen Walsh (Oxford: Oxford University Press, 1991), 276.

10 Laurence D. Berman, '*Prelude to the Afternoon of a Faun* and *Jeux*: Debussy's Summer Rites', *19th-Century Music* 3/3 (1980), 225–38.

11 Pasler, 'Timbre, Voice-leading, Musical Arabesque', 234, n. 6.

12 See for example Glenn Watkins, *Pyramids at the Louvre: Music, Culture, and Collage from Stravinsky to the Postmodernists* (Cambridge, Mass.: Harvard University Press, 1994), 297–8.

13 See ibid.; Georgina Born and David Hesmondhalgh (eds.), *Western Music and Its Others* (Berkeley, Los Angeles and London: University of California Press, 2000).

14 See Arnold Whittall in Stephen Banfield (ed.), *The Blackwell History of Music in Britain. The Twentieth Century* (Oxford: Blackwell, 1995), 9–11. See also Whittall, *Musical Composition in the Twentieth Century* (Oxford: Oxford University Press, 1999), 8–13.

15 Pierre Boulez, *Conversations with Célestin Deliège* (London: Eulenburg, 1976), 96.

16 Whittall, *Musical Composition in the Twentieth Century*, 22–7, n. 14.

17 Holloway, *Debussy and Wagner*, 235.

18 See below for David Schiff's ascription of 'new classicism' to the later music of Elliott Carter. For discussions of 'modern classicism'

see James Hepokoski, *Sibelius: Symphony No. 5* (Cambridge: Cambridge University Press, 1993), especially chapter 2, and Whittall, *Musical Composition in the Twentieth Century*, 30 and 32, n. 14.

19 Ayrey, 'Debussy's Significant Connections: Metaphor and Metonymy in Analytical Method', 128.

20 Ibid., 131.

21 Ibid., 129.

22 Roger Scruton, *The Aesthetics of Music* (Oxford: Oxford University Press, 1997), 176.

23 Parks, *The Music of Claude Debussy*, 233.

24 Robert Morgan, *Twentieth–Century Music* (New York: Norton, 1991), 48–9.

25 Nichols, *The Life of Debussy*, 163.

26 Ibid., 163 and 164.

27 Jonathan Bernard (ed.), *Elliott Carter: Collected Essays and Lectures, 1937–1995* (Rochester, NY, 1997), 123.

28 Ibid., 124.

29 Ibid., 133.

30 Ibid., 270.

31 Derrick Puffett, 'Debussy's Ostinato Machine'; Jonathan Cross, *The Stravinsky Legacy* (Cambridge: Cambridge University Press, 1998), 89–93.

32 For Carter's 'new classicism', see David Schiff, *The Music of Elliott Carter* (London: Faber & Faber, 1998), 29–31. See also Arnold Whittall, 'Modernist Aesthetics, Modernist Music: Some Analytical Perspectives', in James M. Baker, David W. Beach and Jonathan W. Bernard (eds.), *Music Theory in Concept and Practice* (Rochester, NY: University of Rochester Press, 1997), 157–68. For Carter's chordal vocabulary, see Schiff, *The Music of Elliott Carter*, 324–7.

33 Paul Griffiths, *György Ligeti* (London: Robson Books, 1997), 121.

34 Cross, *The Stravinsky Legacy*, 110, n. 31.

35 Griffiths, *György Ligeti*, 121, n. 33.

36 Risto Nieminen and Renaud Machart, *George Benjamin* (London: Faber & Faber, 1997), 35.

37 See Caroline Potter, *Henri Dutilleux: His Life and Works* (Aldershot: Ashgate, 1997), 204.

38 Nichols, *The Life of Debussy*, 166–7, n. 25.

39 Jonathan Dunsby, 'The Poetry of Debussy's *En blanc et noir*', 150–1.

Select bibliography

Abbate, Carolyn, '*Tristan* in the Composition of *Pelléas*', *19th-Century Music* 5/2 (1981), 117–41.

Austin, William W., 'Debussy, Wagner, and Some Others', *19th-Century Music* 6/1 (1982), 82–91.

Austin, William W. (ed.), Norton Critical Score, *Debussy: Prelude to 'The Afternoon of a Faun'* (New York: Norton, 1970).

Ayrey, Craig, 'Debussy's Significant Connections: Metaphor and Metonymy in Analytical Method', in Anthony Pople (ed.) *Theory, Analysis and Meaning in Music* (Cambridge: Cambridge University Press, 1994), 127–51.

Bardac, Raoul, 'Dans l'intimité de Claude Debussy', *Terres Latines* 4/3 (March 1936).

Berman, Laurence D., '*Prelude to the Afternoon of a Faun* and *Jeux*: Debussy's Summer Rites', *19th-Century Music* 3/3 (1980), 225–38.

Briscoe, James R. *Claude Debussy: A Guide to Research* (New York and London: Garland, 1990).

 'The Compositions of Claude Debussy's Formative Years (1879–1887)', Ph.D. thesis, University of North Carolina at Chapel Hill, 1979.

Briscoe, James R. (ed.), *Debussy in Performance* (New Haven and London: Yale University Press, 1999).

Casella, Alfredo, 'Claude Debussy', *The Monthly Musical Record* (January 1933).

Cobb, Margaret G. (ed.), *The Poetic Debussy* (Rochester, NY: University of Rochester Press, 1994).

Copeland, George, 'Debussy, the Man I Knew', *The Atlantic Monthly* (January 1955).

Debussy, Claude, *Correspondance 1884–1918*, ed. François Lesure (Paris: Hermann, 1993).

 Correspondance de Claude Debussy et Pierre Louÿs (1893–1904), ed. Henri Bourgeaud (Paris: Librairie José Corti, 1945).

 Debussy Letters, ed. François Lesure and Roger Nichols, trans. Roger Nichols (London, Faber, 1987).

 Debussy on Music, collected by François Lesure, ed. and trans. Richard Langham Smith (London: Secker & Warburg, 1977).

 Lettres à son éditeur, ed. J. Durand (Paris: Durand, 1927).

 Monsieur Croche et autres écrits, ed. François Lesure (Paris: Gallimard, 1987).

 Songs of Claude Debussy, vol. II, a critical edition by James R. Briscoe (Milwaukee: Hal Leonard, 1993).

 Textes, ed. Martine Kaufmann, Denis Herlin and Jean-Michel Nectoux (Paris: Radio France, 1999).

DeVoto, Mark, *Debussy and the Veil of Tonality: Essays on His Music* (Hillsdale, NY: Pendragon Press, 2002).

Dietschy, Marcel, *A Portrait of Claude Debussy*, ed. and trans. William Ashbrook and Margaret G. Cobb (Oxford: Oxford University Press, 1990).

Dunsby, Jonathan, 'The Poetry of Debussy's *En blanc et noir*', in Craig Ayrey and Mark Everist (eds.), *Analytical Strategies and Musical Interpretation* (Cambridge: Cambridge University Press, 1996).

Durand, Jacques, *Quelques souvenirs d'un éditeur de musique*, vol. II (Paris: Durand, 1925).

Eimert, Herbert, 'Debussy's "Jeux"', trans. Leo Black, in *Die Reihe* 5 (Bryn Mawr, 1961).

Forte, Allen, 'Debussy and the Octatonic', *Music Analysis* 10 (1991), 125–69.

Fulcher, Jane F. (ed.), *Debussy and His World* (Princeton: Princeton University Press, 2001).

Gaston de Tinan, Mme, 'Memories of Debussy and His Circle', *Journal of the British Institute of Recorded Sound* 50–1 (April–July 1973).

Goubault, Christian, *Claude Debussy* (Paris: Champion, 1986).

Grayson, David, *The Genesis of Debussy's* Pelléas et Mélisande (Ann Arbor: UMI Research Press, 1986).

Hepokoski, James, 'Formulaic Openings in Debussy', *19th-Century Music* 8/1 (Summer 1984), 44–59.

Holloway, Robin, *Debussy and Wagner* (London: Eulenburg, 1979).

Howat, Roy, 'Debussy and the Orient', in Andrew Gerstle (ed.), *Recovering the Orient* (Switzerland and GB: Harwood Academic Publishers, 1994).

    Debussy in Proportion (Cambridge: Cambridge University Press, 1983).

Jankélévitch, Vladimir, *Debussy et le mystère de l'insant* (Paris: Plon, 1976).

Jarocinski, Stefan, *Debussy: Impressionism and Symbolism*, trans. Rollo Myers (London: Eulenburg, 1976).

Jean-Aubry, Georges, 'Some Recollections of Debussy', *The Musical Times* (1 May 1918).

Laloy, Louis, *Claude Debussy* (Paris: Dorbon-Ainé, 1909).

    La musique retrouvée (Paris: Librairie Plon, 1928).

Lesure, François, *Catalogue de l'œuvre de Claude Debussy* (Geneva: Minkoff, 1977).

    Claude Debussy avant Pelléas *ou les années symbolistes* (Paris: Klincksieck, 1992).

    Claude Debussy: biographie critique (Paris: Klincksieck, 1994).

    Claude Debussy: iconographie musicale (Geneva, Minkoff, 1980).

    Claude Debussy: textes et documents inédits (Paris: Société française de musicologie, 1962).

Lockspeiser, Edward (revised Richard Langham Smith), *Debussy*, Master Musician Series (London: Dent, 1980).

    Debussy et Poe (Monaco: Rocher, 1961).

    Debussy: His Life and Mind, vol. I (1862–1902) (Cambridge: Cambridge University Press, 1978).

    Debussy: His Life and Mind, vol. II (1902–1918) (Cambridge: Cambridge University Press, 1978).

    Music and Painting: A Study in Comparative Ideas from Turner to Schoenberg (London: Cassell, 1973).

Lockspeiser, Edward (ed.), *Debussy et Edgar Poe: manuscrits et documents inédits* (Monaco: Editions du Rocher, 1962).

Long, Marguerite, *Au piano avec Claude Debussy* (Paris: René Julliard, 1960); *At the Piano with Debussy*, trans. Olive Senior-Ellis (London: Dent, 1972).

Nichols, Roger, 'Debussy's Two Settings of "Clair de lune"', *Music and Letters* 48/3 (July 1967), 229–35.

  Debussy Remembered (London: Faber & Faber, 1992).

  The Life of Debussy (Cambridge: Cambridge University Press, 1998).

Nichols, Roger and Richard Langham Smith, *Claude Debussy: Pelléas et Mélisande*, Cambridge Opera Handbooks (Cambridge: Cambridge University Press, 1989).

Orledge, Robert, *Debussy and the Theatre* (Cambridge: Cambridge University Press, 1982).

Parks, Richard S., 'Pitch Organization in Debussy: Unordered Sets in "Brouillards"', *Music Theory Spectrum* 2 (1980), 119–34.

  The Music of Claude Debussy (New Haven and London: Yale University Press, 1989).

Pasler, Jann, 'Debussy, *Jeux: Playing with Time and Form*', *19th-Century Music* 6/1 (1982), 60–75.

Pomeroy, Boyd, 'Toward a New Tonal Practice: Chromaticism and Form in Debussy's Orchestral Music', Ph.D. thesis, Cornell University (2000).

Puffett, Derrick, 'Debussy's Ostinato Machine', *Papers in Musicology* 4 (Nottingham University, 1996).

Roberts, Paul, *Images: The Piano Music of Claude Debussy* (Portland: Amadeus Press, 1996).

Ruschenberg, Peter, *Stilkritische Untersuchungen zu den Liedern Claude Debussys* (Hamburg: University of Hamburg, 1966).

Smith, Richard Langham, 'Debussy and the Pre-Raphaelites', *19th-Century Music* 5/2 (Fall 1981), 95–109.

Smith, Richard Langham (ed.), *Debussy Studies* (Cambridge: Cambridge University Press, 1997).

Trezise, Simon, *Debussy: La mer*, Cambridge Music Handbooks (Cambridge: Cambridge University Press, 1994).

Vallas, Léon, *Claude Debussy: His Life and Works*, trans. Maire and Grace O'Brien (New York: Dover, 1973).

  The Theories of Claude Debussy, Musicien Français (London: Oxford University Press, 1929).

Wenk, Arthur B., *Claude Debussy and the Poets* (Berkeley: University of California Press, 1976).

  Claude Debussy and Twentieth-Century Music (Boston: Twayne Publishers, 1983).

Index

LaVergne, TN USA
06 October 2010
199825LV00003B/16/A